THE PEACEMAKERS

ARMS AND ADVENTURE
IN THE AMERICAN WEST

THE
PEACEMAKERS

ARMS AND ADVENTURE
IN THE AMERICAN WEST

R.L. WILSON

Photography by Peter Beard,
G. Allan Brown, Susan Einstein, and Douglas Sandberg

CHARTWELL
BOOKS, INC.

Other Books by R. L. Wilson

Winchester: An American Legend
Colt: An American Legend
Winchester Engraving
Colt Engraving
Winchester: The Golden Age of American Gunmaking and
    the Winchester 1 of 1000
Samuel Colt Presents
The Arms Collection of Colonel Colt
L. D. Nimschke Firearms Engraver
The Rampant Colt
Colt Commemorative Firearms (two editions)
Theodore Roosevelt Outdoorsman
Antique Arms Annual (editor)
The Book of Colt Firearms (with R. Q. Sutherland)
The Book of Colt Engraving
The Book of Winchester Engraving
Colt Pistols
Colt Handguns (Japanese)
Paterson Colt Pistol Variations (with P. R. Phillips)
The Colt Heritage
The Deringer in America (with L. D. Eberhart, two volumes)
Colt's Dates of Manufacture

Copyright © 1992 by R. L Wilson
Photographs © 1992 by Peter Beard, G. Allan Brown,
Susan Einstein, and Douglas Sandberg
All rights reserved under International and Pan-American Copyright Conventions.

This edition published in 2004 by CHARTWELL BOOKS
A division of BOOK SALES, INC.
114 Northfield Avenue, Edison, New Jersey 08837

Published by arrangement with R. L. Wilson

Book design: Martin Moskof
Design assistant: George Brady
Book production: Linda Kaye
Printed in China

Library of Congress Cataloging-in-Publication Data

Wilson, R. L. (Robert Lawrence)
The peacemakers: arms and adventure in the American West/R. L.
Wilson; photography by Peter Beard . . . [et al.].—1st ed.
p.   cm.
Includes bibliographical references and index.
ISBN: 0-7858-1892-8
1. Americana—West (U.S.)   2. Weapons—West (U.S.)
3. West (U.S.)—Social life and customs.   I. Title.
F596.W62   1992
978—dc20   92-6049

Endpaper: From the Greg Martin Americana Collection. An elaborate Buffalo Bill Cody saddle, by G. H. & J. S. Collins, Omaha, Nebraska, serves as centerpiece for a potpourri of Western memorabilia and arms. At *top left*, the Stevens 10-gauge double-barrel shotgun used by Wyatt Earp and Wells Fargo special agent Fred Dodge, number 927; to its *right*, Buffalo Bill's engraved Savage .32 automatic, number 33177. *Above and to the right*, the Captain Jack Crawford Winchester Model 1873 .22, presented to him by the factory, number 499609. *Beneath* Captain Jack's rifle is the most elaborate badge known from the West, in various colors of gold, and inscribed to Sacramento Police Chief Oliver Cowdery Jackson, March 13, 1885. At *center left*, a gold-plated and Ulrich-engraved Marlin Model 97 .22 lever-action rifle used by Annie Oakley, number 288890. *Below and at left*, the Texas Jack Omohundro S&W American, a presentation by him to the Earl of Dunraven, engraved on the backstrap *Earl Dunraven/from Texas Jack*, number 4868. To its *left*, a gold watch presented to Sheriff Pat Garrett for killing Billy the Kid, the fob with gold star badge inscribed: PAT F. GARRETT/SHERIFF/DONA ANA CO./N.M. Badge at right also Garrett's, of gold, and inscribed on the back *To/Pat Garrett/with the best/Regards of/A. J. Fountain/1881*.

At *lower left*, Indian flintlock trade musket of exceptional quality, decorated with silver and brass, c. 1820. Model 1878 Colt Frontier revolver *below*, number 33233, was made by the factory for Captain Jack Crawford and is inscribed on the backstrap *Presented to Capt. Jack Crawford/by the Colt's Patent Fire Arms Mfg. Co.* Pair of Williamson deringers at *lower left*, numbers 4808 and 4811, are similar to pistol carried by Wild Bill Hickok. Half-plate ambrotype of Lt. Col. George Armstrong Custer at *left center* never previously illustrated.

At *top right*, the Winchester Model 1892 .44-40 carbine with large-loop cocking lever used by Chuck Connors in *The Rifleman*, number 985658. *Beneath* is a Michael Price San Francisco Bowie knife, mounted in ivory and gold, with silver scabbard. *Below*, the left-handed Sharps Model 1853 Sporting Rifle, made by the factory for exhibition purposes and richly engraved by Gustave Young; shown at the Paris Universal Exposition of 1856. *Below at right*, a Smith & Wesson Schofield .45 revolver, made for Wells Fargo & Co., and marked on the barrel W.F. & CO. EX. 1878. *Beneath at right*, the oil painting of W.F. & Co. bulldog "Guarding the Goods," by J. Walcom, San Francisco, 1885 (12 by 14 inches). Colt Model 1862 Police revolver *at left* has cut-down barrel and is inscribed *Wells, Fargo & Co.* on backstrap, number 39251. Revolvers and painting rest on rare Wells Fargo Mug Book of the 1860s–70s, showing California desperadoes. California gold quartz watch, chain, and fob from gold rush era, to *left* of bulldog painting. *Beneath*, a presentation-inscribed, ivory-gripped dragoon-size pepperbox by Allen & Co., number 37, dated 1849 and inscribed to soldier of fortune William Walker by his friends of the Boston & Maine Railroad. At *right center*, Annie Oakley's J. Stevens presentation target rifle, with gold-plated and engraved frame, number 25640. Annie's show belt is draped across the barrel. Rifle *below* is the Kickapoo Indian presentation .22 Colt Lightning, deluxe-engraved and finished in half nickel and gold, number 10570. *Below* Annie's photograph is Stagecoach King Ben Holladay's Winchester Model 1866 rifle, inscribed with his name and Ulrich-engraved, number 38586. *Beneath* is a California Bowie knife, with silver hilt and scabbard, made in San Francisco, engraved on the scabbard with the inscription *Presented by/Mr. Ithamar Witing,/to/Capt. Jeremiah S. Silva,/while in Command of Sloop Velos,/on the Sacramento River,/California.* (Douglas Sandberg photograph)

Frontispiece: Lieutenant Colonel George Armstrong Custer, with scouts and white interpreter, two years before the "Last Stand" at the Little Bighorn. Pointing at the map on the general's lap is Bloody Knife, Custer's chief scout. Remington rolling-block rifle, Bowie knife, and Colt Single Action revolvers carefully positioned for camera. Two of Custer's hunting dogs reclined comfortably. *At left*, nickel-plated Colt Single Action (echoing those of the scouts) rests on period holster. Indian hunting knife, with well-worn blade, accompanied by beaded scabbard. Flintlock trade musket shows evidence of considerable use in Indian hands. Photograph positioned on rare unexposed daguerreotype plate, of silver-plated copper. (Peter Beard photograph)

CONTENTS

Charles Schreyvogel at his easel, imaging the American West. Costumed as a cavalryman, the model posed on the artist's Hoboken, New Jersey, apartment rooftop (1903). The revolver was the classic Colt Peacemaker, the *de riguer* handgun for the vast majority of Western action paintings.

INTRODUCTION

The American West: an adventure, a way of life, a spirit, and a time and place symbolized around the world by the cowboy, the frontiersman, and the gunfighter, and by their arms. Among the latter are chiefly the Colt Peacemaker revolver and the Winchester Model 1873 rifle. These "peacemakers," and thousands more "shooting irons" are also captivating props playing before countless millions of Wild West buffs in the arena, on stage and the radio, in the cinema and on television.

Historian Frederick Jackson Turner stated that the three major tools in the development of America were the plow, the axe, and the gun. Plows and axes do not make for colorful or intriguing collector's items, but the gun has a magnetic, magical attraction and has captivated the hearts and minds of aficionados around the world since the days the Great Western Adventure began.

Many a history-maker of the West itself had an infatuation with firearms and other weaponry. The affection and care devoted to trusty arms sometimes led to anointing favorites with nicknames: "Lucretia Borgia" for Buffalo Bill Cody's trusty buffalo rifle, "Sam Colt" for artist George Catlin's tried-and-true Paterson Colt revolving rifle, and the "Widow" for scout and showman Texas Jack Omohundro's Plains rifle. Countless diaries, letters, and other documents—and thousands of surviving period photographs—attest to the importance of these peacemakers. Often arms proved to be instruments of life insurance, whether or not they bore out the frontier poem about the Colt:

Do not be afraid of any man,
no matter what his size,
just call on me in time of need,
and I will equalize.

Among early collectors of arms were Buffalo Bill Cody, Lieutenant Colonel George Armstrong Custer and General Nelson A. Miles, Captain Jack Crawford, Colonel Samuel Colt, Oliver Winchester, and Theodore Roosevelt.

And while the West was nearing the end of the trail, Thomas Edison's motion pictures gave to our culture a fresh entertainment medium in which some of the West's players became stars in the fictionalizing of the great saga. A few of these stars had also played key roles in yet another phenomenon: Wild West shows. Still later, radio and talking pictures were joined by television. Through it all, scarcely a Western program was presented without arms as important elements of the entertainment.

Generations of arms collectors have been weaned on such programming. With the dawn of the video industry, collecting Westerns has become an international pursuit—and many enthusiasts would agree that not a few of the best films in the genre have been done in modern times, despite liberties taken with reality, and skyrocketing production costs.

Like millions of devotees, the author grew up immersed in Westerns. First, the Saturday matinees of Gene Autry and Roy Rogers, Johnny Mack Brown and Monte Hale. Then the TV with the tried-and-true matinee heroes, plus the Lone Ranger, James Arness and

Gunsmoke, Bonanza, Rawhide, ad infinitum, and simultaneously with such films as *Shane* (Alan Ladd), *Winchester '73* (James Stewart), and *Rio Bravo* (John Wayne).

Researching *The Peacemakers* has been a great adventure for the author: firearms and their accessories (knives particularly) were so necessary in the Western saga that many have become icons. The fascination of millions of Americans to arms of the West is an understandable phenomenon, for the art and craftsmanship, history, mechanics, and romance are unequaled by any other artifact associated with the West. Further, most of the objects are of American manufacture, and thus are part of our national pride. Our culture created what came to be termed as the "American system of manufacture," and it was the firearms industry that was the principal creator. It should also be noted that the vast majority of firearms were devoted to positive uses. As in today's society, the "good guys" vastly outnumber the "bad guys," notwithstanding the preponderance of media coverage that bad news is given versus good.

The author is hopeful that the extraordinary appeal of these peacemakers, the arms of the American West —and of their adventurous users—transcends the pages of the present book and instills a feeling of respect and admiration for the positive contributions of America's extraordinary pioneer spirit, and the spirit of respect and admiration which is an underlying factor in the production of the vast majority of Western entertainment.

—R. L. Wilson

To That Uniquely Exciting World
of Collectors, Dealers, Historians, Historical Societies, and Museums
Devoted to
Studying, Documenting, and Interpreting
the Arms and Adventures
of the American West
● ● ●
Their Passion
Made the Dream of This Book
into Reality

And in Memory of
Dr. John M. Wilson, Sr.
1916–1991
Who Early Encouraged His Son's
Fascination with the Exciting
World of Arms and Armor

THE PEACEMAKERS
ARMS AND ADVENTURE
IN THE AMERICAN WEST

Delegation of Ponca Chiefs, Washington, Nov. 15, 1877.

INDIANS: ARMS AND THE FIRST AMERICANS

T he Emperor Napoleon's sale of the Louisiana Territory played a vital role in the westward expansion of the youthful United States. This signal event symbolized the shift
in power from France, Spain, and Great Britain to the fledgling nation, and was the
beginning of the end of Indian domination of the American West.

Slowly but surely, the tribes of the West would be crushed into submission. First came the
explorers, the missionaries, the entrepreneurs—Spaniards and Russians, French and English,
and the Americans. The dawn of the nineteenth century saw the Lewis and Clark Expedition
(1804–06), followed by Zebulon Pike, and soon the near-legendary mountain men. Slowly but
surely, the cornucopia of the Great West opened to reveal a wealth in natural resources and
grandeur that was an irresistible magnet to Easterners and to emigrants and adventurers
from around the world.

Against this onslaught the Indian was doomed. His traditional weapons—the war club,
tomahawk, lance, and bow and arrow—were fearsome at close range, but a poor match for
the white man's muskets, rifles, pistols, and even cannon.

Native American ingenuity and access to new weapons led to an improvement in arms and
equipment for fighting and hunting, but never in a sufficiently organized, effective sense.

Superior firepower, and sheer numbers, would prevail. Although the Indian tribes had the
advantage of knowing their habitat intimately, that in time was negated by the force of arms

Ponca chief Standing Bear led his tribe in peaceful resistance to white injustice after forcible removal from their Nebraska homeland to an
unwanted reservation in 1877. After suffering from mistreatment and neglect at the hands of federal agents, the Ponca's plight became
known through newspaper articles; conscientious whites worked on their behalf. In 1879, Standing Bear and his people were returned to
land in northern Nebraska. The winter 1879–80 tour of the East, recorded here in a poignant photograph taken in Washington, D.C., led to
public pressure to improve government treatment of all Indian peoples. Standing Bear's passive resistance was in marked contrast to the
armed response of most tribes. Silver peace medals (honoring "peace and friendship") bore President's bust on obverse, were useful government gifts to Indians.

Detail from page 8.

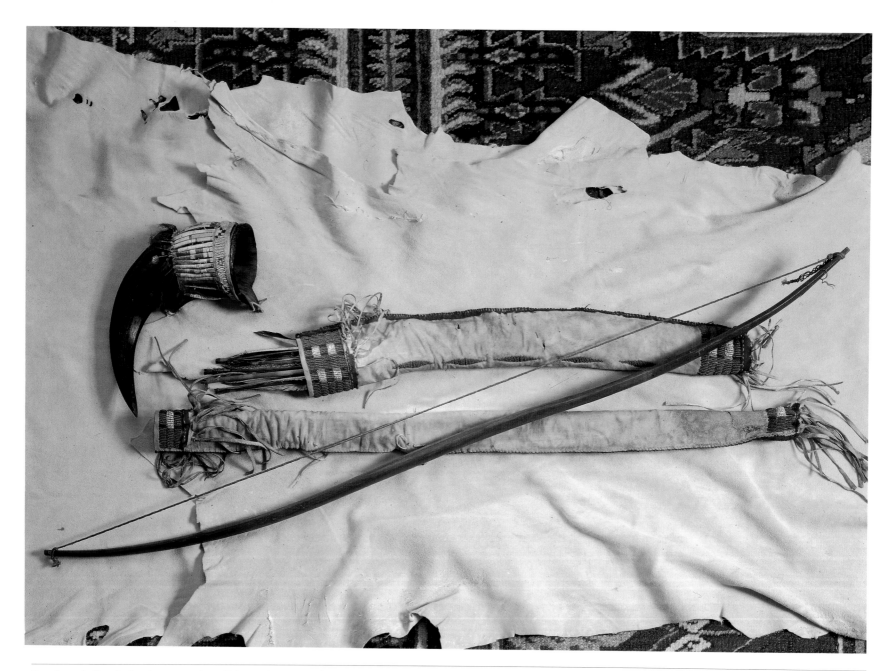

Sioux bow, of self or single-peice construction, with bow and quiver case, beaded buffalo horn used for warpoint; c. 1880s. Bows and arrows present difficulty in dating since they changed little over generations.

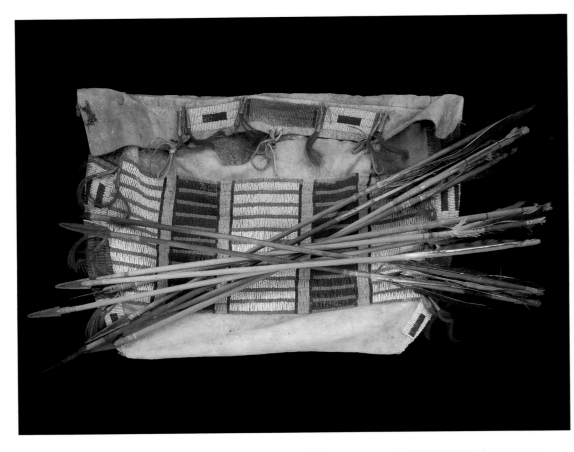

and men of the U.S. Army and in the organized and well-armed masses of pioneers. Mountain men and traders, their numbers limited, were dependent on an uncanny sense of self-preservation. Many were inclined to take up Indian ways to save their fur trade, and themselves.

"War Now. War Forever."

The Shawnee warrior Tecumseh was a forceful advocate of Indian resistance. With his brother, Tenskwatawa, a coalition of Midwestern tribes was organized. Tecumseh set the stage for resistance to the white man, a long-playing tragedy which would dominate much of the nineteenth century: "Burn their dwellings. Destroy their stock. The red people own the country." He went on to call for "War now. War forever. War upon the living. War upon the dead; dig up their corpses from the grave; our country must give no rest to a white man's bones."

Tecumseh's forces, the Creek Confederacy, numbered upward of 15,000 warriors. The death of Tecumseh and ultimate defeat of the Creeks, signified by the Treaty of Ghent (ending the War of 1812), were the death knells of Indian nationalism. After 1815, the Indian's fate was sealed. Western Indians would fight on, but resistance by the last Indian tribes would effectively be quelled by 1890.

What had taken the white newcomers some 200 years east of the Mississippi would require only about a century west of the Mississippi. Thomas Jefferson, who was sympathetic to the Indians' plight, had anticipated hundreds of years for the process.

Spain's sale of her American property and claims east of the Mississippi (1819) added to the U.S. grip on the West. William Henry Harrison represented popular sentiment when he said: "Is one of the fairest portions of the globe to remain in a state of nature, the haunt of a few wretched savages, when it seems destined by the Creator to a large population and to be the seat of civilization?"

A policy of forced removal saw such scandalous events as the "Trail of Tears," along which some 15,000

Sioux possible bag, c. 1880. With selection of Plains Indian hunting arrows.

Hunting buffaloes with white wolf skins as camouflage. Watercolor by George Catlin, c. 1840. How an Indian might shoot a buffalo from horseback with a muzzle-loading rifle was described by Solomon Carvalho, who accompanied John Charles Frémont's expedition of 1853–54: "A Delaware Indian [sited in Kansas], in hunting buffaloes, when near enough to shoot, rests his rifle on his saddle, balances himself in the stirrup on one leg; the other is thrown over the rifle to steady it. He then leans on one side, until his eye is on a level with the object, takes a quick sight and fires while riding at full speed, rarely missing his mark, and seldom chasing one animal further than a mile."

Catlin pen-and-ink drawing, in which bows and arrows, war clubs, lances, tomahawks, and knives are all in hand. Scalp, held aloft at *lower right*.

Cherokees were forcibly moved, most on foot, from Georgia to Oklahoma. It is estimated that as many as 1,500 died in the trek, overseen by troops under General Winfield Scott. Other tribes were also forcibly removed into the West. Often tribes native to the new areas were hostile toward the interlopers and opposed them by the same violent means used against whites.

Pre–Civil War Indian hostilities in the West were of such breadth and scope that they are not easily categorized. Post–Civil War encounters are another matter: these were the wars of the Great Plains and adjacent Texas and the Rocky Mountains, the great Southwest of New Mexico, Arizona, and environs, and the Northwest.

Changes in the federal government's Indian policy during the nineteenth century were influenced by such factors as rapid westward movement of population, added U.S. territories, the California gold rush and California's statehood, and the development of the Overland Trail. Moving the Indians out of the way led to forced containment on reservations. To say that the majority of negotiated treaties were unfair to the Indians is an understatement. The attempted containment on reservations was a major cause of Indian resistance.

The Civil War offered a glimpse of hope to the Indians, and 15,000 fought on the side of the Confederate States of America. About 3,000 were recruited to fight for the Union. The Confederacy made some concessions to the Indians, while the preoccupation of the Union forces dealing with the South allowed several uprisings in Western areas where troop strengths were reduced. Over 500 settlers in Minnesota were killed in an uprising by the Sioux, led by Chief Little Crow. In response, General John Pope (recently defeated at Second Bull Run) launched a campaign summed up by such statements as "It is my purpose utterly to exterminate the Sioux if I have the power to do so." They were "to be treated as maniacs or wild beasts, and by no means as people with whom treaties or compromises can be made." Thirty-eight of the Indians were executed: 303 had been condemned to hang, but most

The Pursuit, by Currier & Ives, 1856. The red man's lance versus the single-shot pistol of the frontiersman, also armed with a half-stock plains rifle.

Nostalgic *Cheyennes Among the Buffalo*, crayon-and-ink drawing from ledger sketchbook by Montana-Wyoming Indian, done while incarcerated in Florida, c. 1880. A handful of such books are known; this one is from collection of Brigadier General E. D. Townsend, who retired from Army at about time drawings were made.

had their sentences commuted by a compassionate President Lincoln.

A second uprising during the Civil War was by the Cheyenne and Arapaho tribes of the Colorado Territory, in response to gold and silver mining begun in the 1850s. Hostilities by the Indians led to the infamous Sand Creek Massacre of 1864, a dawn attack by Colonel John M. Chivington and the 3rd Colorado Cavalry. Despite being greeted by Chief Black Kettle raising the American flag and a white flag of surrender, Chivington ordered the slaughter of men, women, and children. The senseless carnage was a low point in the national conflict between whites and Indians. Of Black Kettle's village of 500, some 300 managed to survive.

Chivington's brutality backfired, inspiring the Indians to a renewed vigor. It would take another twenty-five years of unrest before most of the Indians of the West would be pummeled and coerced into submission.

Large-scale Indian victories in the West were few and far between. Easily the most dramatic was that at the Little Bighorn, popularly known as Custer's Last Stand, or the Custer Massacre. The aftermath for the Indians was a renewed intensity of the white onslaught, particularly by a shaken U.S. Army.

Although direct confrontations between whites and Indians were not infrequent, there was a subtle and more effective means to undermine the Indians of the Plains: elimination of the buffalo herds.

The end of the Civil War found America an industrial giant, with an experienced armed force and hardened veterans who could homestead on land available from the government. Further, there was the appeal of

Great Lakes pipe tomahawk of c. 1840, *upper right,* with iron bowl and spontoon blade; iron tacks, and braided Germantown yarn drop or lanyard. *Lower right,* eastern Plains tomahawk, with iron and brass head, c. 1860. The elaborate, heavy pipe tomahawk at *left* is from late nineteenth century; steel blade inserted in brass head. Articulated Comanche horse stick, *bottom center,* and beaded Blackfoot leggings are c. 1860.

mining, commerce, and all the other elements of conquering the most vital continent on the face of the earth. Great fortunes would be made, and a uniquely American adventure would unfold.

The Indian, in the minds of many, would be in the way. Policy dictated that the tribes must accept containment or be dealt with militarily.

The post–Civil War years proved the warrior prowess of the Plains tribes, which conducted successful raids and easily evaded their military antagonists. An attempted peace conference at Fort Laramie (spring 1866) led to Sioux Chief Red Cloud's comment on the government's request for free use of the Bozeman Trail: "Great Father sends us presents and wants new road, but White Chief goes with soldiers to steal the road before Indians can say yes or no!" At that point the chief and his warriors abruptly departed in disgust. The government Indian agent nevertheless concluded a treaty, but it was not signed by those who could have held their people in check.

Red Cloud and his forces responded with repeated attacks, and Fort Phil Kearney on the Bozeman Trail (headquarters for commanding Colonel Henry B. Carrington) would be under siege more than any other U.S. post, of any period.

A clear-cut victory for the Indians was the Fetterman Fight (December 1866), in which Crazy Horse and his men lured Captain William J. Fetterman and eighty men into an expertly orchestrated ambush. Crazy Horse's decoys led the impetuous and foolhardy Fetterman over a hill and straight into a force of 2,000 Dakota and Cheyenne warriors. To a man the command was annihilated, in the space of about half an hour. Even a dog accompanying Fetterman's column was killed. One of the warriors had shouted, "Do not let even a dog get away!"

Terrified at the thought of a slow death by torture, Fetterman and Captain Frederick H. Brown took their own lives with their revolvers. Other men were so horrified they were killed without fighting back. Two civilians with Fetterman had been armed with Henry

repeating rifles. Around their bodies were expended cartridges (50 by one of them), and one of them had no less than 105 arrows in his body.

The Fetterman Massacre led the federal government to attempt to improve its conduct of Indian affairs. The Bozeman Trail was closed, forts were abandoned, and other attempts were made to pacify Red Cloud and his forces. Another treaty was signed, and more Indians joined reservations—this time in the Dakota Territory.

The Fetterman debacle also helped in cleaning up the generally unprincipled bureaucracy of federal Indian agents. Even George Armstrong Custer had been appalled by the corruption. But the Bureau of Indian Affairs would remain largely unchanged until the turn of the century.

Besides the slaughter of the buffalo and military confrontations, another powerful influence on the Indians was what they saw in Midwestern and Eastern cities on junkets organized by the federal government. In such places, teaming with so many whites and burgeoning with technology, the power of the Great Father and his people was overwhelmingly evident.

Demonstrations by huge cannon and Gatling guns made an impression. Visits to the Washington, D.C., arsenal revealed guns by the tens of thousands. However, most of the Indians became homesick, and urged their hosts to complete the tour quickly, so the delegations could get back to their homes and families in the West.

"Conquest by Kindness" was the official federal government Indian policy following the Civil War. However, such events as the Fetterman fight and the murder of General E. R. S. Canby and Peace Commissioner Eleasar Thomas by Modoc Indians under a flag of truce (April 1873) contributed to a return to hostilities. Raids in Texas by Kiowa and Comanche tribes, from the reservation near Fort Sill, Indian Territory, led to the Army's becoming more active in Indian affairs. Thereafter until the 1880s the Indians who refused reservation life were dealt with summarily.

(*above*) Somewhat stylized Indian, shot at close range by frontiersman, armed with a Colt revolver; Currier & Ives, 1858. Stag-handled Bowie knife on shooter's belt. Lance, bow, and shield on ground at *right*.

(*opposite left*) Ojibwa knife and sheath, Michigan, c. 1830–50, at *right* loom-beaded and with silk edging, contrasts with Plains weaponry: Sioux war club, c. 1880, has carved face at ball and spike end, grip bound with braided, dyed quills. At *center*, mountain man knife with beaver tail sheath, c. 1850. Stone war club has fetish and cowrie-shell drop; Blackfoot, nineteenth century. Beaded horse blanket from Nez Pierce, c. 1860.

(*opposite right*) Accompanied by a Cheyenne pipe bag at *left* (c. 1880) and a Flathead pipe bag (colored with red ocher) at *right* (c. 1860), the tomahawks are all of the Plains Indian Wars period, with the Blackfoot at *right* wrapped in brass wire, and of c. 1860.

Custer's defeat at the Little Bighorn was bad timing for the Indians. Falling just prior to the opening of the Centennial Exhibition in Philadelphia—designed to demonstrate America's might to the world —the annihilation of Custer proved both a tragedy and an embarrassment. Only the crushing of the Indians would dispel this blight on the nation's international image, or so it was felt by many in power at the time.

Innumerable instances of the heroic resistance of native tribes are recorded. Celebrated in literature and film, and in the lore of Indian descendants, is the fight for freedom of Chief Joseph and his Nez Perce tribe. Known to the Lewis and Clark Expedition, the tribe had a long history of peace, and had never killed a white. A dispute with squatters led to the killing of four whites (1877). To escape their pursuers, Joseph and his band of 800 headed for Canada from Oregon, eluding, defeating, and fighting to a draw the U.S. Army along the way. The campaign offers a case study in military strategy and won Joseph's Nez Perce the respect of their adversaries.

Part of their route cut through Yellowstone National Park (to the surprise of tourists). Finally General Nelson A. Miles forced a surrender. Some 300 of the Nez Perce reached Canada shortly before Chief Joseph made his famous statement: "... It is cold and we have

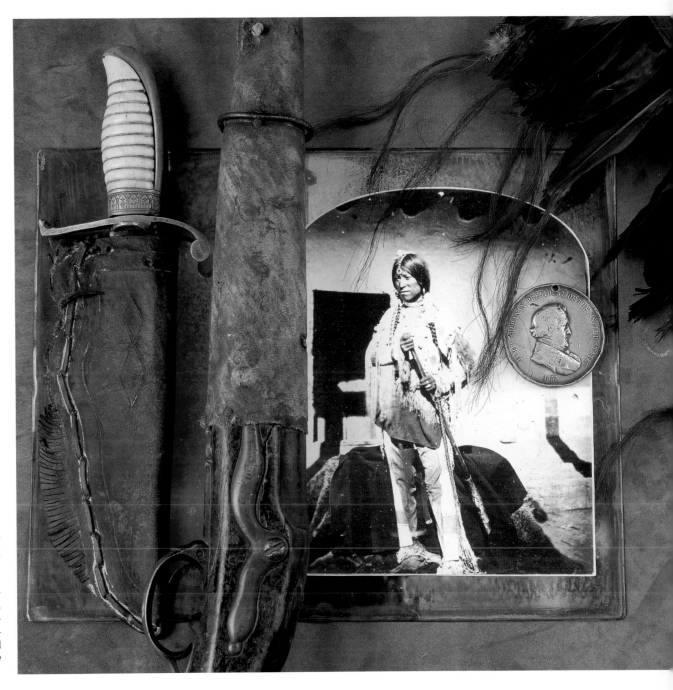

Displayed on a Sioux saddle cloth are, *from left*, Plains ball-headed war club with iron spike and five tomahawks of western Plains, from 1850 to the 1870s; curved blade example at *right* rare. *Far right*, knife sheaths with skinning knives. *Lower left*, "Beaver tail" general-purpose knives. Heads and blades obtained from traders; the lower knife marked on blade with New York maker's name. Tacks obtained from traders, also taken from travel chests and luggage of victims.

Jicarilla Apache Shee-zah-nan-tan, holding half-stock muzzle-loader; breech wrapped with rawhide, as is Brown Bess musket at *left*, converted from flintlock to percussion, the stock cut down, and barrel reduced to 31-inch length. Some shortened lengths were the result of burst barrels; the warrior would simply cut the barrel behind the point of bursting. Knife made by Indian from military sword by shortening blade and cutting off knuckle bow.

no blankets. The little children are freezing to death. . . . Hear me, my chiefs! I am tired. My heart is sick and sad. From where the sun now stands, I will fight no more forever."

Members of the Chiricahua Apache tribe were the final organized body of Indians fighting the government in the early to middle 1880s.* Raiders along the Mexican border could simply escape across the border when they were pursued by either Mexican or American units. Eventually a treaty was signed with Mexico which eliminated that advantage.

It was General Nelson A. Miles who was responsible for ending the Apache menace. After a determined campaign, Miles was able to ship off the offending Apaches and their relatives to camps in Florida. The famed Chief Geronimo was one of the last to surrender, and he too was exiled to Florida.

Fierce and courageous fighters that they were, the Native American warriors struck absolute terror in the hearts of their victims. Troopers are known to have committed suicide rather than endure the torture they could expect from their captors.

On the other hand, atrocities were perpetrated by so-called civilized troops, and among the most barbaric were those of Colonel Chivington's men at Sand Creek. An eyewitness stated that Indians were "scalped, their brains knocked out . . . men . . . ripped open women, clubbed little children . . ." Chivington

---

*By c. 1885, over 240,000 Indians were in place on approximately 180,000 square miles, divided up into 180 reservations.

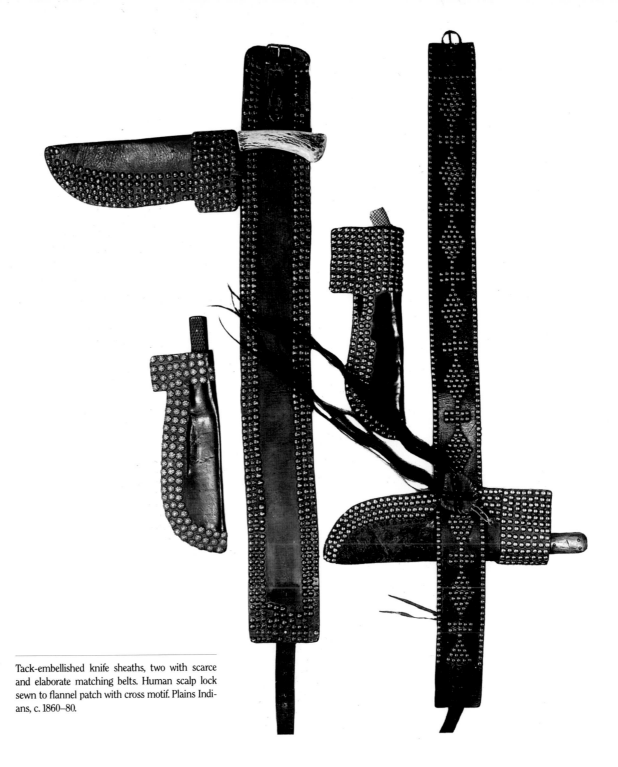

Flintlock trade muskets (*top* marked by U.S. maker), with Plains Indian tomahawk, its haft decorated with brass tacks and by branding with red-hot file. Scalp lock from red-haired human kill. Artifacts rest on buffalo hide. English-made trade guns continued to have the lion's share of the Western market until c. 1840. With the support of federal government contracts, this changed to American domination, particularly by such makers as Henry Deringer, Jr., Henry E. Leman, and George and Edward Tryon.

Tack-embellished knife sheaths, two with scarce and elaborate matching belts. Human scalp lock sewn to flannel patch with cross motif. Plains Indians, c. 1860–80.

displayed some one hundred Indian scalps on a Denver stage, before an audience of applauding whites.

The culmination of the Great Plains wars is symbolized by the tragic death of Sitting Bull and a mass killing at Wounded Knee, December 1890. Such leaders as holy man and chief Sitting Bull had incited Indian revolt. "Look at me" he said to an assemblage of reservation Indians. "See if I am poor, or my people either. . . . You are fools to make yourselves slaves to a piece of fat bacon, some hard-tack, and a little sugar and coffee." Sitting Bull was killed by Indian police, December 15, 1890.

Two weeks later, at Wounded Knee, the 7th Cavalry avenged their defeat at the Little Bighorn by firing into several hundred Indians. Deluded by the Ghost Dance mystics who claimed protection from soldiers' bullets, the Indians had refused to be disarmed. The slaughter wiped out more than 200 men, women, and children. Not a few wounded were left on the battlefield; they froze to death the next evening in a blizzard.

Except for isolated incidents, the Indian Wars were over.

Indian pride survived and the warrior traditions continued to modern times through service in the U.S. Army and other armed services. Herman J. Viola's *After Columbus* quotes a modern-day Ute: "We Indians are grateful that the United States became such a militaristic country because it has provided us with an acceptable way to continue our warrior ways." During the Vietnam War, while thousands of young Americans

Trade musket at *top* acquired by collector on an Indian reservation; barrel engraved in script, *"Montreal"*; among silver overlays are beavers, a snake, turtle (other side), cross, bleeding heart, and fleur-de-lis. Skin repair at wrist; c. 1800. Treasured objects, guns would pass down through generations. Trade rifle at *bottom* by Leman, with lock dated 1840, in .50 caliber, stock artificially striped for added appeal. Profits from trading a "Northwest Gun," as the type came to be called, were substantial. From the winter of 1812–13, such a gun from the Pacific Fur Company post, Spokane, would trade for at least twenty beaver pelts. Wholesale a gun would run £1 20 shillings; the value of the pelts was approximately £25!

fled the country to avoid military service (mainly heading to Canada), not a few Canadian Indians came to the United States to enlist. As in past wars, including World Wars I and II, the presence of Indians in fighting units tended to ensure high fighting morale.

The Indians' bows, arrows, trade muskets, and other largely nineteenth-century firearms have been replaced by high-tech modern weaponry, like the Colt M-16 rifle. But that Indian spirit and fighting instinct, courage and pride, remain—all are components in the present rejuvenation of the Indian peoples in America, symbolized by the Smithsonian Institution's new National Museum of the American Indian, on the Mall in Washington, D.C., and the revitalization of the Heye Foundation as the National Museum of the American Indian, New York City.

Bows and Arrows

The warrior tradition was instilled in Indian children from birth. From childhood, Indian boys played with bows and arrows, the scaled-down sizes often made by fathers for their sons. The boys could shoot moving targets with uncanny accuracy. For most Indians of the West, hunting was a way of life, and to some, so was warfare.

Firearms were early introduced to Indians, but a proliferation of guns did not occur until the nineteenth century, when they were supplied by traders,

Plains Indian artifacts. Tomahawk attributed to Joseph Jourdain, c. 1855, its pipe bowl forged from rifled gun barrel. Beaded drop of sewn calico. Rifle by Henry E. Leman, .50 caliber, with 31-inch barrel; rawhide repair to shattered forestock. No aperture for ramrod; ball would be spit into barrel while hunting buffalo from horseback; c. 1850. Breastplate of hair pipe. Quirt with brass-tacked wooden handle. Trade knife with skull and horseshoe mark, believed early work of the renowned Russell; sheath of buffalo hide.

Scarce presentation rifle for an Indian chief; made by Leman. Silver-mounted, engraved with bow, arrow, and pipe tomahawk on the toeplate; marked U.S. on the barrel, and with an ordnance inspector's mark behind the sideplate.

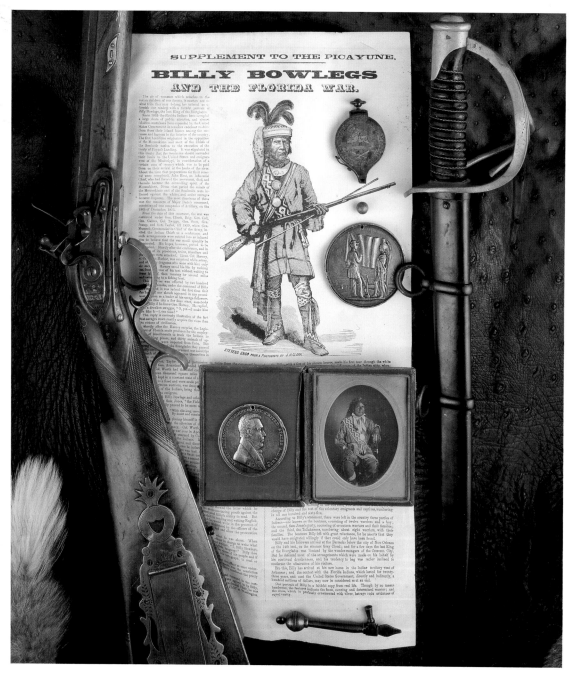

taken as trophies of war and in raids on whites, and even given or issued by the U.S. government.

Bows and arrows would remain as common weapons. In retreat from battles, guns might be abandoned, but not bows and arrows. As breechloaders and repeating guns came in vogue, however, bows and arrows tended to assume a role primarily as backup.

By 1875, many older warriors had guns of rather high quality and serviceability—such as the Winchester 1866 and 1873 lever-actions at the Little Bighorn. Ammunition, however, would remain scarce, and the Indians lacked the tools and mechanical ability for most repairs.

Exactly how Indians held the bow and bowstring and released their arrows is unknown. There were various holds with fingers, thumbs, and hands. Chief Plenty Coups described shooting an arrow, which was best done from the right-hand side of the bow:

> Both hands and both arms must work together—at once. The left must push and the right must pull at the same time if an arrow is to go straight or far. The [right] hand, palm toward one, its fingers straddling the arrow, must know and keep the center of the bowstring without the eyes having to look.

The design and manufacture of arrows was important, with the straightness of each arrow paramount. Shafts were given identifying markings in paint, so an archer's affiliation and person could be identified. The type of feathers also could serve to determine a tribe.

For shooting practice, buffalo chips were useful, and could be rolled for moving targets. Boys sought first to develop distance, then worked on precision and accuracy.

Experienced archers could shoot with speed and force. A mortal wound could be made from twenty yards, and as many as eight arrows could be kept in the air simultaneously, with arching shots. There was such force in the snapping bowstring that a gauntlet was needed for wrist and arm protection. The bow hand also gripped a cluster of arrows (tips pointed downward) for quick reloading. Extra arrows could also be held in the mouth, plus the customary quiver.

(*opposite*) Though most of life was spent in his native Florida, Billy Bowlegs was one of thousands of Indians to be relocated West. In 1858 he and a number of fellow Seminoles moved to Oklahoma. During Civil War served with the rank of captain, 1st Regiment, Indian Home Guard, a Kansas unit. Contemporary with long-running Seminole War are Colt Paterson, capper, and combination tool at *top* and *bottom right*, and New England rifle. Note peace medal worn in a daguerreotype of 1852, and U.S.-issue sword chief is holding. The model 1860 saber represents the Civil War era.

(*above left*) Brass tacks and signs of hard use, and the beaded sheath, identify this Model 1841 U.S. Mississippi rifle as an Indian service arm. Firing a .54-caliber projectile, gun could readily kill a buffalo.

(*above right*) Trade musket at *bottom* contrasts with government contract trade flintlock gun, of more graceful construction and with longer barrel. Commercial production of Indian trade guns from American makers went to Western market. These were referred to as "Lancaster pattern" (as in the Leman pictured *above*) and "English pattern." The former were of Kentucky rifle styling, the latter on lines of contemporary English inexpensive sporting guns (as on *top* gun shown here). These arms were of sufficient quality to also attract white trappers as end-users. The flintlock Northwest guns were still in production as late as the 1870s, even though many Indians had switched to breech loaders and to various types of repeating firearms. Plains tomahawk with file-burned handle; chief's war bonnet, of the late 1870s.

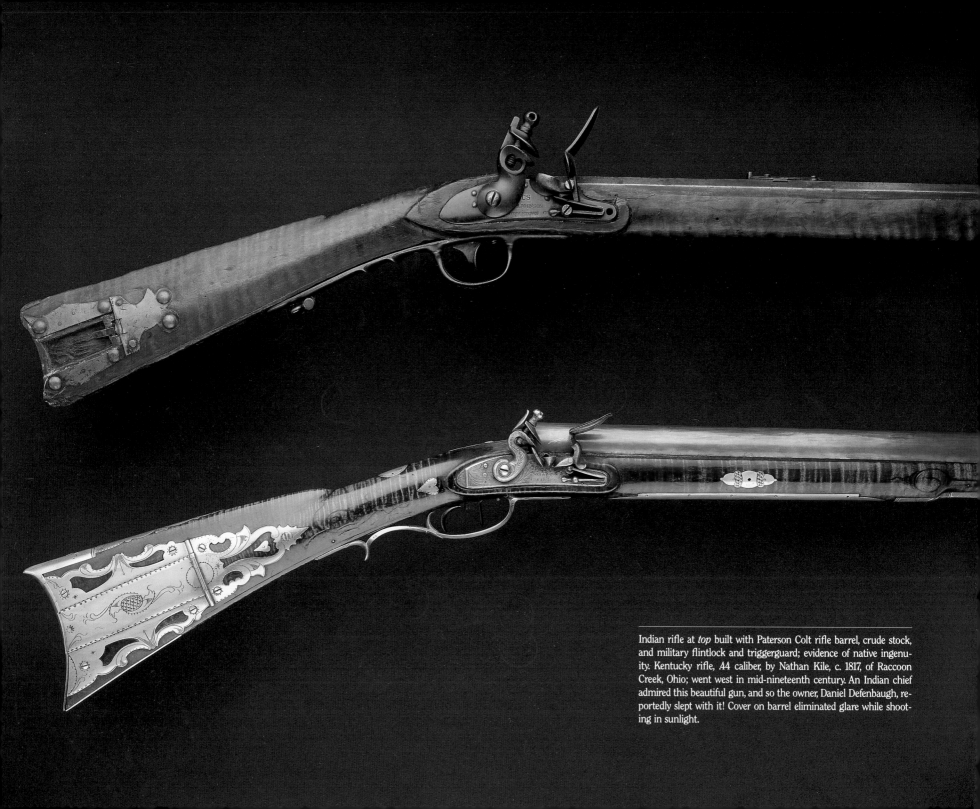

Indian rifle at *top* built with Paterson Colt rifle barrel, crude stock, and military flintlock and triggerguard; evidence of native ingenuity. Kentucky rifle, .44 caliber, by Nathan Kile, c. 1817, of Raccoon Creek, Ohio; went west in mid-nineteenth century. An Indian chief admired this beautiful gun, and so the owner, Daniel Defenbaugh, reportedly slept with it! Cover on barrel eliminated glare while shooting in sunlight.

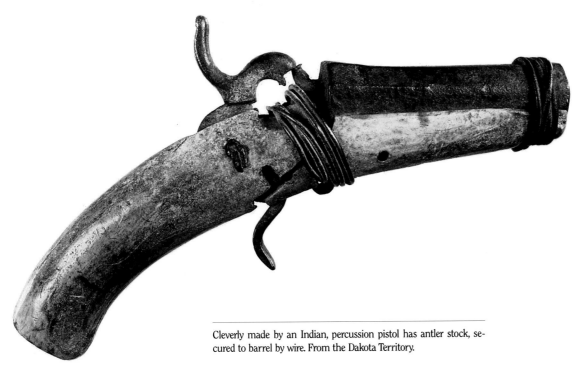

CHOCTAW NATIONAL BANK OF CADDO

Cleverly made by an Indian, percussion pistol has antler stock, secured to barrel by wire. From the Dakota Territory.

Cannon, a wounded horse, guns, lances, bow and arrows, bullets, and at *lower left* the staff (to identify assistant leaders in a war party) are evident in this scene of a charge against what is likely U.S. Army. Note shields; Colonel Richard I. Dodge paid tribute to the subject in *33 Years Among Our Wild Indians*: "...the shield is the head and front, the topmost summit of warlike paraphernalia. On it he bestows infinite patience, care and thought.... it is his shield, his protector, his escutcheon, his medicine, almost his God." Usually made of buffalo hide, shields were felt to have magical powers, even to be capable of stopping the white man's bullets. By an Indian artist on a bank ledger, from Caddo, Indian Territory.

Indians preferred to be as close to their prey as possible, to conserve arrows and avoid wasted shots. Young archers would graduate from flint to iron arrowheads as they gained shooting skills.*

Lances

As backup to the bow and arrow, Plains Indians relied on lances, tomahawks, clubs, and knives. Firearms became increasingly important, but they were generally more difficult to obtain and maintain, and they demanded skills not all Indians could master.

Lances for hunting, primarily for buffalo on horseback, typically were tipped in iron (about 10 inches or more) and measured between 7 and 9 feet long, with wood hafts from 1 to nearly 3 inches in diameter. The hunter would ride up next to the buffalo, and thrust the lance deeply into a point just behind the shoulder or behind the rib cage. Then the hunter would hang on to the lance and try to ride alongside the buffalo for a short while. Then he would pull out the lance and move on to another buffalo. Decor for hunting lances was plain, though some bore brass or iron tacks, feathers, and paint.

Lances for war were generally smaller in diameter (5/8 inch to 1 1/4 inches) and shorter (6 1/2 to 7 1/2 feet), and were elaborately decorated. Decorative materials ranged from animal-hide wrappings (strong and fast beasts, like beaver, weasel, mink, and otter), colorful cloths, beads, fringes, feathers from eagles or other birds, and tacks. Horsehair streamers might be attached to the butt. Scalps might also be attached, or colorful ribbons.

Like the Knights of the Round Table, the Indian lancer held his weapon under the arm, secured and aimed by the hand. The closer one could be to the enemy or animal, the better. Lances could also be held in two hands above the head for jabbing. Throwing was an alternative; such lances would have a feather spiral decor running the shaft's length.

Apertures or thongs on the lance allowed for attaching to the horse and for ease in holding. Seasoned wood was needed for the lance, preferably ash, hickory,

---

*For more detail on the bow and arrow, see Appendix.

(*opposite*) Indian at *right* holds Colt Richards Conversion Model 1860 Army revolver and a noncommissioned infantry officer's sword. At *left*, Apache scout Jim, with his three-barrel rifle-shotgun, and Colt Model 1878 Frontier double-action revolver. Indian police badge of c. 1880s. Trade gun at *top* of American manufacture, studded with 202 brass tacks. Buttplate and forend cap of pewter; pewter arrow, brass quarter moon, and five-pointed star inlaid on left side of buttstock. Has 30-inch barrel; mid-nineteenth century.

(*above*) From the collection of General Nelson A. Miles, Henry rifle number 7136 bears presentation inscription from President Grant, to Sitting Bull the Minor—chief from another Plains tribe, and not *the* Sitting Bull. The beaded and fringed scabbard was not supplied by the donor.

(*top right*) Cree chief Poundmaker, his Model 1866 Winchester with shoulder sling.

(*bottom right*) Most armed with muzzle-loaders, these Indians are gathered together in Salt Lake City, 1869.

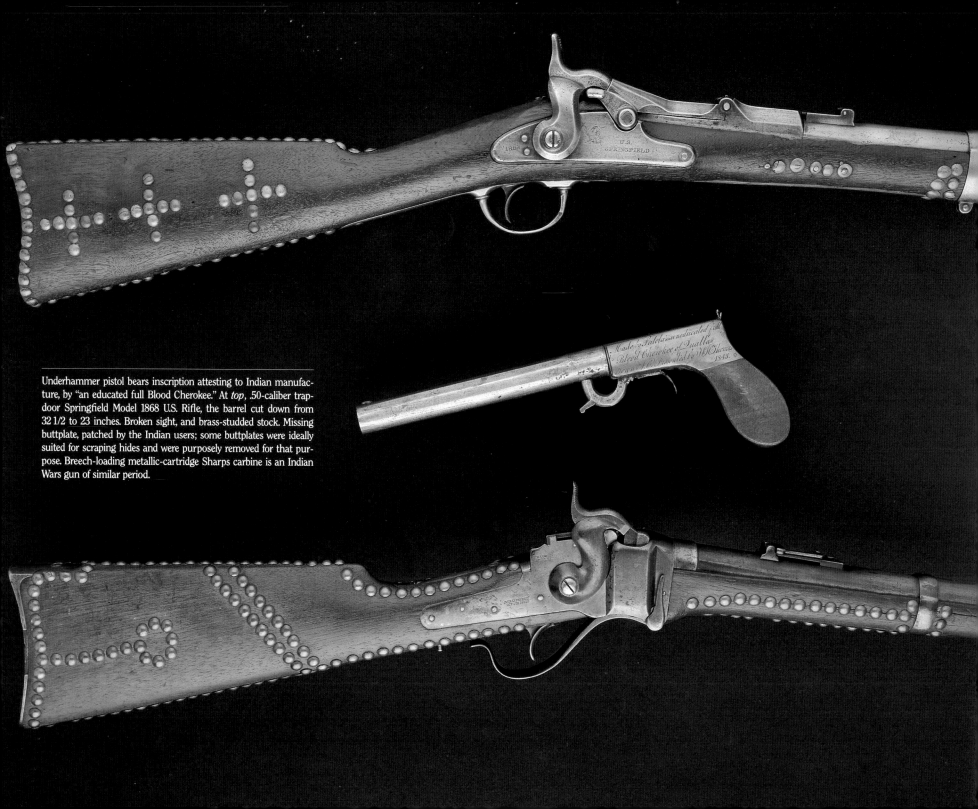

Underhammer pistol bears inscription attesting to Indian manufacture, by "an educated full Blood Cherokee." At *top*, .50-caliber trapdoor Springfield Model 1868 U.S. Rifle, the barrel cut down from 32 1/2 to 23 inches. Broken sight, and brass-studded stock. Missing buttplate, patched by the Indian users; some buttplates were ideally suited for scraping hides and were purposely removed for that purpose. Breech-loading metallic-cartridge Sharps carbine is an Indian Wars gun of similar period.

The Battle of the Little Bighorn

The story of Custer's Last Stand or the Battle of Little Bighorn, has been told and retold innumerable times; it is one of the most famous battles in American history. Here is a rare version—a battle memoir from the Ogalalla chief Low Dog, quoted in the *Leavenworth Weekly Times*, August 18, 1881. Low Dog was one of the key battle leaders of the victorious Indian confederation. The interview was conducted by a Captain Howe, of the 17th Infantry, at a conference of chiefs, all of whom, the *Times* reporter stated, had been in the battle.

"We were in camp near Little Big Horn river. We had lost some horses, and an Indian went back on the trail to look for them. We did not know that the white warriors were coming after us. Some scouts or men in advance of the warriors saw the Indian looking for the horses and ran after him and tried to kill him to keep him from bringing us word, but he ran faster than they and came into camp and told us that the white warriors were coming. I was asleep in my lodge at the time. The sun was about noon [pointing with his finger]. I heard the alarm, but I did not believe it. I thought it was a false alarm. I did not think it possible that any white men would attack us, so strong as we were. We had in camp the Cheyennes, Arapahoes, and seven different tribes of the Teton Sioux—a countless number. Although I did not believe it was a true alarm, I lost no time getting ready. When I got my gun and came out of my lodge the attack had begun at the end of the camp where Sitting Bull and the Uncpapas were. The Indians held their ground to give the women and children time to get out of the way. By this time the herders were driving in the horses and as I was nearly at the further end of the camp, I ordered my men to catch their horses and get out of the way, and my men were hurrying to go and help those that were fighting. When the fighters saw that the women and children were safe they fell back. By this time my people went to help them,

Springfield trapdoor carbine, number 20140, documented through forensic research as present at Battle of the Little Bighorn, evidenced by a cartridge casing fired by the gun, found 350 meters northeast of Last Stand Hill. Believed used by an Indian firing on Custer's command. Cavalry picket pin found c. 1930 by a coyote trapper, on battlefield. Beaded moccasins and stone war club are Sioux, and of the Little Bighorn period. Scabbard for Indian knife crudely fashioned from top of Model 1872 cavalry boot; many of dead soldiers at the Custer battle had tops of boots cut away for use of the leather. Leather cartridge belt for .45 cartridges has iron stirrup strap buckle from McClellan saddle, an indication it was made up before arsenal-produced belt issued early in 1877. Belt virtually identical to that worn by Private George Walker, shown in photograph taken prior to his death at Little Bighorn. Cartridge belts, which were acid-tanned, caused extraction problems due to verdigris buildup on cases from reaction of leather to copper. Cartridge box same as those used by 7th Cavalry at the battle. Cavalry officer's buckskin gauntlets from estate of General Ranald Mackenzie, a contemporary of Custer. Mackenzie led the 4th Cavalry regiment in attacking and defeating Dull Knife's Cheyenne village in Wyoming, November 1876. The gauntlets may have been from the Custer battlefield, and picked up in the village along with several other 7th Cavalry items found by troops before they torched the village. Since Mackenzie was missing two fingers from his right hand, it is unlikely he wore these gauntlets himself.

and the less able warriors and the women caught horses and got them ready, and we drove the first attacking party back, and that party retreated to a high hill [Custer and men to Last Stand Hill]. Then I told my people, not to venture too far in pursuit for fear of falling into an ambush. By this time all the warriors in our camp were mounted and ready for fight, and then we were attacked on the other side by another party. They came on us like a thunderbolt. I never before nor since saw men so brave and fearless as those white warriors. We retreated until our men got all together, and then we charged upon them. I called to my men, 'This is a good day to die: follow me.' We massed our men, and that no man should fall back, every man whipped another man's horse and we rushed right upon them. As we rushed upon them the white warriors dismounted to fire, but they did very poor shooting. They held their horses reins on one arm while they were shooting, but their horses were so frightened that they pulled the men all around, and a great many of their shots went up in the air and did us no harm. The white warriors stood their ground bravely, and none of them made any attempt to get away. After all but two of them were killed, I captured two of their horses. Then the wise men and chiefs of our nation gave out to our people not to mutilate the dead white chief, for he was a brave warrior and died a brave man, and his remains should be respected.

"Then I turned around and went to help fight the other white warriors, who had retreated to a high hill on the east side of the river. [This was Reno's command.] I don't know whether any white men of Custer's force were taken prisoners. When I got back to our camp they were all dead. Everything was in confusion all the time of the fight. I did not see Gen. Custer. I do not know who killed him. We did not know till the fight was over that he was the white chief. We had no idea that the white warriors were coming until the runner came in and told us. I do not say that Reno was a coward. He fought well, but our men were fighting to save their women and children, and drive them back. If Reno and his warriors had fought as Custer and his warriors fought, the battle might have been against us. No white man or Indian ever fought as bravely as Custer and his men. The next day we fought Reno and his forces again, and killed many of them. Then the chiefs said these men had been punished enough, and that we ought to be merciful, and let them go. Then we heard that another force was coming up the river to fight us [General Terry's command], and we started to fight them, but the chiefs and wise men counseled that we had fought enough and that we should not fight unless attacked, and we went back and took our women and children and went away."

The *Leavenworth Times* account continued:

"This ended Low Dog's narration, given in the hearing of half a dozen officers, some of the Seventeenth Infantry and some of the Seventh Cavalry—Custer's regiment. . . . Officers were there who were at the Big Horn with Benteen, senior captain of the Seventh, who usually exercised command as a field officer, and who, with his battalion, joined Reno on the first day of the fight, after his retreat, and was in the second day's fight. It was a strange and intensely interesting scene. When Low Dog began his narrative, only Capt. Howe, the interpreter, and myself were present, but as he progressed the officers gathered round, listening to every word, and all were impressed that the Indian chief was giving a true account, according to his knowledge. . . ."

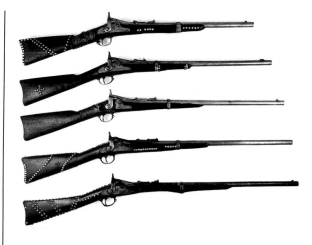

Indian-used Springfield trapdoor carbines and cut-down rifles, from collection of the late William O. Sweet. Any or all of these could have been at the Little Bighorn. Note extensive saddle wear on bottom gun.

Winchester Model 1866 carbine number 39618 *(bottom)* and Sharps Model 1874 military rifle C54586, both proved by forensic testing to have been present at the Little Bighorn. The 44 rimfire case matching the Winchester was found in 1985 at the Reno-Benteen defense site around Sharpshooter's Hill or Wooden Leg Hill. The .50-70 casing from Sharps was found in 1984 at Henryville or Henry Ridge area, an Indian position near Calhoun Hill. Both guns were used by Indians against Custer and his command. Photographs show Chief Gaul, Two Moon, and Sitting Bull, all principals in the battle.

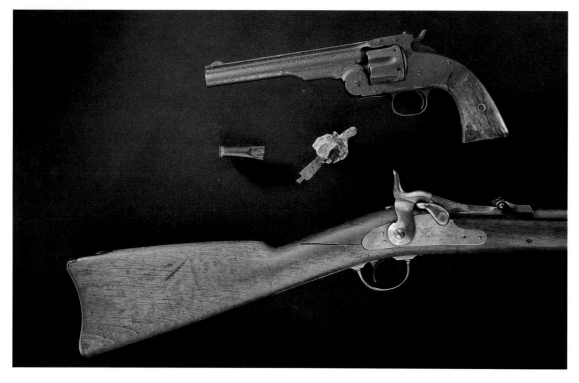

Chief Gall's Model 1876 Winchester rifle, .45-60 caliber. PEZI is carved on stock, his Sioux-language name. A Hunkpapa Sioux Chief, Gall was one of the field leaders at Little Bighorn. Realizing whites were impossible to defeat, he was not in favor of Ghost Dance religion and is credited with encouraging his followers toward education and adapting white ways.

Smith & Wesson Schofield .45 revolver picked up at Little Bighorn battlefield site by party of surveyors, summer of 1883; gun found loaded. Springfield trapdoor carbine, number 17025, documented by Major William B. Wetmore as "A carbine from the battle of Little Big Horn. Touch-in-the-Clouds Chief of the Minneconjous got it in the Custer fight. He gave it to Lieutenant Frederick G. Schwatka, 3rd Cavalry, about the middle of October 1876. The latter gave it to Wm. [B.] Wetmore, late 6th Cavalry. It looks as though the soldier having used up his ammunition clubbed his carbine and thus using it broke the stock before he fell." Cartridge casing from battlefield; some trapdoor casings split, and required prying loose from the breech manually. Upper thoracic vertebra of adult male, picked up at Custer battlesite, 1877, by Second Lieutenant George S. Young, 7th U.S. Infantry. At the time, removal of remains of Custer and other officers was under way, for reburial. Reburial on the site was also undertaken for troops who had not received adequate burial shortly after battle. Young picked up this grisly relic, as well as two cartridge cases, and one other arrow point.

ironwood, oak, or white elm. Although stone and bone were first used, the iron tip was preferred, and came to the tribes from traders or blacksmiths. Tips came in a variety of shapes and sizes; some were knife blades. On the warpath, by horse, not a few warriors carried lances. These were held in the hands, or attached across the warrior's back, or attached to the saddle.

Knives

Essential equipment for the Indians, knives were commonly of iron, supplied by traders. Blades were either single- or double-edged, the latter similar to a spear tip. Unlike the whites, Indians generally fought with the blade held downward, allowing for overhead blows or sideswipes at the midsection. Throwing was another fighting technique.

Early knives were often traded or sold to the Indians as blades only; it was up to the Indian to make his own handle. Bone, wood, and horn were commonly fitted. Often blades were so heavily used and frequently sharpened, they ended up in quite abbreviated form.

Handles supplied with traders' knives, like the John Russell Company "Green River" skinning and hunting style, were of hardwood. A presentation knife might feature mounts or inlays of silver or pewter.

An ingenious blade was fashioned by Indians from files and saws, then usually fitted with bone or antler handles. An identifying characteristic of Indian skinning knives was the grinding off of the edge in sharpening, with one side only beveled; this made them more serviceable for skinning.

Cases are often strikingly beautiful and were designed to engulf most of the knife. This way it was much harder to lose and was protected against the elements. Decoration ranged from brass tacks to sturdy rawhide, and/or combinations of beads, paints, quills, hairs, and stitching. Knife cases rank among the most striking of Indian artifacts.

These sheaths were carried in a number of ways, most on belts around the waist, but occasionally on a neck strap. Even the belts and straps were often richly

(*above*) Undated photograph at Blackfoot Indian Agency of tribal leaders. *From left*, Stabs-by-Mistake, White Antelope, Neck Blood Indian, unidentified, Moves Out, and Rides-at-the-Door. The unidentified chief holds Model 1876 Winchester carbine and has handsomely tacked belt.

(*top right*) Photograph by Rodman Wanamaker (of Philadelphia department store family), a student of the Custer battle, in 1913. *Left to right*, four Crow scouts of Custer: White-Man-Runs-Him, Hairy Moccasin, Curley, and Goes Ahead. They are on Last Stand Hill.

(*bottom right*) Plains Indians armed with Single Action Colt and Model 1873 Springfield trapdoor carbines. Possibly Army scouts; c. 1880.

decorated, and might match the sheaths, some with disks hammered from silver coins.

Clubs and Tomahawks

Clubs were intimidating and varied, some of colorful stones (smoothed from streams or riverbeds), some of wood with knife or spike heads, others with wood ball heads, buffalo horns, and the so-called gunstock wooden club with threatening lance blades. The clubs with stone heads generally weighed between 2 and 8 pounds, with the stone secured by sinew to a sturdy wood or leather handle. A slingshot club featured a flexible handle, and could be swung like the medieval military flail.

Handles were often long enough to allow for wielding from horseback, sometimes measuring 30 inches; wood was common, with leather and bone also in use. Skins and cloths, paints, quills, horsehair, rawhide, and tacks were used for decoration.

Tomahawks are the most recognizable of American Indian artifacts, and the pipe tomahawk is unique to Indian culture. Whether weapon or tool, pipe or symbol of rank, the tomahawk is associated with warfare, craftsmanship, prestige, ceremony, and comfort: an instrument of both peace and war. Except among the Southwest Indians, tomahawks were in wide use throughout the West.

To the Indians of the nineteenth century, the tomahawk as a weapon was of less importance than to their predecessors, or to Eastern, Southern, or Midwestern groups of previous centuries. However, the trapper Osborne Russell was attacked by Indians with "battle axes" late in the 1830s, Marcus Whitman was killed in 1847 by a tomahawk-wielding Cayuse warrior at Waiilatpu, Oregon Territory, and skulls in the Army Medical Museum that show evidence of tomahawk blows are in date as late as 1869.

Throwing the tomahawk was an effective Indian technique. George Catlin referred to the weapon's being thrown "with unerring and deadly aim." Evidence suggests that Indians practiced by hurling tomahawks at trees. A self-portrait by Cheyenne Chief Yellow Nose (c. 1880) shows him throwing a tomahawk and striking a fleeing victim in the back.

The tomahawk was used symbolically to challenge another tribe to war. And the weapon became a metaphor in such figures of speech as "taking up the hatchet" (war) and "burying the hatchet" (peace).

Presentation tomahawks were highly prized by chiefs, were symbolic of friendship, and served to lend solemnity to treaties. Some were handed down through generations; Six Nations Chief G.H.M. Johnson carried one as an indication of authority. His tomahawk was a presentation dating from the eighteenth century, and was written about by an author in 1860.

The pipe tomahawk (first adopted c. 1700) was ideal for ceremonial use, doubling to allow for smoking on special occasions. That function actually became more important than use as a weapon, and was a reason for the tomahawk's survival through the nineteenth century.

A particular style of tomahawk with historical documentation by Lewis and Clark is the Missouri war hatchet. In January 1805 the explorers found the style in use by the Mandan Indians. It was also popular with the Comanche, Dakota, Fox, Iowa, Kansa, Osage, and Oto tribes.

A Clark journal entry from January 1805 includes a drawing and notes that a request of their camp had come from several Indians to have "war hatchets" of that design made. The expedition's blacksmith proceeded to make such axes, in order to trade for corn. The tomahawk was described in a Lewis journal entry of February, which concludes by remarking that "the great length of the blade [7 to 9 inches] of this ax, added to the small size of the handle renders a stroke uncertain and easily avoided, while the shortness of the handle must render a blow much less forcible even if well directed, and still more inconvenient as they uniformly use this instrument in action on horseback." The styling of this weapon is similar to that illustrated on page 12.

A spontoon-style ax was also drawn in the Lewis and Clark journal in the same period. The pattern of that tomahawk is as illustrated on page 7. The expedition blacksmith also made heads of this pattern for the Mandan Indians. Lewis referred to these as of an "older fassion."

Tomahawk haft decoration ranged from scallops on the lower surface to brands made with a hot file, brass tacks, wrappings in wire (usually brass or copper, and sometimes from the telegraph), beaded flaps, feathers, eagle claw charms (rare), and brass tinkling devices attached to thongs threaded through a piercing on the haft bottom. Cloth wrappings are sometimes present. Presentation pipe tomahawks are likely to exhibit silver inlays, sometimes gold, and possibly engravings and inscriptions. A silver chain denoting friendship (rare) might run from a silver band at the mouthpiece to a band a few inches away, or near the head.

Firearms

Long before Lewis and Clark explored the Louisiana Territory, flintlock guns from white traders had been available to the Indians. A standard style, designed by the Hudson's Bay Company, was light in weight, cheaply made, short in its smoothbore barrel, large in triggerguard (allowing it to be shot wearing gloves), and of about .66 caliber. These weapons had a particular profile, and were produced in quantity by such English gunmakers as Barnett, Bond, Ketland, Parker

---

Pipe tomahawk at *top* believed made by riflemaker; old identification on haft, "Fort Snelling Minn. Sioux 1865." Blade mark a wolf or horse motif, and other stampings. Winchester Model 1873 rifle, in .44-40 caliber, likely belonged to a reservation Indian of note; wrapping on butt may be from a vest, reused on revered object. Model 1873 carbine inscribed on left sideplate: "Chief Spotted Tail/from/ Louis Boucher." The recipient, a French métis gun trader, married one of the chief's daughters. Spotted Tail was a principal leader of the Brulé Sioux and an uncle of Crazy Horse. Tomahawk at *bottom* of Plains origin, c. 1870. Quirt at *center* has handle fashioned from chair leg; decorated with numerous tacks, trade tokens, saddle nails, and shields (one of the shields marked "Wests Baggage Transfer 21 Grand Island"). J.S.B. tokens remain unidentified as to trader. Lashes fashioned from split reins.

Field & Co., and Sargent Brothers, and later by American makers like Henry's Bolton Gun Works.

A recognizable feature was the brass serpentine sideplate mounted on the left side, opposite placement of the lock. Lewis and Clark, as well as explorer Zebulon Pike, observed many guns of this type on their expeditions. Lewis wrote that through trading with whites the "Sioux managed to be well supplied enabling them to maintain their superiority on that section of the Missouri." Superior firepower was essential in tribal rivalries. Those best armed had distinctly superior security. The gun and the horse were among the Indian's most revered and coveted possessions.

These guns were available to Indians from government posts, as well as from various traders. The Indians became so knowledgeable of quality that they preferred the English trade guns, actually looking for the distinctive serpentine sideplate, and for markings like a fox seated in a tombstone (Hudson's Bay Company) or a fox in a circle (North West Company).* A chief's gun was also made, of better than the standard quality, sometimes with a silver escutcheon on the stock.

Trade rifles were also introduced, influenced by the styling of the muskets. These were normally of .52 caliber, flintlock, with short barrels, at times shortened even more by Indians. Since they were accustomed to shooting at close range, their preference was for the trade musket—especially since it was easier to load and could dispatch buffaloes from horseback readily. It was also less expensive than the rifles, some of which

*Many Belgian and American makes were stamped with similar marks, as deceptive marketing aids.

Modoc scout taking aim with Spencer carbine; note 1858 pattern Army hat on lava rock. Noted journalist Henry M. Stanley wrote from Kansas (1867) that "the Indians . . . are armed with Spencer rifles, and their first attempts to use them appear to have resulted in several of them getting their hands injured by the explosion of the metallic cartridges, while they attempted to force them into the muzzle by pounding, not being posted in the breech-loading business."

were made by Kentucky rifle builders the likes of Christopher Gumpf, Henry Deringer, Jr., and Jacob Dickert.

Thousands of muzzle-loading rifles destined for Indians were manufactured on government order. Over 10,000 such guns in flintlock had been given to warriors emigrating West by 1837. A rifle, powder, and balls were part of the treaty agreements with several tribes, for warriors who were relocating West. Henry Deringer, Jr., was so prominent a maker that as early as 1829 the Superintendent of Indian Affairs wrote that "the Indians all seek his guns, and know his name as well as if they could read. . . ."

The means by which Indians obtained guns were often ingenious. In the late 1860s in Nebraska, Cheyenne warriors derailed a handcar and took its cargo of Spencer repeating rifles. Other sources of guns were more routine. Military weapons were given on discharge to Indians serving in the Civil War. Some guns were presented by the federal government to Indians on signing treaties. And Indians on reservations were frequently given arms for use in hunting game.

Although the types of firearms owned by the Indians were varied, in not a few instances—such as Custer's fight at the Little Bighorn—the Indians were better armed than their white adversaries. Their facility on horseback was exceptional. The horseman could reload by spitting a ball from his mouth into the muzzle of a flint or percussion musket, and then could shoot while riding at full stride. Because of the high cost of powder, ball, and (in later years) metallic cartridges, target practice was a luxury for Indian shooters.

Since the Indian could shoot arrows with such rapidity, and with as lethal effect at close range, there were times when the bow and arrow would be chosen over the gun. Rain or moisture could hamper his use of the muzzle-loader, or he might lose his percussion caps.

Upkeep on guns also was problematic. Broken stocks were repaired with wet hide, left to dry, often making the stock stronger than ever. Some lock re-

The profusion of weaponry may have been supplied these Indians for photography. Experts Charles Worman and Louis A. Garavaglia, in their landmark two-volume work *Firearms of the American West*, have noted similar Wesson carbines in several posed scenes found in Smithsonian Institution and National Archives collections of photographs.

pairs were also ingenious. Equally clever was an alteration to powder horns: the sides were scraped to translucent thinness so that the amount of remaining powder could be checked by holding them to the light. An easy and quick measurement of the proper charge was to pour powder over the ball held in the hand until the ball was covered.

Indians had even devised a means of reloading metallic cartridges, by using percussion caps as primers. Powder and projectile could be adapted by breaking up cartridges of a different caliber. Some cartridges were reused with frequency.

Indian favorites in the dawn of repeaters from the percussion era were the Colt and Remington (1850s–1860s) and in metallic-cartridge arms both the above makers (1870s–1880s), as well as the Springfield U.S.-issue trapdoor carbine or rifle, the Spencer repeating rifle and carbine, and, especially, the Winchester Model 1866 "Yellow Boy" and the Model 1873.

Scabbards were often richly decorated, expressing the reverence held for the piece, and pride of possession. Designs can reveal the tribe of the owner, and some tribes, like the Crow, could be identified from a distance by the way they held their longarms. Scabbards were long, to envelop all of the weapon and protect it against the elements.

As the Indian's arsenal expanded to metallic-cartridge breechloaders, the need for the lance, tomahawk, club, and bow and arrow diminished. But access to the new technology would not last long enough or be great enough to save his nomadic and free way of life.

In the twilight years of conflicts with the white man, Indian firearms became increasingly breechloaders and repeaters. But after the Civil War and through the early 1870s the majority of Indians with firearms had smoothbore and rifled muzzle-loaders. The government policy of providing guns to tribes continued, and traders did not let up their dealings of arms either. Even Colt revolvers had fallen into some hands. A major with the 3rd Infantry at Fort Dodge

Holstered Colt Single Action Army revolver and Officers Model Springfield rifle (special version for officers who liked to hunt) draped on pommel of Lieutenant Britton Davis's mule. Faithful Apache scout held reins.

wrote in January 1867 in a letter to the War Department:

Between the authorized issue of agents and the sales of the traders, the Indians were never better armed than at the present time. Several hundred Indians have visited this post, all of whom had revolvers in their possession. A large majority had two revolvers, and many of them three. The Indians openly boast that they have plenty of arms and ammunition in case of trouble in the spring. The Interior Department does not seem to appreciate the danger of thus arming those Indians. The evil of presenting a revolver to each of the chiefs of bands would hardly be appreciable but when the whole rank and file are thus armed, it not only gives them greater courage to murder and plunder, but renders them formidable enemies.

The letter went on to state: "For a revolver the Indian will give ten, even twenty times its value, in horses and furs. . . ."

Sales by licensed traders had gotten out of hand. Soldiers as high-ranking as Brigadier General Philip St. George Cooke, Commanding Officer, Department of the Platte, issued an order for Indian agents to cease transactions in firearms, while post commanders were to "take vigilant and decisive measures for the prevention of all sale, barter, or gift of arms or ammunition to Indians within reach of their power."

There were others who favored continuing to provide guns and ammunition to the Indians. The ensuing debate pitted the policy of the Department of the Interior (in favor of sales) against that of the War Department (against).

Some agents put restrictions on the more advanced weapons and ammunition, while permitting "the ordinary muzzle loading Indian trade rifle and ammunition. . . in quantities sufficient for hunting purposes."

That the hostiles were well armed was the conclusion of an Army sergeant on duty in Texas, c. 1870–1876: "There is a common belief among people of this day and time that the Indians fought solely with bow and arrow, but in all my Indian fighting, which amounted to seven pitched battles, besides several skirmishes, I have always found them well equipped with good guns and plenty of ammunition."

A number of other eyewitness accounts attest to the quality and quantity of armaments. From the Black Hills, 1876: "The adult men were splendidly armed—indeed much better than the average man of our party...."

The frustration of many frontier personnel was evident in the statement of Captain Charles King:

No end of silk-hatted functionaries have hurried out from Washington, shaken hands and smoked a pipe with a score of big Indians; there has been a vast amount of cheap oratory and buncombe talk about the Great Father and the guileless red men, at the end of which we are told to go back to camp and bury our dead, and our late antagonists, laughing in their sleeves, link arms with their aldermanic friends, are "dead-headed" off to Washington, where they are lionized at the White House, and sent the rounds of the great cities, and finally return to their reservations laden down with new and improved rifles and ammunition....

The defeat of Custer at the Little Bighorn proved the merit of Captain King's concerns. Testimony at the Reno court of inquiry from Lieutenant Charles Varnum noted that in Reno's retreat across the river and running fight to a hilled sanctuary "a great many Indians [were] riding along the column with Winchester rifles across saddles, firing into the column." As many as about 25 to 30 percent of the attacking Indians were estimated to have been armed with modern repeating rifles.

The *Army and Navy Journal* reacted with sarcasm in an editorial which must have made Oliver Winchester's blood boil:

We advised the Winchester Arms Company to act upon the suggestion offered them by Capt. Nickerson of Gen. Crook's staff, and prosecute the Indians for infringement of their patent. The cap-

Police sergeants of the Yankton Sioux Standing Rock Agency; Red Tomahawk at *left*, and Eagle Man. It was Red Tomahawk who killed Sitting Bull. The men are armed with Model 1875 Remington revolvers and an 1873 Winchester (*left*) and a Whitney-Kennedy, both carbines.

Spencer rifle believed one of Apache war leader Geronimo's firearms, and reportedly surrendered to peace officer and Wells Fargo guard Jeff Milton. Stock richly embellished with pierced overlay; in .56-46 caliber with 30-inch octagonal barrel.

tain testifies, with others, that Winchester rifles are plenty among them; the agency people and the traders solemnly affirm that they don't furnish them; so it can only be inferred that the Indians manufacture them themselves. If Gov. Winchester could get out a preliminary injunction, restraining the Indians from the use of his rifle, it might be of signal service to our troops in the next engagement.

Further, from the Little Bighorn battle the Indian forces went away with approximately 592 Springfield trapdoor carbines and Colt Single Action Army revolvers, and assorted ammunition.

Congress reacted in August 1876 with a joint resolution which authorized President U. S. Grant to take steps "to prevent such special metallic ammunition being conveyed to such hostile Indians." And further, to "declare the same contraband of war in such district of the country as he may designate during the continuance of hostilities."

These and other restrictions were futile for many Indians. Colonel Richard Irving Dodge noted:

Every male Indian who can buy, beg, borrow, or steal them, has now firearms of some kind. . . . The trade in arms is entirely illicit. The trader slips into the Indian country, now here, now there, and not knowing beforehand the caliber of the ammunition re-

quired, takes that which is most commonly in use. Some guns of a band were almost always out of use on this account, but necessity . . . has so stimulated the ordinary uninventive brain of the Indian, that if he can only procure the moulds for a bullet that will fit his rifle, he manages the rest by an ingenious method of reloading his old shells peculiar to himself. He buys from the trader a box of the smallest percussion caps . . . forces the cap [into the cartridge casing] until it is flush. Powder and lead can always be obtained from the traders; or, in default of these, cartridges of other calibers are broken up, and the materials used in reloading his shells. Indians say that the shells thus reloaded are nearly as good as the original cartridges, and that the shells are frequently reloaded 40 or 50 times.

The errant traders had no regard for the law. Manuel Garcia wrote of an 1878 trade to the Blackfeet, boasting that "two Pen d'Oreilles came and I robbed one of them of seven buffalo robes for a second-hand needle gun and for two buffalo robes I gave him three boxes of fifty-caliber cartridges, and I got two robes from the other buck for three boxes of Henry cartridges."

Better Armed Than Whites?

A government report in 1879 maintained that the Indians' superiority to white troops in armament was

largely a myth. The report's basic conclusion was that "[repeaters] and like arms are comparatively few, while a very considerable number of muzzle-loaders greatly reduce the average of Indian armament below that of the troops."

However, the report conceded, that "the Sioux and Cheyennes have had some fine breech-loaders, giving color to the opinion that they are better armed than the cavalry, is undoubtedly true."

Records of captured guns from hostilities are revealing. Surrendering to a patrol of cavalry near Camp Robinson, Nebraska, Cheyennes under Dull Knife were incarcerated at the post. The warriors were thoroughly searched. In January 1879, they attempted to escape, unsuccessfully. The following firearms were subsequently surrendered, having been ingeniously disassembled and hidden with the women and children, some parts worn as ornament: Springfield trapdoor .50-caliber rifles (seven), Springfield .45-70 carbine, Sharps .50-caliber carbine (three), Sharps rifle (Old Reliable), Colt .36-caliber revolver, Colt 1851 Navy revolver, and Remington Army revolver.

The 1879 Ordnance Report listed such varied shoulder arms surrendered by incoming Indians (mainly Sioux and Cheyenne) as miscellaneous muzzle-loaders (160), ninety-four of which were by Henry Leman, six by Samuel Hawken, ten by J. P. Lower, six by J. Henry & Son, four by Henry Folsom & Co., and two Northwest trade guns. Additionally, there were recorded forty-nine Springfield breechloaders, twenty-three Spencer repeaters, thirteen Sharps breechloaders, twelve Winchester lever-actions of .44 caliber, and four Henry rifles, as well as various single-shot breechloaders. Many were in poor condition, but "could be used by so enterprising an enemy as the American Indian."

Finally, the 1879 report recorded 125 revolvers and single-shot pistols. All but a converted Colt and a single-shot Remington rolling-block were percussion: seventy-two Colts, thirty-seven Remingtons, five Whitneys, four Starrs, a Manhattan, a Pettengill, and a Savage (all of U.S. manufacture).

Indians as Marksmen

The general consensus was that Indians were excellent close-range shots, but were usually poor at distance shooting. Corroboration for that is provided by Captain O. E. Michaelis:

> As General Miles states of the Nez Perces, the use of fine sights and measurement of distances is the result of civilization. The typical Indian is a point-blank marksman. The use of bright muzzle and buckhorn sights proves this. He steals upon his quarry and fires *at* it. Hence they prefer arms with long dangerous spaces [ranges], an attribute that overcomes the difficulty attending fine sighting and the accurate estimation of distances.

Tests at the Springfield Armory (1879 report) showed that on average the Springfield trapdoor could be operated at about the same rate of fire as the Winchester magazine repeater. Accuracy and penetration were superior in the Springfield, while in two minutes a trapdoor fired twenty-nine shots, the Winchester thirty-three.

An 1883 statement by Lieutenant Britton Davis identified the arms of an Apache band in Arizona:

> This party was armed, as in fact were nearly all the hostiles in Mexico, with the latest models of Winchester magazine rifles, a better arm than the single-shot Springfield with which our soldiers and scouts were armed. The Indians obtained their arms from settlers and travelers they killed, or purchased them from white scoundrels who made a business of selling arms, ammunition, and whiskey to Indians.

Resourceful and brave warriors, generally ill-equipped at first against the invading whites, the Indians of the West put up a determined fight against increasingly overwhelming odds. Their legacy of courage, ingenuity, spunk, grit, and romance has imbued each weapon in their varied arsenal with a spirit and color that have captivated every collector's imagination since the days of Lewis and Clark and their patron, Thomas Jefferson, and even before.

Geronimo with rare Confederate-made revolver, the Dance Dragoon. Likely a prop provided by photographer. Back of cabinet photograph dated August 26, 1901.

TRAILBLAZERS AND MOUNTAIN MEN

As early as 1783, Thomas Jefferson was possessed with the thought of exploration of the American West, even asking General George Rogers Clark if he would "like to lead such a party." In 1792 the idea resurfaced when the eighteen-year-old Army officer Meriwether Lewis requested of Jefferson that he be permitted to join such an expedition.

As President, and after the Louisiana Purchase of 1803, Jefferson was in a position to make his dream come true. Though he himself would never travel farther west than Harpers Ferry, West Virginia, Jefferson had made one of America's most extraordinary acquisitions of real estate: 830,000 square miles from Louisiana and the Mississippi River to the Rocky Mountains and the Canadian border, a vast wilderness comprising the whole or portions of what would become thirteen states.

Acquisitions and annexations in 1845 (Texas, parts of what later became New Mexico, Colorado, and Wyoming), 1846 (later Washington, Oregon, Idaho, and part of Wyoming), and 1843–53 (to be California, Nevada, Utah, Arizona, and parts of Texas, New Mexico, Colorado, and Wyoming) would complete America's possession of the West.

Conquest of that vast area of picturesque scenery, rich farmland and mineral resources, lakes, rivers, and deserts took the rest of the century, however, and the true pioneer trailblazers of that effort were explorers the likes of Meriwether Lewis and William Clark and the moun-

Breathtaking Thomas Moran–style landscape would appear to show mountain man of c. 1840, but is of Harry Yount, the first ranger of Yellowstone National Park; taken c. 1874, at Berthoud Pass looking north to Colorado, by renowned frontier photographer William Henry Jackson. Yount held a percussion rifle, possibly with over-and-under barrels. Swivel-breech rifle by J. Kunz, Philadelphia, and so signed; 36-inch half-round, half-octagon barrels. Unusual double triggers, or set trigger (cock hammer, then push forward trigger, whose pull has been "set" for lightness by tiny screw, then fire).

By Albert Bierstadt, *Mountain Man* illustrates characteristic carrying position of rifle, across front of saddle. The artist's first trip to the Rocky Mountains was in 1859, the year he painted this picture.

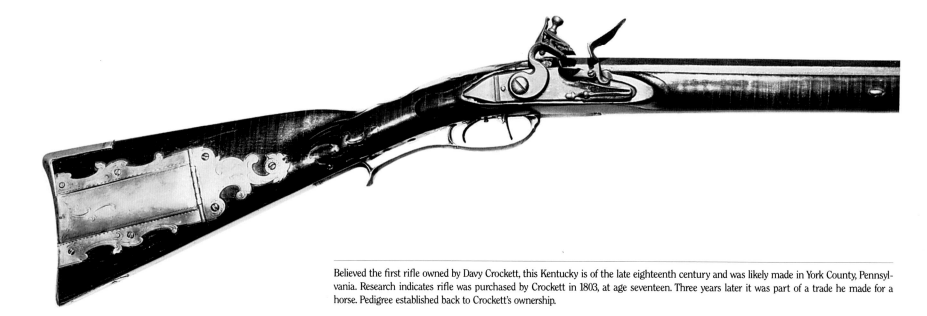

Believed the first rifle owned by Davy Crockett, this Kentucky is of the late eighteenth century and was likely made in York County, Pennsylvania. Research indicates rifle was purchased by Crockett in 1803, at age seventeen. Three years later it was part of a trade he made for a horse. Pedigree established back to Crockett's ownership.

tain men, not a few of whom attained heroic reputations in their own time: Jim Bridger, Jedediah Smith, Kit Carson, and Jim Beckwourth.

In anticipation of the long-desired expedition into the West, Jefferson hired U.S. Army Captain Meriwether Lewis as secretary-aide, two weeks prior to the Presidential inauguration, 1801. In the course of the next two years, the expedition became the subject of intense discussion. William Clark was selected by Lewis as co-commander, to share in "it's fatiegues, it's dangers and it's honors."

Plans for the expedition were so thorough that Lewis was trained in botany, astronomy, surveying, anatomy, mathematics, and other branches of science. Besides exploration, making friends with the Indians and impressing them with the sovereignty of the United States were goals of the undertaking. Approximately one hundred silver peace medals were to be given to Indians along the way.

The expedition departed St. Louis in May 1804. Lewis and Clark were accompanied by soldiers and interpreters, by Clark's slave, York, and by a pet Newfoundland dog. By November 1805 the party had reached the Pacific Ocean; it returned to St. Louis late in September 1806. Their courageous guide for much of the trip had been the Shoshoni chieftain's daughter Sacajawea, who thereby became one of the first heroines in American history.

The epic achievement of Lewis and Clark revealed to America a breathtaking expanse of beasts and exotic native peoples, with a beckoning richness guaranteed to attract further exploration and commerce; the stage was set for the adventurer-pioneers: traders and the mountain men.

The Arms of Lewis and Clark

Weapons taken on the expedition were clearly prerequisites for survival. They featured Kentucky rifles,

which had been specifically made by Lancaster, Pennsylvania, gunmakers. Clark's own, referred to as his "small rifle," was of only about .33 caliber. Lewis's portrait, on returning from the expedition, shows him in full frontier regalia, with a slender full-stock Kentucky flintlock, on its butt a near-oval patchbox, the triggerguard elegantly curved, and the stock with sling swivels. Lewis also obtained fifteen rifles, rifle slings, powder horns, and sundry accessories and spare parts, from the Harpers Ferry Armory. Muskets were also on the trip, and Clark ordered that "every man have 100 balls for their rifles and 2 lbs. of buckshot for those with musquets etc." Two blunderbusses rounded out the battery of longarms.

Lewis had a pair of "Horsemans Pistils" along, likely the first U.S. military-issue pistol, the Model 1799 North & Cheney, and "1 Pair Pocket Pistols Secret Triggers," by Robert Barnhill. One of these pistols (the "Secret Triggers" dropped down upon cocking the

Frontiersman's fringed buckskin jacket, one of only a handful extant. Beaded buckskin bag often held tobacco or a strike-a-light. Choker of hair pipe bone and buffalo horn beads, with shell and beaded drop. Chief's grade trade musket by E. K. Tryon, with 42 1/2-inch barrel, c. 1830–40. To facilitate fast reloading, touchhole from flashpan into barrel could be enlarged, permitted knocking gun on butt, which would spill powder into pan. Loading blocks could be used, with balls in position to be rammed into muzzle. To avoid loading with patch, ball could be moistened in mouth.

Cheekpieces of two early-nineteenth-century New England guns, with silver, silver wire, and ivory inlays. Equally elegant frontiersman's tomahawk with silver monogram inlay on head; attributed to a Kentucky rifle maker, and of c. 1790. Besides the Indian, trappers and mountain men, explorers, soldiers, and even some early settlers found the tomahawk useful. Tomahawks on Lewis and Clark Expedition appear to have been products of Harpers Ferry Armory. Also an issue item for period with U.S. Army rifleman, c. 1808 through War of 1812. Tool common with trappers, traders, and mountain men up through mid-century; implements likely to be used way beyond date of original manufacture.

hammers) he gave away to an Indian. The horseman's pistols served Lewis well. When Indians tried to steal some rifles, Lewis and two of his men set after them. Lewis himself retrieved his own rifle, at pistol point, after a determined chase.

Tomahawks and knives for trades with Indians were also purchased, plus 123 pounds of "English Cannister Powder."

The most intriguing gun on the trip was Lewis's air gun. Lewis fired a demonstration (one of several) in August 1805, on the Ohio River, in which he

fired myself seven times fifty five yards with pretty good success; after which a Mr. Blaze Cenas being unacquainted with the man-

---

(*opposite, top left*) The American eagle adorned this advertisement for the J. J. Henry gun works; c. 1830.

(*opposite, bottom left*) From the Thomas Gilcrease Institute of American History and Art, Tulsa, Alfred Jacob Miller's *Lost Trapper*, a watercolor executed in his position as artist with the expedition of William Drummond Stewart, a Scottish lord, 1837.

(*opposite, right*) Flintlock Kentucky pistols, with silver-inlaid tomahawk. The Kentuckys of 1820, and of classic form and workmanship. *Top* possibly by John Walker, Lancaster County; *lower* pistol also attributed to Pennsylvania manufacture. It was the custom to make Kentucky pistols in matched pairs. Pistols were not as important on early frontier as rifles and muskets. With short barrels, they were for close range, as backup, and lacked long-range accuracy or striking power. Pistol also, in military terms, symbolic of rank; primarily for officer and dragoon issue. In terms of scarcity, experts have estimated that one pistol was made for every hundred Kentucky rifles.

Over-and-under swivel-breech Pennsylvania-made rifles. *Top* in flintlock, marked PK and believed by Peter Kunz; German-silver mountings. *Lower* rifle marked CD and attributed to Christian Derr, Jr.; silver inlays, with rare Indian motif to right of cheekpiece. Symbolism on Kentucky rifles has long tradition in gunmaking; early inlays on these arms have origin in nature and God, e.g., the star, eagle, fish, crescent, heart, and flower. Later inlays are more inclined to have been inspired primarily as decorative elements; they are not considered to have a tie-in with hex signs of the Pennsylvania Dutch. American eagle first appeared on firearms late in the nineteenth century and signified patriotism and pride in the United States.

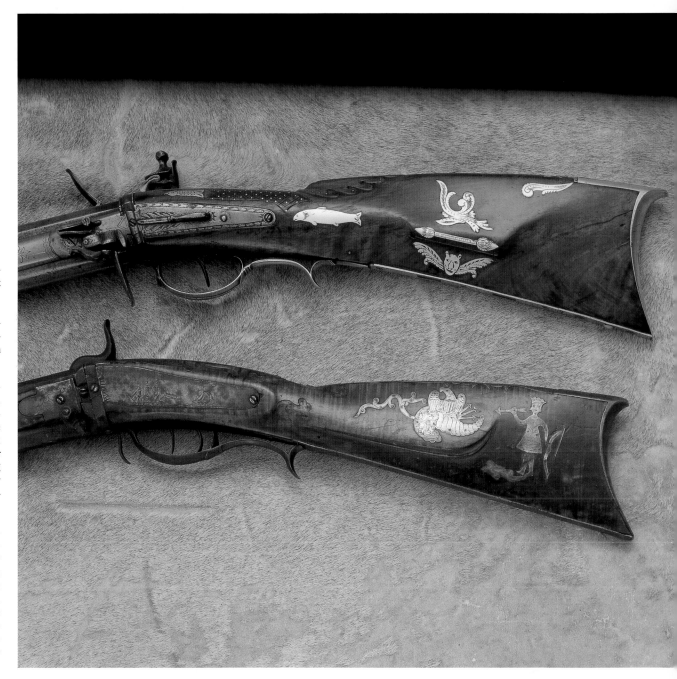

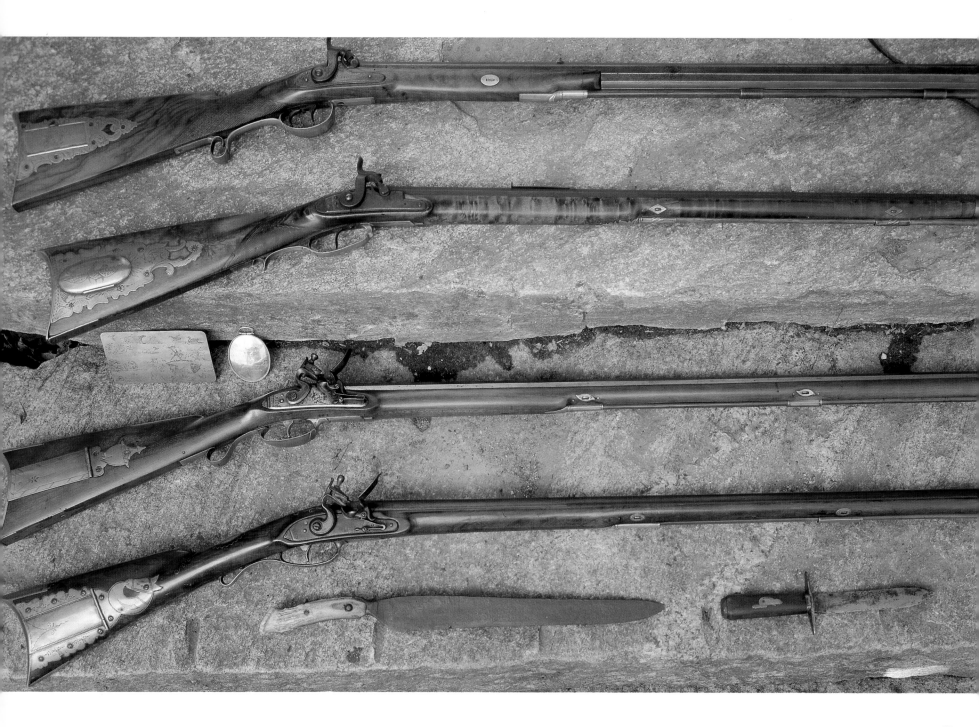

American Frontier Life, by Currier & Ives, 1862. Scene could well depict an event as long as twenty-five years earlier. Based on painting by A. F. Tait. Traveling together in groups was advisable, permitted staggered shots, so in fighting with Indians some guns would remain loaded. Wily Indians waited to charge until whites' guns were likely empty.

Mixture of muzzle-loading guns that went west in the first half of the nineteenth century. Flintlocks at *bottom* of Lewis and Clark and Zebulon Pike period, and of New England manufacture. That with horsehead patchbox is marked AA (possibly Asabel Allen, who later worked in Wisconsin); fires buckshot or round ball, and is smoothbore. Shortest rifle is marked "J. Ridout & Co." on lock, also New England–made, c. 1820; converted from flintlock, and barrel cut down by about 10 inches. Stock of bird's-eye maple. *Top* rifle by J. Kunz, Philadelphia, .48-caliber, sturdy but elegant construction; c. 1840. Large rifleman's knife of Pennsylvania manufacture; skinning knife at *right* made from file, grip with silver beaver inlay.

American-eagle-engraved oval patchbox, from rifle on page 42; daguerreotype of Mexican War–period soldier. Folding dirk with ivory handle, marked "Berkshire Cutlery Company" (English) and of c. 1850s; handy pocket companion.

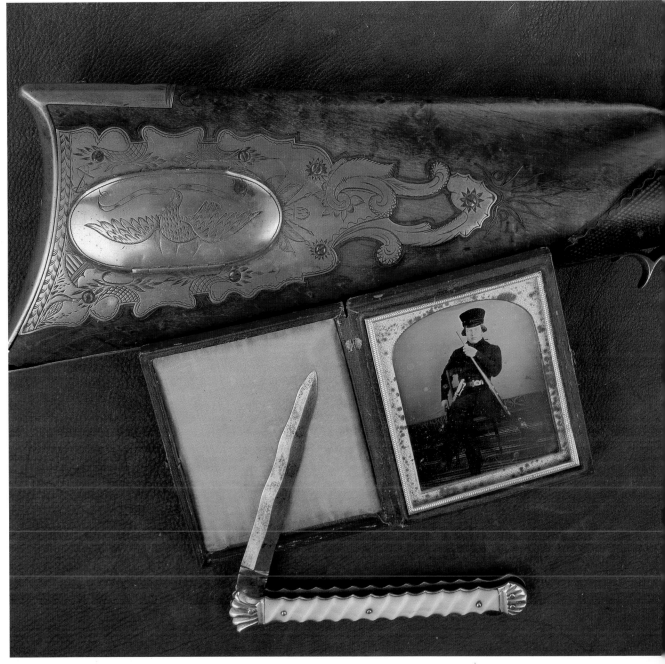

Also from an A. F. Tait painting, *Life on the Prairie* captured thrill of hunting buffalo from horseback. Historian Francis Parkman knew the challenge, from own experience (c. 1846): "The chief difficulty in running buffalo...is that of loading the gun or pistol at full gallop. Many hunters for convenience's sake carry three or four bullets in the mouth; the powder is poured down the muzzle of the piece, the bullet dropped in after it, the stock struck hard upon the pommel of the saddle, and the work is done. The danger of this is obvious. Should the blow on the pommel fail to send the bullet home, or should the bullet, in the act of aiming, start from its place and roll towards the muzzle, the gun would probably burst in discharging. Many a shattered hand and worse casualties besides have been the result of such an accident. To obviate it, some hunters make use of a ramrod, usually hung by a string from the neck, but this materially increases the difficulty in loading. The bows and arrows which the Indians use in running buffalo have many advantages over fire-arms, and even white men occasionally employ them."

Mountain man scene, with rugged large-caliber guns, Slotter & Co., Philadelphia, large-size deringer, traps, and accouterments. Iron-mounted flintlock suitable for struggling trapper, unable to afford better-quality firearm. Tack-decorated percussion musket converted from flintlock; barrel proofmarked PW and NR; lock dated 1801; American-made, based on French Charleville military pattern. Flint-locks remained popular on frontier until 1840s; early percussion caps were of poor quality and flints were more available. Percussion was nevertheless better; flintlocks made visible flash in exposed pan, and wind and rain could prevent firing. After bad luck with flintlock in trying to shoot bear six feet away from his muzzle, H. H. Sibley (1839) wrote: "[A]nyone calling himself a sportsman who will not use a percussion, when he can procure one, in lieu of a flint-lock, should be...furnished with a strait jacket at the public expense."

Iron-mounted J. Henry & Son Plains rifle at *bottom*. At *center* the historic Henry Deringer, Jr., rifle used in duel between Congressman Cilley of Maine and a William Graves; shot at distance of eighty yards, on Annapolis Road, near Washington, D.C. On third round of shooting, Cilley fell with mortal wound in abdomen. *Top* by Samuel Hawken, and so signed; full-stock, and converted from flintlock to percussion. One of earliest Hawken Plains-style rifles known.

(above and opposite) A Hawken rifle of Kit Carson's, in classic frontier mountain man style, by Jake and Sam Hawken. In 1882 the latter reminisced: "Kit gave me an order for a rifle and I didn't see him again for several years. One day he walked into the shop—I didn't know him—and asked if I had any rifles. I told him there was one on hand, and that was made for Kit Carson. That's my name, he said, and took the rifle for $25. He would have readily paid twice as much, for all my guns were made to kill at 200 yards." Like many distinguished Westerners, Carson was a Mason.

agement of the gun suffered her to discharge herself accidentally the ball passed through the hat of a woman about 40 yards distant cutting her temple about the fourth of the diameter of the ball; shee fell instantly and the blood gusing from her temple we were all in the greatest consternation suppose she was dead . . . in a minute she revived to our expressable satisfaction, and by examination we found the wound by no means mortal or even dangerous. . . .

The gun thoroughly impressed the Indians, who termed it "great medicine." Clark wrote that they "cannot comprehend it shooting so often and without powder."

Zebulon Pike and Others

Another explorer, Zebulon Pike, was not so fortunate with his firearms. In August 1805, Pike began an expedition on the upper Mississippi with rifled guns unable to bring down big game: "My Rifle was too small a Ball to kill Buffalo. The Ball should not be [smaller] than 30 to the pound; or an Ounce Ball would still be preferable; and they should be hunted on horse Back." Thirty to the pound meant .54 caliber, and an ounce ball was .66 caliber. Pike and his men appear to have had Kentucky rifles of about .40 caliber.

Muskets on the expedition were incapable of long shots for game, and the men were shooting at elk from distances of as much as 400 yards. In response to an impending attack by Indians, Pike instructed his men to hold their fire "until within five or six paces, and then to charge with bayonet and sabre. . . ."

Blunderbusses were also part of the equipment, as were pistols, likely the North & Cheney Model 1799, like Meriwether Lewis's pair.

Gunpowder was another headache. Pike tried to dry out some gunpowder from an overturned canoe and "in attempting to dry the powder in pots, blew it up; and nearly blew a Tent and two or three men with it. Made a dozen new cartridges with the old wrapping paper."

A later river accident destroyed all of Pike's cartridges and "four pounds of double battle Sussex powder. . . . Fortunately my kegs of powder were preserved dry, and some bottles of common glazed powder. . . . Had this not been the case, my voyage must necessarily have been terminated, for we could not have subsisted without ammunition."

In his next expedition, along the Arkansas River west to the Rockies, Pike was adequately armed, but experienced other problems. At least three guns burst,

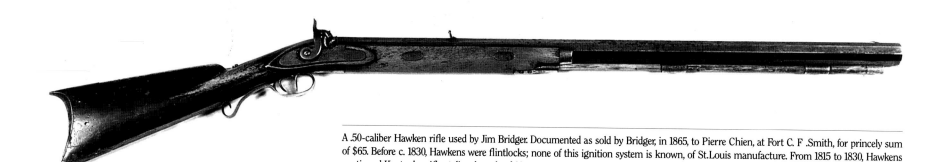

A .50-caliber Hawken rifle used by Jim Bridger. Documented as sold by Bridger, in 1865, to Pierre Chien, at Fort C. F .Smith, for princely sum of $65. Before c. 1830, Hawkens were flintlocks; none of this ignition system is known, of St.Louis manufacture. From 1815 to 1830, Hawkens continued Kentucky-rifle styling, barrels of 40 to 44 inches, and of about .50 caliber. After c. 1830, barrels were shorter and caliber about .50 to .53. Octagonal barrels standard in all periods. Post-1830 rifles also had sturdier stocks, thick at wrist, of straight-grained maple or walnut.

and at least five broke: "one of my men was now armed with my sword and Pistols."

The next federal-government-sponsored expedition into the West was Stephen Long's, which left St. Louis in June 1819. Contemporary journals described the profusion of armaments:

> The hunters, interpreters, and attendants, were furnished with rifles or muskets; the soldiers were armed exclusively with rifles, and suitably equipped. Our stock ammunition amounted in all to about 30 pounds of powder, 20 pounds of balls, and 40 pounds of lead, with a plentiful supply of flints, and some small shot.
>
> We were well armed and equipped, each man carrying a yauger or rifle gun [believed the Model 1803 Harpers Ferry rifle], with the exception of two or three who had muskets; most of us had pistols, all tomahawks and long knives, which we carried suspended at our belts.

An air gun complemented the arsenal, likely as "great medicine" with the Indians.

Long's troops were encouraged to practice on targets. The best shots were expected to "hit the same mark [3 inches in diameter offhand] one hundred yards. . . . [Those doing so] three times in six are raised to the first Class. . . . There are but few who are not in the first class."

The Mountain Men

Others who explored the early West were in that celebrated species known as mountain men. Some acted as privateers and some worked for a fur company on wages. Among this unique breed were John Colter of

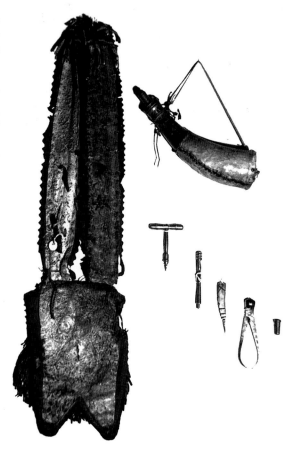

the Lewis and Clark Expedition (he left to take up trapping; he was the first white man to see the Yellowstone), Manuel Lisa (who reached the Bighorn, and traversed part of the Oregon Trail, 1811–12), William Henry Ashley (a fur trader, and himself the employer of several mountain men), and the renowned Jim Bridger and Kit Carson.

The market for beaver pelts, to be made into hats for the fashionable, encouraged men to brave the West and work their traps. In the process these hardy souls became unofficial explorers. They were of many nationalities—American, Spanish, French —and the total number of mountain men, in the active period 1820–1840, was only about 1,000. Thomas James recalled his initiation, 1809, working on contract to the Missouri Fur Company:

> We Americans were all private adventurers, each on his own hook, and were led into the enterprise by the promise of the Company, who agreed to subsist us to the trapping grounds, we helping to navigate the boats, and on our arrival there were to furnish us each with a rifle and sufficient ammunition, six good

Mountain man Mariano Modena's game bag, powder horn (reinforced with rawhide), and worming device (for removing bullets), cleaning-rod tip, horn powder measurer, bullet mold, and empty case for measuring powder. Modena's Hawken rifle has oval silver plaque on cheekpiece, inscribed "Purchased St.Louis/1833/Mariano Modena/Gen. A. H. Jones/Big Thompson Colo./1878."

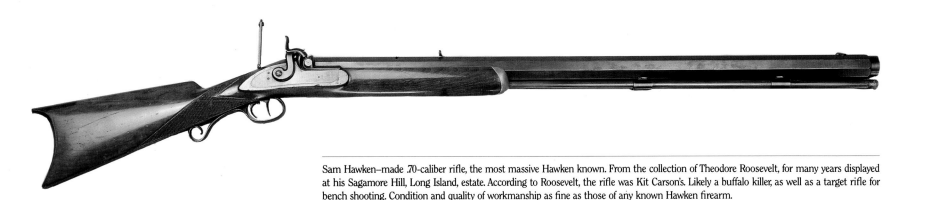

Sam Hawken—made .70-caliber rifle, the most massive Hawken known. From the collection of Theodore Roosevelt, for many years displayed at his Sagamore Hill, Long Island, estate. According to Roosevelt, the rifle was Kit Carson's. Likely a buffalo killer, as well as a target rifle for bench shooting. Condition and quality of workmanship as fine as those of any known Hawken firearm.

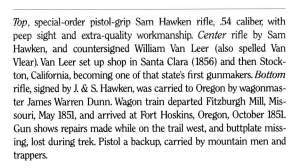

Top, special-order pistol-grip Sam Hawken rifle, .54 caliber, with peep sight and extra-quality workmanship. *Center* rifle by Sam Hawken, and countersigned William Van Leer (also spelled Van Vlear). Van Leer set up shop in Santa Clara (1856) and then Stockton, California, becoming one of that state's first gunmakers. *Bottom* rifle, signed by J. & S. Hawken, was carried to Oregon by wagonmaster James Warren Dunn. Wagon train departed Fitzburgh Mill, Missouri, May 1851, and arrived at Fort Hoskins, Oregon, October 1851. Gun shows repairs made while on the trail west, and buttplate missing, lost during trek. Pistol a backup, carried by mountain men and trappers.

Thomas Tate Toben, scout, guide, Indian fighter, and mountain man, with his Samuel Hawken rifle and fringed and beaded outfit. In 1863, Toben tracked down and killed two Mexican murderers, for whom a $2,500 reward had been offered by the governor of Colorado. The wanted men were one of the notorious Espinosa brothers

and a companion. In scout's own words: "I took a step or two in front and saw the head of one of the assassins. At this time, I stepped on a stick and broke it; he heard it crack, he looked and saw me, he jumped and grabbed his gun. Before he turned around fairly, I fired and hit him in the side; he bellowed like a bull and cried out, 'Jesus favor me,' and cried to his companion, 'Escape! I am killed.' I gave a whoop and sung out, 'Yell, boys, I've got him, so if there is more of them, they will make their appearance.' I tipped my powder horn in my rifle, dropped a bullet from my mouth into the muzzle of my gun while I was capping it. A fellow came out of the ravine, running to an undergrowth of quaking aspen. I sung out, 'Shoot, boys.' The three fired (two soldiers and [a] Mexican) and missed him. I drew my gun up and fired at first sight and broke his back about his hips. I sent the Mexican boy off on a run to tell . . . what had happened . . . . Espinosa had started to crawl away. He did not go very far. He braced himself up against some fallen trees, with pistol in hand waving it over his face, using a word in Mexican that means 'base brutes.' I had run down to where he was; his reply was 'base brutes.' A soldier went to lay his hand on him. I said, 'Look out, he will shoot you!' He fired, but missed the soldier. I caught him by the hair, threw his head back over a fallen tree and cut it off. I sent the Mexican boy to cut off the head of the other fellow; he cut it off and brought it to me. We rushed into their camp, the soldiers gathered their baggage. I took a diary and all the letters and paper[s] I could find in the camp and the rifles, pistols and butcher knives. . . . I put their heads in a sack. . . . On the eleventh of September, fifth day out, came into Fort Garland with Lieutenant Baldwin and six soldiers. I rode up in front of the commanding officer's quarters and called for Colonel Tappan. I rolled the assassins' heads out of the sack at Colonel Tappan's feet. I said, 'Here, Colonel, I have accomplished what you wished. This head is Espinosa's. This other is his companion's head and there is no mistake made.' Lieutenant Baldwin spoke, 'Yes, Colonel, there is no mistake, for we have this diary and letters and papers to show that they are the assassins.' The diary showed that they [including another Espinosa, shot earlier] had killed about thirty . . . altogether."

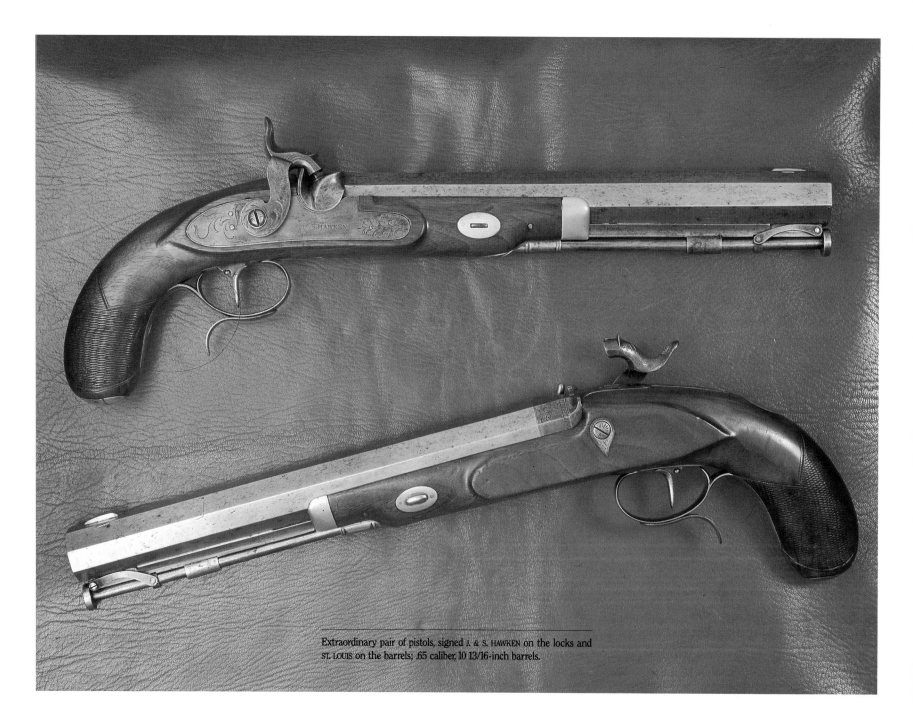

Extraordinary pair of pistols, signed J. & S. HAWKEN on the locks and
ST. LOUIS on the barrels; .65 caliber, 10 13/16-inch barrels.

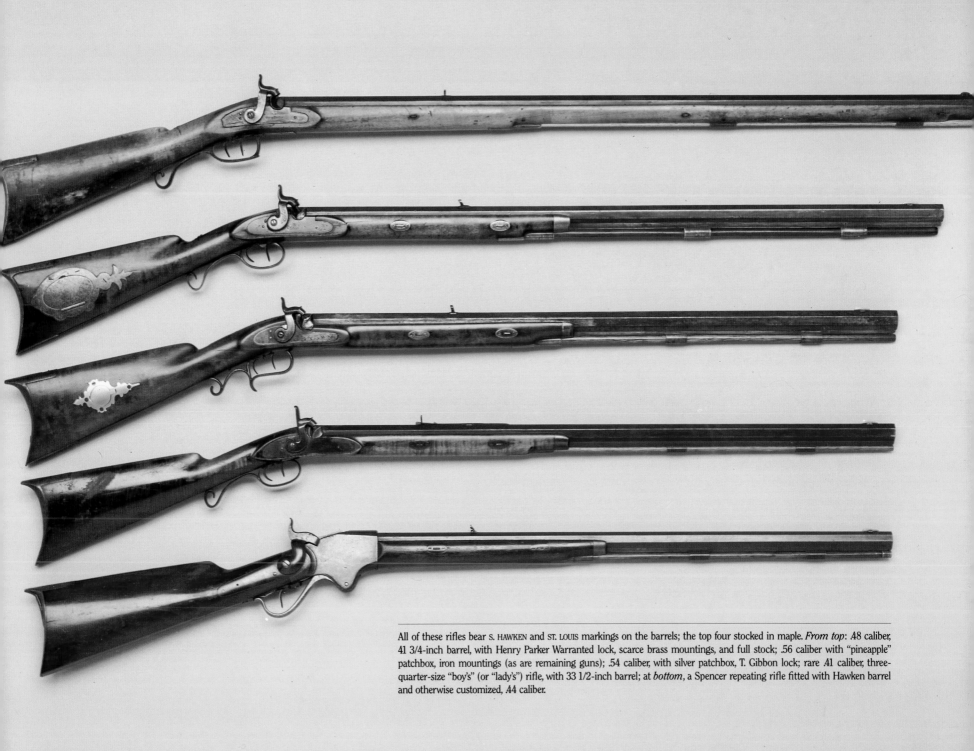

All of these rifles bear S. HAWKEN and ST. LOUIS markings on the barrels; the top four stocked in maple. *From top*: .48 caliber, 41 3/4-inch barrel, with Henry Parker Warranted lock, scarce brass mountings, and full stock; .56 caliber with "pineapple" patchbox, iron mountings (as are remaining guns); .54 caliber, with silver patchbox, T. Gibbon lock; rare .41 caliber, three-quarter-size "boy's" (or "lady's") rifle, with 33 1/2-inch barrel; at *bottom*, a Spencer repeating rifle fitted with Hawken barrel and otherwise customized, .44 caliber.

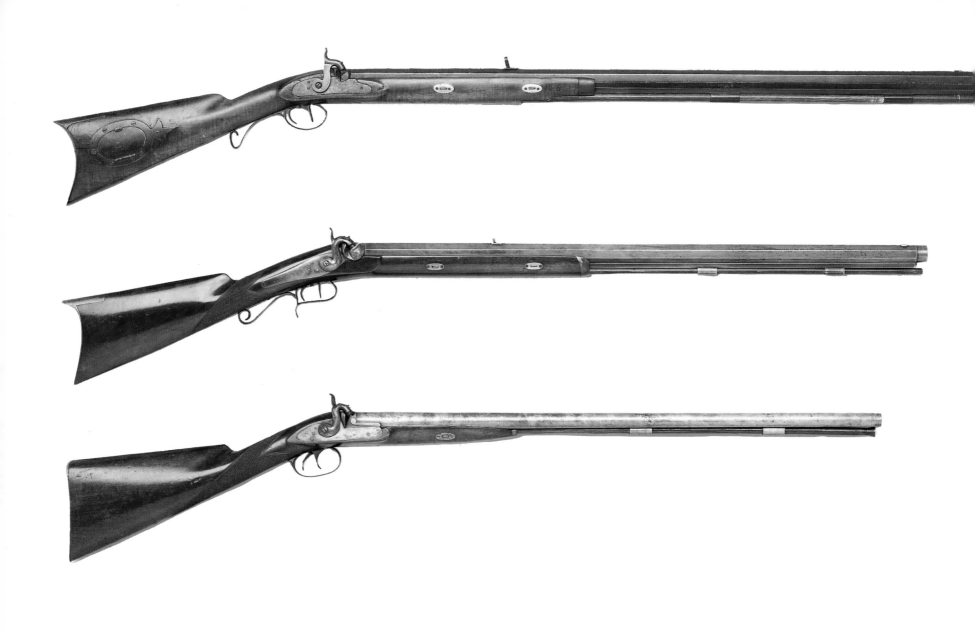

St. Louis gunmakers. *From top*, S. Hawken .54-caliber rifle, iron mounts and German-silver escutcheons, Goulcher lock, 36 1/2-inch barrel; .38-caliber sporting rifle by H. E. Dimick, muzzle turned to accept bullet starter, iron mountings; double-barrel 12-gauge shotgun by J. P. Gemmer, damascus twist barrels, and iron mounts. All guns from mid-century.

beaver traps and also four of their hired French, to be under our individual commands for a period of three years.

Besides the promise of adventure, these men sought profit with solitude, and sensed they were part of America's westward growth and expansion. Free agents, of course, needed capital for supplies, not the least of which were rifle and accessories. The rifle of choice itself reached legendary rank and is known to this day as "the Mountain Man's Rifle": the Hawken.

The Hawken Rifles

Located in St. Louis, gateway to the West, Jacob Hawken had come to the city from Maryland and had once worked at the Harpers Ferry Armory. He and James Lakenan, of Virginia, were in St. Louis by 1819, apparently set up as partners. Although frontier rifles were supplied by Eastern makers, especially from Pennsylvania, gunmakers located in St. Louis had a distinct advantage: knowing the users meant immediate market access and the benefit of their views on design and performance.

In 1822, Samuel Hawken joined his older brother in St. Louis, establishing a business a few blocks away. When Lakenan died, the brothers set up the J. & S. Hawken shop. Guns with their markings span the years c. 1825 to 1850.

These rifles were of rugged proportions and substantial caliber, could take the pounding of the frontier, and were accurate. The second quarter of the nineteenth century proved boom years for the Hawkens and other St. Louis gunsmiths.

It was the Hawken which became the standard by which all "Rocky Mountain" rifles were measured. Quoting Samuel Hawken himself: "Paul Anderson's expedition was the first one I fitted out. He and [trader/adventurer Samuel] went to Santa Fe and gave such good reports about my guns that everyman going west wanted one." Other keen Hawken patrons were Jim Bridger, Kit Carson, John C. Frémont, Mariano Modena, and trader–mountain man Josiah Webb.

Englishman George Frederick Ruxton wrote of his

Pistols made in St. Louis, with CHEVALIER-marked Bowie knife made in New York. *Top*, .45-caliber target pistol by H. E. Dimick; buttcap of ivory; 10-inch barrel. Deringer at *left* attributed to Dimick, but unmarked; .45 caliber. Other deringer marked H. E. DIMICK on barrel, and .52 caliber; note patriotic shield on lockplate, mountings of silver. *Bottom* pistol marked S. HAWKEN ST. LOUIS; .46 caliber; iron mounts. Bowie knife of pre-1850 date, and with handsomely checkered rosewood hilt.

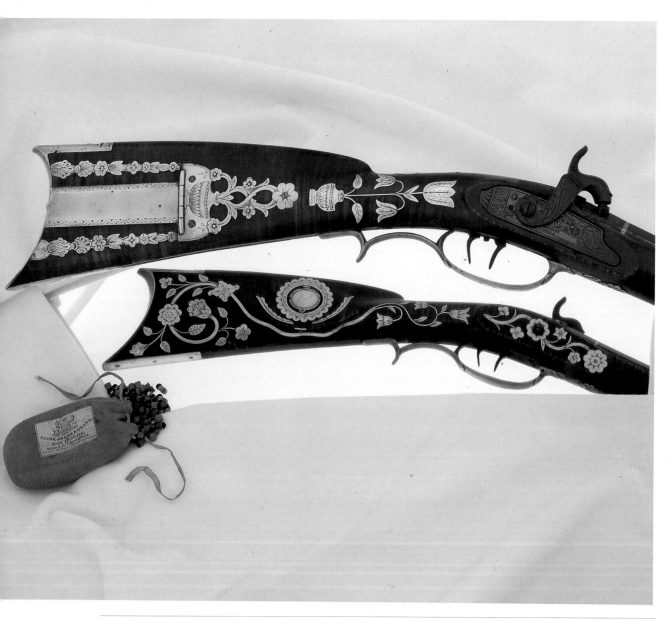

Deluxe Henry Deringer, Jr. Kentucky rifle, embellished in engraved and inlaid silver, and with brass patchbox and mountings; 58 1/2-inch overall length, with 43-inch octagonal barrel, inlaid at muzzle and breech with silver band. Of .31 caliber, and made as a percussion. Lock marking on inlaid copper plate. Full-length stock in curly maple. Compartmented cheekpiece inlay contains removable brass compass, in specially fitted housing.

Although photographed in the 1870s, the huntsman's rifle is of Wesson type, and of mid-century manufacture. Wesson rifles were respected for their craftsmanship and accuracy. U.S. Boundary Commission of 1850 had Wessons along on its journey exploring the Southwest. In skirmish with Apache adversaries, one Delgadito, the leader, was pouring out "torrents of the vilest abuse upon the Americans. . . . Among our party was Wells, the Commissioner's carriage driver—an excellent, brave and cool man, and a crack shot. I pointed Delgadito out to Wells, and handing him my [Wesson target] rifle, told him to approach as nearly as possible, take good aim and bring the rascal down. Wells glided from tree to tree with the utmost caution and rapidity, until he got within two hundred and sixty or seventy yards of Delgadito, who, at that moment, was slapping his buttocks and defying us with the most opprobrious language, while in the act of exhibiting his posteriors—a favorite taunt among the Apaches—he uncovered them to Wells, who took deliberate aim and fired. This mark of attention was received by Delgadito with an unearthly yell and a series of dances and capers that would put a *maître de ballet* to the blush."

54

By Krider, Philadelphia, rifle made with short barrel, in .75 caliber, and probably for use in the West. Silver mounts, including oval inlay on cheekpiece inscribed "Presented to/Capt. W. H. Owen/by/Major M.Chevallie/April 9th 1852."

"Old Sally" was the name given this heavy rifle by mountain man Joe Meek. Right side of buttstock carved "J. Meek, Rocky Mountains"; left side similarly carved "Death," "A. Kelly," and with a running-deer motif.

By Frederick Hellinghaus, St. Louis, double shotgun was Kit Carson's. Capable of firing shot or balls, smoothbore longarms (especially those with heavy barrels) could fire patched balls with accuracy up to 80 yards. Some guns made with straight-grooved barrels, to facilitate loading.

Meek with a double-barrel shotgun or rifle, as well as Colt Dragoon revolver and Bowie knife. Double-barrel or multibarrel guns were expensive, and, in rifles, difficult to make. Over-and-under or swivel barrels were a better system, allowing individual sights for each barrel. Swivel-barrel guns, however, were prone to breakage. Jim Bridger was a double rifle user.

From an A. F. Tait painting, Currier & Ives issued this lithograph, *The Last War-Whoop*, in 1856. Arrow stuck in frontiersman's leg and bedroll.

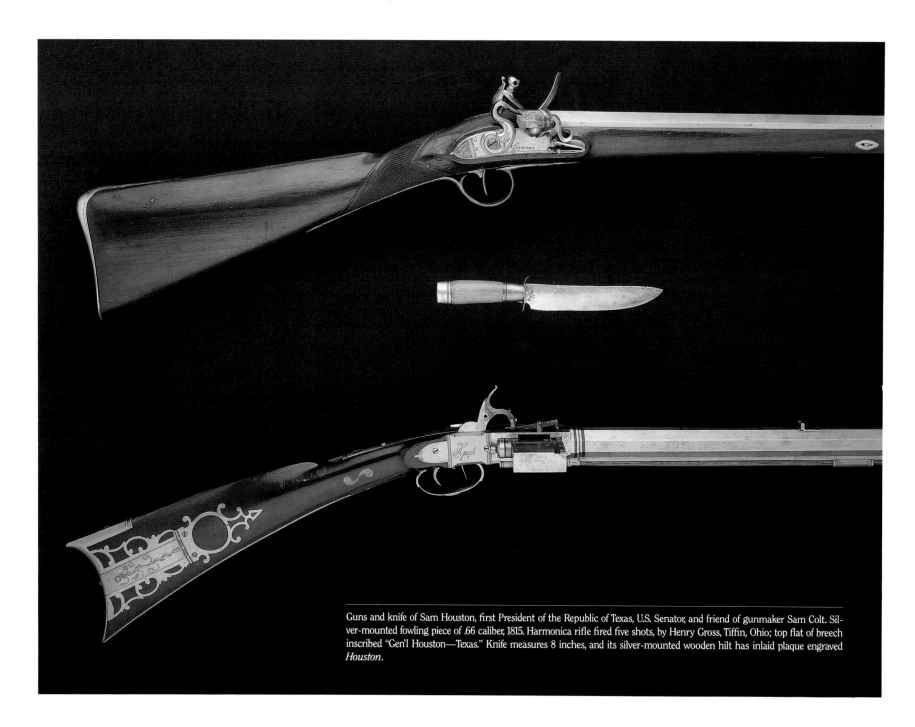

Guns and knife of Sam Houston, first President of the Republic of Texas, U.S. Senator, and friend of gunmaker Sam Colt. Silver-mounted fowling piece of .66 caliber, 1815. Harmonica rifle fired five shots, by Henry Gross, Tiffin, Ohio; top flat of breech inscribed "Gen'l Houston—Texas." Knife measures 8 inches, and its silver-mounted wooden hilt has inlaid plaque engraved *Houston*.

"Remember the Alamo"

In 1835 a revolt broke out among Texans—including a significant number of newly arrived Americans from various Southern states—to establish their independence from Mexico. Initially garrisoned by a force of Mexicans, the Alamo—a mission transformed into a military fort—had surrendered to Texan troops. The Texans released their foes, armed them for defense against Indians, and sent them on their way back to Mexico, hoping that the Mexican leadership would adopt a reasonable attitude toward independence. But Mexican dictator General Antonio López de Santa Anna, a vindictive egomaniac though a sometimes skillful soldier and politician, was determined to force the Texans to remain under Mexican domination.

Santa Anna's attempt to deal with the Texans led to the premier battle in Texas history: the Alamo. On February 24, 1836, a siege which would last thirteen days was launched by Santa Anna and his force of more than 4,000 troops. The fortress was defended by 187 Texans, under command of the twenty-six-year-old Colonel William Barret Travis and forty-year-old James Bowie. The already nationally famous heroes Bowie and Davy Crockett were most prominent of the band which defended the nearly three-acre site against overwhelming odds. The deadly accuracy of the frontiersmen and their rifles, like Crockett's favorite Kentucky, "Betsy," combined with an eighteen-gun array of 4-, 6-, 8-, 12-, and 18-pound cannon (loaded with cut-up horseshoes and other projectiles) and raw courage, made the Mexicans pay dearly for their victory.

Colonel Travis, hoping for reinforcements, sent an appeal for help, carried through Mexican lines by Captain Albert Martin. The stirring letter was a clarion for freedom which received international attention:

To the People of Texas and All Americans
Fellow Citizens and Compatriots:
I am besieged by a thousand or more of the Mexicans under Santa Anna. I have sustained a continued bombardment for twenty-four hours and have not lost a man. The enemy have demanded a surrender at discretion; otherwise the garrison is to be put to the sword if the place is taken. I have answered the summons with a cannon shot, and our flag still waves proudly from the walls.

I shall never surrender or retreat.

Then, I call on you in the name of liberty, of patriotism, and of everything dear to the American character to come to our aid with all despatch. The enemy are receiving reinforcements daily and will no doubt increase to three or four thousand in four or five days. Though this call may be neglected, I am determined to sustain myself as long as possible and die like a soldier who never forgets what is due to his own honor and that of his country. *Victory or death! . . .*

A Mexican officer described one of the valiant defenders at battle: "a tall man, with flowing hair [who] wore a buckskin suit and a cap all of a pattern entirely different from those worn by his comrades. This man would rest his long gun and fire, and we all learned to keep at a good distance when he was seen to make ready to shoot. He rarely missed his mark, and when he fired he always rose to his feet and calmly reloaded his gun, seemingly indifferent to the shots fired at him by our men. He had a strong, resonant voice and often railed at us. . . ."

In the final assault, which lasted an hour and a half, waves of Mexican regulars and militia stormed the walls (at some places 12 feet thick, and at the chapel as high as 22 feet) and killed every single defender. As the Mexican army band played the "Deguello," the fire and death call for no quarter, Santa Anna's troops broke into the plaza.

The death of one revolutionary was described by a Mexican sergeant: "He was a tall American of rather dark complexion and had on a long buckskin coat and a round cap without any bill, made out of fox skin with the long tail hanging down his back. This man apparently had a charmed life. Of the many soldiers who took deliberate aim at him and fired, not one ever hit him. On the contrary, he never missed a shot. He killed at least eight of our men, besides wounding several others. This being observed by a lieutenant who had come in over the wall, he sprang at him and dealt him a deadly blow with his sword, just above the right eye, which felled him to the ground, and in an instant he was pierced by not less than 20 bayonets."

The death of Jim Bowie was equally tragic; though reports vary, he was apparently too ill to defend himself, and was shot repeatedly (even after death). Colonel Travis had been struck in the forehead while fighting on the top of a wall, armed with a shotgun.

Another Mexican soldier remembered the scene within the walls: "I can tell you the whole scene was one of extreme terror. . . . After some three quarters of an hour of the most horrible fire, there followed the most awful attack with hand arms."

The final defense was in the chapel, the original walls of which remain standing in San Antonio, open to hundreds of thousands of tourists annually. One of the defenders tried to torch the powder magazine, but was killed before he could do so. The widow of another was captured, and instructed by Santa Anna to take news of the massacre as a warning to Texans what they could expect from resisting Mexican domination. A few women and children were also spared, as was Travis's slave, and a San Antonio citizen.

Although evidence of the battle is sometimes contradictory, it seems clear that Davy Crockett survived, was captured, and almost talked himself to freedom. A Mexican officer suggested to Santa Anna that it would be a fine gesture to the Americans to spare Crockett's life. At the last minute Santa Anna ordered his death, along with those of five other male survivors: "I do not want to see those men living. Shoot them." Several Mexican officers were shocked at the brutality; one later recalled: "I turned away horrified in order not to witness such a barbarous scene. . . . I confess that the very memory of it makes me tremble and that my ear can still hear the penetrating, doleful sound of the victims."

Santa Anna ordered the Texans' remains, many of them horribly mutilated, to be stacked up like cordwood and burned. The losses of the Mexicans were enormous: an estimated 1,500 killed, although the number is speculative, since Santa Anna ordered their bodies buried. Most Mexican casualties came from friendly fire and from grapeshot. The quality of rifles used by the defenders and their effectiveness against the Mexican army is largely a myth.

News of the Alamo had an exactly opposite effect from that Santa Anna wanted, for the Texans now swore a steely resolve to follow the dictum of the martyred Travis: "Victory or Death!"

The chance for revenge came quickly, when General Sam Houston and nearly 800 men confronted Santa Anna in the Battle of San Jacinto. The proud Mexican general misjudged his foe and saw his force of some 1,400 soundly whipped in just eighteen minutes. Before the battle, the Texans, itching for a fight, had been inspired by Houston, astride his white stallion: ". . . Victory is certain! Trust in God and fear not! The victims of the Alamo and the names of those who were murdered at Goliad [an earlier battle, in which the Texans surrendered, only to have most of them massacred on Santa Anna's orders] cry out for vengeance. Remember the Alamo! Remember Goliad!"

The Texans outfoxed their foe, attacking them while many were taking a siesta. A participant wrote: "We marched upon the enemy with the stillness of death. . . . No fife, no drum, no voice was heard." When the attack began, the Texans' fife-and-drum corps played the ballad "Will You Come to the Bower?" and the men charged to "Remember the Alamo! Remember the Goliad!" When just 60 yards from the enemy's defenses, the Texans opened fire. Two horses were shot out from under Houston, but he remounted and led the charge,

waving his sword. The defeat was total. A sergeant called it the "most awful slaughter I ever saw . . . the Texans pursu[ing] the retreating Mexicans, killing on all sides, even the wounded. . . . I had a double-barrel shotgun and had shot only four times when we crossed the breastworks. After that I shot no more at the poor devils who were running." Santa Anna was observed by one of his aides to be "running about in the utmost excitement, wringing his hands and unable to give an order." The general managed to escape, but was later sighted, disguised and bewildered, not far from the battlefield. When brought before Sam Houston, reclining and not well because of a bullet wound, Santa Anna trembled with fear (though he too was in bad health) and requested his medicine kit. A dose of opium revitalized the vanquished general. (Houston was also under the influence of opium, a sedation by his doctor.) In a sharp exchange, Houston reminded the cunning Santa Anna of events at the Alamo, and at Goliad. Fortunately, Santa Anna soon found that he was worth more to the Texans alive. Houston later explained his decision: "My motive in sparing the life of Santa Anna . . . was to relieve the country of all hostile enemies without further bloodshed, and secure his acknowledgement of our independence, which I considered of vastly more importance than the mere gratification of revenge."

The victory assured the independence of the Republic of Texas, and nine years later statehood would be granted. Ironically, Santa Anna would soon brave something like a grand tour of the United States, being greeted more like an exiled statesman than a villain. He was well received by members of the Kentucky legislature, businessmen from Philadelphia and New York, and even dined at the White House, as guest of President Andrew Jackson. Jackson then arranged for Santa Anna's return to Vera Cruz, aboard the U.S. Frigate *Pioneer.*

travels and adventures in Mexico and the far West. He described a Mississippi rifleman of c. 1825, in St. Louis, who

first of all visited the gun-store of Hawken, whose rifles are renowned in the mountains, and exchanged his own piece, which was of very small bore, for a regular mountain rifle. This was of very heavy metal, carrying about thirty-two balls to the pound, stocked to the muzzle and mounted with brass, its only ornament being a buffalo bull, looking exceedingly furocious, which was not very artistically engraved upon the trap in the stock.

Standard mountings on the Hawkens were iron, which was stronger than brass. But Ruxton's description suggests that the earlier St. Louis rifles had brass mounts.

The ultimate Hawken evolution was reached from late in 1830s early into the 1840s, with a 38-inch barrel (some shorter, some longer) of heavier weight and in about .50 to .53 caliber. The half stock was of maple, with distinctive cheekpiece of oval contour and mounts of iron. Rifle weight was a hefty 11 pounds.

An element contributing to the highly accurate barrels was their composition of soft iron and the rifling of a slow twist. The rifle was considered accurate to over 200 yards, and mountain man Bill Hamilton wrote that "in those days the best rifles used were the Hawkins and they carried three hundred and fifty yards."

Although the Hawken shop and other St. Louis gunmakers had a marketing advantage over their rivals in the East, those craftsmen too had a generally loyal following. Among the best such makers were Henry E. Leman, James Henry, E. K. Tryon, and Edwin

---

A .50-caliber Plains rifle, c. 1865, made in shop of San Antonio dealer Charles Hummel; 35 1/2-inch barrel. Parts for manufacture believed shipped to San Antonio, from the East, by way of New Orleans. Rare glass powder flask, marked "N. A. Johnson & Co./Seguin, Tex." Large Bowie measures 17 1/2 inches overall; sheath of boot leather. Rifle bag, c. 1840, of saddle-skirting leather, sewn with rawhide thongs; homespun burlap shoulder strap, with dyed borders; note TEXAS marking on brass star. Small rifleman's knife fashioned from a saw blade.

One of the earliest Bowie knives, this one inscribed on throat of scabbard *R. P. Bowie/to/H.W. Fowler/U.S.D.* (Dragoons). Knife made by Searles, of Baton Rouge, Louisiana, for Jim Bowie's brother, Rezin. On display at the Alamo.

(*bottom left*) Frontier character brandishing early Bowie knife, with another on his belt, along with a holstered Dragoon Colt and unidentified longarm. Daguerreotype, c. 1850.

(*bottom right*) John S. "Rip" Ford in buckskin coat, with gauntlets and a pair of what appear to be Colt Walker revolvers in tooled holsters. Ford, a rough and ready Texan, and adjutant and physician with Captain Jack Hays's regiment of Texas Rangers, earned his nickname by signing Mexican War death certificates "John S. Ford. R.I.P." The redoubtable Ford was credited by historian Walter Prescott Webb with the statement: "A Texas Ranger rides like a Mexican, trails like an Indian, shoots like a Tennessean and fights like the devil." Ambrotype of c. 1855.

Wesson. Wesson, of Northborough, Massachusetts, became renowned for the target accuracy of his finely made rifles. Gunmakers of talent were in virtually every city, and many towns and villages, throughout the South and East. They existed because of a ready demand, and the client's realization that a fine rifle or gun might well prove to be the most important object he would ever own.

Of rifles with fur trade histories, few could rival "Old Blackfoot," the favorite rifle of trader and mountain man Josiah J. Webb. In his book *Adventures in the Santa Fe Trade 1844–47*, Webb left a vivid history of this remarkable weapon, which he had received in a swap:

> Many years before, a trapper employed by the American Fur Company had taken it on a trapping expedition in the Blackfoot country. The Indians killed him and took his gun. Years after, Messrs. Bent, St. Vrain and Company sent an expedition to that nation on a trapping and trading trip, and traded for the old rifle. At the fort it was re-stocked (full length), and altered from flint-lock to percussion, and kept at the fort for a target rifle for several years. In 1846 I had it newly grooved [rifled], half stocked, and [added] a new lock and breech pin [all done by J. & S. Hawken, of St. Louis, and so marked], and have carried it in all my travels in the trade except on my last trip. . . . [It was] my old and trusty friend, companion, and bedfellow, who never went back on me—"Old Blackfoot"—the name it was known by at the fort and which I have always retained.

James B. Marsh in *Four Years in the Rockies* (1884) paid as fine a tribute to the Hawken (and its mountain man user) as any: "[I]nstinctively does a Rocky Mountain trapper, in moments of peril, grasp his trusty rifle. It is his companion and his best and truest friend. With a Hawkins rifle in his possession he feels confident and self-reliant, and does not fear to cope with any odds, or encounter any danger."

Other Arms, and Colts

A variety of arms vied with the Hawken and other Plains single-shot rifles. These ranged from double-barreled, to revolving-chambered, to harmonica-breech rifles, and other bizarre mechanical contraptions.

Smoothbore guns also had their place on the early

By John Chevalier, c. 1840, this giant Bowie measures 17 1/2 inches overall, with a 1/2-inch-thick blade, and mountings of ivory, silver, and silver-plated brass. German-silver mounts to scabbard. Weight of knife: 2 1/2 pounds!

Though made for use by the U.S. Navy on the Wilkes South Seas Expedition (1838–42), some Elgin Cutlass pistols made their way west. Billed as the "Elgin patent Bowie knives with pistol attached which will shoot and cut at the same time," the bizarre pistol was covered by an 1837 patent, and the naval pattern was made in a quantity of only 150, by C. B. Allen, Springfield, Massachusetts. Specimens of the type were sold in St. Louis, December 1838. Other stylings made by Morrill, Mossman, & Blair, and Mossman & Blair, in neighboring Amherst; those had barrels of about 3 to 6 inches and were in calibers .34 to .54. Serial number 100 is the finest known example of the large-size pistols; overall length of approximately 17 inches, weight 2 pounds 4 ounces, caliber .54 smoothbore.

Western and Southern Bowie knives, all but two of English manufacture (most in Sheffield); at *left*, by Samuel Bell, Knoxville, Tennessee. Reading to *right*, makers are Unwin Rodgers, Mappin & Webb, W. H. Grainger (probably dealer), "manufactured for F. C. Goergen New Orleans" and possibly American, W. F. Jackson, Ibbotson Peace & Co., R. Bunting, unidentified, S. C. Wragg, and Theodore A. Meyer. Folding knives by A. Davys (note half-horse, half-alligator motif), and unidentified maker (note pelican motif of state of Louisiana). These knives, marked with mottos such as "Real Ripper Kentucky Fashion To Cut Thro All," "For Stags and Buffaloes," "Far West Hunting Knife," and "Hunter's Companion," were clearly made for the American market. Earliest specimen, by Bell, dates c. 1835; latest is post–Civil War.

Looking every bit like a mountain man of 1840, photograph of Charles S. Stobie dates from 1866, in Colorado. Plains rifle with full stock; his knife scabbard fringed, and probably quilled to match his moccasins. Hat forebodes cavalier look cultivated by Buffalo Bill and others.

SETH KINMAN AND SON CARLIN,
CALIFORNIA HUNTERS AND TRAPPERS.

(*top left*) William H. Jackson photograph of "A half blood [hunter and trapper] Indian wife and children." His rifle a mid-century Plains muzzle-loader, with extra-long barrel.

(*top right*) Three-barrel rifle, with iron mounts, c. 1850, the barrels revolve to fire from a single lock. Multibarrel rifles and rifle-shotgun combinations were a carryover from the Kentucky rifle days. Those used in pioneer West were usually by American makers and had disadvantage of excessive weight. Their future was cut short by rash of breech-loading percussion and metallic cartridge arms in 1850s and 1860s. An 1862 traveler, Dr. William Dibb, described his combination rifle-shotgun and its performance against Plains buffalo: "I tried a shot with the big bullet . . . the shot barrel carried a 1 1/3 [ounce] ball while running—which had the effect of stopping without hitting him—he wheeled about and stood ready. I stopped, & took a steady pull with the rifle. This time I heard the bullet 'thug' as it struck him."

(*bottom left*) Kinman and son amply supplied with scalps, knives, guns, tomahawks, bow and arrows, and hunting trophies, c. 1855. Carlin held a Model 1851 Navy Colt for the camera.

(*bottom right*) Revolving guns had a short life span in the West, c. 1835–50. *From top,* by William Billinghurst, credited as most prolific maker of manually revolving percussion arms in America. Next the J. & J. Miller, which, with William Billinghurst guns, set standard and pattern for arms of this type. Rifle with German-silver eagle patchbox by Benjamin Bigelow, Marysville, California. *Bottom* rifle by W. H. Smith features exceptional craftsmanship. The Millers, Bigelow, and Smith were all protégés of Billinghurst.

Henry Deringer's son, Calhoun M., presented this superb set of dueling pistols to the Honorable Alex Ramsay in midcentury. Ramsay served as governor of the Minnesota Territory at that time and appears to have had long friendship with young Deringer. One of Ramsay's functions as governor was as superintendent of Indian affairs. Market for Deringers in Minnesota was then quite active. Other contemporary Minnesotans known to have ordered large-size Deringer pistols were Hercules Dousman, Henry M. Sibley, and Joseph Rolette.

John James Audubon, by his sons John and Victor, c. 1845. An inveterate hunter, Audubon is said to have shot 500 birds as a sportsman for every bird he shot to paint. His expeditions to the West, as revealed by journals and diaries, document thorough delight in sport of shooting. Portrait reflects importance of his gun and dog, and dedication to the hunt.

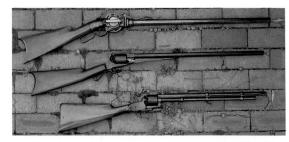

Notable other attempts at revolving percussion shoulder arms. *From top*: P. W. Porter "turret rifle," Remington revolving rifle, and LeMat. Porter always had one chamber or more aimed in direction of shooter, as did an earlier make, the Cochran. A nine-shot gun, probably a Cochran, was stolen by Indians from a traveler in Utah in 1846. Gun later recovered because thief was shot accidentally trying to fire the contraption; his chief ordered gun returned to the next immigrant party!

Heavily armed gentleman with Bowie knife, pepperbox (rare bikini holster), Massachusetts Arms Company revolver, and half-stocked sporting rifle. The Bowie's scabbard rests between the latter two firearms. Daguerreotype of early 1850s.

Indians caught up with the four surveyors at *right*, in civilian finery, killing and scalping them, in 1868. The men had been sent by the federal government to survey a site in northern Oklahoma. False-fronted building was the "Summit Street Market."

frontier. Some were blunderbusses, swivel guns (mounted on boats), shotguns, and (more often) muskets. An arsenal at a trading post on the Columbia River, Fort Nez Perce, was made up of "four pieces of ordnance from one to three pounds besides ten wall pieces or swivels, sixty stand of muskets and bayonets, twenty boarding pikes, and a box of hand grenades."

Shotguns had a devastating effect for self-defense, and black mountain man Jim Beckwourth told of a night fight with Indians in the 1820s in which his party of four fired into the dark. In the morning they "discovered two dead Indians lying where we had directed our aim.... We knew they had been killed by our guns, for the other two men fired with shot-guns loaded with buck-shot. [They hit other Indians] but their wounds were not serious."

What appears to have been a musket was involved in an incident with a bear, as told by Jedediah Smith: "[T]he Bear ran over the man next to me and made a furious rush on the third man Joseph Lapoint. But Lapoint had by good fortune a Bayonet fixed on his gun and as the Bear came in he gave him a severe wound in the neck which induced him to change his course."

In his memoirs, T. D. Beckwourth recalled with poignancy that time, which he had been a part of, as a member of W. J. Ashley's spring 1822 trapping expedition:

> Buried amid the sublime passes of the Sierra Nevada are old men, who, when children, strayed away from our crowded settlements, and, gradually moving farther and farther from civilization, have in time become savages—have lived scores of years whetting their intellects in the constant struggle for self-preserva-

Geologist John F. Steward, armed with a Winchester Model 1866 rifle, stood within the Glen Canyon of the Colorado River, 1871.

Looking more like the James and Younger Gang than a fossil-seeking expedition to the West from Yale University, this group of students was led by Professor Othniel Charles Marsh (standing at *center*), in 1872. Marsh also led parties in 1870, 1871, and 1873. Besides their own arsenal, the men were escorted by armed U.S. Cavalry units.

tion; whose only pleasurable excitement was found in facing danger; whose only repose was to recuperate, preparatory to participating in new and thrilling adventures.

Explorers, traders and mountain men found pistols attractive as added insurance, though often expensive. They were usually in pairs, and some hardy souls might have more, with various places to carry or conceal them. Size ranged from the large military types (of .50 to .70 caliber), to medium "belt" pistols, to pocket types. Most elegant of these were the Kentucky pistols, usually of .40 to .54 caliber, and with about 6- to 10-inch barrels, rifled or smoothbore. Smaller guns were about 5 to 7 inches in length; some were in caliber as large as .50. Beginning c. 1825 the most famed of these, the Deringer (by Henry Deringer, Jr.) rose rapidly in popularity.

Dueling pistols were also widely sold, standard in cased pairs, with full accessories. Most were of European or English make; American-made duelers were not common. Most barrels were smoothbore, as dictated by the "Code Duello." When Comanches killed Jedediah Smith in 1831 on the Cimarron River, his pistols were a percussion pair of dueling pattern, mounted in silver.

Handgun uses were varied. James Clyman and party, while trapping in 1824, failed to cut a hole in the frozen Big Sandy River with tomahawks, so Clyman drew one of his pistols and when he "fired into the hole up came water plentifull for man & horse."

Kit Carson wielded a pistol in self-defense against a

Selected equipment of a locating engineer who surveyed railroad lines in Texas, Colorado, Oregon, and South America. This weaponry, purchased from a dealer in Texas, made up of a Manhattan Cutlery Company Sheffield Bowie knife, a 44-40 Colt six-shooter (number 58774), and a matching-caliber Model 1873 Winchester (number 60825).

Holding a .50-70 trapdoor Springfield Officer's Model rifle, frontier photographer William H. Jackson strikes a cavalier pose in this 1872 picture.

71

mean-spirited Frenchman at the Green River rendezvous* in 1835:

> I would rip his guts. He said nothing but started for his rifle, mounted his horse, and made his appearance in front of the camp. As soon as I saw this, I mounted my horse also, seized the first weapon I could get hold of, which was a pistol, and galloped up to him. . . . I was prepared and allowed him to draw his gun. We both fired at the same time, and all present said that but one report was heard. I shot him through the arm and his ball passed my head, cutting my hair and the powder burning my eye, the muzzle of his gun being near my head when he fired. During the remainder of our stay in camp we had no more bother with this French bully.

The most impressive of all Plains pistols is a massive pair by J. & S. Hawken, with 10 13/16-inch octagon rifle barrels, of a potent .65 caliber. As in the Hawken rifles, the English influence in their styling was strongly evident. These extraordinary arms are among the most remarkable of all Hawken guns. Judging from their fine condition, the set likely was spared from years of mountain man use.

Taking a buffalo from horseback with a pistol was a sport ideally suited to mountain men or a visiting Englishman. Eyewitness George Wilkins Kendall described the technique. The huntsman would "sally out after them on horse-back, armed with heavy holster-pistols, run alongside, while under full speed, and shoot from the saddle. Of all hunting in the world, this is probably the most exciting, at the same time involving the sportsman in no little danger."

Traveler and adventurer Bill Hamilton observed (1842) trappers armed with two pistols, rifle, tomahawk, and a knife of large proportions. Increased firepower was offered to mountain men and explorers near the end of the trailblazer era, with the improved Hartford-made Colt revolver and Allen's pepperbox. The Colt had appeared first as the diminutive Pocket Paterson, followed by two belt sizes, and a holster size, in .28, .31, and .36 calibers respectively. The small and medium pistols did not prove suitable for frontier use, but the Texas pistol, as the .36-caliber came to be called in Colt's own lifetime, made a distinguished record, mainly in the hands of Texans.

A few mountain men tried the early Colt revolvers, the "Patersons," despite their cost and mechanical fragility. Josiah Gregg and brother headed to Santa Fe, each armed "with one of Colt's repeating rifles, and a pair of pistols of the same, so that we could, if necessary, carry thirty-six ready-loaded shots apiece; which alone constituted a capacity of defence rarely matched even on the Prairies." Records show the American Fur Company in 1839 acquired two Colt Paterson revolving handguns and a revolving shotgun, to be shipped to its representative in St. Louis. A year later the Paterson Colt New York agency sold a .36-caliber holster pistol with "Rifle Stock & Barrel" to a Mr. Gilpin of St. Louis.

And in 1841, Kit Carson and over two dozen trappers rescued a wagon train on the Santa Fe Trail. Several of the trappers relied on their Paterson Colts to save the day. The Indians disappeared from the scene, surprised and, for once, in a state of panic.

The Allen, a heavy multibarreled revolver, known as a pepperbox, was a double-action, or self-cocker, with no need to line up a chamber with a single barrel (as in the Colt). However, the Allen best suited for the frontier, the so-called Dragoon size, was heavy, cumbersome, and effective only at short ranges. Further, the .36-caliber barrels were smoothbore, and loading was slow. Other makes soon entered the market with their pepperboxes, notably New York's Blunt & Syms.

Possibly it was an Allen pepperbox which John James Audubon, no stranger to firearms, presented to a steamboat captain at Fort Union on the Missouri River (1843). The gift was "a 'handsome' six-barrelled pistol, the only thing we have that may prove of service to him," and it was mounted in silver.

Wagon trains along the Santa Fe Trail in the 1840s saw leaders advising men of the companies to have a tomahawk in their armament. Many of these were the simple belt ax or hatchet, rather than the Indian-style trade tomahawk. A quite deluxe ax with a hammer poll (top where the pipe bowl often fit) was presented to Davy Crockett by a group of young men from Philadelphia.

Some rather elegant examples were likely by Kentucky rifle makers, for pioneer riflemen, explorers, trappers, traders, and mountain men.

Civilization would appear to be not too far away, however, when U.S. Boundary Commissioner John R. Bartlett (1850) moved about the Southwest in a "Rockaway" carriage, accompanied by six wagons pulled by mules, with the carriage interior fitted out like a traveling armory:

> First, there was suspended at the top a doubled-barrelled gun, while to one of the uprights was affixed my rifle, one of Sharp's repeaters; a heavy revolver, one of Colt's six-shooters, was strapped to each door; and Dr. Webb (who rode with me) and I were both provided with a pair of Colt five-shooters. My carriage driver carried a pair of Deringer pistols. We were thus enabled, in case of necessity, to discharge a round of thirty-seven shots without reloading; besides which, [the] Sharp's rifle could be fired at least six times in a minute.

---

*Annual summer gathering of mountain men, Indians, and traders in carnival atmosphere, at which pelts were sold, outfitting done for future trips, and news and gossip exchanged, amid consumption of liquor and considerable revelry. Held from 1825 for at least fifteen years, the first at Henry's Fork on the Green River, Wyoming territory; others at various sites.

John "Liver-Eating" Johnston's Winchester Model 1876 sporting rifle, number 9989. Extra wood fitted onto toe of buttstock may have been to facilitate quick removal from saddle scabbard. The 6-foot-5-inch, 250-pound trapper, wolfer, lawman, scout, and Indian fighter is alleged to have taken a bite out of livers of Indians he slew, in revenge for murder of wife and child. Evidence makes story doubtful, though he was a rough-and-ready fellow.

THE ARMY:
AN EVOLVING ARSENAL

The early effectiveness of the Army against the Indians was limited by the small number of forts and outposts on a vast frontier, and use of only infantry units—there was no cavalry until 1832, when Congress authorized the formation of mounted rangers and the groundwork was set for the most effective offense against the mounted warriors of the West.

In 1838 the Army established the Corps of Topographical Engineers, leading toward surveying the West and creating reliable maps. At that time, as a point of reference, the strength of the regular Army (as opposed to militia units) was only 10,000 men, not a few of whom were in Florida, fighting the Seminole Indians. Beginning in 1842, some five expeditions led by John C. Frémont, "the Pathfinder," appreciably opened America's eyes to the potential of the West for agriculture and ranching.

Veterans of the Mexican War of 1846–48 were tough and thoroughly experienced fighters, but America had acquired a vast new territory: the great Southwest. These lands, including California, all had Indian populations, among them the traditionally hostile Apaches and Navajos. Their presence inevitably led to combat, with campaigns initiated by the United States to tame the tribes.

Yet insufficient troop strength, bored soldiers with poor morale and laden with heavy gear, and the superior fighting capability of the Indians meant the balance of power remained in favor of the native warriors until the mid-1850s. A New Mexico–based Indian agent wrote in

No nineteenth-century military figure has captured the public imagination more than Lieutenant Colonel George Armstrong Custer. These artifacts from Civil War and Indian Wars all have personal significance. Cased Remington New Model Army revolver a presentation from the company, the flag a gift from wife, Libbie, by family tradition sewn from her petticoats, the pitcher inscribed to her from the 7th Cavalry, and the journal at *left foreground* one kept by "Yellow Hair" himself, of campaigns and adventures in the West.

"California Joe" Milner, one of Custer's trusted scouts. see page 99.

1852: "The Indians have nothing but their bows and arrows and their ponies are as fleet as deer. Cipher it up. Heavy Dragoons on poor horses who know nothing of the country sent after Indians who are at home anywhere and who always have some hours start. How long will it take to catch them?"

Artillery and Guns

When cumbersome cannon or mortar could be taken afield, the Army had an advantage; fearsome artillery was an effective persuader against Indian attackers. Even civilian shotguns were occasionally used. Once Pathfinder Frémont, challenging another Army officer to a duel, was confronted with shotguns as the choice of weapons. Luckily the duel was quashed by action of another officer.

Until the mid-1850s, riflemen were secondary to infantry with muskets, and were assigned skirmishing duty, firing with accuracy until troops closed within musket and bayonet range. Slowness of loading was a limitation in dealing with the quick-moving Indians, and a musket could be fired nearly twice as fast as the rifle.

An exception was the Hall Model 1819 breechloader:

Selection of U.S.-issue longarms and accouterments that saw Western service. *From left*, Model 1817 flintlock rifle; Model 1819 Hall breech-loading flintlock rifle; Model 1836 Hall percussion carbine; Jenks "Mule Ear" carbine by N. P. Ames; Model 1841 Mississippi rifle by Robbins & Lawrence; Model 1863 Remington Zouave contract rifle with bayonet; Model 1855 rifled carbine; Model 1847 sapper's musketoon and bayonet; and Model 1861 rifle-musket. At *right*, Model 1833 foot artillery sword, by Ames Mfg. Co., and based on French design, in turn inspired by Roman infantry sword. Total made of all models of guns was in excess of 475,000.

Holster or "Texas" Paterson Colt .36-caliber revolver, its *WAT* ordnance inspector mark visible on left side of 7 1/2-inch barrel. Initials are those of William A. Thornton, ordnance inspector, whose mark is often found on Colt and other government-purchased arms of period c. 1840–61. Thornton was an admirer of Samuel Colt and a source of helpful advice on improvements in Colt firearms. Cavalry saber is the Dragoon Model of 1833, made under contract by Ames.

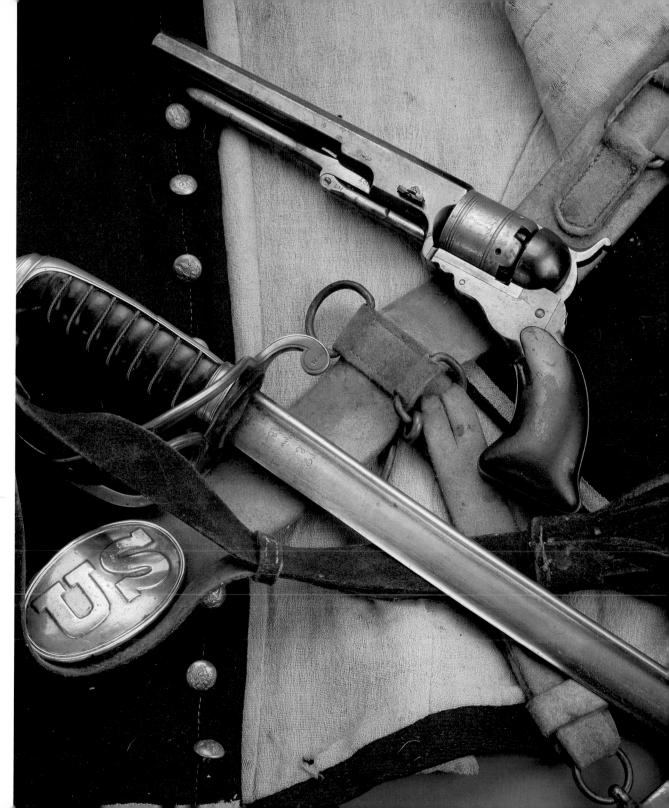

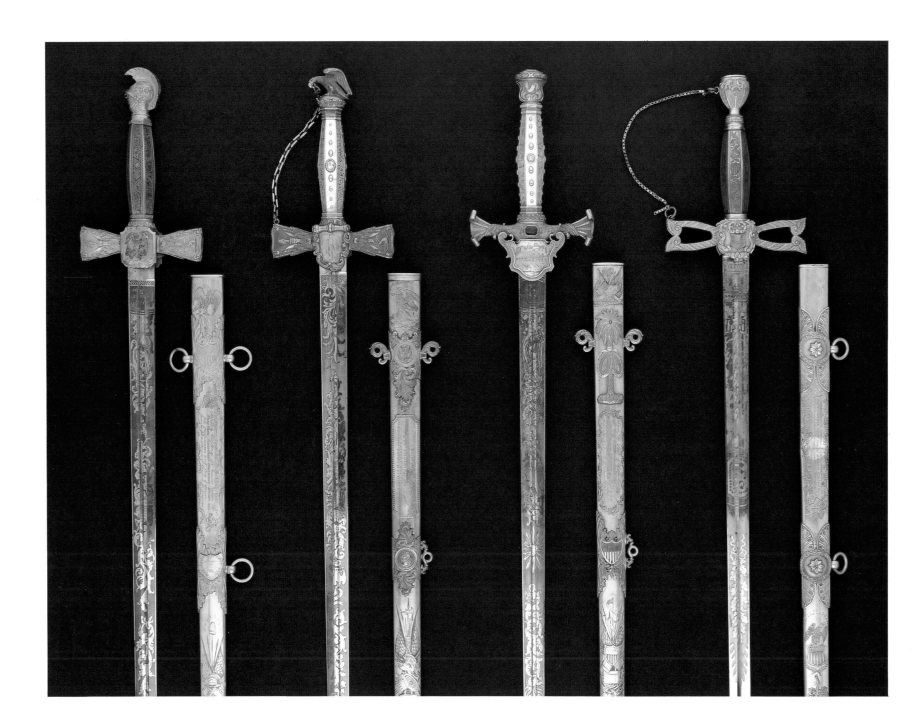

the gun could shoot faster than a musket (by about 33 percent) and was more accurate. But the guns were slow to make, and expensive. Rifles were also useful to the Army for hunting, a recreation which kept soldiers on the alert and yielded fresh meat for the mess.

With the Model 1841 "Mississippi Rifle" the Ordnance Department adopted one of the most aesthetically pleasing and popular of nineteenth-century military firearms. The sobriquet came from the successful use of this gun by Jefferson Davis and his Mississippi volunteers during the Mexican War. It was of .54 caliber and had a 33-inch barrel; its brass patchbox gave it a distinctive identifying feature. With a production total of over 70,000, the Model 1841 was one of the more common midcentury military arms.

Short-barreled guns, suited for dragoon use, were another frontier military staple. The percussion Hall breech-loading carbine, in calibers from .52 to .64, mainly a smoothbore, was often loaded with shot instead of an individual ball. The dangerous problem of gas leakage caused some accidents of blown-out stocks at the breech, and disturbing flashes in the face. Nevertheless the Hall carbine remained the dragoons' issue shoulder arm for approximately thirty years.

A rival to the Hall, the Jenks breechloader proved difficult to load after fouling. Pulling upward on a mule-ear-like aperture revealed a channel in the breech, into which powder and ball could be inserted. On closing the lever the gun was ready to be capped and fired. One officer praised the Jenks "very much for buffalo guns, from the facility of handling them at speed, being lighter than [Hall's carbine]."

Problems with both weapons helped create a prejudice against any breechloaders. Colt's Paterson revolving rifles, carbines, and muskets, as tested from 1837 on for many years, never surmounted such opinions, to the frustration of the dynamic and determined inventor. Multidischarges were a common concern, and rapid reloading was a problem. Carrying extra cylinders, loaded, allowed for faster firing, but until the

Sam Chamberlain holding Mexicans at bay with the breechblock of his Hall percussion carbine. His diary, in the West Point Museum, remains a stirring, folksy, and lengthy memoir of Mexican War.

(*opposite*) Recognition of Mexican War and Civil War service in the form of exquisite presentation swords, each inscribed on scabbard. A form of male jewelry, these magnificent objects vied with richly decorated guns in capturing the strong patriotic spirit of the time. *From left*, the Colonels Magruder and Garland and the Brigadier General Shields swords, by Ames Mfg. Co., Chicopee, Massachusetts; the Captain Johnson by Mitchell & Tyler, Richmond, Virginia.

Hartford-made 1855 solid-frame models, this meant removing the barrel first.

There were some favorable government test reports for the Paterson Colts, but government purchases remained limited (a Navy report on Colts complained of "the deafening sharpness of the report, which must injure the hearing of those who use them"). Colt himself went to the Seminole War site and managed a direct sale of fifty Ring Lever rifles, though he lost a substantial check in payment when the boat he was in capsized. It took months to get the sum replaced through the horrendous (even then) Washington, D.C., bureaucracy. Additional orders of one hundred Model 1839 .525 carbines (for the Navy) and sixty for dragoon trials, plus one hundred carbines and fifty revolvers for Army ordnance officers, represent most sales for federal government forces of Paterson Colt production.

A number of these Colts saw service in the Mexican War, and in points west, and it was the use of the Paterson Colt revolver, especially by Texas Rangers and dragoons in the Southwest, which inspired Captain Samuel H. Walker to contact Samuel Colt, in 1846, to collaborate on what became the mighty Walker .44 revolver.

Still another service arm was the musketoon (a shortened and lightened musket), made for mounted men, artillery, and engineers (a.k.a. sappers; brass mounts to the guns signified dragoons, iron mounts were for artillery and sappers). This gun was not popular, and was termed by the experienced Colonel J.K.F. Mansfield as "almost worthless." Excessive recoil and poor accuracy were but two reasons for its unpopularity.

Another military arm, with a bright future of nearly thirty years' duration, was the invention of a one-time employee of the Harpers Ferry Armory: Christian Sharps. The falling-block percussion breech-loading action, actuated by a lever doubling as triggerguard, was capable of handling powerful loads. After a paper cartridge was inserted into the breech, raising the lever cut off the back end, exposing the powder. A mechanical system of priming was commonly employed.

Orders from the federal government began as early as 1852, with 200 carbines. Reports from the field favored the Sharps over the Hall, the musketoon, and the Jenks for cavalry use. Although such defects as burning cartridge paper left in chambers after firing presented concerns, the Sharps could be operated at about ten shots a minute. Among the reports reaching ordnance officers were such statements as "I have had five of Sharps' carbines on hand six months, and am satisfied that they are superior to any firearm yet furnished the dragoons."

The Army and Ordnance Adapts

By act of Congress, 1855 marked an increase in size of the U.S. Army. More serious clashes with the Indians called for greater manpower and more arms and ammunition. "Bleeding Kansas," strife with the Mormons, and the differences which would lead to the Civil War called for more men and more arms.

The guerrilla tactics of Indian raiders challenged the military's tactics. Indians did not need to stand and fight, in the traditional phalanxed way. The Army also suffered from low pay, morale problems, desertion, and occasionally miscreant officers and noncommissioned officers, as well as dissension between those with loyalties to the North and to the South.

The Civil War gave the Indians a breather of nearly five years. Most of the regular Army returned East, with volunteer units remaining in the West to deal with the Indians. Still, clashes took place on the frontier, notably in Texas, Kansas, Missouri, and even New Mexico and Arizona. Campaigns were fought against the Mescalero Apaches, the Navajos, and the Comanches and Kiowas.

One of the most prominent of volunteers fighting against Indians during the Civil War was Kit Carson. Once Carson's force would have been wiped out, but was saved by the commanding presence of two mountain howitzers.

The Sand Creek Massacre embittered the Indians and instilled them with a new resolve. One chief vowed: "We have now raised the battle-axe until death." Toward the end of the Civil War the Sioux, Arapaho, and Cheyenne were raiding with regularity. But to suppress the tribes of the Plains would demand another decade of fighting.

Reorganization and enlargement of the U.S. military, beginning 1855, also meant a general rearming. Influenced largely by French military innovations, a new projectile design would become one of the most famed technical advances in military history: the minié ball, a conical projectile with a hollow base; upon firing, the bullet expanded into the rifling grooves of the barrel. The bullet was named after French army officer Captain Claude Minié, who had experimented with a system in which a plug was inserted into the bullet's base. The American James H. Burton, of the Harpers Ferry Armory, determined the plug to be unnecessary after experiments lasting more than four years. The Minié ball permitted rapid loading, without patches, and hits with substantial accuracy and energy.

One of the guns using the minié ammunition was the Mississippi rifle. The system permitted adopting rifled muskets for infantry use, the rifling adding noticeably to accuracy. A satisfied Secretary of War, Jefferson Davis, reported to Congress in December of 1855: "[T]he improved ammunition, to which mainly is due the increased range recently obtained by small arms, has been issued to troops bearing grooved [rifled] arms, and its use in actual service has fully realized all the advantages that were anticipated."

Smoothbore muskets were dropped; the new combination of arms, all suited to the "Minié-Burton" system, were the 1855 .58-caliber rifle, the .58-caliber rifle-musket, and the 1855 pistol carbine with attachable shoulder stock (the latter credited in design to Jefferson Davis, a firearms enthusiast). Rifling was introduced to selected smoothbore muskets. Conversions of flintlocks, and the adding of automatic primers, were also ordered.

Other noteworthy events were the development of a new-model musket, the 1861, made without an automatic primer system (it had not been working well on previous guns), and the razing of the Harpers Ferry Armory to prevent its capture by the Confederacy. In the process approximately 15,000 longarms were destroyed. That was the end of the Model 1855 rifle, as well as of the armory itself.

The Civil War period saw a profusion of arms, with a legion of muzzle-loading types imported from Europe and England, as well as supplied by U.S. makers fulfilling government demands. Further, there were conversions of flintlock arms, and even some sporting arms were bought on U.S., state, and territory contracts.

Confederate and Union purchases totaled well into the hundreds of thousands—an arsenal that would, following the war, help to supply the flood of immigration to the West.

Inventories recorded of arms at various posts in the West were often quite detailed. These records help to reveal the advantage in arms held by the Yankee juggernaut—decidedly in favor of the Union, in buying power, opportunity, and in quality of domestic manufacture. However, the mix of calibers was so varied that ordnance officers had to be careful to provide ammunition of the proper projectile and charge.

For U.S. cavalry issue, two popular Model 1855 creations were the Springfield rifled carbine, of .54 (later .58) caliber, and the .58-caliber pistol carbine. About 1,000 were made of the former and 4,000 of the latter. Other brands, like the Sharps, Greene and Merrill, and Colt's Model 1855 sidehammer longarm, also saw mounted service.

However, the proliferation of types was quite con-

Percussion carbines, .52 caliber, with a 26-bore (approximately .58 caliber) shotgun and its bayonet. Note coffee grinder in stock of Model 1859 carbine. At *top*, the Model 1851, one of the earliest of Sharps. Below the coffee-mill gun, a Model 1852 (pronounced slant to breech), one of the rarest and most unusual of nineteenth-century military arms.

fusing, prompting Lieutenant Colonel Philip St. George Cooke to write (1857): "The armament of the Cavalry arm has been so varying that there would seem to have been no controlling authority on the subject." Still one more design to enter the fray was the Burnside breech-loading carbine, soon to be joined by the Maynard, another breechloader.

An advocate of the Colt was Lieutenant J.E.B. Stuart; he wrote to Colonel Colt from a camp on the Missouri River:

> As I expect to try to campaign in the Indian Country next spring, I am anxious to equip myself with the best Rifle-arm; judging from the reputation of your revolving Rifle that it fills the ticket, you will please send me by U.S. Express Co to Fort Riley Kansas— one of your Revolving Rifles with all the necessary fixtures and tolerable supply of cartridges. . . .

In a May 3, 1861 order for a shoulder-stocked Model 1860 Army revolver, Stuart (soon to be an officer of the C.S.A.) closed his letter with: "I take pleasure in adding my testimonial to the superiority of your arms over all others."

A myriad of domestic and imported carbines were made and used in the Civil War period, with the

Breech loaders of the Civil War era. *From left,* Henry rifle behind unique wooden stagecoach-style case; Spencer repeating military rifle with period Texas markings, painted on stock; percussion carbines by Maynard, Cosmopolitan, Burnside, Starr, and Smith. First made during the Civil War, McClellan military saddle retained its basic configuration throughout period of use, well into twentieth century; that pictured is of c. 1903.

Array of U.S. martial pistols, all of which saw service in the West. *Top to bottom, from left*: Model 1805 Harpers Ferry flintlock, Model 1808 Navy and Model 1813 Army and Navy, both by Simeon North. *Next* row, Model 1816 and Model 1826 by North, Model 1836 by Asa Waters, Model 1855 pistol-carbine, a Model 1842 percussion pistol, and a conversion of the Model 1836 flintlock to percussion. *Third* row, Model 1842 Navy pistol by Henry Deringer, Jr., and Model 1842 pistol by R. Johnson. Total made of these pistols exceeds 94,000 specimens. Powder container termed peace flask, because of shaking-hands motif. Ames rifleman's knife of 1849 has 11 3/4-inch blade, made for U.S. mounted riflemen, in quantity of 1,000.

(*above*) Daguerreotype, c. 1848–50, of Californians, one with a holstered Walker Colt revolver and riding quirt dangling from his wrist.

(*right*) Captain Samuel H. Walker, in only known daguerreotype portrait of him in uniform. The revolver is his Walker Colt number 1009, from presentation pairs sent by Samuel Colt. Walker was killed by a Mexican lancer in a skirmish at Huamantla, in October 1847. His last words were: "Although your captain has fallen, never surrender, my boys." Revolver awarded one of ten silver medals for outstanding antique firearms, at National Rifle Association exhibition, 1990.

(*opposite*) Magnificent presentation sword and historic pistols of Colonel George Washington Morgan, a hero of the Mexican War. The sword by Ames Mfg. Co., and inscribed on the scabbard from citizens of Ohio "as a Testimonial of Their Regard for His Distinguished Military Services During the War in Mexico." Colt Whitneyville-Hartford Dragoon revolvers with inscribed silver grips, ordered from the factory by Moore & Baker, New York: on backstraps, HONOR TO THE BRAVE. Serial numbers 1118 and 1123. The Model 1836 flintlock pistol with silver grip plaques commemorating service use by Morgan; other side inscribed *Col. George W. Morgan U.S.A. to his father/ Thomas Morgan. Washington, P.A. Dec. 1847*.

Sharps remaining the preferred brand. Over 80,000 carbines of various makes were acquired by the U.S. government by war's end.

A carbine which commanded the respect of the Confederates was the Spencer lever-action repeater, with its magazine loaded through an aperture in the buttplate. President Lincoln test-fired a Spencer rifle near the White House (on the Mall), with respectable accuracy for a President.

A Union cavalry trooper stationed in Nebraska (July 1865) wrote of his unit's affection for the Spencer: "A [Confederate] prisoner once asked how we wound the d——ish things up, and when asked to explain, he said he supposed that we wound them up in the morning and shot all day." Similar sentiments were expressed for the Henry repeating rifle, forerunner of the first Winchester. However, despite their high volume of fire, Army Ordnance continued to issue single-shot carbines and rifles, not trusting the troops with magazine repeaters.

Double-barrel shotguns were popular with both

Colt .36-caliber Model 1851 Navy (*bottom* three) and Model 1861 Navy revolvers, and the 8-inch .44-caliber Model 1860 Army (*top*), all U.S.-issue handguns. U.S. mark not present on all service revolvers, but initials of inspectors and grip cartouche stamps standard. Military blue finish contrasts with brighter blue used on civilian Colts of the period.

Frontier violence was bred in pro- and antislavery hotbeds like the rapidly growing Kansas and Nebraska territories of the 1850s. Presentation Navy Colt was from inventor to Kansas Territorial Governor R. J. Walker, and is inscribed on triggerguard strap. Model 1853 Sharps carbine is one of one hundred "Beecher's Bibles," shipped to Kansas by New England abolitionists in boxes marked as books and Bibles. Clergyman Henry Ward Beecher was quoted in the *New York Tribune* (February 1856) lauding the Sharps: "You might just as well," he wrote, "read the Bible to Buffaloes as to those fellows who [were pro-slavery in Kansas]; but they have a supreme respect for the logic that is embodied in Sharps rifles." Photo shows armed antislavery Missouri ruffians, with Dr. John Doy, the morning after their rescue of him from a St. Joseph, Missouri, jail, 1859. Doy had been arrested for liberating slaves.

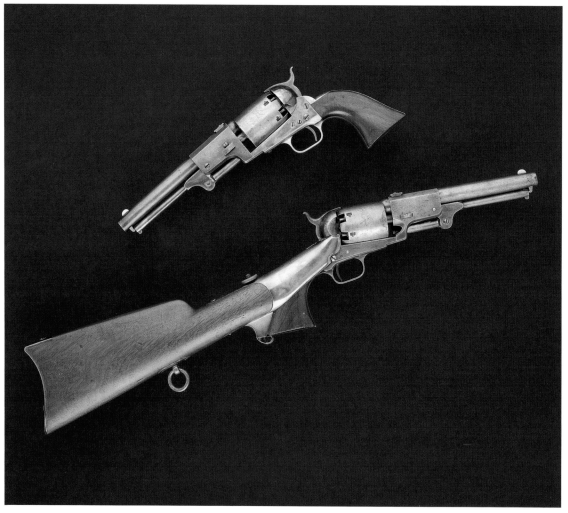

Matched pair of Colt Third Model Dragoons, inscribed and presented by Samuel Colt to his friend Colonel Charles A. May, of the U.S. Army. Colt also gave May an inscribed and cased pair of Model 1860 Armys, numbers 2259 and 2260, with matching shoulder stock. May was involved in the testing which led to adoption of the Model 1860 Army by the U.S. Ordnance Department. Also a longtime friend of Samuel Colt, and a pallbearer at the inventor's funeral.

From a group presentation by Colonel Colt, in November 1861, to approximately fifteen U.S. Army officers. Gifts were cased pairs of Model 1860 Army revolvers and cased 1861 Navy and 1862 Police revolvers. That shown here inscribed on backstraps *Genl J. W. Ripley/with Compliments of Col. Colt*. Ripley was then Chief of Ordnance, and among earlier posts had been commandant of the Springfield Armory. Other recipients were Generals A. E. Burnside, J. K. F. Mansfield, R. B. Marcy, T. W. Sherman, Andrew Porter, George B. McClellan, and Irvin McDowell. Civilians E. S. Sanford and Lincoln's first Secretary of War, Simon Cameron, were also given pistols.

Navy Colts are in W. F. N. Arny's flap holsters, in this picture of c. 1856. According to court testimony on John Brown, Arny sent "twenty-five navy revolvers of Colt manufacture" for the Abolitionists. One of these, number 51010, used by Brown.

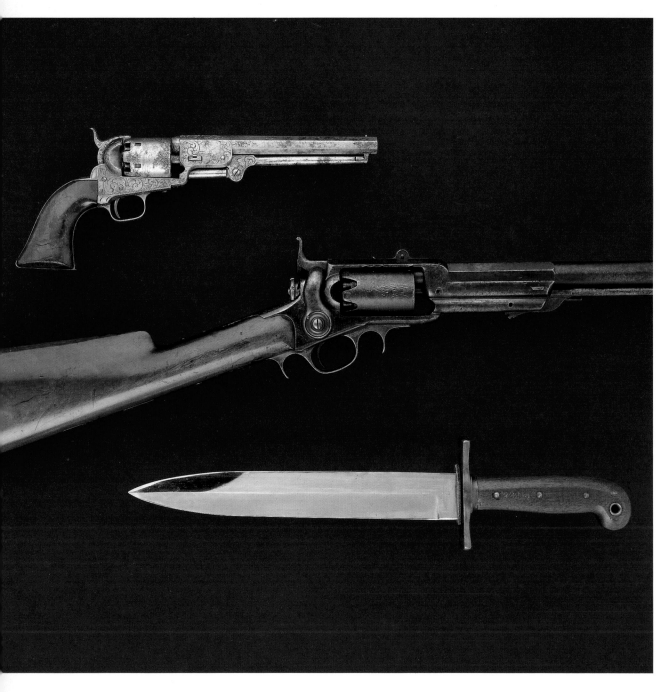

Union and Confederate cavalry, usually with cut-off barrels for maneuverability. Their disadvantage was inaccuracy at long range. But at short range they were devastating.

Military Pistols

Makers like Simeon North, R. Johnson, and the Harpers Ferry and Springfield armories supplied most of the single-shot service pistols. Officers and mounted troops, always a minority of the total armed men in service, were issued these guns. These heavy-caliber smoothbore handguns could knock down a running buffalo with a single shot and boasted spine-tingling recoils. Models were made in various patterns, which reveal a logical evolution from flintlock through to percussion.

Taking a buffalo from horseback with the old 1805 Harpers Ferry flint pistol was described by Philip St. George Cooke: after indignantly reholstering a pepperbox "patent play thing," he drew his "old Harper's Ferry 'buffalo slayer,'" and select[ed] a barren cow—round behind as a barrel—and at five paces—all at full speed—deliver my fire; the shot soon stops her."

Backstrap of the well-used Navy revolver bears inscription GENL HARNEY, U.S.A./FROM SAM COLT; serial 7980. The sporting rifle, number 84, inscribed on the upper tang General Harney U.S.A./with Compliments of Col. Colt/Hartford, Jan. 8th 1857. Harney had been a loyal proponent of Colt firearms since the Seminole War days. Ames rifleman's knife one of finest examples extant.

Ornate Civil War presentation swords, General William Tecumseh Sherman's at *left*, given in recognition of services at Battle of Shiloh. At *center*, to General Philip H. Sheridan, by officers, honoring service in four battles. At *right*, to Major General Winfield Scott Hancock, at Mississippi Valley Sanitary Fair, 1864. Sherman and Hancock swords designed and made by Tiffany & Co., New York. Sheridan's marked by C. R. Kirschbaum, Solingen (Germany). Over 125 presentation swords were made by Tiffany & Co. during the Civil War, most creations by distinguished designer Edward C. Moore, and about thirty of them supremely deluxe. Several of recipients also distinguished themselves in the West.

Defiant Quantrill guerrillas, pro-South, sporting cigars and heavily armed with Colt revolvers. *From left*, Arch Clement, Dave Pool, and Bill Hendricks. Jesse and Frank James served with men like these— Frank with Quantrill's force, and Jesse with Bloody Bill Anderson.

Arms and memorabilia of John Gilbert Wray, a construction engineer with the Union Pacific Railroad. Wray was present at Promontory Point, Utah, when the transcontinental railroad was joined and the golden spike driven in celebration. Tintype shows him wearing holster, Colt Army revolver, and Bowie knife. On back of photograph at right he wrote: "going east, wood, going west, coal."

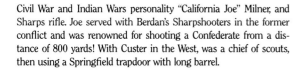

Civil War and Indian Wars personality "California Joe" Milner, and Sharps rifle. Joe served with Berdan's Sharpshooters in the former conflict and was renowned for shooting a Confederate from a distance of 800 yards! With Custer in the West, was a chief of scouts, then using a Springfield trapdoor with long barrel.

Lieutenant Colonel Custer admiring his Spencer sporting model rifle. Taken near Fort Dodge, in 1868.

Hank Wormwood, believed a scout for General George Crook at time photo taken, c. 1875. He held an 1873 Winchester and had at least one holstered S&W revolver.

Officers Model Springfield trapdoor rifle, Model 1875, with 1872 officer's cavalry saber, and training manuals. Hits were possible at ranges of 1,000 yards. Officer's customized gauntlets boast Indian beadwork.

Selection from thirty years of evolution in U.S. military arms, all Springfield Armory–made. *From left*: Model 1873 trapdoor rifle, in .45-70 caliber, 32 5/8-inch barrel; Model 1870 carbine of .50 caliber; Model 1881 Forager shotgun, in 20 gauge; and Model 1875 officer's rifle. Bolt-action .30-40 Krag carbine, and the .30-06 Model 1903 rifle, with scarce rod-bayonet extending from aperture in stock. Nearly 550,000 of all types of Springfield trapdoor rifles and carbines were made.

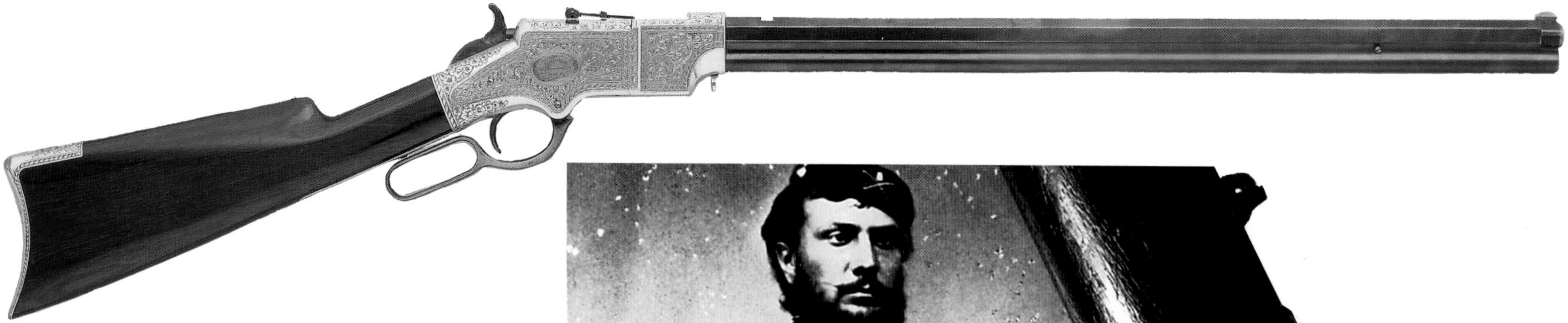

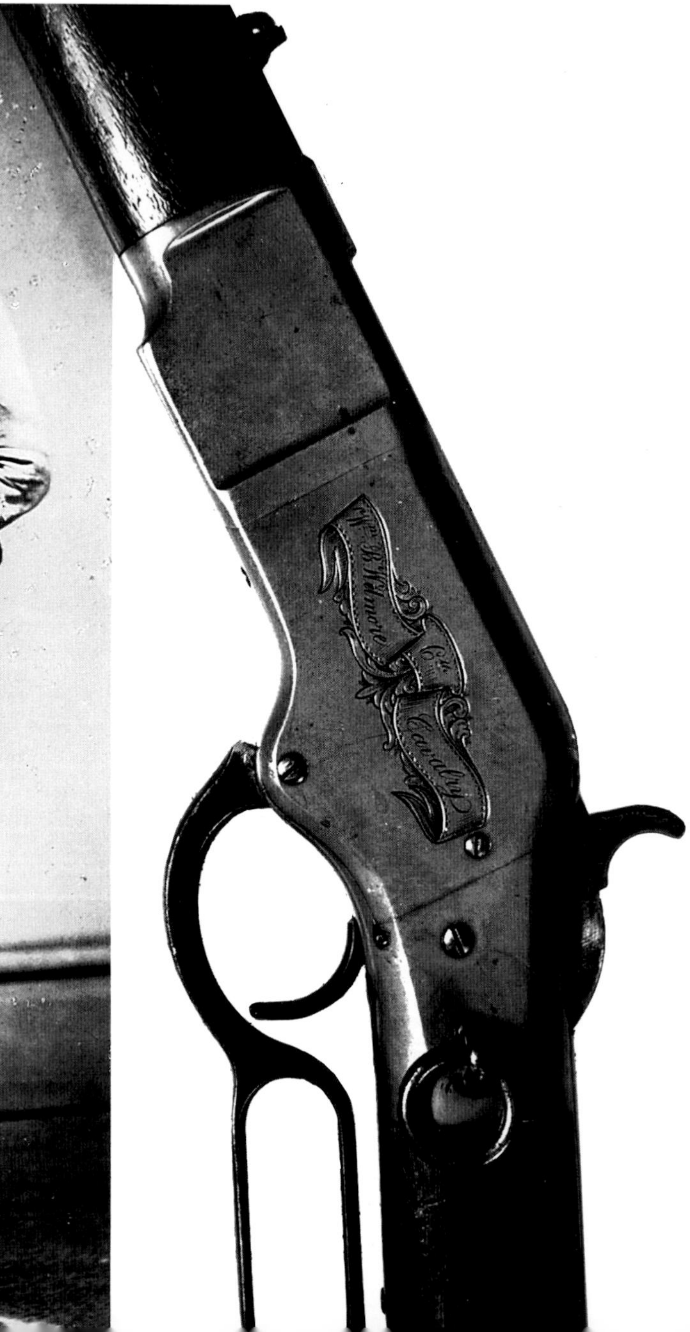

(*top*) Important Henry rifle, number 6, presentation by New Haven Arms Company to President Abraham Lincoln; engraved and gold-plated brass frame and buttplate; stock of rosewood. Standard-model Henrys distinguished themselves in the Civil War and the West. In the Hayfield fight (Big Horn Mountains, Montana Territory, August 1867), a Henry rifle shooter spent a day killing Indians. According to participant Finn Burnett: "I don't believe there is another man living, or that ever lived, who has killed as many Indians in a day as [D. A. "Al"] Colvin did on the occasion of the hayfield fight. He was armed with a sixteen-shot repeating [Henry] rifle, and had a thousand rounds of ammunition. He was a dead shot, and if he missed an Indian in that fight none of us ever knew it. He fired about three hundred shots that day. . . . As he did most of his shooting at distances of from twenty to seventy-five yards, it was almost impossible for him to miss. . . . He was shooting steadily from nine-thirty in the morning until five o'clock in the afternoon, and the ground around where he was stationed was literally covered with empty shells from his rifle."

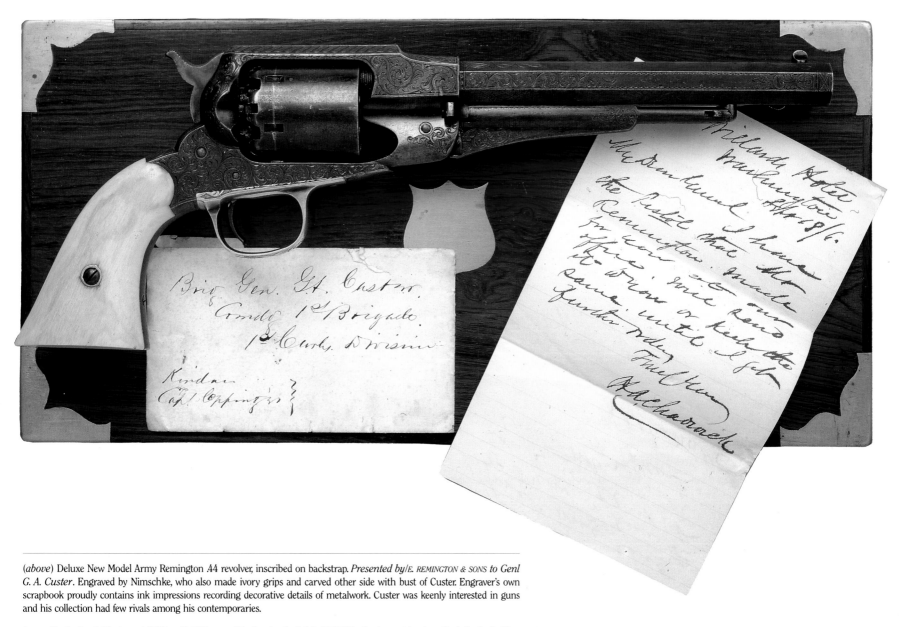

(*above*) Deluxe New Model Army Remington .44 revolver, inscribed on backstrap. *Presented by/E. REMINGTON & SONS to Genl G. A. Custer.* Engraved by Nimschke, who also made ivory grips and carved other side with bust of Custer. Engraver's own scrapbook proudly contains ink impressions recording decorative details of metalwork. Custer was keenly interested in guns and his collection had few rivals among his contemporaries.

(*opposite, bottom*) Lieutenant William B. Wetmore, 6th Cavalry, had this 1866 Winchester carbine inscribed (by L. D. Nimschke, prominent New York engraver), as well as a Smith & Wesson American Model revolver and a Model 1873 Winchester. During his frontier service, 1872–75, Wetmore killed leader of bandits attempting to rob an Army paymaster and was cited for bravery in a skirmish with Indians. Note two revolvers in military flap holsters, and beaded pouch or sash on cartridge belt.

Tintype from Custer's effects shows four of his trusted scouts. *From left*, Will "Medicine Bill" Comstock, Ed Guerrier (Cheyenne half-breed), Thomas Adkins, and "California Joe" Milner. All heavily armed.

Cased presentation No. 2 Smith & Wesson revolvers, given Custer in appreciation of hunt put on for J. B. Sutherland and friends. Pistols appear in photograph of Custer and wife in library at their Fort Abraham Lincoln, Nebraska, residence. Etching and silver-plating attributed to Tiffany & Co., New York. Gold hat cord was Custer's; 7th Cavalry cap and shoulder knot belonged to Captain Miles W. Keogh, also killed at Little Bighorn.

The traditional horse pistols, issued in pairs and carried in saddle holsters would meet their match in the invention of Samuel Colt—first in the 4-pound-9-ounce Walker, tried and proved in the Mexican War, followed by the smaller but similar .44-caliber, six-shot Dragoon or Holster revolvers. Follow-up orders to the initial 1,000-gun Walker contract (1847) amounted to over 10,000, with most of these repeating hand cannons heading west for service with the Regiment of Mounted Rifles. These revolvers were also the first practical repeating pistols, with an internal mechanism that was basically the same as that later used in the Single Action Army "Peacemaker" of 1873.

So accurate and powerful was the Walker that Sam Walker himself wrote that the pistols tested "as effective as the common rifle at one hundred yards and superior to the musket even at two hundred yards." Mexican War trooper Sam Chamberlain carried a Colt Walker, and in one of his escapades, attacked several guerrillas,

> rather carelessly I held by revolver in my left hand and my Sabre in my right. . . . one brutal looking greaser cried out, "American soney-bitchey" and fired on me point-blank with a huge flintlock pistol. Fortunately he missed, but then lunged out with a machete while his companions closed on me. A shot from my "Colt's" brought him down, and then there was a shout and a dozzen Dragoons came pouring onto the roof.

Burst cylinders in service help to account for the scarcity of Walker pistols, with approximately 300 damaged because of the excessive cylinder length. Sam Colt's recipe for loading was to fill the chambers to the maximum, and fit the round or conical ball flush with the muzzle of each chamber. Some barrels also burst at the muzzle, one reason not a few revolvers had their barrels shortened.

Shortened barrels (from 9 to 7 1/2 inches) and cylinders (from 2 7/16 to 2 3/16 inches) corrected these two major shortcomings in subsequent Dragoon revolvers, and the Colt remained the most highly prized of handguns in the West thereafter.

While Colt's Dragoon pistols were preferred by most

troops, some still were enamored of the horse pistols. Issue of these single-shots to regular troops continued in quantity into the mid-1850s. Further, the U.S. government purchased and sold some thousands of Dragoon Colts to emigrants headed west. The St. Louis Arsenal was one such public source of these arms.

Endorsing Colt pistols among the military were luminaries the likes of Brigadier General William S. Harney, Major Ben McCulloch, Colonel Charles A. May, and General (later President) Franklin Pierce. All of these gentlemen (and many more) are known to have received presentation revolvers from Samuel Colt, who early on recognized the value of gifts of arms, placed where they would do the most good.

In 1855, the U.S. government bought Colt Model 1851 Navy revolvers. Perhaps Colt's presents helped pave the way. These arms joined the Dragoon revolvers and rapidly replaced single-shot horse pistols. One source noted that Indians fighting the mounted troops with Colt revolvers "charge them suddenly, are in contact with them but a few minutes, and in that time must do all the execution they expect to do, and for that purpose the revolving pistol is absolutely necessary."

Among other revolvers in service, though they never rivaled the Colt, were the English-designed Adams and the North & Savage, Whitney, Beal, Starr, Joslyn, Rogers and Spencer, and LeFaucheux.

Of all the varied handguns, only the Colt Model 1860 Army and the Remington .44 New Model Army remained in service for nearly a decade following the war. Despite the advantages of their solid-frame design, the Remington Army Model revolvers were not well received on the frontier. In a January 1867 report to Chief of Ordnance Major General A. B. Dyer, General C. C. Augur, Commanding Officer, Department of the Platte, complained of poor materials, of bursting, of weak mainsprings, and of hammers which would not reach the nipples to fire the caps. He went on to quote from a field report by Brevet Brigadier General I. N. Palmer, at Fort Laramie:

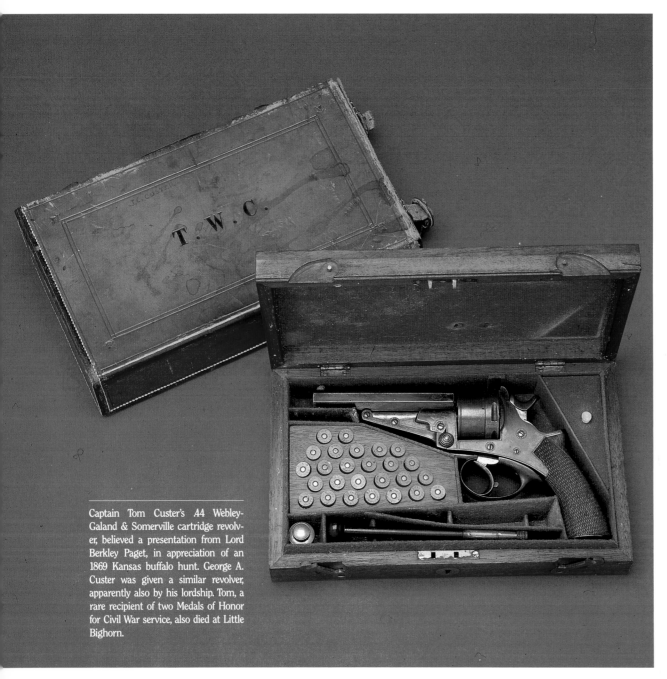

Captain Tom Custer's .44 Webley-Galand & Somerville cartridge revolver, believed a presentation from Lord Berkley Paget, in appreciation of an 1869 Kansas buffalo hunt. George A. Custer was given a similar revolver, apparently also by his lordship. Tom, a rare recipient of two Medals of Honor for Civil War service, also died at Little Bighorn.

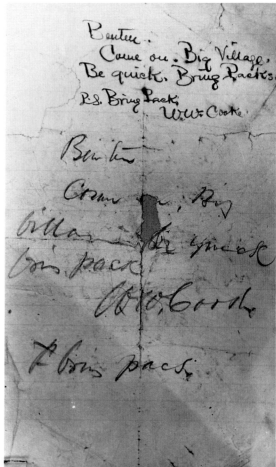

Last message from Custer, written at his order by adjutant W. W. Cooke; within thirty to forty-five minutes, Custer and five companies of 7th Cavalry were annihilated. Sent to Captain Frederick W. Benteen, who would survive battle, with Major Marcus A. Reno, from their position on bluffs overlooking the Little Bighorn River, about three miles from where Custer and men made their "Last Stand."

[The Remington revolvers are] almost a useless weight for the men to carry . . . on the whole if it were left to Company commanders, they would not take them into the field. . . . The defects reported in the Remington revolvers are of great consequence, and destroy the confidence of the men in their arms, which in view of the approaching Indian campaign is to be avoided by all means. . . . The Cavalry should by all means have revolvers and these should of course be reliable. Colts have never to my knowledge been found fault with in any important particular, and it is possible as Colts cannot be supplied that there are on hand at some convenient arsenal a sufficient quantity of Remingtons which have been thoroughly tested and found perfect to replace those found deficient.

Post–Civil War

The postwar Army was increased in strength to accommodate stations in the South, as well as the press of Indian fighting in the West. There were ten cavalry regiments and forty-five infantry regiments* authorized in July 1866. The makeup of these units ranged from emigrants to adventurers to ex-slaves (there were four black regiments with white officers) to ex-convicts.

Government policy on Indian affairs pitted "conquest by kindness" against the views of hardened veterans like General William Tecumseh Sherman: "The more we can kill this year, the less will have to be killed the next war, for the more I see of these Indians the more convinced I am that they all have to be killed or maintained as a species of paupers. Their attempts at civilization are ridiculous."

The Army was actively engaged against the Indians for more than two decades after the Civil War. Much of the fighting was in the form not of pitched battles, but

---

*Decreased to twenty-five in 1869.

From Gary Owen to Glory, oil by Ralph Heinz, detailing Custer near death, attended to by Tom and Lieutenant Cook, within circle of horses shot by troopers to set up barricade. Though speculative, Heinz painting far surpasses the vast majority of Custer battle paintings, most of genre heavily laced with artist's license.

Gatling gun and troops at Fort McKean, Dakota Territory, 1877. By spring 1876, there were fifty-four Gatlings at thirty-four posts around the West, from Mississippi to Rocky Mountains. Heavy to move about, and thus not with Custer at Little Bighorn, the guns served mainly for post defense.

In pursuit of hostiles, fall 1885, near Willcox, Arizona Territory. Trackers armed with Springfield trapdoor carbines, the Model 1884, appear to be on the trail in this posed shot.

Training horses to provide protection for their riders and to be accustomed to gunfire, 6th Cavalry exercise photographed at Fort Bayard, New Mexico Territory.

U.S. paymaster with his armed guards, on the Deadwood Road to Fort Meade, Dakota Territory.

of skirmishes. The strategy of winter campaigns to eliminate sources of food and to wreck Indian encampments was combined with decimation of the buffalo. At the same time the Army played a key role in surveying the West, protecting railroad crews, constructing roads, and helping to extend civilization.

Breechloader Superiority

The Civil War proved the superiority of breechloaders over muzzle-loaders. No more would panicked troops load a barrel up with powder and ball, but fail to cap and fire, as had happened to about 12,000 soldiers at the Battle of Gettysburg. A veteran from 1864 challenged champions of the muzzle-loader to come "to the front armed with one Springfield musket, and oppose themselves to an equal number of Rebs, armed with repeaters or breech loaders. If they can stand that, let them go to the picket line, and while fumbling for a cap and trying to get it on the cone one of these cold days, offer themselves as a target to some fellow on the other side who has nothing to do but cock his piece and blaze away." A breechloader also permitted loading without having to leave cover. Only one cartridge would chamber at a time. And in a charge or retreat there was no risk of losing one's ramrod. The muzzle-loader, noted the veteran, was a "bungling, slow-shooting gun."

In 1865 the U.S. Ordnance Department ordered 5,000 rifled muskets to undergo conversion to what is commonly termed the "trapdoor." The inventor of the system, E. S. Allin, described the simple procedure: "All that is necessary is to cut away the barrel on the top at

Troopers from black 25th Infantry Bicycle Platoon, Fort Missoula, Montana, posed with their Krag .30-40 rifles, 1896. A beginning at mechanizing troop movements. Name "buffalo soldiers" supposedly given black troops by Indians, from their short, curly hair and comparing them to sacred buffalo. White soldiers called them "brunettes." Buffalo soldiers had a distinguished service record in West, served in 9th and 10th Cavalry and 24th and 25th Infantry regiments; led by white officers, among them "Black Jack" Pershing.

the breech and add the [breech cover or block] and [extractor], cut the recess in the breech-screw, and modify the hammer. All other parts remain the same."

This potent gun, known today as the Model 1865 Springfield, fired a 500-grain bullet, with 60-grain powder charge. Various improvements were made to the trapdoor Springfields. U. S. Grant himself wrote: "There being such a large number of arms on hand capable of economic alteration, it seems unnecessary at present to experiment with new arms. . . . "

Over 52,500 guns were rebuilt, in .50-70 caliber, by converting muzzle-loaders. Ironically the Army was slow in getting these out into the West where they were sorely needed. Near the end of 1867 the Springfield Model 1866 was issued.

Model 1866s performed admirably against the Sioux near Fort C. F. Smith, August 1867. The fight lasted all day. Twenty infrantrymen and their six civilian companions turned back frequent Indian charges. Not only did the brand-new guns perform well, but their accuracy and quick rate of fire, according to an official report, tended to keep the troops "calm, composed, and confident under fire."

The famous Wagon Box Fight (also August 1867) pitched twenty-six infantrymen and four civilians against Red Cloud and hundreds of Indians. The men were from Fort Kearney and had recently received the Model 1866 Springfields. So sure were they of imminent death that some of the men were preparing to kill themselves. A sergeant later remembered two men "fixing their shoestrings into loops to fit them over the right foot and from thence to the triggers of their rifles . . . to kill themselves when all hope was lost . . . rather than be captured and made to endure the inevitable torture."

Hotchkiss bolt-action rifles, the first production made jointly by Springfield Armory and Winchester, in hands of troops at Bisbee Canyon, Arizona Territory; mid-1880s. Indian scouts with Springfield trapdoor, *top*, and 1876 half-magazine rifle, *right*.

Tiffany-gripped Colt .38 rimfire Model 1862 Police conversion, factory-engraved and silver- and gold-plated, used by Cyrus McNeeley Scott of Arkansas City, Kansas. Scott served as a special scout for the adjutant general of Kansas, against Indians. Photo shows Scott, with his revolver, number 23773/E, tucked under his left arm, with an Idaho scout named Chapman and the Nez Perce chief Yellow Bull.

Picnic lunch during a hunting foray near Fort Thomas, Arizona Territory, February 1886. Lieutenant Colonel Anson Mills, of the 10th Cavalry, seated at left of cactus.

At *top*, the first Colt Single Action Army revolver, number 1, in .44 S&W caliber. A small **s** accompanies the number on frame, perhaps denoting "sample." Factory cutaway bears serial 15407; in .45 Colt caliber. Production gauges from various periods of manufacture; catalogue of 1893. Serial 1 made 1872, taken to England as sample by General William B. Franklin, Colt's vice president and general manager.

106

COLT'S PATENT FIRE-ARMS MANUFACTURING COMPANY, HARTFORD, CONN., U. S. A.

SINGLE ACTION ARMY REVOLVER.

.45 Calibre, Central Fire.

Half size of Revolver.

`45 COLTS`

Price, $16.00.

The length of the Revolver is 12½ inches; length of barrel, 7½ inches; its bore or calibre, .45. Weight, 2 lbs. 5 oz.

It has a solid frame, case-hardened.

Length of barrel is 4¾, 5½, and 7½ inches, with ejectors.   Length of barrel is 3½ and 4 inches, without ejectors.

We can also furnish this arm to use the .44 Russian, .44 target and gallery, .41 calibre long and short, .38 calibre long and short, and .32 calibre cartridges.

To take Apart the Pistol.—Half-cock the pistol, loosen the catch-screw which holds the centre-pin, draw out the centre-pin, open the gate, and the cylinder can then be withdrawn.

To remove the ejector, turn out the ejector tube screw, then push the front end away from the barrel and pull it towards the muzzle. The barrel can then be un-screwed.

The stock can be removed by turning out the two screws just behind the hammer, and that at the bottom of the strap. All the parts of the lock are then displayed, and can be readily separated.

The cylinder bushing should be pushed out for cleaning.

To remove the gate, turn out a screw in the lower side of the frame (hidden by the trigger guard), then the gate spring and catch can be withdrawn, and the gate can be pushed out. The best sperm oil should be used for oiling the parts.

To Eject the Cartridge Shells.—1st motion: holding the pistol in the left hand, half-cock with the right hand and open the gate. 2d motion: eject the shells in succession with the ejector pushed by the right hand, moving the cylinder with the thumb and fore-finger of the left hand. When the shells have been ejected, the pistol is ready for loading.

N. B.—There are three notches in the hammer of this pistol. The first is the safety-notch, the second is the half-cock notch, and the third is the cock-notch. The pistol cannot be fired when the hammer rests in the safety-notch or half-cock notch and can be fired by pulling the trigger when the hammer rests in the cock-notch. The pistol should be carried habitually with the hammer resting in the safety-notch.

`32 CAL. COLTS NEW LIGHTNING MAGAZINE RIFLE`   `38 CAL. COLTS NEW LIGHTNING MAGAZINE RIFLE`   `44 CAL. COLTS NEW LIGHTNING MAGAZINE RIFLE`

"THE FRONTIER."—This most popular Revolver is the same as that described above, and is designed to fill the want of a Revolver using the same ammunition as a magazine rifle and thus avoid the necessity of carrying two kinds of ammunition, besides the many other apparent advantages which make this arm a necessity to the practical sportsman and frontiersman.

"THE FRONTIER" is made to use the 32-100, 38-100, and 44-100 Standard Magazine Rifle Cartridges. All of above revolvers can be furnished with case-hardened frame and blued barrel, or nickel plated, and with wood or rubber stocks as desired, at same prices.

All barrels over 7½ inches long, $1.00 extra for each additional inch.

(5)

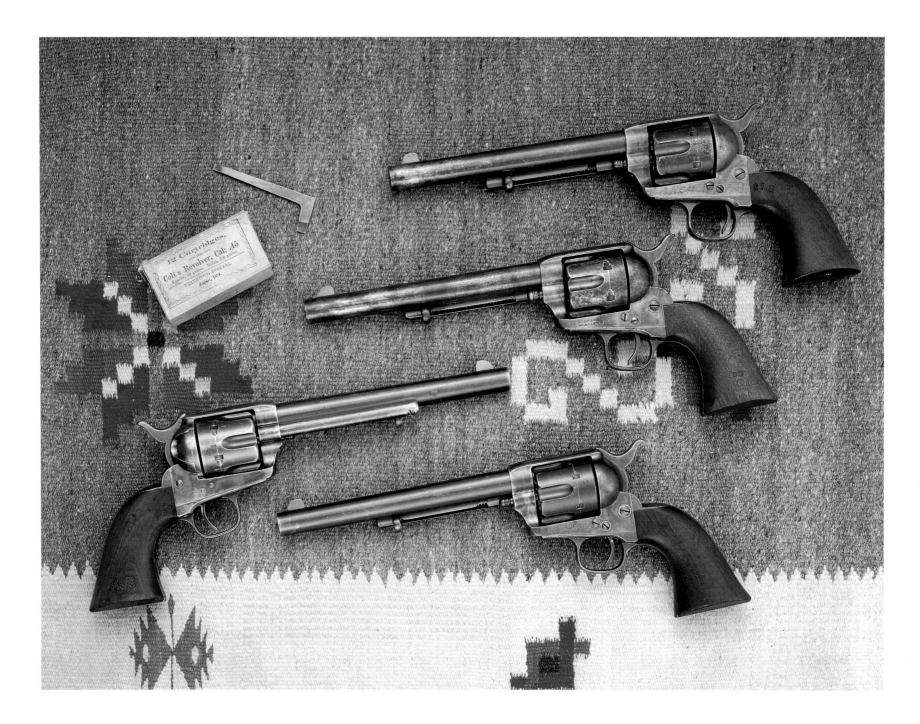

The Model 1866s gave the Indians a surprise:

A great number of the Indians rode in very close—probably within a hundred and fifty yards, and sitting on their ponies waited for us to draw ramrods for reloading, as they supposed we were yet using the old muzzle-loaders but, thanks to God and Lieutenant-General Sherman, the latter had listened to the appeals of Colonel Carrington . . . and we had just been armed with the new weapon . . . we simply threw open the breech-blocks of our new rifles to eject the empty shell and slapped in new fresh ones. This puzzled the Indians, and they were soon glad to withdraw to a safe distance.

The Army continued to refine the 1866 and to test various other innovations. The Remington rolling-block (a simple, near-foolproof action, with the breech-block rolling under the hammer to load, then rolling forward to close the breech for firing) was tried, as were the Sharps, Ward-Burton (a bolt-action), Martini-Henry, Spencer, and others—all metallic-cartridge breechloaders.

In a historic fight at Beecher's Island, Kansas, fifty men under Brevet Colonel George A. Forsyth held off a spirited attack from Cheyenne and Sioux warriors. The troops were armed with Spencer rifles and Army Colts, and also three Springfield trapdoors and at least one Henry rifle. The repeated fire eventually forced the Indians to leave (Chief Roman Nose was left dying on the field of battle). Nine days after the fight, rescuers came on the scene. The scouts remaining alive had survived by eating horses and mules; instead of pepper, gunpowder was used to kill the taste.

The Spencer also fared admirably in George Armstrong Custer's attack in November 1868 on the luckless Black Kettle and his camp of Cheyennes on the Washita River. Over one hundred Indians were killed, and over 1,100 buffalo robes and skins were captured, plus thirty-five revolvers and forty-seven rifles. The Indians also lost some 875 mules and horses. Custer had trained a crack unit of forty marksmen, who put down a withering fire with their Spencers into the camp. The colonel had a Spencer sporting rifle in his gun collection, ordered specially from the factory in 1866.

Battery E, 1st Artillery, who were at Wounded Knee, December 1890. Armed with Single Action Colts, Model 1880 knives, and a Hotchkiss breech-loading cannon.

(*opposite*) U.S. martially marked Single Actions, top three with inspector cartouches on grips, U.S. frame stamps (left side), and individual letter inspector markings. Standard .45 caliber, 7 1/2-inch barrels, walnut grips, and finishes. From the 1870s and 1880s. *From top*, numbers and inspectors: 114028, David F. Clark; 31663, Lewis Draper; 48815, Henry Nettleton; 3543 (Custer period), O. W. Ainsworth.

New Springfield Trapdoors

At an Ordnance Board meeting in New York City in September 1872, over eighty guns were evaluated. At the same time a caliber study was undertaken, by another board. The caliber chosen was .45, recommended in brass casings. The gun selected was the trapdoor Springfield—even though the board recognized that "the adoption of magazine-guns for the military service, by all nations, is only a question of time. . . ." *

The Model 1873 Springfield, in .45-70 caliber, fired a 405-grain bullet at 1,350 feet per second muzzle veloc-

---

* Tests were made of various breechloaders in the field, and reports came back to ordnance officials. The Spencer lost out largely because its rimfire cartridge was too short, and the guns could not be changed to accept cartridges the likes of the potent .50-70.

ity in the rifle and 1,100 f.p.s. in the carbine. The new guns were blue, instead of the standard bright finish found on nearly all predecessor trapdoors. Deliveries to troops in the field commenced late in 1873, and over 10,000 carbines and 18,000 rifles were completed by July 1874.

The Springfield Armory tried to satisfy the sporting needs of officers by making a special series of Officers Model Springfields. By 1875, however, not more than twenty such rifles had been made, one of them for General Grenville M. Dodge, Union Pacific Railroad empire builder. George Armstrong Custer also had a Model 1866 Officers Model, documented in a photograph with Russia's Grand Duke Alexis, who had come to the United States in 1872, hoping to hunt the Great American West. Custer wrote about his gun in a letter to wife Libbie (June 1873):

Well, [brother Tom's] latest dodge is to obtain possession of my Springfield rifle, which I allow my orderly, Tuttle, to carry. Night before last he carried it off to his tent without saying any thing about it; but Tuttle slipped down while Tom was at breakfast and recaptured the Rifle! Tuttle killed two antelope with my Springfield at pretty long range.

Tuttle was later killed in a sharpshooting exchange with Indians across a river, in Montana. As Custer described it, Tuttle

took a sporting Springfield Rifle and posted himself, with two other men, behind cover on the river bank, and began picking off the Indians as they exposed themselves on the opposite bank. . . . It was while so engaged that he observed an Indian in full view near the river. Calling the attention of his comrade to the fact, he asked him "to watch him drop that Indian," a feat which he succeeded in performing. Several other Indians rushed to assistance of their fallen comrade, while Private Tuttle, by a skillful and rapid use of his breech-loading Springfield, succeeded in killing two other warriors. The [Indians], enraged no doubt at this rough handling, directed their aim at Private Tuttle, who fell pierced through the head by a rifle-bullet. He was one of the most useful and daring soldiers who ever served under my command.

In 1875 an Officers Model was designed and made that was to become a standard type, rather than a cus-

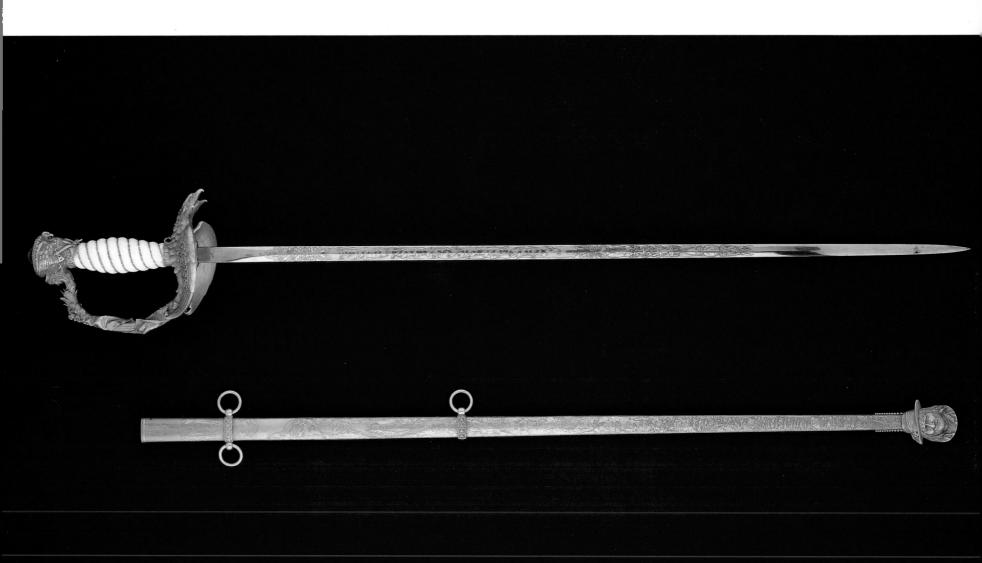

Described in *Frank Leslie's Illustrated Weekly*, September 10, 1887, as "A grateful and well-deserved honor bestowed upon General Nelson A. Miles by his Arizona admirers," this exquisite sword was designed and made by Tiffany & Co., in 1886–87: "[T]hey state that in real artistic excellence it is one of the best, if not the very best [sword], they have ever made." Presentation made on first anniversary of surrender of Geronimo and his Apaches. Grip of enamel; scabbard and sword mounts of gold, with a 56-karat sapphire asteria on the pommel; blade of etched steel.

(*opposite*) Two Colts belonging to Captain Jack, an 1878 Frontier double action .45, number 8127, and Lightning .38 slide-action rifle, number 29649. Crawford was twice wounded as Union soldier in Civil War and became a scout in Black Hills. Later he performed in plays and Wild West shows, sometimes with Buffalo Bill Cody.

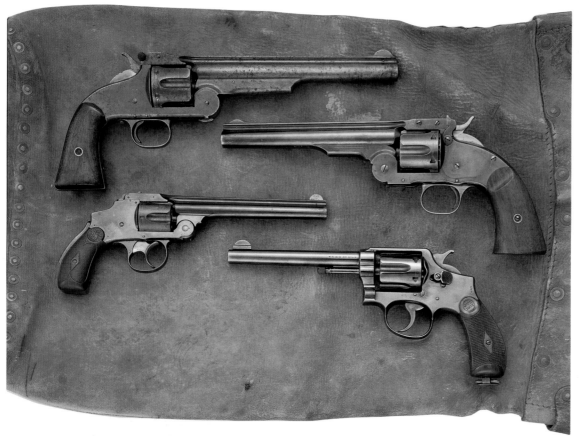

tom rifle. Among its features were a 26-inch round barrel, engraved breech and mountings, wood ramrod, half stock, peep sight on stock behind the tang, and single set trigger; it was in .45-70 caliber.

The merits of the Springfield carbine and rifle were disparaged in the press and in ordnance discussions following the crushing defeat of Custer and his men at the Little Bighorn. Copper cartridges were bursting and would fail to extract, the rimmed head often breaking free, leaving the empty case stuck in the chamber. To quote Major Marcus Reno, present on that fateful day:

> An Indian scout, who was with that portion of the regiment which Custer took into battle, in relating what he saw in that part of the battle, says that from his hiding place he could see the men sitting down under fire, and working at their guns—a story that finds confirmation in the fact that officers, who afterwards examined the battle-fields as they were burying the dead, found knives with broken blades lying near the dead bodies. . . .

A debate ensued, which was summed up by an officer from the command of General A. H. Terry: "Who knows best what the cavalry soldier wants, the officer at his desk in Washington or the soldier in the field? Is it not time for a reform, or must we still *advance backwards*?" Not until 1882 would the cartridge-case problem be corrected.

Complaints over the single-shot Springfield trap-door carbine, combined with 4th Cavalry Colonel Ranald S. Mackenzie's request for ordnance issue of Winchesters, led to a Springfield Armory test. The findings showed the .44-40 Winchester 1873 lacked sufficient power in comparison to the .45-70 trap-doors, and the Model 1866 carbine also did not fare well overall. The best range for the 1866 and the 1873 was 100 yards. The success of the lever-action Winchesters in America was primarily with sportsmen, not the military.

Still another vexing problem was that of marksmanship. An experienced frontier officer offered these observations:

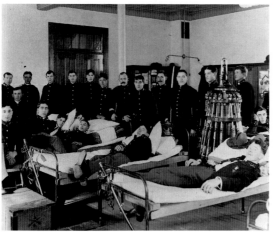

Smith & Wessons with histories of U.S. military service. *From top,* American Model, number 1621; Schofield .45, First Model, number 2873; double action .38 Safety Second Model; .38 Hand Ejector, Military & Police, First Model.

Arsenal rack among Troop A, 6th Cavalry, has locked-up Colt .38 double actions and Krag carbines. Sabers attached to bed frames, with one trooper holding his at attention. Fort Robinson, Nebraska, c. 1898.

Compared with the white hunter of the plains, the Indian is a wretched shot. He is about equal to the United States soldier, being deficient for the same reason—lack of practice. The Government and the Indian are each too poor to afford to waste more than ten cartridges a month on drill, and no man ever became an expert marksman on that allowance. . . .

With deadly marksmen a theory of fighting the Indians was to hit them at long ranges, thus preventing their capability of close-in attack. The best shots, who could estimate range, would be able to advise comrades the distance settings for their sights.

Continuing to test for improved service arms, an Ordnance Board in 1878 considered repeating rifles of .45-70 caliber. Among the entrants were the lever-action Winchester and Whitney-Burgess, and bolt-actions like the Hotchkiss (by Winchester). Franklin (by Colt), Keene (by Remington), and Vetterli (by Sharps). The Hotchkiss was selected, and production was done jointly by Winchester and the Springfield Armory. Both carbines and rifles were in field tests by early 1879.

Meantime, improvements continued with the Springfield trapdoor; even a few single-barrel shotguns were produced. The Army also ordered double-barrel shotguns by various makers, including the renowned Parker. Some of these arms were intended for dealing with road agents, and thus were "for use with Escorts for Paymasters."

Officers sometimes ordered shotguns on their own. With the 25 percent discount available to them from the Colt company, there was incentive to order either the Model 1878 hammer gun or the 1883 hammerless, both side-by-side doubles.

As of March 1882 the Springfield trapdoor 20-gauge shotguns were to be issued two per infantry company in some parts of the West, for commanders to "encourage [their] men to use them freely for hunting game, birds, ducks, and anything else that will contribute to their comfort and increase their skill in quick shooting."

A Gradual Switch to Bolt-Actions

Still another Ordnance Board commenced in July

Troopers of 10th Cavalry, escorts to General Wesley Merritt and party, St. Mary's, Montana, 1894. The revolvers are .38-caliber double-action Colts, newly issued.

Custom-made by the Colt factory for George S. Patton, number 332088 Single Action .45 was in his hands on the Texas-Mexican border. He shot two border bandits with it, and notched the ivory grip—a *rare* example of notching a gun for a human kill. Patton wrote of the shooting to his wife.

1881. This time three bolt-action rifles were selected, including an improved Hotchkiss. By 1886, reports from field testing were filing in—largely negative. The other two contestants, the Lee and Chaffee-Reece, fared no better than the Hotchkiss: "complicated mechanism," "too easily fouled with dust," "liable to accident," "reloaded ammunition works badly" (copper cases were still in use), and so forth.

A Hotchkiss did provide some amusement, however. Leonard Wood (later an organizer of the Rough Riders with Theodore Roosevelt) showed his Hotchkiss to Chief Geronimo, during negotiations for surrender (1886):

Geronimo came to me and asked to see my rifle. It was a Hotchkiss and he had never seen its mechanism. When he asked me for the gun and some ammunition, I must confess I felt a little nervous, for I thought it might be a device to get hold of one of our weapons. I made no objections, however, but let him have it, showed him how to use it, and he fired at a mark, just missing one of his own men, which he regarded as a great joke, rolling on the ground, laughing heartily and saying "good gun."

By the middle of 1886 the bulk of the repeats had been returned to the East. But experiments and developments with the venerable trapdoor continued. A new variant featured a rod bayonet, sliding out from the front of the full stock. The Springfield hung on as the prime service longarm on the frontier into the mid-1890s.

Developments in improved gunpowder, the so-called smokeless, and advanced mechanisms for magazine guns made the trapdoors obsolete while they were still in service. Brass cartridge cases replacing the common copper were also a step forward. Late in 1890 another Ordnance Board test series began. Fifty-three firearms were considered. Most were bolt-actions, and high-velocity, small-caliber ammunition was predominant.

Winner of the trials was the bolt-action side-magazine Krag-Jorgensen, capable of magazine fire, or of single-loading with a cutoff for the loaded magazine. Designated the Model 1892, its caliber was .30-40

Krag, firing a 220-grain bullet at 2,000 feet per second. Carbine and rifle versions were produced.

Thanks partly to the interest of small-arms expert and President Theodore Roosevelt, the Krag was replaced by the Springfield Model 1903 bolt-action, standard in .30-06 caliber, which would remain the service rifle until the semi-automatic Garand of the late 1930s. The trend to small calibers with high- velocity cartridges continued.

Handguns in the Service

Military handguns played a less important role in the post–Civil War West than their longarm counterparts. And these handguns remained primarily percussion through into the 1870s, while the longarms were increasingly chambered for metallic cartridges. Trooper John Donovan, running a gauntlet on horseback out of an Indian trap near Fort Phil Kearney in 1866, "was armed with a Colt [1860] Army revolver, and a single shot Star[r] Carbine. . . . The revolver. . . was all that saved him when the Indians were on each side of him trying to pull himself off his horse, for just in the nick of time he shot one on each side."

Smith & Wesson had a stranglehold on metallic-cartridge revolvers with bored-through cylinders, and these patent rights would not expire until 1869. However, S&W's small-caliber revolvers were insufficient for military use. Jim Bridger was quoted on the pocket S&W: ". . . I've seen that kind, but never handled 'em. Was afeard I'd break it."

Pressure was mounting for a large-caliber breech-loading military handgun. The March 1867 *Army and Navy Journal* published a letter on the subject:

> We want a pistol of the size and weight of the present Army pistol to use the metallic cartridge, of the calibre to be adopted for the

---

Serial number 1 Model 1911 .45 ACP Automatic pistol, from government serial series. Commercial-issue pistols of this model are marked with a C prefix. Both types saw much action in Texas and Mexico, and do to this day, though the largest legal automatic pistol caliber permitted for private ownership in Mexico is .38 Super.

new carbines (.45 and 50); on the Colt and Remington pistols might be altered to use metallic explosive cartridges, by cutting off the rear of the cylinder, so as to make it similar to Smith & Wesson's pistol cylinders.

The Springfield Armory even made up a few trapdoor pistols, in .50 caliber, but these were never adopted. Colt's tried a Thuer (front-loading) conversion, which also had no future. Remington paid royalties to S&W, and produced a functional Army conversion, chambered for a five-shot .46-caliber rimfire cartridge. Officers were also free to purchase their own handguns. The mix was substantial: one of the best collections was that of George Armstrong Custer, including a pair of .32-caliber Smith & Wessons, a Remington New Model Army, and a Galand and Sommerville .45 centerfire "Bulldog" revolver—all of them presentations from admirers.

An Ordnance Board meeting in St. Louis, 1870, considered several entrants in the military handgun test sweepstakes. Of the six (a S&W, four Remington revolvers, and a Remington rolling-block single-shot pistol) the Remington single-shot was recommended as best all around.

Orders were placed for the Remington rolling-block pistol and for the S&W No. 3 (later known as the American) in .44 centerfire caliber. The Americans were being issued in the West by the fall of 1871.

At the same time, Colt was moving toward its own service pistol design, by converting 1860 Army percussion revolvers using the Richards and Richards-Mason system, designing the "Open Top Frontier" (all .44s), and then, the *pièce de résistance*, the Single Action Army Peacemaker.

Mexican *rurales* or *federales* of rank often were attracted to fancy guns, such as Tiffany-gripped engraved and plated Colts. At *left*, .38 rimfire Model 1862 conversion has Mexican eagle pattern grips. Open Top .44 rimfire is fitted with Civil War battle scene grips. Both revolvers Nimschke-engraved and plated in nickel. Monogrammed south-of-the-border holster is decorated with silver and gold thread.

The Colt Peacemaker

A triumph of design and performance, the Single-Action Army won an Ordnance Department trial in the fall of 1872, against the S&W .44 American. Captain John R. Edie reported: "I have no hesitation in declaring the Colt's revolver superior in most respects, and much better adapted to the wants of the Army than the Smith & Wesson." Still another test pitched the Colt against the new S&W Schofield .45—and the Single Action won again, decisively.

Purchases, which began in quantity with the contract of July 1873, of some 8,000 revolvers, would be renewed in various numbers repeatedly over the next seventeen years. Over 35,000 Single Actions were acquired by the government in that period, and most went to the Army. The six-shot revolver was in .45 centerfire caliber, fired a 250-grain bullet, had a 7 1/2 inch barrel and blue and case-hardened finish, and was fitted with walnut grips.

Ordnance endorsement and adoption of the Single-Action as the Model 1873 military revolver was a springboard for sales to civilian markets and law enforcement worldwide. To this day the Single Action Colt is the most recognizable handgun in the world, a classic form and function, star of stage and screen, and favorite of millions of buffs of the Wild West.

It also proved a favorite of the services, even to deserters who (according to an 1875 War Department document) stole about two-thirds of the handguns lost to the cavalry. The guns were not to be left in the hands of troops while not on duty.

Military trials of revolvers continued to be held, and the S&W Schofield was ordered in a quantity of several thousand. But the Single Action Army would remain the dominating service handgun for over two decades.

Other Handgun Choices

Private purchase of handguns by officers and enlisted men covered a variety of pistols and revolvers. Suicide was a reason for some of these:

Even officers of the United States have not disdained when engaged in Indian warfare to carry with them a small pocket Derringer pistol, loaded, to be used in the event of capture as a *dernier ressort*, so as to escape by self-inflicted death the torture to which captives are invariably subjected.[*]

Once, George Armstrong Custer was given such a weapon before going into an Indian encampment under a truce.

Custer's pistols at the Little Bighorn were described by a lieutenant with Captain F. W. Benteen as "two Bulldog, self-cocking, English, white-handled pistols, with a ring in the butt for a lanyard." These stubby but powerful self-cocking (double action) revolvers had a good following in the West, primarily in the 1870s.

Another Little Bighorn casualty, Captain Miles W. Keogh, also apparently had an English revolver. A Sioux brave in Canada was reported to have been observed by a trader with such a revolver, the grip inscribed with Keogh's name, rank and unit, the 7th Cavalry. But most nonissue military handguns were by American makers: double action Colts like the 1877 Lightning and 1878 Frontier, pocket an holster S&Ws, Merwin and Hulberts (double and single action, featuring forward-sliding barrels for automatic extraction), Remington Model 1875 and 1890 single actions, and many more.

Enter the D.A. Revolvers

The .45 Long Colt was the cartridge of choice, but the Ordnance Department also was looking into .38 caliber revolvers for issue. These arms in double actions, with swingout cylinders and a simultaneous ejection system, were being perfected by Smith & Wesson and Colt. An 1889 Ordnance Board test recommended the newfangled revolver for issue in limited numbers, in field tests against each other and against the single actions.

There were questions of stopping power as well between the .38 D.A.s and the .45s. Writer A.C. Gould endorsed the .45:

After the Wounded Knee fight, the body of Captain Wallace was found at the entrance of an Indian Lodge, and there was every evidence that the officer had sold his life very dearly. Five Indian warriors lay dead around him, each of them with a single bullet wound. The captain had a six-chambered revolver in his hand empty, and it is therefore presumed that, before he was overpowered by the savages, he had a desperate fight, and emptied the revolver upon his adversaries, each shot having fatal effect. The revolver used by Captain Wallace was a Colt .45 army pattern.

Field tests of double action .38 Colts and S&Ws (one hundred of each) were conducted in 1890–91, and these concluded that the Colt was sturdier and better suited to service use.

Consequently, the Model 1892 D.A. Colt .38, improved from the test revolvers, was ordered by the Army in a quantity of 5,000 revolvers. Service experience settled the debate between .38 and .45 caliber. The New Service Colt of 1897 was built on a frame which accommodated the .45, and at the turn of the century that .45 became the caliber of choice (.45 ACP, for Automatic Colt Pistol) in the adoption of Colt military automatic pistols. It would remain so with the U.S. automatics until the 9mm Beretta XM/9 was adopted in the 1980s. The debate continues.

---

[*] "William Blackmore, introduction to Colonel Richard Irving Dodge's *The Plains of the West* (1876).

Serial number 0 Model 1905 Colt Automatic "Model Gun" for the first production pistol chambered in the .45 ACP cartridge. Surrounded by photos from early-twentieth-century Mexico. At *center*, a Colt advertisement just prior to World War I. Bandoliered American at *top right* was Buck Connor, a mercenary who later appeared in Hollywood Westerns.

Gen. Francisco Villa
the cause of it all

COLT'S
Revolvers and Automatic Pistols
Adopted by the
U. S. Army and Navy,   State National Guards,
Municipal Police Dep'ts,   Foreign Governments.

COLT
"NEW SERVICE"
REVOLVER

COLT
AUTOMATIC
PISTOL

Caliber .45—Government Model

California gold! Daguerreotype at *left* of goldfield scene, c.1850–52; diary at *right* kept by prospector Julius A. Harris, in daguerreotype at *lower left*, by Robert H. Vance, foremost California photographer of the day. The mining scene is one of the most sought-after Currier & Ives lithographs. Deringer by Slotter & Co., the pepperbox by Allen.

IN SEARCH OF GLITTER

When James Marshall found raw gold forty-four miles upstream from Sutter's Fort, January 1848, word spread east, and the seekers of glitter soon gave history and folklore the great California gold rush of 1849. The lure of California gold precipitated a migration west which dwarfed the numbers of all previous explorers, mountain men, emigrants, and travelers. Whether by the Santa Fe and Gila trails, by the Oregon Trail and Humboldt River, by ship around Cape Horn, or by ship and land and ship through the Isthmus of Panama to San Francisco, these hardy souls risked everything—even on arrival at the gold fields they were in danger.

California's population increased fivefold in 1849, from 20,000 to 100,000. It took only another year to gain statehood, and by 1852 a mail route had been established connecting California to Santa Fe and Independence, Missouri.

Although most miners never struck it rich, their presence inspired a rapid development of farming, ranching, industry, and commerce—even a thriving wine industry. Freighting and stagecoaching became big business, with the first trans-West operation set up by John Butterfield, known as the Overland Stage Company (1858). The route took approximately twenty-four days from St. Louis to San Francisco.

Still other mining strikes were made in 1859, first gold in Colorado ("Pikes Peak or Bust") and then silver and gold in Nevada (the "Comstock Lode").

To accommodate the demand for quicker mail service to California, one of the West's most colorful enterprises was launched: the Pony Express. Run only from April 1860 to the fall of 1861, the small army of youthful and daring riders (W. F. Cody among them) could relay between Independence and California in just ten days. It was the Western Union Telegraph Company which closed down the Express, at a loss to the organizers, Russell, Majors, and Waddell, of some $200,000.

"Wild Ben" Raymond, a mine guard, rakishly held a .44 Merwin & Hulbert and wore holstered No. 3 New Model S&W, plus Bowie knife from neck chain. Leadville; c. 1879.

Buying out the owners of the Pony Express was another entrepreneur profiting from rapid Western expansion: Ben Holladay, "the Stagecoach King," whose Overland Express & Mail Company held a near monopoly on the stage and freight business over much of the West.

Gold strikes in Idaho and Montana and later in the Black Hills all added to Western migration. A competitor to Holladay grew to be the giant of the express business: Wells, Fargo & Co. Established in 1852, the firm would buy out Holladay some fourteen years later. In 1869, completion of the transcontinental railroad symbolized the welding together of East and West. The lure of gold and silver served as a catalyst for these extraordinary developments. And few dared head into the frontier in those times without an instrument of portable life insurance: the gun.

The Demand for Arms

Lawlessness was concentrated in camps and communities which attracted a mix of humanity, not a few consumed by greed, and not a few ruthless criminals. Mark Twain described the mining town of Virginia City, Nevada, in *Roughing It*:

> There were military companies, fire companies, brass bands, banks, hotels, theatres, "hurdy-gurdy houses," wide-open gambling palaces, political pow-wows, civil processions, street fights, murders, inquests, riots, a whisky mill every fifteen steps, a dozen breweries, and half a dozen jails and station-houses in full operation, and some talk of building a church.

Gold and silver fever accelerated the demand for firearms. Sam Colt wrote: "When the California gold fever broke I had a bigger demand for guns than I could meet. . . ." Unlike a number of dealers and makers, the Hawkens were fair in their pricing, but sellers of Colt revolvers could demand several times the normal price, especially in California. Business in St. Louis remained brisk; foremost of that city's gunmakers were T. J. Albright, J. & S. Hawken, and H. E. Dimick. An advertisement from 1850 noted Dimick's target and hunting rifles, with the invitation "Gentlemen don't be bashful, call and see me."

Forty-niner bedecked with military shako; waistband with single-shot percussion pistols; rifle a full stock of Plains style, also percussion.

The Forty-niner, watercolor sketch by John Woodhouse Audubon. Saddle holsters for pistols; Plains rifle across pommel.

Few of the inexperienced seekers of fortune heading west were unfamiliar with firearms. Some bizarre accidents took place. Within a group from Pittsburgh heading to the gold fields a guard shot a youngster pretending to be an attacking Indian. A guidebook for emigrants seeking Colorado gold advised against "the dangerous practice of placing a loaded gun, with the cap on, in any. . . wagons. More accidents occur on the plains from this practice than from any other."

A whole trade in arms mushroomed in California. In San Francisco, A. J. Plate, Charles Curry, A. J. "Natchez" Taylor, Robert Liddle, and Charles Schlotterbek were well established by the late 1850s. Some maintained private target ranges, and supplied not only guns but gunsmithing services. Taylor, for instance, would load guns like Deringer pistols for a varied clientele of miners, businessmen, politicians, judges, travelers—and prostitutes. Alas, poor Natchez was accidentally shot by a careless customer who didn't know a Colt revolver was loaded.

The popular sport of target shooting also grew. San Francisco had more than a dozen shooting clubs by the mid-1850s.

The magnetic attraction of the gold and silver fields meant that arms were moved about the West and often soon abandoned or otherwise changed hands, since they were sometimes no longer needed on arrival at the mining sites. This was also true at the sites of later discoveries, like Cripple Creek in Colorado, the Alaskan-Canadian Yukon and the Canadian Klondike, and finally Goldfield and Tonopah, Nevada. Additionally, in the second half of the nineteenth century, about 15,000 Americans headed to Australia for their mining strikes, taking along tons of guns and Bowie knives, creating what would become a treasure hunt in modern times for collectors.

Gunsmiths and Dealers

The precious metal stampede also inspired gunsmiths to set up shop on location in the West. Besides those established in San Francisco and St. Louis, the gunmaker Benjamin Bigelow, formerly of Rochester,

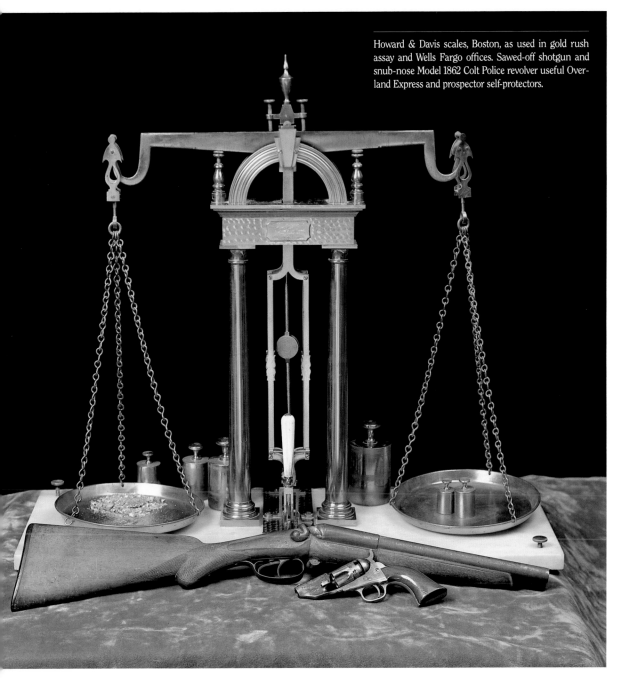

Howard & Davis scales, Boston, as used in gold rush assay and Wells Fargo offices. Sawed-off shotgun and snub-nose Model 1862 Colt Police revolver useful Overland Express and prospector self-protectors.

New York, moved to Marysville, California; J. M. Browning set up in Ogden, Utah; and Carlos Gove settled in Denver. These entrepreneurs and others established shops in the boom years of 1852 to 1863. Even Sam Hawken moved to Denver, first as a miner and then as a gunmaker. He returned to St. Louis two years later. Henry Folsom of St. Louis established himself in Denver, becoming one of the biggest dealers in the arms trade, and by 1870 Folsom and company had expanded to New York City, New Orleans, and Chicago.

Enterprising gunsmiths and dealers sprang up in major cities, and many in villages and towns, throughout the West. Some of these firms would remain in business in one form or another (some as hardware merchants) until into the twentieth century.

Military-style guns were serviceable for prospectors and had the advantage of being simple and sturdy. Many types were readily available, and were common in dealers' stocks. Such guns as the Model 1841 Mississippi rifle were sold in great numbers. An 1848 veteran of an expedition with Kit Carson (Los Angeles to Taos) noted:

> We numbered twenty hired men, three citizens, and three Mexican servants, besides Carson and myself [Lt. George Brewerton], all well mounted and armed for the most part with "Whitney's rifle,"* a weapon which I can not too strongly recommend for every description of frontier service, from its great accuracy and little liability to get out of order—an important point in a country where no gunsmith can be found.

By authorization of Congress in 1849, service arms and ammunition were directed to be available at cost to emigrants whose destinations were New Mexico, as well as California and Oregon. Many of these guns were brand-new. Sales of surplus arms also took place, as they had for years, to arms dealers.

Companies like Sharps owed part of their success to the search for glitter. An April 1850 advertisement in the St. Louis *Missouri Republican* offered: "Just Re-

---

*One of the makers of the Model 1841 was the armory of Eli Whitney, Jr.

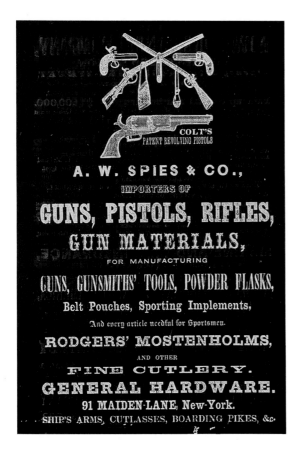

Spies' broadside illustrated mixed array of arms for prospectors, the Colt Dragoon with utmost prominence.

Prospecting was definitely the goal of this portrait sitter; in his belt, a Model 1851 Navy Colt.

His pistols a Colt Baby Dragoon revolver and a Stocking bar-hammer single shot, George Northrup was ready for the goldfields. Records show he never made the trip.

Ed Schieffelin and his Sharps custom sporting rifle; barrel of extra-
heavy weight; number 162329. Holster rig and S&W of equally special quality. Schieffelin hit the jackpot, discovered rich silver ore in
Tombstone, Arizona Territory, 1877.

Ed. Schieffelin

California rifles by Benjamin Bigelow, Marysville. Wesson-style for target shooting at *top*; revolving gun more for defense or *sporting purposes.*

ceived by Express, Sharp's Patent Rifle, a splendid article for California emigrants. This Rifle is entirely new in construction, differing from all other firearms; is loaded at the breach, caps itself, and is warranted to shoot ten times in a minute."

Colt, Allen, Smith & Wesson, and many other marques could also thank the gold and silver rushes for the explosion in the arms market.

The fate of some Hawken rifles, which could not compete in time with the developments in breechloaders and repeaters, was told by former mountain man Bill Hamilton, seeking California gold in about 1853. He and five sidekicks "traded our Hawkins rifles for Sharps rifles, brought in by emigrants. The barrels of the Hawkins rifles made good substitutes for crowbars. . . ."

Wagons West

Immigrant wagon trains carried (according to an 1856 observer, in Kansas) "about one 'gun' to a wagon, those being mostly western rifles, some few being shotguns." Advertisements to sell guns often promoted the seeking of gold: "Pike's Peak. Gold in Abundance. Also, 100 Sharp's Rifles, for sale at cost by Child, Pratt, & Co." (*Missouri Democrat*, fall 1858). Colonel Colt countered promotions of breechloaders like Sharps and competing revolver arms with advertisements boasting his guns did not

> endanger your eyesight and brain. . . . they do not stick fast . . . as do the guns which open like molasses gates or nut crackers. . . . They leave no burning paper in the barrel after a discharge, to blow the next cartridge into your face. . . . they are always worth what they cost—in the Far West much more, almost a legal tender! . . . Ask any ranger who has tried the cutting slide guns [Sharps], what he thinks of them. . . .

One way Colt responded to competitors was re-

Volcanic breech-loading pistols, firing self-contained lead cartridges. At *top*, by Smith & Wesson, in .38-caliber, with 8-inch barrel. *Bottom* by New Haven Arms Co., in .30 caliber.

Pepperbox in daguerreotype likely by Allen & Thurber; that *above*, by Robbins & Lawrence. Ivory-gripped Bowie knife with appropriately etched and gilded blade.

This Western character grasped his Bowie knife with knuckle-bow, has powder flask hung from shoulder cord near Colt Dragoon (brand-new, as indicated by bright in-white cylinder), and clutched Hall breech-loading carbine. Daguerreotype c. 1850.

Colt Model 1849 Pocket revolver, number 14228, inscribed in remembrance by owner. Matching "slim Jim" holster. Knife by San Francisco's Michael Price; handle of elk horn. Ivory-handled cane engraved with mining scene, reflecting photograph in the diggings.

Dragoon pepperboxes, with historic gold ring inscribed inside and: "*Presented to/CAPT. E. WAKEMAN/by his Passengers on Ste./INDEPENDENCE/from San Francisco/to/San Juan Del Sur/Oct. 19, 1851.*" Gold fragments under crystal. Reward to captain from grateful pilgrims.

vealed in an 1860 letter he wrote to an associate in Arizona (the spelling characteristically Sam Colt):

I am noticing in the newspapers occasionally complimentary notices of the Sharp & Burnside Rifles & Carbines, anecdotes of there use upon Grisley Bares Indians, Mexecans, &c&c Now this is all rong it should be published Colts Rifles Carbines &c When there is or can be maid a good storrey of the use of a Colts Revolving Rifle Carbine Shotgun or Pistol for publication in the Arizzonan the opertunaty should not be lost & in the event of such notices being published you must always send me one hundred Copes If there is a chance to du a few good things in this way give the editor a Pistol or Rifle complement in the way it will tell You know how to du this & Do not forget to have his Colums report all the axidents that occur to the Sharps & other humbug arms. I hope soon to see the evidence of your usefulness in this line of business.

An early repeater, designed for cartridges with powder and primer inside the hollow back of the ball, was the Jennings, later succeeded by the S&W and Volcanic–New Haven Arms Company lever-actions. Although they were largely impractical (gas leaking at the breech, and low-velocity projectiles), they did lead to development of the Henry rifle, "The Best Arm for protection against bush-wackers and guerillas, [and] at the same time a superior hunting rifle," according to T. J. Albright, the St. Louis gunmaker and dealer.

The sixteen-shot .44-caliber Henry quickly earned a reputation on the frontier. M. O. Davidson wrote:

The recent experience of my men on their journey through Sonora and Arizona armed with [Henry rifles] gives me a high idea of their value. . . . In the Indian country, so great is the dependence placed upon them, that none of our men care to go on escort duty unless there is one or more of these powerful and accurate weapons in the party. . . .

The Spencer repeater joined the Henry rifle in Western popularity, each having its own proponents. From the Arizona Territory governor (June 1864):

[My Spencer carbine] of the large size. . . . In range and accuracy in firing, simplicity of structure, and the rapidity with which it can be loaded and fired . . . surpasses any arm I have ever heard of. The old mountain-men and hunters in the territory have seen and used it, and some of them speak even more warmly in its

Ambrotype with wayfarers; one held cocked Wells Fargo Model Colt Pocket revolver, his hand held eagle flask.

"George J. Cross, Sac City, California," inscribed on backstrap, alluded to Sacramento. State seal on ivory grip. Gold quartz jewelry, native to California, and symbolic of affluence. Made from gold rush days, until 1906 earthquake.

praise than I. . . . No one of them has a word to say in favor of any other breech-loading gun.

Because of Civil War demands, however, Henrys and Spencers were not available in any quantity in the West until as late as 1864.

Metallic cartridge arms, though they had disadvantages in early low-velocity ammunition and weak cartridge casings, offered advantages over muzzle-loaders in rapidity of fire, and an effective gas seal (lacking in many breech-loading percussion guns). Large rifle calibers worked better in single-shot breech-loading longarms, since mechanisms of lever-actions like the Henry and the Winchester Model 1866 could not accept the large-sized cartridges.

Popularity of Shotguns

Smoothbore guns were effective companions to the westward-moving emigrants and miners, whether shotguns, muskets, or rifle-style sporting arms lacking rifling. Of these, shotguns had the greatest popularity. Many scatterguns were of foreign make, particularly English. In a May 1854 advertisement, St. Louis dealer and gunmaker H. E. Dimick offered some 400 muskets and 1,300 single-barrel guns, as well as 2,400 doubles.

Traveler and writer (later landscape architect and designer of New York's Central Park) Frederick Law Olmsted wrote of a trip through Texas in the late

Ill-fated gold rush figure, William McKnight, in daguerreotype taken in 1851; Los Angeles. Writing to his mother (letter beneath Bowie knife), McKnight complained of "great pain being unable to sit up for more than a few minutes at a time. . . . I am now five hundred miles away from my wife and not a person about me who would do any thing without pay—the mail is about to close and I must bid Farewell *perhaps forever*. . . . —God bless you is the prayer of your dying Son." On the same letter a note from McKnight's wife, dated mid-August: "Alas he is gone. Died last night about ten oclock. . . . it was the Lords will to take him. . . . I have always felt a strong desire to have the picture you sent to your sister. It is the only good one that has ever been taken. . . . Oh how terrible it is to see the grave close over those you love. . . . (Do try and get me that picture. Margaret)." Picture widow alluded to is that illustrated. Pepperbox by Robbins & Lawrence; .31 caliber.

1850s, noting that "two barrels full of buckshot made a trustier dose . . . than any single ball for a squad of Indians, when within range, or even in unpractical hands for wary venison." Richard Burton had been advised by Mormon Porter Rockwell (in 1860, preparatory to traveling from Salt Lake City to California) to arm himself with "a double-barrelled gun loaded with buckshot; to 'keep my eyes skinned,' especially in Kanyons and ravines; to make at times a dark camp—that is to say, unhitching for supper and then hitching up and turning a few miles off the road . . ." Burton regarded the best gun for fighting Indians "without any exception, is a ponderous double barrel, 12 to the pound, and loaded as fully as it can bear with slugs."

Miners had a predilection for the shotgun. A duel was witnessed by Henry X. Biedler while in Denver on the 1859–60 gold rush, in which the "fight was for blood all the way through, the contestants using double barrel shotguns and ounce balls. Lew Bliss killed his man [a Doc Stone]." The guns also served, of course, for hunting, with birds the customary game.

Road agents who preyed on the miners also preferred shotguns. Montana bandits of the 1860s were commonly armed with

> a pair of revolvers, a double-barreled shotgun of large bore, with the barrels cut down short, and to this they invariably added a knife or dagger. Thus armed and mounted on fleet, well-trained horses, and being disguised with blankets and masks, the robbers awaited their prey in ambush. When near enough, they sprang out on a keen run with level shotguns, and usually gave the word, 'Halt! Throw up your hands, you sons of b———s!' If this latter command was not instantly obeyed, there was the last of the offender. . . .

Eventually vigilantes responded to the Montana road agents, likewise armed with shotguns.

The first breech-loading cartridge shotguns were the doubles by French makers like LeFaucheux, but firing pinfire cartridges, their following on the Ameri-

One of finest pairs of Southern-made Deringers, by Stephen Odell, Natchez, Mississippi. Solid gold mountings.

131

Varied-size pocket pistols by Henry Deringer. In his own words: "I adopted this stamp 'DERINGER PHILADELA' as my particular trade-mark, and as such it is known amongst all persons dealing in or familiar with fire-arms, both in this country and in Europe.... It is a pistol manufactured by me and well known here and in Europe by my name.... It is a single barrel pistol with a back action percussion lock, patent breech, wide bore and a walnut stock. It varies in length from 1 1/2 to 6 inches for the ordinary pistol, and from 6 to 9 inches for the duelling pistol. It is commonly mounted with german silver. The barrels used are all rifled. The locks vary in size and proportion to the length of the barrels...." Third pistol in *from top left* measures 5 inches overall.

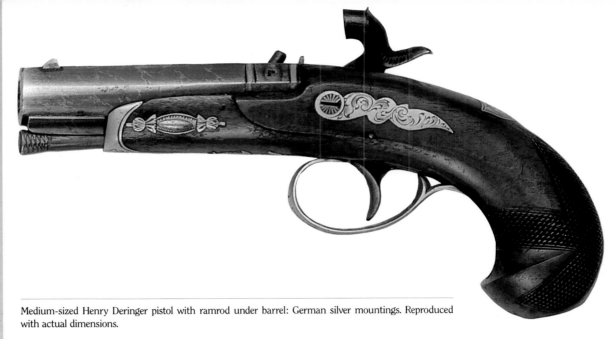

Medium-sized Henry Deringer pistol with ramrod under barrel: German silver mountings. Reproduced with actual dimensions.

can frontier was limited. Muzzle-loading percussion doubles would hold sway until the coming of practical breech-loading metallic cartridge guns, like the Parker and Colt.

Handguns Through 1865

Colt dominated the repeating handgun market through the expiration of the Colonel's master patent protection (1857) and beyond. Some marques tried to compete even before the expiration, among them British double action makers, and the Massachusetts Arms Company. The latter firm lost a suit brought by Colt, which discouraged a number of other would-be rivals.

Pocket protectors like the Deringer-style single-shot pistols grew in demand in gold rush days, as did the pepperboxes (notably Allen's designs) and even the massive government-issue single-shot pistols.

The Colt line was the best developed, in pocket, belt, and holster sizes. Counting longarms, over one million Colt percussion guns (mostly revolving pistols) were made during the inventor's lifetime. Colt died

January 10, 1862, his business running night and day, and his aides admonished to "make hay while the sun shines."

Many travelers would buy their guns in St. Louis, as did Englishman William Kelly, Jr., part of a group of eight Americans and two dozen British, all headed for the gold fields: "Acting on Mr. W——'s advice, we only purchased our rifles, pistols, broadswords, and bowie-knives [in St. Louis]."

By 1850, Colts were bringing as much as $500 in San Francisco. An advantage of the company was its production facility, geared for quality and volume, which could meet demand. T. Butler King of San Francisco wrote in 1850 that "[Colts] were undoubtedly of the greatest service in enabling the Americans to maintain their superiority among greatly superior numbers of Mexicans and other foreigners, during the early part of the gold-digging season, when the foreigners outnumbered the Americans three or four to one...."

In early California gold rush days the Colt's leading rival was the multichambered pepperbox, despite the

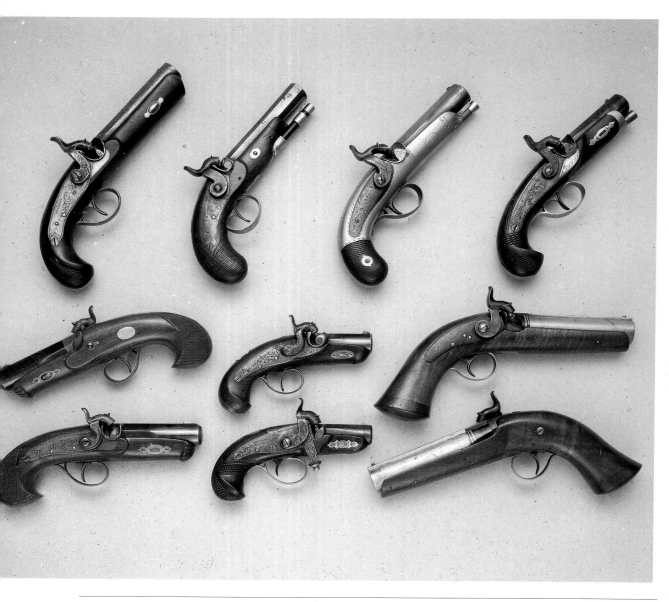

Competitor pistols to the genuine Deringer, by various makers; *from top left*, Gillespie of New York, R. Constable of Philadelphia, Blunt & Syms (possibly made in Liège Belgium), and Seaver of New York; *bottom row, from left*, matched pair by Charles M. Siebert of Columbus, Ohio, A. G. Genez of New York (*top*) and Jesse S. Butterfield of Philadelphia, and matched pair with New York markings. Genez pistol measures 5 inches overall, superbly engraved by Nimschke.

All of these pistols by Deringer's archrival, Slotter & Company, Philadelphia firm established by former Deringer employee Henry Schlotterbeck. Landmark trademark infringement suit brought by Deringer against California dealer A. J. Plate and the resultant testimony (*Deringer v. Plate*, brought 1863, the conclusion published 1870) are a remarkable source on Deringer, Slotter, and dealers and gunmakers involved in San Francisco and Philadelphia gun business at the time. Some Slotter pistols are blatant copies of Deringer originals, even down to markings. Others were sold marked J. DERINGER/ PHILADELA, and still others with SLOTTER & CO. markings. Pistol at *bottom* is an unfinished example, measures 8 1/8 inches overall.

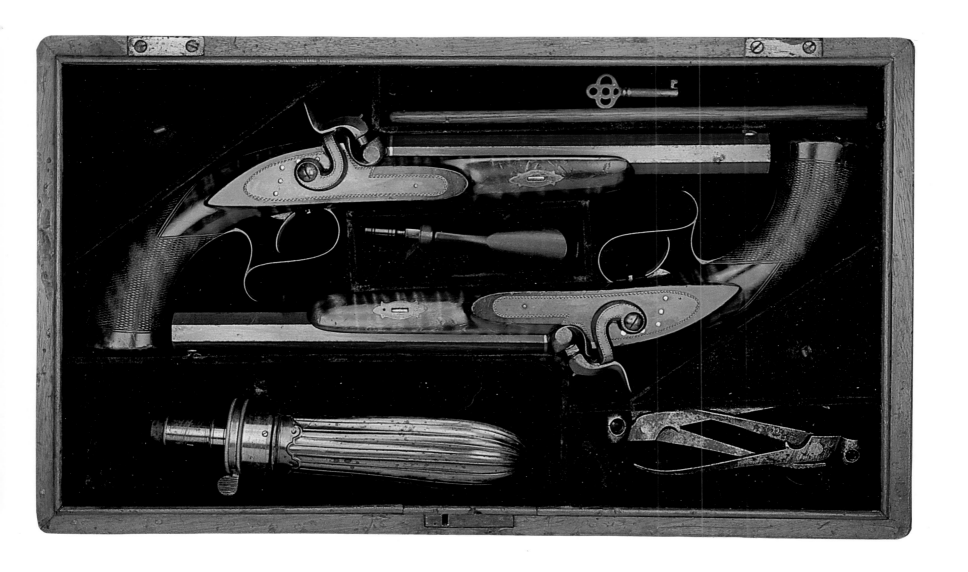

Classic American dueling pistols, by Memphis gunmaker Schneider & Co. Stocks of curly maple, iron mounts, with silver plaque stock inlays inscribed sv, for original owner, Samuel Vance; c. 1855.

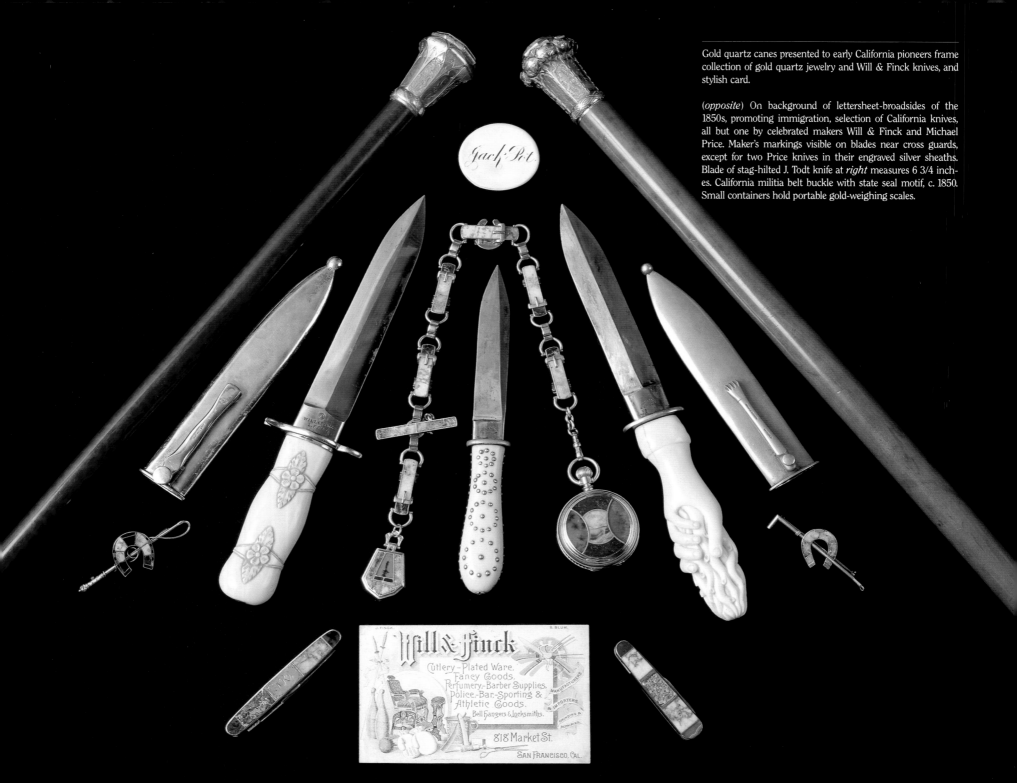

Gold quartz canes presented to early California pioneers frame collection of gold quartz jewelry and Will & Finck knives, and stylish card.

(*opposite*) On background of lettersheet-broadsides of the 1850s, promoting immigration, selection of California knives, all but one by celebrated makers Will & Finck and Michael Price. Maker's markings visible on blades near cross guards, except for two Price knives in their engraved silver sheaths. Blade of stag-hilted J. Todt knife at *right* measures 6 3/4 inches. California militia belt buckle with state seal motif, c. 1850. Small containers hold portable gold-weighing scales.

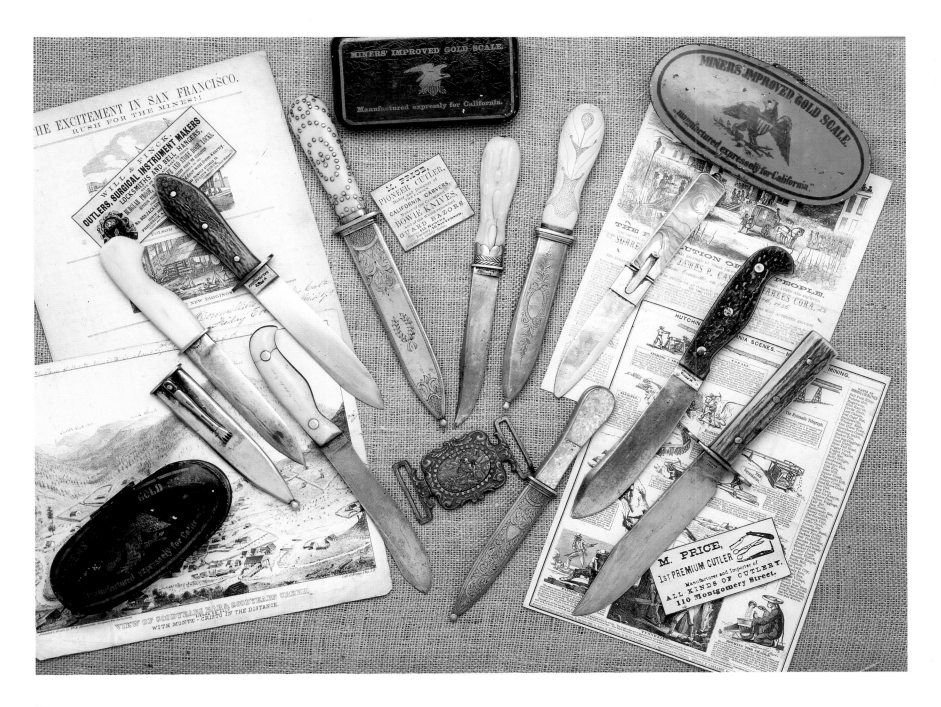

Matched pair of exceptional double action Adams patent (English) revolvers, by Massachusetts Arms Co.; barrels engraved *W. J. SYMS & BROR.* Finely engraved with frontier and patriotic motifs, as well as English crowns. Perhaps show guns, or made for visiting English travelers—or fine pistols a prospector might splurge on after striking it rich. Serial numbers 693 and 746.

fact that this clumsy revolver was rated by some as unsafe. A miner's letter from San Joaquin (1849) sided with the Colt:

> One of Colt's large pistols is sufficient for each man to protect him from either marauding Mexicans or Indians, and are more dreaded than any other arms. No man who values his life should carry Allen's revolvers, for they are more to hurt the person who fires them than the person fired at.

One justice of the peace even ruled an Allen pepperbox failed to qualify as a dangerous weapon!

Mark Twain wrote about the Allen from firsthand observation (1861):

> George Bemis...wore in his belt an original "Allen" revolver, such as irreverent people called a "pepperbox." Simply drawing the trigger back, cocked and fired the pistol. As the trigger came back, the hammer would begin to rise and the barrel to turn over, and presently down would drop the hammer, and away would speed the ball. To aim along the turning barrel and hit the thing aimed at was a feat which was probably never done with an "Allen" in the world.... as one of the stage-drivers afterward said, "If she didn't get what she went after, she would fetch something else."... It was a cheerful weapon the "Allen." Sometimes all its six barrels would go off at once, and then there was no safe place in all the region about, but behind it.

Besides by Allen, pepperboxes were made by such American firms as Manhattan, Blunt & Syms, Marston, and Bacon. Various imports were also on the

California knives made in New York, Massachusetts, and Sheffield, England, with clipper ship cards, advertising speedy voyages to San Francisco in the 1850s. *From left*, two knives by J. D. Chevalier of New York; 8 3/4-inch-blade Bowie with half-horse, half-alligator pommel by G. Woodhead of Sheffield (opposite side of blade with Indian shooting buffalo scene, over "American Bowie Knife" and miners scene under motto "California Gold at the Diggings," plus spread-wing eagle and patriotic legend); another Chevalier; a J. Walters & Co./Globe Works of Sheffield; a G. Wostenholm & Son–Washington Works I*XL Bowie; another G. Woodhead, its blade including legend "I Can Dig Gold From Quartz"; a Joseph Law of Sheffield; an Ames Mfg. Co., Chicopee, Massachusetts, with California bear pommel; and, at *bottom*, folding knife by Unwin & Rodgers of Sheffield. Bowies offered some of the most stirring patriotic inscriptions and motifs in nineteenth-century arms.

French broadside heralding "The Gold Mines of California," with French bronze "Le Miner," "Foreign Miners License," ambrotype of well-armed prospector, and Bowie knives by Sheffield makers honoring California and its miners. Even whiskey bottle paid silent tribute..

Miner ready to try luck and his kit. Surrounded by knives that could be used to pick gold from quartz. Overall length of fancy Bowie on *left* is 11 inches. Most of Sheffield manufacture, for the Western market.

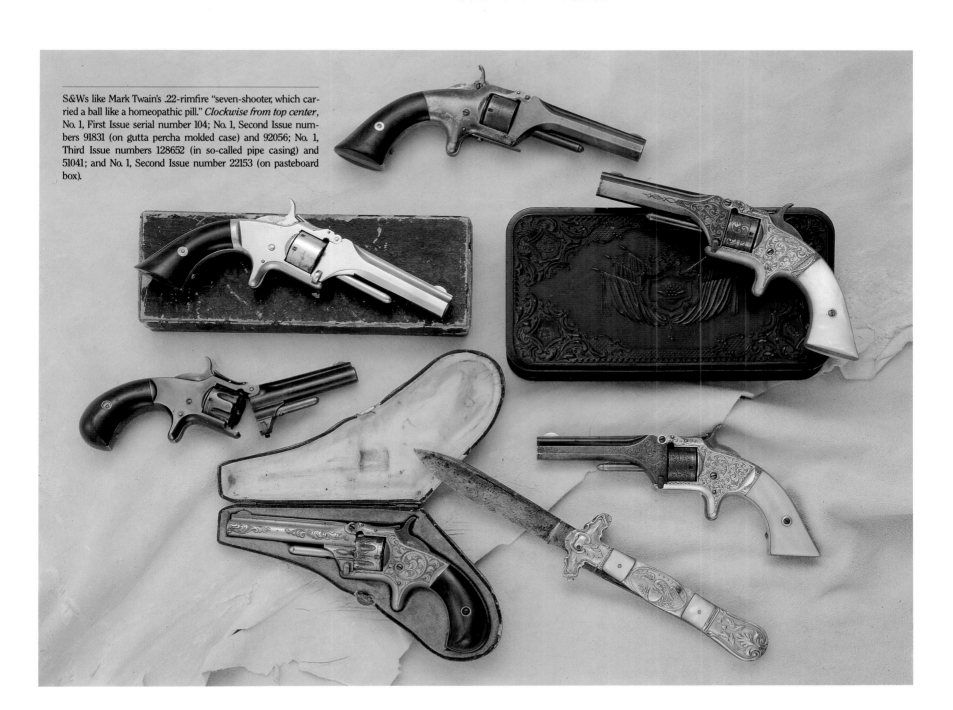

S&Ws like Mark Twain's .22-rimfire "seven-shooter, which carried a ball like a homeopathic pill." *Clockwise from top center*, No. 1, First Issue serial number 104; No. 1, Second Issue numbers 91831 (on gutta percha molded case) and 92056; No. 1, Third Issue numbers 128652 (in so-called pipe casing) and 51041; and No. 1, Second Issue number 22153 (on pasteboard box).

market, generally by English and Belgian makers. Single-barrel guns of pepperbox styling were also available, known as bar hammer pistols, usually with screw-off barrels for ease in loading.

The Deringer Pistol

A favorite of miners, and a gun whose name became part of our language as the name for a pocket pistol, was the Deringer. Already renowned for his Kentucky rifles and military pistols, Henry Deringer, Jr., began manufacturing percussion pocket pistols in the second quarter of the nineteenth century. Their popularity exploded onto the scene with the heavy demand of miners, and of hangers-on such as gamblers and ladies of the evening. California proved to be the pistol's prime market.

Made in various sizes, the standard Deringer was about .41 caliber, measuring small enough to fit easily into a man's hand. Mounts were usually German silver, with decorative engraving. Already in 1848 they were described in a Santa Fe gambling den:

> Between the wall and the tables were placed chairs for the convenience of the dealer, or dealers—for these gentry usually hunt in couples; while upon the board was displayed not only the *lure* in the shape of Mexican dollars and Spanish doubloons . . . but a *preventive* to interference (or, as is sometimes the case, just complaints of unfair dealings) in the shape of Bowie knives, "Derringers," and "six-shooters," which latter weapons lay prepared for instant use, being loaded and capped so as to be ready to the hand.

An 1852 San Diego dinner party incident between two duelists ended up in firing "Derringer pistols across the dining-room table." One antagonist, a doctor, shot first, before the signal to fire, and then begged for mercy. His opponent, unhurt, placed a few kicks on the doctor's person, and emitted a few expletives. No one was shot since the seconds deemed to use corks instead of bullets!

A California forty-niner's arms *equipe* of fashion was a complement of deringers (sold in pairs), Colt revolvers, and/or the Allen pepperbox, and a Bowie knife.

Motley crew of grizzled prospectors, load carted by overworked mule. Three men sport holstered large-frame Colt percussion revolvers.

Believed at Camp Verde, Arizona Territory, prospectors ready to seek their fortunes. Mount at *right* sported Spencer military rifle on saddle.

California theaters were prone to request that patrons check their arms on entering. As reported by a New Yorker (1851):

> If any man declared that he had no weapon, the statement was so incredible that he had to submit to be searched; an operation which was performed by the doorkeepers; who . . . were occasionally rewarded for their diligence by the discovery of a pistol secreted in some unusual part of the dress.

The New Yorker went on to say that

> miners were so greedy, treacherous, and unreliable that no man's life was safe. Law and order were unknown; fights occurred daily; and anyone who could not protect himself with his fists was unfortunate. Every man carried a gun, and all types of weapons that could shoot, cut, or stab—plain pocket pistols, Colt revolvers, double-barreled guns, repeaters, daggers, and double-edged swords—were used. . . . Robbery and murder were commonplace, because men still preferred to steal gold dust rather than work for it and did not hesitate to take human lives if necessary.

To distribute these guns in the mining areas, and elsewhere, dealers from the East, as well as those in Western and Mississippi River cities, aggressively advertised their wares. Deringer pistols were occasionally found stamped on the barrel flat with such markings as "MADE FOR *A. J. Plate* SAN FRANCISCO." And the sale of Colts was made easier by such florid endorsements as from F. X. Aubrey, an explorer, describing an incident against Garroteros Indians near the Colorado River (August 1853):

> . . . our party must necessarily be destroyed; but some of us having disengaged ourselves, we shot them down so fast with our Colt's Revolvers, that we soon produced confusion among them, and put them to flight. We owe our lives to those firearms, the best ever were invented, and now brought, by successive improvements, to a state of perfection

Colonel Colt himself could not have better stated the superiority of his revolving pistols.

Dueling and Colt Competitors

In California's rip-roaring gold-mining days, dueling was commonplace. Duelists were a speciality of arms dealer A. J. Taylor, whose indoor shooting range could accommodate challenger or challenged for pre-event practice. Newspapers published notes in advance of some duels. An engraved announcement sometimes invited friends to observe. Taylor was known as one who "would then supply weapons for both sides at a price." An 1856 advertisement advised the public of "genuine Derringer Pistols, and a large assortment of English Duelling and Colt's Pistols," available at Taylor's emporium.

Dueling pistols might be the traditional kind by English, French, Belgian, German, or American makers, or could be Colt revolvers or virtually any other kind of gun. For Westerners there was no strict code governing what firearms it was proper to shoot at one another in formal circumstances. Normally the participants stood facing away from one another, backs adjacent, then on signal walked five paces and turned around to fire at close range. If firing revolvers, the duelists would continue until one of them was hit or the guns were empty! Dueling as a recognized means of settling disputes, however, was seldom practiced after the Civil War.

The Deane, Adams, & Deane English percussion revolvers were made (like the Colt) in pocket, belt, and holster sizes and in .31, .44, and .50 calibers. These solid-frame guns were standard as double-actions, and set out to compete with the Colts. In 1856 the British firm came to be known as the London Armoury Company, but the guns continued to be called the Deane, Adams, or Deane and Adams, in the United States. Another English revolver, the Tranter, also had a respectable Western market.

Not infringing on the U.S. patent, the English revolvers were sold here before the 1857 Colt patent expiration. Thereafter the number of American revolvers entering the market was substantial. Most successful of these would be Remington, which soon had a line rivaling Colt's, and a solid-frame design on most models which was superior to that of the Colts. Remingtons too appeared in pocket, belt, and holster sizes, calibers .31, .36, and .44, and were made in large numbers.

Miner with poor choice of cheap revolver, but handsome Model 1894 Winchester with pistol-grip stock on pack. Photograph by Brisbois, Leadville, Colorado.

Smith & Wesson's New Revolver

A truly revolutionary development in handguns was the bored-through-cylinder Smith & Wesson tip-up barreled revolver,* which entered the market in 1857. Though the cartridge was a mild .22 rimfire, the advantage was that primer, powder, projectile, and casing were together as one unit. This spelled the end of muzzle-loaders, although not for the immediate future.

Colt's monopoly on revolvers therefore expired in the year that S&W's monopoly on cartridge revolvers (with bored-through cylinders) began. The muzzle-loading percussion revolver was being replaced by the breech-loading metallic cartridge system. Colt would not be able to legally make a practical revolver for the new ammunition until 1869.

Despite rivals who had the audacity to market guns infringing on their patent rights, S&W brought out an expanding line of revolvers, with tip-up barrels, in .22 and later in .32 rimfire calibers.

Mark Twain couldn't resist ridiculing the S&W .22 (1861) in writing about travels in the West:

> I was armed to the teeth with a pitiful little Smith & Wesson's seven-shooter, which carried a ball like a homeopathic pill, and it took the whole seven to make a dose for an adult. But I thought it was grand. It appeared to me to be a dangerous weapon. It only had one fault—you could not hit anything with it. One of our "conductors" practiced awhile on a cow with it, and as long as she stood still and behaved herself she was safe....

A line of bored-through-cylinder cartridge revolvers was offered by Allen, and they proved to be formidable competitors to Smith & Wesson. Suits from S&W interfered with Allen and other makers as much as possible. Settlements were sometimes made by turning over the infringing makers' revolvers to S&W, which was then free to sell them. In some instances S&W's name would be stamped on the guns before they were sold. Such makers as Bacon, Moore, Pond, Warner, and Allen were sued by S&W. Examples of each manufacturer were known and used in the West. S&W also was faced with foreign makers like LeFaucheux and its pinfire, plus cartridge deringer makers and producers of pistols with barrels ranging from one on up to clusters of four or more.

Cartridge Pepperboxes

Pepperbox cartridge guns were common in the 1850s, with Sharps the leading manufacturer. The Sharps four-barrel pistol was loaded by sliding the barrel cluster forward; the firing pin revolved on the face of the hammer each time it was cocked to shoot. These .22-, .30-, and .32-caliber rimfire pistols were made in the tens of thousands. One owner of a .22 was Lord George Berkeley (St. Louis, 1859):

> [It was] the most perfect little *bijou* of a revolver I ever saw in my life. The makers of this perfect little weapon, which is highly finished and handsome enough to be worn on a chain at a lady's waist, are Sharp & Co., Philadelphia, and for which in [1849] they had a patent. In size it is so small that I carried it in my waistcoat-pocket, and in execution so effective that at eight yards I

---

*Patented by former Colt employee Rollin White, and licensed to S&W.

could shoot as correctly, if not more so, than I could with my favorite pair of John Manton duelling-pistols. . . . I have been told . . . that this deadly little weapon is made to come into play in those brutal and bloody "difficulties," as they call them . . . which, I regret to say, so frequently disgrace society in the United States.

As of 1862, Sharps had taken on a partner, William Hankins, and the pepperboxes thereafter carried their names together.

Remington soon brought out a pepperbox series of cartridge pistols, as did Starr, Bacon, and Rupertus. Added to the burgeoning array of cartridge pistols were numerous deringers, with mechanisms having side-swing, or swing-up, or swing-down, or pivoting barrels, or those that slid forward, or stationary barrel units with various breech mechanisms.

Cartridge Deringers

By 1860 the .41-caliber rimfire metallic cartridge was on the market, and there would appear in the next few years at least two models of pistol firing that diminutive round which would remain in their makers' catalogues into the twentieth century: the Colt Thuer deringer and the Remington over-and-under Vest Pocket double deringer. From the dawn of the .41 rimfire in 1860 to the end of the era over fifty years later, there were over seventy-five makers, and over 300 variant models of cartridge deringers were built in the United States.

Such weapons were effective only when fired at point-blank range, much like their muzzle-loading predecessors. A vignette repeated from time to time in mining communities and in seedier parts of Western cities and towns was recounted by peace officer Frank Canton, dealing with an unruly prisoner (1894):

I had a heavy pocket derringer that I usually carried in my hip pocket when in town. It was a forty-one-caliber Colt. I thought it was a good one, but had never tried it out. . . . [Canton pushed

Members of the first party that discovered gold in the Black Hills, Dakota Territory, 1874. H. N. Ross (1) armed with Sharps military rifle; Dick Stone (2) with scope-sighted Model 1874 Sharps; Jack Cale (4) has Model 1866 Winchester carbine.

away the attacking criminal], and at the same time drew my derringer and fired at his head. The bullet struck him in the forehead just over the left eye. He fell on his back, and I supposed from the appearance of the wound that he was shot square through the head. [However, on the doctor's examination], he found that the bullet had not penetrated his head, but had glanced around the skull under the skin, and come out at the back of his head. He was unconscious for twelve hours, then commenced to improve. . . . I threw away this derringer that I had, and have never carried one since.

Despite their lack of consistently lethal power, cartridge deringers have a history closely associated with gamblers, madams, and soiled doves. The miner was an easy prey for those frontier parasites. Gunfighters and outlaws, two other hard types of the Western life-style, favored heavy-caliber revolvers.

Charles M. Russell's *The Wagon Boss*. Choice selection of rifles: the Sharps. Note whiskey bottle and deep wagon-wheel ruts at picture bottom.

Faro gaming chip rack holds selection of pocket protectors, in .22 rimfire unless indicated otherwise. At *center*, Sharps four-shot pepperbox, *top left and top right*, Marston three-barrel Deringers; second and third *down from left*, Rupertus and Bacon pepperboxes; *next*, Remington Elliott five-shot Deringer; squeezer pistol in .32 rimfire by Chicago Fire Arms Co.; next *to right* unidentified, Irving, and unidentified, single-shot Deringers. Turn-barrel Deringer to their *right* by American Arms Co., with .22 rimfire caliber in one barrel and .32 rimfire in other.

Number 138813 from a matched pair of Model 1851 Navy Colt revolvers, the back-strap inscribed: *J. B. Hickock, 1869*. Two full-standing portrait photographs of Hickok, in which he is armed with Navy Colts, the butts thrust forward for quick access, have been identified. This prized icon of the West's premier gunfighter is displayed by the Gene Autry Western Heritage Museum.

GAMBLERS, MADAMS, GUNFIGHTERS, AND OUTLAWS

The Civil War serves as a ragged dividing line between muzzle-loading arms and the acceleration of advancements in firearms design and ammunition that occurred during and after the conflict. For enthusiasts of the craftsmanship, mechanics, history, and romance of arms, the remaining years of the nineteenth century were the Golden Age of American gunmaking.

These years coincide with the rapid settling of the West. Even during the distractions of the Civil War, migration continued—drawn by the lure of gold and silver strikes. Wagon trains were as long as 1,200 wagons, facing the largely unknown wilderness with guns at the ready and nerves on edge. At war's end the migration increased dramatically, from both North and South, and was swelled by immigrants from Europe. Federal legislation, notably the Homestead Act of 1862, encouraged the common man to move west, claim a tract of land of up to 160 acres, and own the land after five years, if he made particular improvements and met other reasonable conditions. Special benefits were allowed for Civil War veterans, whose years of military service could be counted against the five-year residency requirement.

The Great Plains beckoned as the last great frontier, and were settled principally in the 1870s and 1880s. That period saw the largest populations of pioneers moving west. At first harboring a vast cattle industry, later the range was substantially replaced by farming. Completion of the transcontinental railroad joined the nation together through the Iron Horse. Improved transportation furthered the Army's strategy of destroying the vast buffalo herds and weakening the hostile Indian tribes. Barbed-wire fences and changes in the beef industry (including elimination of the long trail drives from Texas) left farmers gradually dominant over ranchers. Droughts, grasshopper plagues, depressions, devastating winters, and range wars, as well as rampaging Indians, outlaws, slick gamblers, gunfighters, and prostitutes, were all components in the taming of the West. Almost to a man (and woman), firearms continued to play a central role.

Hickok expert Joseph G. Rosa dates this famed portrait at c. 1873–74, while Hickok was touring with Buffalo Bill's Combination theatrical group. The buckskin outfit therefore would be a stage costume. Libbie Custer described Wild Bill: "Physically, he was a delight to look upon. Tall, lithe and free in every motion, he rode and walked as if every muscle was perfection. . . . He was rather fantastically clad, of course, but all that seemed perfectly in keeping with the time and place. He did not make an armoury of his waist, but carried two pistols. He wore top-boots, riding breeches, and dark blue flannel shirt, with scarlet set-in front. A loose neck-handkerchief left his fine, firm throat free."

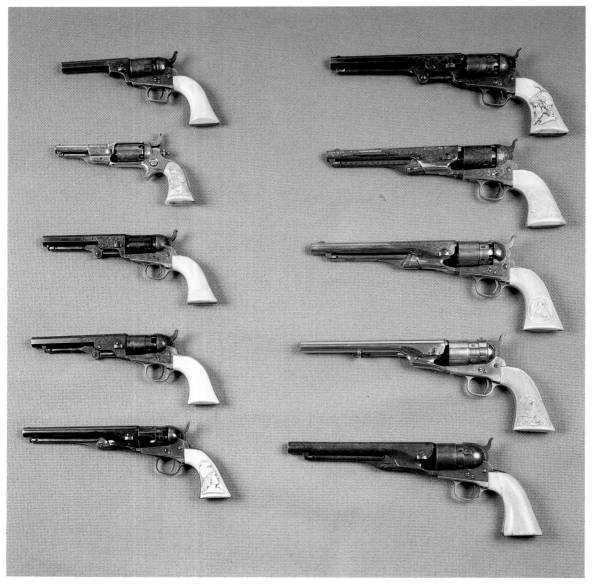

Colts fitted with ivory grips. *From top left*, .31-caliber Baby Dragoon, Model 1855 Sidehammer, and 1849 Pocket; .36 Model 1862 Pocket Navy and 1862 Police. *From top right*, 7 1/2-inch-barrel .36 Model 1851 Navy, 1861 Navy; 8-inch-barrel .44 percussion Model 1860 Army, .44 metallic-cartridge Richards conversion, and .44 Model 1860 Army Thuer conversion.

Tools of the Trade

Gunfighters,* gamblers, and outlaws—men of daring, chance, and fate—plied their trades in the era of the six-gun, which lasted from after the Civil War until the early twentieth century. Expertise with firearms was a matter of survival. The preference in handguns was the Colt, and in longarms the Winchester.

Following the Civil War, the muzzle-loading Colts maintained a steady popularity, even as late as the 1870s. John Wesley Hardin's capture by Texas Rangers in 1877 showed he still had a percussion revolver: "[One of the Rangers asked:] 'Have you taken his pistol?' They replied no, that I had no gun. Jack Duncan said, 'That's too thin' [i.e., "I don't believe it"], and ran his hand between my over and undershirt, pulling out a .44 Colt's cap-and-ball six-shooter, remarking to the others, 'What did I tell you.'"

The full array of Civil War and prewar-era arms remained in vogue, partly because of availability, partly because of their merit, and partly because shooters were used to these guns and comfortable with their operation. Further, paper cartridges and loose powder, balls, and caps were commonly purchasable throughout the West. The percussions also offered greater power and punch than most early metallic-cartridge guns.

Smaller-framed arms began the inroads on percussion handguns, and some, like the Sharps .22 and .32 pepperboxes, would reach a total in excess of 140,000 by the inventor's death in 1874. Remington's pepperboxes, the Marston multibarrel, and the Reid "My Friend" knuckleduster also had large markets. These arms, and the myriad of deringers, were hardy backups for men who relied mainly on bigger handguns, and for hideaways in the city where only small pistols might be carriable.

Prostitutes with deringers were described by journalist Henry M. Stanley, in Julesburg, Colorado (1867): "These women are expensive articles, and come in for

---

* Term known to have been used in the West as early as 1874.

Large-frame percussion revolvers, with competitor Colt Third Model Dragoon cased set (*top center*), Blunt & Syms trade label in lid. *From top left* (all .44s unless indicated otherwise): Joslyn, Massachusetts Arms Co., Wesson and Leavitt patent .40 caliber, North and Savage .36 "Figure Eight," and Rogers and Spencer. Beneath Dragoon Colt, a Savage .36, Freeman, and Butterfield .41. *From top right*, Pettingill, Starr single-action, Allen and Wheelock, and Starr double action.

Miscellaneous percussion revolvers, the Navys in .36 and all but one of the Pockets in .36 caliber. *From top left*, Allen & Wheelock Navy and Pocket; Springfield Arms Co. Navy and .28 Pocket; Cooper Navy and Pocket. *From top right*, Colt Model 1849 Pocket, cased set; close copies of Colts, the Manhattan Navy and Pocket; the Alsop Navy and Pocket. All but Colt and Manhattans made in limited numbers.

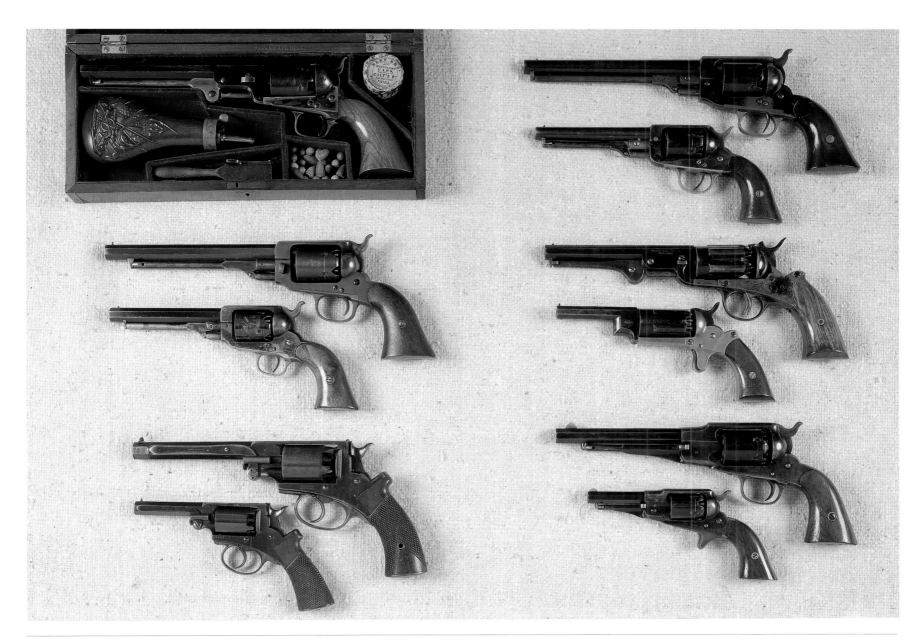

More percussion revolvers, the Navys in .36 caliber, the Pockets in .31. *From top left*, Colt Model 1851 Navy, cased set; Whitney Navy and Pocket; Massachusetts Arms Co., Adams Patent, Navy and Pocket. *From top right*, Navy and Pocket by Union Arms Co., Walsh (twelve- and ten-shot), and Remington.

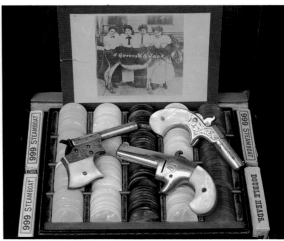

Some communities issued licenses for prostitution. While price for "services" of whore was about $2, her license per month, in Tombstone, 1894, was only $7. Portrait of lady by C. S. Fly, by whose gallery "Gunfight at the O. K. Corral" took place. Petite pistols, all in .22 caliber, by (*from left*) Stafford (*above*) and Frank Wesson "Watch Fob" model (*below*), Remington Vest Pocket (with etched frame), and Marlin.

(*top right*) Some favorites of soiled doves and madams. *From left*, Remington .30 rimfire Vest Pocket deringer, National and Remington-Elliott deringers, both in .41 rimfire. Finishes in gold and silver plating, and grips of mother-of-pearl.

a large share of the money wasted. In broad daylight they may be seen gliding through the sandy streets in Black Crook dresses, carrying fancy derringers slung to their waists, with which tools they are dangerously expert."

Deringers were even carried by two who dared to try capturing John Wesley Hardin (Texas, 1869): "When they came, I covered them with a double-barreled shotgun and told them their lives depended on their actions, and unless they obeyed my orders to the letter, I would shoot first one and then the other." Both men put down their arms: "One had a double-barreled gun and two six-shooters; the other had a rifle and two derringers. They complied with my request under the potent persuasion of my gun levelled first on one and then the other."

The growing popularity of the .22 and .32 cartridge revolvers, like the S&Ws, is evident in the recollection of William Dixon, in Leavenworth (1866): "All our acquaintance in this city urge us to get more and better arms; a suggestion in which the mail-agents cordially agree. The new arm of the West, called a Smith-and-Weston [sic], is a pretty tool; as neat a machine for throwing slugs into a man's flesh as an artist in mur-

der could desire to see." He added: "We buy a couple of these Smith-and-Westons, and then pay our fare of five hundred dollars to Salt Lake [by stagecoach]."

The Colt and Others

Although pocket protectors had a brisk sale, the preferred holster arm for serious shooters was the large-frame revolver. Conversions from percussion had a ready market, and were turned out in largest quantities by Remington. In many Remington arms the user could fire either a percussion cylinder or an interchangeable metallic cartridge, made under license from S&W.

Colt's Thuer conversion—a front-loader to circumvent the S&W patent rights—was not a popular frontier item, though that too permitted interchanging percussion and cartridge cylinders. The .44 Richards and Richards-Mason conversions had good markets, and quantities into the thousands (even military sales), followed by the Open Top Frontier .44, immediate predecessor to the serious revolver shooter's favorite, the Single Action Army .45 Peacemaker. For design and performance, and line and form, no more practical and sculpturally handsome a Colt has ever been devised. The starring role the Single Action has played in film and TV Westerns is a fitting tribute to

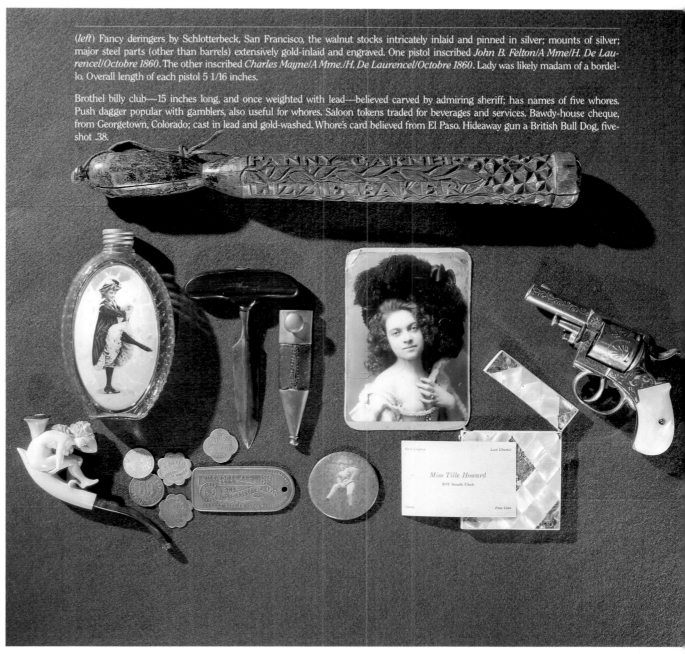

(*left*) Fancy deringers by Schlotterbeck, San Francisco, the walnut stocks intricately inlaid and pinned in silver; mounts of silver; major steel parts (other than barrels) extensively gold-inlaid and engraved. One pistol inscribed *John B. Felton/A Mme/H. De Laurencel/Octobre 1860*. The other inscribed *Charles Mayne/A Mme./H. De Laurencel/Octobre 1860*. Lady was likely madam of a bordello. Overall length of each pistol 5 1/16 inches.

Brothel billy club—15 inches long, and once weighted with lead—believed carved by admiring sheriff; has names of five whores. Push dagger popular with gamblers, also useful for whores. Saloon tokens traded for beverages and services. Bawdy-house cheque, from Georgetown, Colorado; cast in lead and gold-washed. Whore's card believed from El Paso. Hideaway gun a British Bull Dog, five-shot .38.

Remington double deringer and mother-of-pearl garter dagger, with bordello accessories. Porcelain-faced Elgin topless-cowgirl pocket watch inscribed on back "For the Good Times—D." January 1879 *Ford County* (Kansas) *Globe* wrote up a "desperate fight . . . at the boarding house of Mrs. W., on 'Tin Pot Alley,' last Tuesday evening, between two of the most fascinating doves of the roost. When we heard the noise and looked out the front window, which commanded a view of the situation, it was a magnificent sight to see. Tufts of hair, calico, snuff and gravel flew like fir in a cat fight, and before we could distinguish how the battle waned a chunk of dislocated leg grazed our ear and a cheer from the small boys announced that a battle was lost and won. The crowd separated as the vanquished virgin was carried to her parlors by two 'soups.' A disjointed nose, two or three internal bruises, a chawed ear and a missing eye were the only scars we could see."

(*top right*) Ideal for soiled dove self-defense: Smith & Wessons *from top left*, double action Second Model, Safety Hammerless, Hand Ejector, all .32s. *Top right*, .32 double-action First Model, and *below* Wells Fargo & Co. stamp, the First Model Ladysmith, in .22 rimfire; D. B. Wesson himself designed this model, both delicate and attractive.

the actual role of this six-shot equalizer in the winning of the West. Then and now, the Colt Single Action has been the handgun of choice.

Made in barrel lengths from 2 1/2 to 16 inches and in calibers from .22 rimfire to .476 Eley, the Single-Action set the standard against which all others were measured. Every class or type of no-nonsense gun-toter in the West had a Single Action Colt—if he did not, the Colt was usually his wished-for sidearm.

Competing against the Colt S.A.A. were the Remington Single Action Model 1875 and Model 1890 and the large-framed Smith & Wessons.

Impetus for S&W came from czarist Russia, which ordered 20,000 American models, in .44 Russian caliber. These and other top-break revolvers had a following among some desperate characters. John Wesley Hardin used an Old Model .44 Russian in shooting Deputy Sheriff Charley Webb (1874, Comanche, Texas), and Jesse James is known to have used a Schofield S&W and the Model 1875 Remington.

The attention a gunfighter paid to his hardware is apparent from a series of letters from W. B. "Bat" Masterson to the Colt factory, ordering a total of eight Single Actions. On the Opera House Saloon letterhead, Dodge City, Kansas (July 24, 1885), Bat ordered

Rakish frontier dandy, proud of his plated Colt Peacemaker, hogleg, plowhandle, thumb-buster, equalizer, or six-shooter, to use several of the nicknames earned by the handgun over the years.

S&W Safety Hammerless revolver factory-engraved, its frame inscribed for owner; likely a gift from satisfied client. Reclining maiden cigar cutter removes tip in crotch. Container at *lower right* for condoms, some of which were made of animal intestines. To right of gentleman's "glass label" pocket flask is rare deluxe silver pass from El Paso madams.

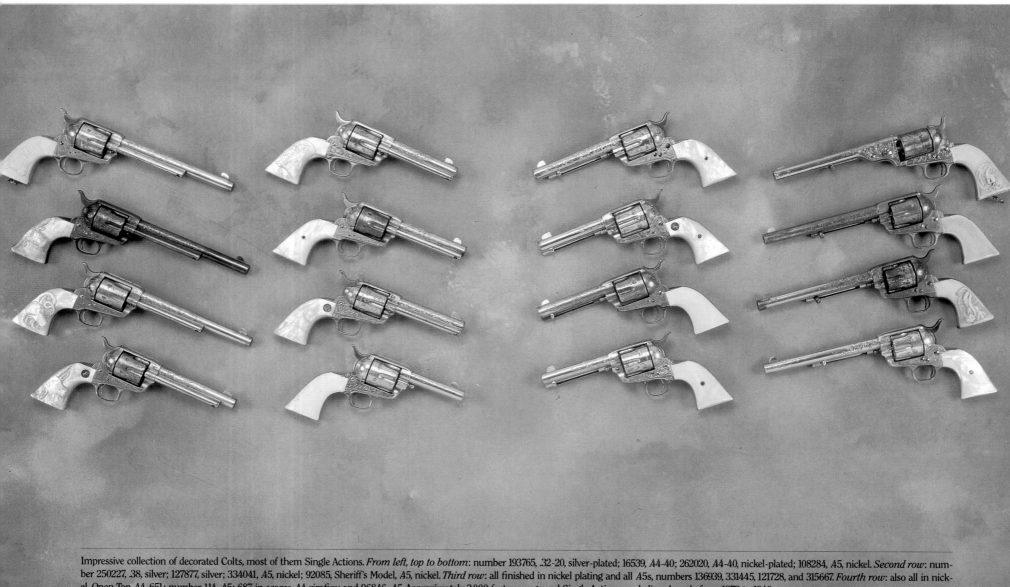

Impressive collection of decorated Colts, most of them Single Actions. *From left, top to bottom*: number 193765, .32-20, silver-plated; 16539, .44-40; 262020, .44-40, nickel-plated; 108284, .45, nickel. *Second row*: number 250227, .38, silver; 127877, silver; 334041, .45, nickel; 92085, Sheriff's Model, .45, nickel. *Third row*: all finished in nickel plating and all .45s, numbers 136939, 331445, 121728, and 315667. *Fourth row*: also all in nickel, Open Top .44, 651; number 114, .45; 687 in scarce .44 rimfire; and 96846, .45. Approximately 3,000 factory-engraved Single Actions are believed made from 1873 to 1940.

156

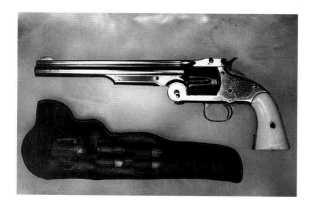

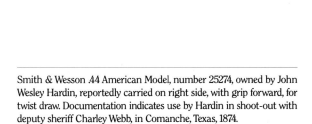

Smith & Wesson .44 American Model, number 25274, owned by John Wesley Hardin, reportedly carried on right side, with grip forward, for twist draw. Documentation indicates use by Hardin in shoot-out with deputy sheriff Charley Webb, in Comanche, Texas, 1874.

First Single Action ordered by W. B. "Bat" Masterson directly from the Colt factory; serial 53684. Originally grips were mother-of-pearl, carved with Mexican eagle motif. Finished in silver plating; backstrap engraved *W. B. MASTERSON*. Deciding that shorter barrel was preferable, Bat had 7 1/2-inch original length chopped back to 5 inches.

Short-lived competitor to the Single Action Colt, Model 1875 Remingtons were made for only fourteen years, in total of about 25,000. Company tried again with Model 1890, of which only 2,000 were made, through 1894. This pair are among fanciest known, likely factory showpieces; numbers 502 and 509.

one of your nickle plated short 45. calibre revolvers [Single Action Army]. It is for my own use and for that reason I would like to have a little Extra pains taken with it. I am willing to pay Extra for Extra work. Make it very Easy on the trigger and have the front Sight a little higher and thicker than the ordinary pistol of this Kind. put on a gutta percha handle and send it as soon as possible, have the barrel about the same length that the ejecting rod is

Masterson's total orders, over a period of years, came to one 7 1/2-inch, two 5 1/2-inch, and five 4 3/4-inch Single Actions, commonly in plated finishes; the first was a deluxe 7 1/2-inch, in silver plating, and engraved, inscribed, and with carved mother-of-pearl grips. In later years, as a sportswriter with a New York newspaper, the great Bat would meet many a New Yorker fascinated by his career in the West. From buffalo hunter to gambler and gunfighter to policeman, sheriff, and deputy U.S. Marshal, Bat Masterson enjoyed one of the more interesting of frontier careers.

Rifles, Shotguns, Carbines

Rifles and shotguns were least vital to gunfighters, gamblers, and outlaws, and of little use to madams and their whores. Since to these professionals guns were critical equipment, selection was directed toward the best that money could buy. Therefore Winchester and Sharps prevailed in rifles, and Parker and better-quality English doubles were preferred in shotguns. These latter tended to have shortened barrels. Richard Townshend, an 1869 arrival to Colorado, commented: "A shotgun's not very handy at close quarters, unless it's a sawed-off. For fighting in a bar-room, let me tell you, or on top of a stagecoach, they like to cut the barrels off a foot in front of the hammers, so the gun handles more like a pistol."

For maneuverability, and as a complement to the revolver, carbines were a favored long gun for the gunfighter and outlaw. But these were usually carried as saddle guns (lawmen did likewise). In the late 1870s, with the increased availability of the .44-40, the concept of cartridges interchangeable between revolvers and longarms became popular.

As a gun and cartridge maker, and with its innova-

One of orders from Masterson, sent directly to Colt's, for Single Actions. Bat's preference for 4 3/4-inch barrel is evident here; .45 was always his favorite caliber.

tive designs, Winchester had a distinct advantage over its longarm competition until into the twentieth century. In 1874 it bought out rival Adirondack Arms Company (which made repeating rifles), and in 1888 it acquired Whitney and a significant share of rival Remington. A number of other firms, like Sharps, Ballard, Bullard, and Massachusetts Arms Company, had disappeared from the scene by the 1890s. The firearms industry continued in a state of flux, as the West itself changed.

The Shoot-out and the Gunfighter

That gunfights and shoot-outs in the West were rare occasions is challenged by the statistic of some 20,000 men killed in gun battles from 1866 to 1900. The gunfighter, a.k.a. mankiller and shootist (the latter term also designated a marksman), was a product of his time, some hardened from Civil War service, and all hardened from the tough frontier.

An 1881 Kansas City *Journal* article described such men:

He may be found behind the bar in a Main Street saloon; he may be seen by an admiring audience doing the pedestal clog at a variety theater; his special forte may be driving a cab, or he may be behind the rosewood counters of a bank. If he has been here any great number of years, his "man" was probably a Pioneer, and died in the interest of "law and order"—at least so the legend runs. And no one dares dispute the verity of the legend, for behold the man who executed a violator of the law without waiting for the silly formalities of a judge and jury, mayhap now sits in a cushioned pew at an aristocratic church, and prays with a regularity, grace and precision only equalled by his unerring aim with a revolver, the great Western civilizer.

Facility with firearms, mainly the handgun, was paramount; but even more so were a steely reserve and calm under pressure. Adrenaline could cause the weak of spine a fatal case of nerves. Gunfighters were prepared to kill if necessary, and if one had a reputation as a mankiller, there were others whose intent it was to kill and assume that mantle on their own shoulders.

The Prince of Pistoleers had advice for would-be gunfighters. In 1865, Wild Bill Hickok, the first "fast gun," stated: "Whenever you get into a row be sure

Presentation Stevens-Lord target pistol, Nimschke-engraved and plated in nickel and gold. Meeting in Austin, Texas, 1879, Buffalo Bill Cody and renowned gunfighter-gambler-lawman Ben Thompson held a friendly shooting contest. Impressed with Thompson's marksmanship, Cody ordered pistol made and sent it along. As reported in *Austin Daily Statesman*, December 10, 1879: "Yesterday morning Marshal Thompson received a very handsome present from Buffalo Bill. It is a . . . costly target pistol, manufactured by Stevens & Co., Chicopee Falls, Massachusetts. The mountings are of gold, handle beautifully tinted pearl, while the glittering steel barrel is most artistically and beautifully carved. It has engraved on the handle [BUFFALO BILL TO BEN THOMPSON] It is the only pistol of the kind in the city, and is a marvel of skilled workmanship."

Contemporary illustration of gunfight between Wild Bill Hickok and Dave Tutt, Springfield, Missouri, July 21, 1865. When asked if he held any remorse for killing Tutt, Hickok reportedly stated: "I had rather not have killed him, for I want ter settle down quiet here now. But thar's been hard feeling between us a long while. I wanted ter keep out of that fight; but he tried to degrade me, and I couldn't stand that, you know, for I am a fighting man, you know."

Gunfighter–lawman–Indian fighter Dallas Stoudenmire's Colt Model 1860 Army conversion hideout revolver, number 6904. Picked up in street after Stoudenmire was killed in El Paso shoot-out. Accompanied by photograph of his sister, which he carried.

J. Braddell & Sons, Belfast, Ireland, double-barrel shotgun, carried by Ben Thompson when city marshal of Austin. Documentation from his aunt, when she presented gun to next-door neighbor Texas Ranger Frank Hamer. Watch was a gift from Thompson to attorney Pendexter, in appreciation for defense in a shooting scrape. Thompson's signature on register book of Hotel Menger, San Antonio.

John H. "Doc" Holliday's Colt Single Action .45 revolver, number 11301. Documenting papers reveal nephew told by his Uncle Doc, on deathbed, that this had been his regular six-gun throughout exploits in the West, the "Shootout at the O.K. Corral" included. The dentist-gambler-saloonkeeper-gunfighter died of tuberculosis, at age thirty-five, 1887.

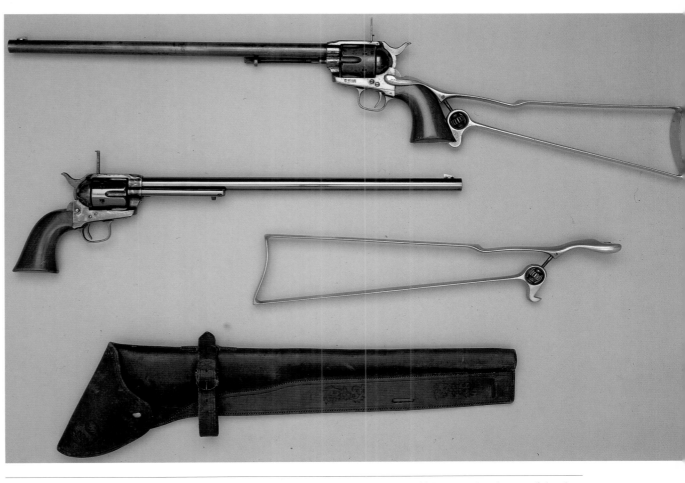

(*top left*) King Fisher, at *left*, gunfighter-lawman-rancher-rustler-saloonkeeper, killed in 1884 in wild San Antonio saloon gunfight, along with his friend Ben Thompson. The shoot-out avenged Thompson's previous killing of a rival, and started when Thompson playfully stuck a revolver barrel into a saloonkeeper's mouth, cocking the hammer! This led to a donnybrook, leaving Thompson dead with nine gunshot wounds, and Fisher dead with thirteen. Fisher's friend Culp armed with S&W American.

(*bottom left*) Commodore Perry Owens, looking the part of the Wild West gunfighter. His rifle a Model 1875 trapdoor Springfield, Officers Model; the Colt Single Action is in unusual holster rig.

(*above*) Buntline Specials, numbers 28802 (*top*) and 28819, both with 16-inch barrels and in .45 caliber. There is much controversy among historians and collectors on whether or not Wyatt Earp and Dodge City lawmen Charlie Bassett, Neal Brown, Bat Masterson, and Bill Tilghman were given wooden-shoulder-stocked long-barreled revolvers by dime-novel author and showman Ned Buntline. The debate pits experts like Lee Silva (pro-story) against William B. Shillingberg (against). Meantime, the Buntlines remain among the most prized variation of any Colt firearm.

(*top left and above*) Buckskin Frank Leslie's custom-made silver-mounted belt, worn by unidentified figure in Tombstone photograph. Well-armed party sported two six-shooters and regal California knife, all appearing to have ivory handles.

(*left*) Johnny Ringo's Single Action Colt, number 222. Ringo was reportedly on a two-week drinking binge with Buckskin Frank just prior to mysterious shooting in Canyon near Tombstone. Revolver found in Ringo's hand at death, and documented in coroner's report, 1882. Photo album found on body; gun further documented from Ringo family.

(*opposite*) Appropriate paraphernalia for professional gambler. Pair pistols *lower left* Belgian-made for U.S. market, signed *Lewis & Tomes* on locks, *London Fine Wire Twist* on barrels. Deringers by Slotter & Co. Massive Bowie knife measures 13 inches overall.

and not shoot too quick. Take time. I've known many a feller slip up for shootin' in a hurry."

An 1867 issue of *Harper's New Monthly Magazine* carried an eyewitness account testifying to Hickok's deadly accuracy: "'That sign is more than fifty yards away. I will put these six balls into the inside of the circle, which isn't bigger than a man's heart.' In an offhand way, and without sighting the pistol with his eye, he discharged the six shots of his revolver. I afterward saw that all bullets had entered the circle." Though historians are skeptical of this account, an expert shot, as was Hickok, could fire with such notable accuracy.

Hickok's favorite arms were a matched set of 1851 Navy Colts, which he carried tucked into his belt, butts forward. He exercised extreme caution in the care and loading of his pistols, and even cast his own bullets, cleaned his guns, and examined such details as a percussion cap before capping the nipples. "I am not taking any chances," he said, "when I draw & pull I *must be sure*."

Hickok told Charles Gross in Abilene, Kansas, about shooting a human adversary: "Charlie I hope you never have to shoot any man, but if you do shoot him in the Guts near the Navel. *You* may not make a fatal shot, but *he* will get a shock that will paralyze his brain and arm so much that the fight is all over."

Hickok's prowess with his Colts was so well known that he was asked to give command performances, several of which were recorded in the memoirs or reports of eyewitnesses. While he was on tour with W. F. Cody's theatrical troupe a demonstration was put on before several local marksmen. Reportedly firing a pair of silver-plated, engraved, and pearl-handled Colt .44s (with a pair of Remington .44s as backup), Hickok

proceeded to entertain us with some of the best pistol work which it has ever been my good fortune to witness. . . . His last feat was the most remarkable of all: A quart can was thrown by Mr. Hickok himself, which dropped about 10 or 12 yards distant. Quickly whipping out his weapons, he fired alternately with right and left. Advancing a step with each shot, his bullets striking the earth just under the can he kept it in continuous motion until his pistols were empty.

Finest known pair of Slotter & Co. deringers, mounted in gold. Made for Barton Jenks, son of a contract maker of U.S. Civil War rifle-muskets. Each pistol 4 3/4 inches overall, and of fine workmanship. Type that would be coveted by better class of professional gambler.

(*opposite*) Percussion deringers by H. E. Dimick; cased pair of Williamsons either fired .41 cartridge or used capsule to fire percussion. Hideaway-sized arms were important to gamblers.

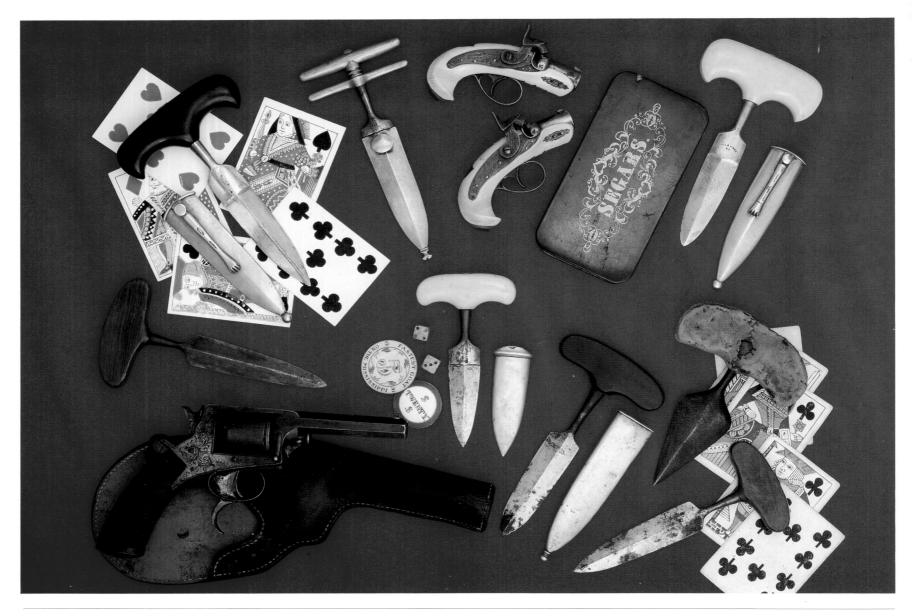

Push daggers prized by gamblers, *clockwise from lower left*: stamped Z. BONHAM on rosewood handle; 4 1/2-inch blade. Next, by Will & Finck, who also made gambling equipment (even cheating devices). Silver-handled dagger by DUFILHO/N. ORLEANS. Another Will & Fink to *right* of ivory-stocked Henry Deringer pistols; silver sheath with patented design features. Homemade dagger appears made from file. Longer dagger *beneath* unmarked, of high quality. *Lower right* with metal sheath, marked WOSTENHOLM & SONS. . . . I*XL CUTLERY (opposite side of blade). *Center* dagger marked M PRICE/SAN FRANCISCO. English-made revolver marked on topstrap MADE BY WILLIAM TRANTER FOR A. B. GRISWOLD & COMPANY NEW ORLEANS, with quick-draw-style holster, its German-silver belt clip marked LOUIS HOFFMAN/VICKSBURG.

(*opposite*) Sharps pepperboxes, in .22 to .32 caliber, each four-barreled, and with carved ivory grips.

166

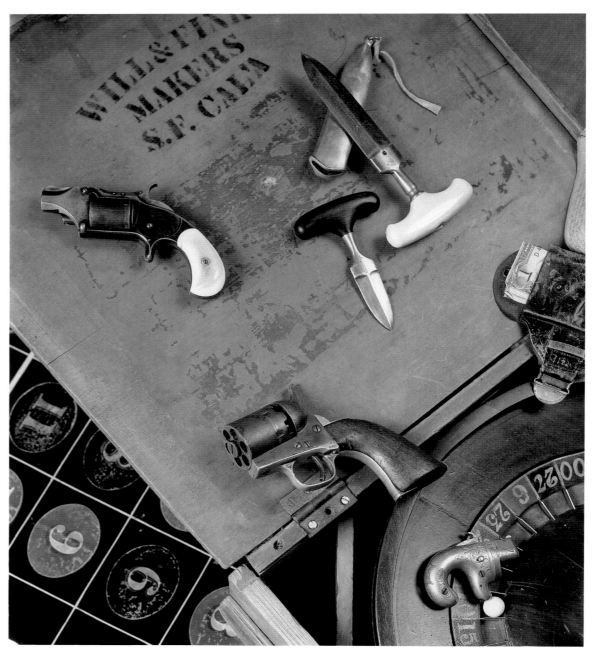

The Dodge City Peace Commission, seated, *left to right*, Charlie Bassett, Wyatt Earp, W. F. McClain, and Neal Brown; standing, W. H. Harris, Luke Short, Bat Masterson, and W. F. Petillon. All would appear to be comfortable in casino environment.

On Will & Finck roulette wheel lid (somehow firm misspelled own name!), ivory-handled push dagger of Will & Finck manufacture, with Michael Price dagger. Colt or National deringer with cut-off barrel; Colt Model 1849 Pocket revolver similarly customized, as has been S&W .32 tip-up pistol.

Whiskey advertisement, encouraging varied reprobate activities; deringers by (*clockwise from upper right*) Ballard, Williamson, Colt, Williamson, and (*center*) Southerner. All in .41 caliber, and smartly made.

Cyrus Noble whiskey advertisement shows faro game in progress at the Orient Saloon, Bisbee, Arizona (1907). Selection of .41 r.f. deringers; *top* pair by Moore; pistols *left and right* a pair by Allen. At *center*, General Abner Doubleday's finely engraved Moore deringer, number 15; after a distinguished Civil War career, the General served commands in Texas and in San Francisco, until retiring in 1873. *Lower left and right*, pistols by Moore.

(*top left*) "This is my last poker game, D.J." written on back of this cabinet photo of cardplayers in a saloon. Suicide special revolver in hand of nonsmoking player, possibly D.J. himself. Saloon appears of notable stature, but not in the same league as the Alamo, of Abilene. A contemporary description noted: "It was housed in a long room with a forty-foot frontage on Cedar Street, facing the west. There was an entrance at either end. At the west entrance were three double glass doors. Inside and along the front of the south side was the bar with its array of carefully polished brass fixtures and rails. From the back bar across a large mirror, which reflected the brightly sealed bottles of liquor. At various places over the walls were huge paintings in cheaply done imitations of the nude masterpieces of the Venetian Renaissance painters. Covering the entire floor space were gaming tables, at which practically any game of chance could be indulged. The Alamo boasted an orchestra, which played forenoons, afternoons, and nights."

(*top center*) Jesse (*left*) and Frank James, with Colt and Remington revolvers; Civil War period.

(*above*) Studio photo suggesting the local lawman drank on duty. Frequently peace officers were on hand in drinking and gambling establishments, as part of their duties to supervise behavior—and because many of them also were gamblers, and most also enjoyed a drink, or two.

(*left*) Simple interior of Albany County, Wyoming, saloon. Note suicide special revolver with bar glass as holster. Gambler probably awaiting arrival of suckers.

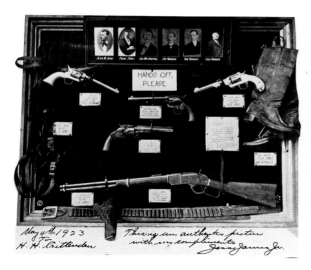

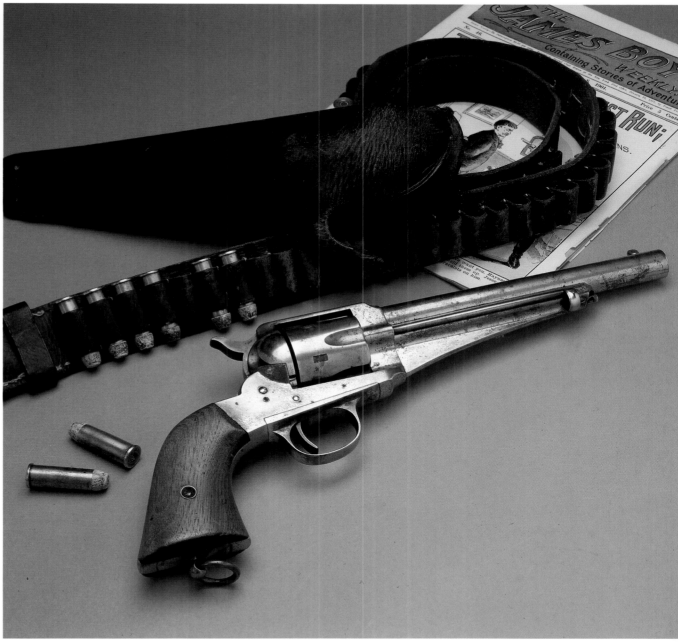

Frontiersman Luther North summed up the essential qualities of the deadly Hickok, qualities required of any true gunfighter: "[Wild Bill] was very deliberate and took careful aim closing his left eye. If he could shoot from the hip he never did it [before North and friends]. . . . Wild Bill was a man of Iron Nerve and could shoot straight enough to hit a man in the right place when the man had a gun in his hand and just between you and me not many of the so called Bad Men could do that." Hickok himself said to Luther's brother Frank: "you can beat the Hell out of me shootin' at pieces of paper, but I can beat you when it comes to hittin' men."

An inveterate gambler, Hickok ended his career in Deadwood, Dakota Territory, in 1876, while in a card

Inscribed by Jesse James, Jr., to H. H. Crittenden of Missouri, photograph shows firearms and memorabilia that belonged to James Gang members.

Holster and belt rig, and Remington Model 1875 revolver given to his doctor by Frank James, at time of his surrender. Serial number 5116.

The Remington Model 1875 of Jesse James, serial number 559, with holster, cartridge-money belt, and vest for loot, obtained by member of Pinkerton family and later donated to the Chicago Historical Society. On Smithsonian-sponsored museum tour for two years as featured display in "America's Star: U.S. Marshals 1789–1989," celebrating the bicentennial of the U.S. Marshals Service.

The "dirty little coward who shot Mr. Howard, and laid poor Jesse in his grave." So ran line in contemporary song, contributing to legendary status of the James boys. Jesse's alias had been Howard, at time of assassination (1882) by Bob Ford, pictured here holding Single Action Colt. According to affidavit sworn by Ford, gun he used in murder was of that model, and bore number 50432.

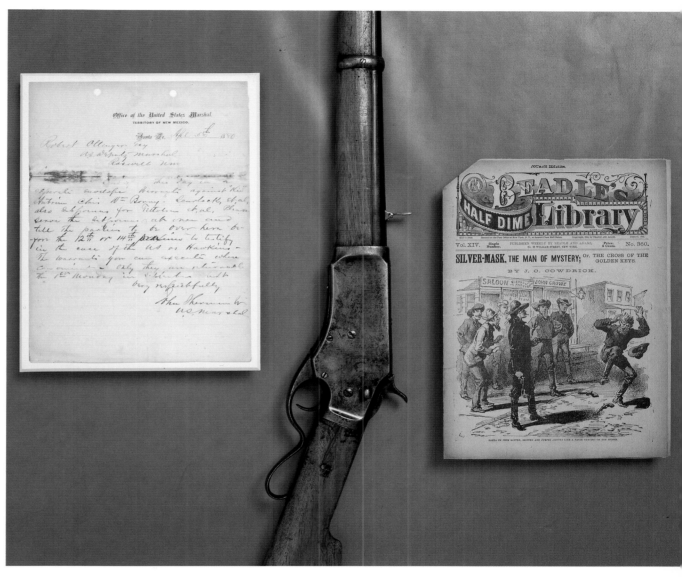

Pat Garrett and posse pictured with their captive, Billy the Kid. Cabinet-size photograph likely of December 24, 1880, the Kid at *right*, with Colt revolver aimed at head by deputy. The Kid and gang had been found holed up in abandoned rock house in Stinking Springs. After killing one of the gang, Charlie Bowdre, and then tempting the remainder with assurance of food and protection from violence, Garrett and his deputies were able to persuade the rest of the outlaws to surrender. At *left*, Pat Garrett, to his *left*, the deputy the Kid grew to hate, Bob Ollinger.

Bisley Colt revolver used by Cole Younger. Given to wife of his cousin, with whom Cole had stayed for about a year. Revolver, serial 194564, dates just prior to release of Bob and Cole Younger (*left and right*) from Minnesota prison. Brother Jim died behind bars.

Billy the Kid's Whitney-Kennedy carbine. Somewhere between myth and reality, the story of the Kid became standard element in lore of the Wild West. Gun and document represent the reality. Dime novel was part of beginning of the myth, which has variously shown the Kid as psychotic killer and harmless boy-man. Carbine given by the Kid after arrest to deputy U.S. Marshal Eugene Van Patton.

game at the No. 10 saloon. Failing to be seated in his preferred manner (back toward the wall), Hickok was shot a few hours later from behind, by a would-be celebrity, Jack McCall. Hickok's card hand, aces and eights of spades and clubs and the jack of diamonds, forever after has been known as the Dead Man's Hand. Death was instantaneous, and contrary to legend, Hickok did not instinctively draw his pistols when hit by the single bullet in the head.

The quick draw was not a myth. One of the first of the West's outlaws to attain notoriety, Henry Plummer of Montana, was said to have been the "quickest hand with his revolver of any man in the mountains," and "could draw the pistol and discharge the five loads in three seconds." Wild Bill Hickok's speed was part of his reputation. An Abilene observer wrote: "He shot six times so quick it startled me, for his six-shooter was in his holster when I said 'Draw.'"

Outlaw Dutch John Wagner was captured by vigilante Neil Howie, and the threat of a quick draw and deadly shooting won the day. Howie was

determined to arrest the robber at all risks, single-handed. He called out, "Hallo, Cap! hold on a minute." Wagner wheeled his horse half round, and Neil, fixing his eyes upon him, walked straight towards him with empty hands. His trusty revolver hung at his belt, however, and those who have seen the machine-like regularity and instantaneous motion with which Howie draws and cocks a revolver, as well as the rapidity and accuracy of his shooting, well know that few men, if any, have odds against him in an encounter with fire-arms. . . . he arrived within a few steps of the Dutchman . . . [and] broke the silence with the order, "Give me your gun and get off your mule."

Modern practitioners of the quick draw have attained remarkable speeds, drawing and firing five shots into a target 10 feet distant in less than two seconds; 1.6 seconds was a record held by Ed McGivern, with a Colt Single Action, in 1934. He could also fan (cocking the hammer with quick movements of the edge of the other hand) five shots into a playing-card-size target at a few yards' distance in 1.2 seconds! But the real test was shooting at another human being, while being shot at in return.

Shoot-outs abounded in the West, although their nature differed from the *High Noon*–style showdowns of Western films and TV programs.

Gambler and dandy Luke Short's shoot-out with gunfighter Long-Haired Jim Courtright is a Wild West classic. On a February day, 1887, in Fort Worth, Short and Courtright drew and shot at each other at point-blank range. Appropriately, the men were near a shooting gallery at the time. Courtright's revolver hammer appears to have caught on the chain of Short's watch —while Short pointed his revolver at Courtright. The first shot smashed the cylinder of Courtright's revolver, and three out of the next five hit his right thumb, shoulder, and heart. No shots hit Short, whose act was considered legitimate self-defense.

A gun battle worthy of Hollywood's best was that between cowboy, gunfighter, and lawman Commodore Perry Owens and the Blevins gang, September 1887, in Apache County, Arizona. Owens, on a Sunday afternoon, came to the Blevins house in search of a Blevins son, a wanted desperado and killer of two sheepmen, in a dispute known as the Pleasant Valley feud.

On approaching the house, cradling his Winchester, Owens spotted the fugitive through one of the two front doors. The killer held a Colt Single Action. Both men fired at the same time; the outlaw was hit, and staggered back into his mother's arms. A brother fired from the house at Owens, whose return fire scored a hit in the right shoulder. Owens sprinted around to the side of the house and shot a Blevins brother-in-law (armed with a revolver) in the shoulder as well. Next Owens shot in the heart the youngest of the Blevins boys, who was also brandishing a revolver. Mrs. Blevins and two other women in the house were not hit; all of Owens's adversaries died except one of the Blevins brothers. Owens walked away unscathed. Alas, the arsenal from his shooting days is reported to eventually have been tossed out—down an outhouse privy, after Owens's death, in 1919. In those days the guns would have been secondhand; only early collectors would have recognized their rarity and historical interest.

Colt Single Action Army .45 with which Pat Garrett killed Billy the Kid, July 14, 1881; serial number 55093. Gold badge a gift from A. J. Fountain to Garrett, in recognition of his killing the Kid; inscribed on back.

Lightning Colt revolver used by John Wesley Hardin in holdup of crap game at Gem Saloon, El Paso, May 1895. Hardin insisted he was being cheated by dealer, and took back only his gambling losses, $95. Revolver later confiscated by Deputy Sheriff Will J. TenEyck, and retained by his office. Hardin fined $25 for "carrying a pistol." Serial 73728; .41 caliber, nickel-plated.

Backstrap of this Colt Model Lightning revolver inscribed "J.B.M. to J.W.H.," a presentation to John Wesley Hardin (1895) from his cousin James B. Miller. An Elgin watch also presented by Miller to Hardin. Both were in appreciation of his assisting in prosecution by state of Texas of George "Bud" Frazer, for shooting at Miller. Miller would later ambush Frazer, killing him with a shotgun. Revolver, number 84304, in its El Paso–made holster.

Guns of hard characters from Texas. Single Action Army at *top* used by John Wesley Hardin, serial number 126680. Ivory-gripped Colt Lightning *below* also of Hardin; .41 caliber, number 68837. Winchester Model 1887 shotgun of George Scarborough, G.S. on right side, number 6595. A .45 Colt Single Action at *right* owned by John Selman; barrel cut off to 5 inches; number 36693. Selman was killer of Hardin. Single Action with pearl grips was cowboy-lawman-detective George Scarborough's, number 130272; Scarborough shot Selman in an El Paso alley, at 4:00 A.M. on Easter Sunday, 1896.

John Selman's Colt Single Action, number 141805, with which he killed John Wesley Hardin, at the Acme Saloon, El Paso, 1895. S&W .44 double action Frontier, number 352, carried by Hardin when shot. He was rolling dice at the time. Both revolvers documented in El Paso court records.

(*opposite*) Dead members of the Dalton Gang, after townspeople of Coffeyville, Kansas, thwarted double bank robbery attempt, October 1892. *Left to right*, Tim Evans, Bob and Grat Dalton, and Dick Broadwell. Emmett Dalton alone survived. Badly wounded, he served time in prison, and later moved to California, where he became involved in real estate and film business. Ten new Single Action Colts had been purchased by the gang before their ill-fated robbery attempt. Number 147305, one of the ten and pictured here, was recovered by Emmett and given to a friend in later years.

Surely the most famous shoot-out in the West was Tombstone's "Gunfight at the O.K. Corral," October 26, 1881—the culmination of bad blood between the peace officer, gambler, and gunfighter Earps and the Clantons and McLaurys, known rustlers and ranchers. Wyatt Earp, one of the more controversial of Western personalities, and his brothers Virgil and Morgan, accompanied by the tubercular dentist, gambler, and gunfighter "Doc" Holliday, squared off against the unruly Ike Clanton, his younger brother Billy, and Frank and Tom McLaury.

The parties met by Camillus S. Fly's boardinghouse and photographic gallery, in an open space on Frémont Street—not at the O.K. Corral. Facing off at a distance of about 6 to 8 feet, Wyatt barked: "You sons of bitches, you have been looking for a fight, and now you can have it."

In moments the fight broke out. Ike Clanton rushed to Wyatt and declared he was unarmed, to which Wyatt coolly replied: "The fight has now commenced; go to fighting, or get away." Ike ran off to safety.

In the space of about a half minute the McLaurys and Billy Clanton were mortally wounded, Virgil and Morgan Earp were both hit hard, and Doc Holliday was nicked in the hip.

Wyatt alone and the disappearing Ike Clanton were unscathed. A hearing exonerated the Earps, but in the aftermath Virgil was ambushed a few weeks later by a shotgun-wielding avenger, not far from the Oriental Saloon. He suffered crippling wounds. Morgan was murdered from behind in a billiard parlor the following year. In revenge of Morgan's death the surviving Earps saw to killing three men, one of them at the Tucson train station, while Morgan's body was being sent for burial to California.

A remarkable one-hour television recreation of the West's most famed gunfight was made by Wolper Productions for broadcast on national television, 1972. Entitled *The Showdown at O.K. Corral* and narrated by Lorne Greene, the documentary is played on Arizona TV on the annual anniversary of the gun battle.

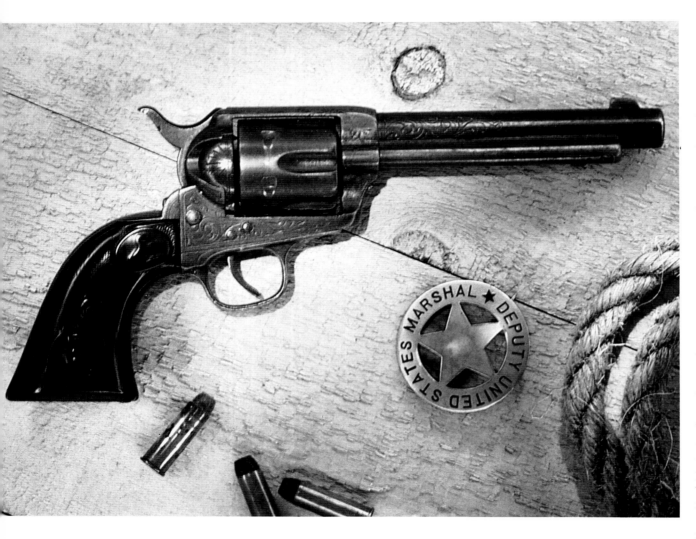

Because of the new guns, Emmett had left behind his old Single Action, number 83073, along with his deputy U.S. Marshal's badge, when the gang headed for Coffeyville. Bob, Grat, and Emmett had been deputy U.S. Marshals in the Oklahoma Territory, before turning outlaw, in 1890. In 1935 Emmett gave the revolver and badge, pictured here, to his best friend, cowboy fiction writer Chuck Martin. Back of badge marked LAMB SEAL & STENCIL C. WASH. D.C.

(*opposite*) Kid Curry's Colt Single Action, with which the notorious outlaw took his own life, 1904. Born Harvey Logan, in Iowa, the Kid was hotly pursued by the Pinkertons and others. Among his sidekicks in crime were Butch Cassidy and the Sundance Kid. Serial number 147144; .45 caliber.

The Gambler

The professional gambler was often also a gun-fighter, and sometimes a peace officer. Some were also outlaws. The *Topeka Daily Commonwealth* (August 1871) offered a generally accurate description: "His divet is principally Navy Plug [chewing tobacco] and whisky, and the occupation of his heart is gambling. . . . He generally wears a revolver on each side, which he will use with as little hesitation as a man as on a wild animal. Such a character is dangerous and desperate, and each one generally has killed his man."

His den of iniquity, the saloon or gambling tent, was a place of crackling action, fueled by the presence of alcohol and often of jaded women, and the forever present possibility of deadly differences over cards, a cheater exposed, or simply bad blood. The Alamo Saloon, Abilene, was described in the *Junction City Weekly Union* (October 1870): "Here in a well lighted room opening on the street the boys gather in crowds around the tables to play or to watch others play. . . . The musicians had to compete with clinking glasses, jangling spurs, ribald shouts, laughter, and the occasional bark of a six-shooter."

Unlike the saloons of Hollywood, these emporiums were generally not larger than 80 feet by 24 feet, with a single bar of about 20 feet. If present, toilet facilities would be at the back (sometimes patrons were expected simply to step outside). Chairs, tables, gambling equipment, a bar, liquor, and soiled doves invited the patrons to relax and have a good time. Many a saloon was in a separate part of town to keep the rowdy element away from the better class of citizens.

The men who plied their trade in these surroundings relied on guns to help maintain peace, and on local law enforcement. Many operators had their own armed guards and bouncers. Luke Short, a partner in the famed Long Branch in Dodge City, became embroiled in a political dispute (1883), which threatened to turn into a shooting war.

A local ordinance against prostitution was used as a pretext for a police raid of the Long Branch. Short and a

policeman shot at each other over the incident (no one was hit), and the feisty gambler was jailed. Released, he was told to stay out of town; instead he wired friends for help, among them Bat Masterson and Wyatt Earp. Dodge City's mayor feared for his life, and sought troops from the governor in defense. The impasse resulted in Luke's return to Dodge, and in celebration one of the West's most extraordinary group portraits was photographed, known as "The Dodge City Peace Commission."

Still another notorious saloonkeeper, gambler, and gunfighter was Rowdy Joe Lowe. In league with his wife (or companion) Kate, Lowe ran a succession of saloons and brothels in Kansas and Texas. In an 1873 gun battle in Wichita, Lowe fired a shotgun at rival saloonkeeper E. T. "Red" Beard, who had just shot a prostitute and had fired a shotgun blast at Joe. Rowdy Joe chased Beard down to a river and leveled his gun at him, causing mortal wounds. Lowe survived three shooting altercations, but succumbed to the fourth, shot by a former policeman, in Denver, 1899.

Outlaws

Folklore aside, outlaws of the West were generally rough and vicious men who chose stealing and killing as a way of life. The world-famed James and Younger Gang were celebrated in their own time. Jesse and Frank were veterans of Civil War guerrilla units and claimed to have entered the world of outlawry when poorly treated by the authorities at war's end.

Enjoying the notoriety of press reports of their exploits, Jesse and Frank visited a Kansas City reporter to give him a gold watch, which was refused, since the frightened journalist thought it stolen. "Heck no," said Jesse; "this'n we bought with our own money!" The journalist still refusing the watch, Jesse then asked, "Well, then perhaps you can name some man around here you want killed?"

Bristling with armaments, the gang finally was split up when an 1876 raid at Northfield, Minnesota, led to the wounding of the Youngers, Cole, Bob, and Jim, and

Rose of the Cimarron, a member of the Doolin Gang. Her revolver the large-framed Model 1878 double action Frontier Colt.

their jailing at Stillwater Penitentiary in Minnesota.

This attempted robbery was so widely reported that it was even covered by the *Times* of London! Bob would die in prison, while Jim committed suicide after being released in 1901. Cole joined his cousin Frank James; they lectured to the public, using their criminal careers as examples of wayward sinners, and organized a short-lived Wild West show.

Frank had surrendered to the governor of Missouri, soon after Jesse, for whom there was a $25,000 reward, was shot in the back by a cousin, Bob Ford, a traitorous henchman in league with the authorities.

Ford, known thereafter as "the dirty little coward who shot Mr. Howard"—Jesse's alias at the time of his death, 1882—spent the rest of his life taunted by the betrayal of the trusting Jesse. Ford himself was shot by an Ed Kelly, ten years later. And Kelly in turn was shot twelve years after that!

For years the James family displayed at fairs guns and accouterments used by members of the most famous of American outlaw gangs. Jesse's Remington Model 1875, serial 559, is a prized possession of the Gene Autry Western Heritage Museum, accompanied by holster, money and cartridge belt, and a buckskin vest in which he stashed his loot.

Equally renowned as a desperate outlaw was Billy the Kid, born Henry McCarty in the East (1859, possibly New York City's Irish slum). He was already in the Wild West by the time he was twelve. A succession of brushes with the law as a teenager led him ultimately, at age eighteen, to join the forces of English rancher John Tunstall, in Lincoln County, New Mexico.

The Lincoln County War was one of the hardest-fought of frontier wars. Gaining a reputation as a fun-loving but cool-nerved rustler, ladies' man, and killer, the Kid was pursued by New Mexico peace officers and his enemies in the Murphy faction of the war. After a failed attempt at amnesty, with Governor Lew Wallace (author of *Ben Hur*), the Kid was soon hunted down by the 6-foot-4-inch Sheriff Pat Garrett, an old friend.

Appointed sheriff in 1880, Garrett arrested the Kid

and four members of his gang just before Christmas. While in prison, sentenced to be hung, the Kid engineered one of the most daring escapes of any Western outlaw. While under escort to relieve himself, Billy slipped out of his handcuffs, knocked down the guard, J. W. Bell, and shot him. The Kid then grabbed the shotgun of Bob Olinger, a bully who had taunted Billy with that very gun, and awaited the deputy's return from a nearby restaurant.

Responding to the shot which killed Bell, Olinger ran to the jail, to be greeted by the Kid, with the welcome "Look up, old boy, and see what you get." With that Olinger was struck by the charges from both barrels, loaded with Olinger's own specially packed buckshot. The vengeful Kid smashed the shotgun and threw it at the hated Olinger's body: "Here's your gun, Goddamn you. You won't follow me with it any longer."

About an hour later a very relaxed Kid rode out of town, after greeting some of the cowed townsfolk, apologizing to the dead Bell, and nudging Olinger's body with his boot: "You are not going to round me up again." An eyewitness reported that the Kid had "at his command eight revolvers and six guns."

Some months later, on the night of July 14, 1881, Pat Garrett again caught up with the Kid, and shot him in a darkened room at the Pete Maxwell house, Sumner, New Mexico. The Kid knew that he was being followed, and was surprised in his pants, shoeless, but armed. Garrett saw the figure: "He must have then recognized me, for he went backward with a cat-like movement, and I jerked my gun and fired." Moving to the door and stepping outside, Garrett hugged the wall and gasped, "That was the Kid that came in there onto me, and I think I have got him."

Garrett, feted far and wide for killing the Kid, was not popular with admirers of the young and spunky outlaw. Guns and watches were presented to Garrett, and years later President Theodore Roosevelt appointed him a customs collector. But Garrett too died violently, in 1908, at the hands of a rival, believed to have been Jim "Killer" Miller. Garrett was shot from behind.

Lady bandit Pearl Hart, known to have used a Merwin & Hulbert .44 Pocket Army revolver (in Arizona Historical Society Museum), and here amply armed with Winchester Model 1873, Colt Single Action, and Model 1877 Lightning. Believed photographed following release from Yuma Territorial Prison, Arizona, after doing time for stagecoach robbery.

Though he was credited by folklore with twenty-one killings, the Kid's tally was likely not more than ten. Garrett's is estimated at more than a half-dozen.

Still another celebrated outlaw-gunfighter was Texan John Wesley Hardin. Despite the Methodist moniker, Hardin had killed a man at age fifteen, and had a total of twelve by the age of eighteen. He is even alleged to have shot a man through a boardinghouse wall, killing him for the annoyance of excessive snoring!

The Texas Rangers put him in jail from 1877 through 1894. On release he set up practice as a lawyer in El Paso, where policeman John Selman shot him from behind in the Acme Saloon.

Hardin's prowess with Colt Single Action revolvers was so respected on the frontier that he was asked to demonstrate his legerdemain by capturing peace officers—with empty revolvers, of course.

The balance of the Colt Single Action is ideally suited for spinning, flipping, switching hands, and other tricks. Although many of the nineteenth-century holsters were not suited for quick-draw and six-gun magic, that such gymnastics took place is fact.

In the matter of accuracy, the sights of revolvers, like the Colt Single Action, were not adjustable; they were a simple notch at the back of the frame top and a blade at the front. With practice, however, shots could be accurately placed at 25 to 50 yards. Most gunfights were at close range, often point-blank. The turn-of-the-century American revolver champion Walter Winans wrote:

> In my opinion revolver shooting is essentially a matter of firing rapidly at short ranges. Deliberate shooting at stationary targets, especially at long ranges, is all wrong. To begin with, the revolver is not accurate enough for such work. When a revolver is used, either in war or in self defense, the shooting is generally done at a few yards' distance, and at a rapidly moving object. Further, it often happens that a succession of shots has to be fired in a few seconds.

Wild Bill Hickok indeed summed it all up when he said: "Take time. I've known many a feller slip up for shootin' in a hurry."

Best-documented outlaw set known to the author, Black Jack Ketchum's .45 Colt Single Action even appears in photograph of the captured outlaw, bloodied from final gun battle. Collection was put together by deputy U.S. Marshal Frank W. Hall, who handled case which led to Ketchum's conviction and execution. Serial number 128145. In the outlaw's confession, he admitted to various crimes, among them some for which others had been imprisoned wrongfully. Just before the gallows were sprung, Ketchum, cool to the end, proclaimed: "I'll be in hell before you start breakfast boys."

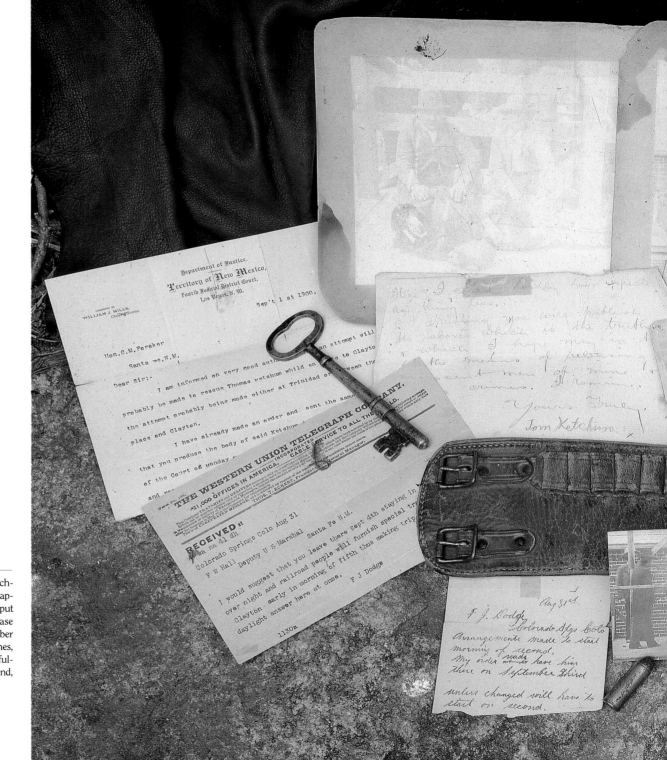

PEACE OFFICERS: BACKING UP THE BADGE

F rom the U.S. Marshals Service, established 1789, the Texas Rangers, established 1835, and sundry local, county, and state law enforcement agencies, the citizens of the West sought peace and security. But first they looked to self-reliance, and sometimes the Army or vigilantes. The West remained largely a lawless frontier after the Civil War era, except in commercial centers like St. Louis. Pockets of lawlessness prevailed even as late as the early twentieth century.

Rapid improvements in weaponry not only served to subdue the Indians, but as an assist in civilizing population centers and bringing about a sense of law and good behavior. It was the Texas Rangers who revived Samuel Colt's dreams as a gunmaker and inventor, by proving the reliability of his revolvers against the Comanches. In 1846, Samuel Walker of the U.S. Mounted Riflemen wrote to Colt requesting redesign of the Paterson revolver:

"The pistols which you made for the Texas Navy have been in use by the Rangers for three years, and I can say with confidence that it is the only good improvement that I have seen [in firearms]. The Texans who have learned their value by practical experience, their confidence in them is unbounded, so much so that they are willing to engage four times their number. In the Summer of 1844 Col. J. C. Hays with 15 men fought about 80 Camanche Indians, boldly attacking them upon their own ground, killing & wounding about half their number. . . . Several other Skirmishes have been equally satisfactory, and I can safely say that you deserve a large share of the credit for our success. Without your Pistols we would not have had the confidence to have undertaken such daring adventures. Was it necessary I could give you

Peace officer Colts, with lawman's "mug book," on copy of *Las Vegas* (New Mexico) *Optic* from period of Pat Garrett's shooting of Billy the Kid. Long-barreled Peacemaker inscribed on backstrap *Patricio Valencia, Santa Fe, 1876*, accompanied by holster and silver badge. The 4 3/4-inch revolver is fitted with patented Bridgeport swivel rig, preference of some professionals on both sides of law. In lawman parlance, a "Good Train Robber" was a dead one.

See page 198

many instances of the most satisfactory results. With improvements I think they can be rendered the most perfect weapon in the World for light mounted troops which is the only efficient troops that can be placed upon our extensive Frontier to keep the various war-like tribes of Indians & marauding Mexicans in subjection. The people throughout Texas are anxious to procure your pistols & I doubt not you would find sale for a large number at this time. . . ."

The result of the Colt and Walker collaboration was the 4-pound-9-ounce super gun, the Walker Model of 1847, fittingly engraved on the cylinder with a scene depicting Jack Hays's big fight.

Though not issued to the Rangers as a law enforcement agency, Colt firearms have remained the standard preferred by most Rangers since the Texas Paterson.

Much of the history of nineteenth-century law enforcement in the West has been punctuated by the bark of Colt revolvers and, from 1867 onward, Winchester rifles and ammunition. In 1844 an Englishman traveling in Texas alluded to the "primitive system of administering justice." Dealing with desperadoes

(opposite left) San Francisco Vigilante sword, truncheon, and watch with silver fob. Watercolor depicts thugs arrested by vigilante enforcers on San Francisco street.

(opposite, top right) Texas Paterson and its successor, the Walker Colt. Earliest known inscribed revolver from Samuel Colt was to Texas Ranger Major Ben McCulloch, and was Whitneyville-Hartford Dragoon. Inscription included date *Jan. 1, 1848* and motifs suggesting Ranger motto: "Free as the breeze, Swift as a mustang, Tough as a cactus."

(opposite, bottom right) Assortment of Western badges, ranging from Indian Police to U.S. and city marshals, city police, deputy sheriff, Texas State Ranger, and private police. In date from c. 1880 to c. 1910. Most were diestruck, and of plated brass. Smallest went on collar of U.S. Marshal.

Silver-mounted knives by Michael Price, one of San Francisco's most renowned cutlery craftsmen. News covered broad spectrum from dancing school to dancing on a rope.

Obvious favorites of these members of Company D, Texas Rangers, were Colt Single Actions and Winchester Model 1873 carbines; c. 1887. Second in *from left, back row*, Bass Outlaw, destined to be shot by John Selman in a gunfight. Care had to be taken not to accidentally put a .45 Colt cartridge into a .44-40 '73. Ranger George Lloyd had that problem against Indians, 1881, and "it jammed, catching him in a serious predicament. However, taking his knife from his pocket the fearless ranger coolly removed the screw that held the side plates of his Winchester together, took off the plates, removed the offending cartridge, replaced the plates, tightened up the screw, reloaded his gun, and began firing. It takes a man with iron nerve to do a thing like that, and you meet such a one but once in a lifetime" (James B. Gillet, *Six Years with the Texas Rangers, 1875–81*).

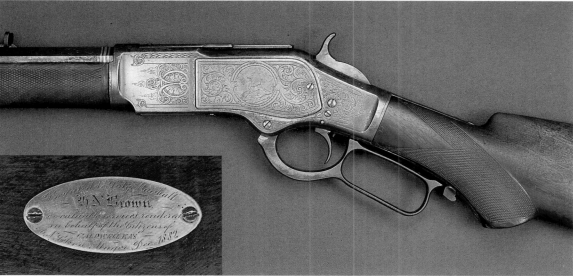

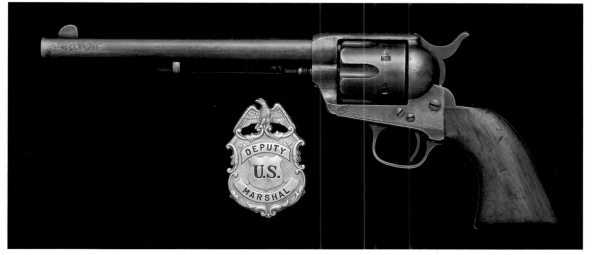

(*above*) Brown and gang of Medicine Lodge bank robbers captured by this posse; most armed with Model 1873 Winchesters. Now in Kansas State Historical Society collection, the town marshall–outlaw rifle is ranked by retired executive director Joseph Snell as one of two most outstanding treasures in the society's museum—the other is the locomotive *Cyrus K. Holliday!*

(*top right*) Presentation Model 1873 Winchester from citizens of Caldwell, Kansas, to City Marshal Brown, described in *Caldwell Post* of January 4, 1883: "A HANDSOME PRESENT. A few of the citizens of this city, appreciating the valuable services of Mr. Henry Brown, city marshal, concluded to present him with a suitable token of their esteem, and so settled upon an elegant gold-mounted and handsomely-engraved Winchester rifle, as an article especially useful to him and expressive of services rendered in the lawful execution of his duties. . . . On the stock of the gun is a handsome silver plate bearing the inscription [illustrated]. Henry is as proud of his gun as a boy of a new top." Brown's treasured rifle is believed involved in his shooting of Pawnee Indian Spotted Horse and of gambler Newt Boyce, and figured in bank robbery by Brown and three accomplices, in neighboring Medicine Lodge, Kansas, April 1884.

Colt .45 and badge of Clair Smith, of the U.S. Marshals. Revolver serial 66094. Intriguing letters sent by lawmen to Colt's ordering firearms include one from W. P. McFarland, U.S. Marshal's office, Austin, Texas, January 1881. He wanted a "single action pistol, .41 cal. but the same size & c, as the 45 cal. With ejector. Barrel 5 inches. Hind sight finer than that commonly made. Plated in the very heaviest manner possible, even if it costs extra. I want you to have blued, a stripe across the frame of the pistol about 1/2 of an inch wide, including the rear sight, and extending behind and below it. . . . Best Pearl handle. . . . And do not forget to fix the price as low as you . . . can, in consideration of my many orders to you, as well as my official position under the U.S."

meant joint action by an outraged citizenry. The San Francisco Vigilance Committee, established 1851, dealt with the criminal element summarily. In response to outrages like the failure of city authorities, outlaws were executed, and others escaped to an environment where they had less fear of reprisals.

The success of vigilantes in California inspired similar bodies in Nevada and Arizona and the Rockies, ranging from mob rule to organized and reasoned committees. Punishment for hardened criminals was swift and certain. The rope was a popular conclusion of many trials. The Squatters' Claim Association, Leavenworth, Kansas, had a committee of thirteen for protecting slaveholders. A vigilance committee was set up in Denver, as well as in other towns in Colorado. The Henry Plummer Gang of Montana, one of the most notorious outlaw operations in the history of the West, was finally wiped out by vigilantes. Though Plummer had operated under his cover of sheriff, in one month in 1864 no fewer than twenty-one outlaws were hanged.

After the Civil War, vigilance committees were active in Kansas, New Mexico, and Texas. As late as the mid-1870s, vigilantes administered justice in some communities. Following arrival of the Missouri, Kansas & Texas Railroad at Denison, the *Denison News* (1874) reported a "neck or two stretched" on outlaws convening there. Two years later, the *Dallas Herald* wrote of a

Topstrap and barrel rib of this .45 c.f. Bulldog revolver inscribed *MADE FOR W. A. PINKERTON BY THOS. M. TRANTER 16 WEAMAN ST. BIRMINGHAM.* Serial number 71. In 1868, Pinkerton and another detective had prisoner in tow, from Galveston, Texas, to Cheyenne. Prisoner leaped overboard from steamer, whereupon Pinkerton "began firing with considerable rapidity, so as to strike the water within a few feet of the man who was so unsuccessfully struggling against the tide . . . [Pinkerton] was provided with two magnificent English Tr[a]nter revolvers . . . and as he could use [them] with great precision he could easily have killed the man in the water . . . as [the prisoner] held up his hand and yelled—'I surrender!' the balls were cutting into the water all about him savagely, and the captain shouted, 'For God's sake, don't kill the man!'"

(*top left*) Gun control, Dodge City, Kansas, the 1880s. *Tombstone Nugget* (1881) editorialized: "The people who are anxious to assert their constitutional right to bear arms ought to do it openly. The revolutionary fathers, who put this into the bill of rights, did not go around with little pistols concealed in their hip pockets; they carried their rifles or muskets over their shoulders like men. If this be thought inconvenient in these undegenerate modern days, there is nothing to prevent the adoption of the old Texas plan of carrying a brace of pistols and a knife or two in the belt. . . . There are numerous ways of carrying arms that are much more picturesque than the hip-pocket plan. . . ."

(*bottom left*) Texas Rangers with Colts and Winchesters, at Amarillo, c.1890. Beginning about 1878 the .44-40 chambering of the 1873 was also available in Colt Single Action, allowing for using cartridge common to both.

(*above*) Hideaway shoulder holster with Smith's patent .32 backup revolver. Opera House police badge represents private security. Palm squeezer pistol is another hideaway. The Gem was a renowned El Paso saloon, site of considerable action over the years. Thomas E. Crawford, a.k.a. the Texas Kid, recalled from the 1880s at Jackson's Hole, Wyoming: "It was quite common among gunmen and sheriffs at that time to carry one pistol upside down in a scabbard under the arm, with the gun hanging by the front sight. There was no drawing to it. You simply reached under your coat, flipped out your pistol, and fired from your stomach. It was all very quickly done."

B. KITTREDGE & CO.,

THE AGENTS OF COLT'S ARMS COMPANY,

OFFER TO THE PUBLIC

SIX NEW MODEL COLT PISTOLS, FIVE POCKET PISTOLS

AND

THE PEACEMAKER.

THE PEACEMAKER.

This pistol, for efficiency, safety, simplicity, and lightness, is far in advance of any military pistol that has yet appeared. After an exhaustive trial in competition with all other pistols submitted (six in all) in 1873, it was adopted as the Cavalry pistol of the United States, on the recommendation of the Board of Officers who made the trials, and the whole of the Cavalry has since been armed with it.

Among seven different military pistols experimented upon at Spandau during the past year by the Prussian Government, the firing of this pistol was the best in all respects.

It is confidently recommended to officers of the Army and Navy, guides, hunters, and all who travel among dangerous communities, as the best weapon to carry on the person that has ever been produced.

EXTRACTS FROM ORDNANCE NOTES.—No. 5,

WASHINGTON, June 27, 1873.

REVOLVERS USING METALLIC AMMUNITION.

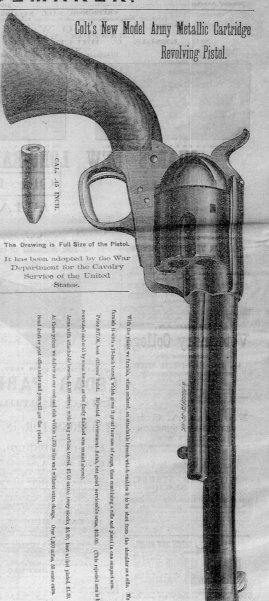

Colt's New Model Army Metallic Cartridge Revolving Pistol.

CAL. .45 INCH.

The Drawing is Full Size of the Pistol.

It has been adopted by the War Department for the Cavalry Service of the United States.

Virgil Earp .44 S&W New Model No. 3 revolver, number 14289. Displayed at the National Cowboy Hall of Fame and Western Heritage Center, Oklahoma City. Virgil survived leg wound at O. K. Corral and shotgun ambush in Tombstone; latter wounds left him with crippled and shortened arm, from which 4 inches of bone were removed.

Advertisement in which the newly popular Colt Single Action Army was touted as "The Peacemaker."

Smith & Wessons of frontier interest. *From left to right, top to bottom:* New Model Russian with scrimshawed ivory grips, 6 1/2-inch barrel, in .44 S&W Russian caliber; New Model No. 3, .44-40, with New York engraving and finishing; New Model No. 3 in half-nickel, engraved by Gustave Young; revolving rifle with shoulder stock, in .320 S&W rifle caliber, rare short barrel without forend (S&W equivalent of Colt Buntline Special); double-action Frontier in .38-40; and Model 1899 Military & Police, in .38 S&W Special.

Pair of Model 1877 Lightning Colts at *left* inscribed on backstrap H. C. LINDSAY/CHIEF/TOPEKA KAS. Numbers 82961 and 86967; .41 caliber. Lightning at right, number 23506, inscribed *Thomas Speers, Chief of Police, from The Force 1882*. Lindsay was a longtime friend of Wild Bill Hickok's.

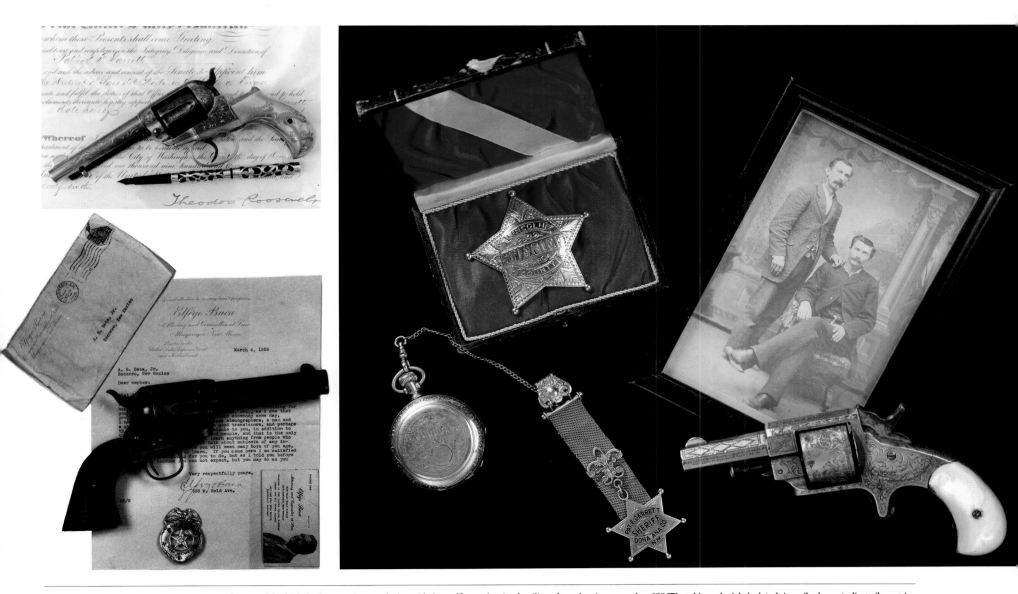

(*top left*) Still another 1877 double action Colt, a model which had a certain popularity with law officers, despite fragility of mechanism: number 138671, gold- and nickel-plated, inscribed on sterling-silver grips *Lincoln, Dona Ana, El Paso*, and on right grip *Customs Collector*. On backstrap: *Pat F. Garrett from his El Paso friends*. Garret's appointment rests beneath revolver, and the inscribed pen used by President Roosevelt in signing the document, 1902. (*bottom left*) Elfego Baca owned this Colt .45, number 272440. The gold badge presented him by the New Mexico Cattle Grower's Association, mounted with three rubies and a diamond, and inscribed with his name on back. As both attorney and peace officer, Baca had remarkable record. Single-handedly held off some eighty cowmen in thirty-three-hour seige, in which he killed four men and survived dynamite blast and estimated 4,000 bullets fired into his defensive position in adobe dwelling. Walt Disney film and TV series made based on his career. (*right*) Swamp Angel .41 rimfire number 4318, by Forehand & Wadsworth, inscribed on backstrap *Pat F. Garrett*. Other presentation items are gold badge back inscribed *To/Pat Garrett/with the best/Regards of/A. J. Fountain/1881/18K*, and watch. Recipient seated in photo, on right. Garrett had collection of firearms and watches, several received as gifts from admirers and friends.

"vigilance committee ... now astonishing the authorities ... by the off-hand way it does business."

By 1880 most communities could rely on local, state, or federal peace officers to keep the law, but occasionally matters were taken into the hands of citizens. And sometimes peace officers themselves turned bad. One of the worst cases in the West was that of Kansas cowtown marshal Henry Brown, a former Billy the Kid gang member gone straight. Not for long, however, since Brown used a presentation Winchester (from the citizens of Caldwell, Kansas) in an attempted bank holdup in nearby Medicine Lodge. Brown and his accomplices were captured. That night a lynch mob took over the jail. Brown attempted to escape and was shot dead. His sidekicks were lynched. Hours before his death, Brown wrote his wife a final letter, urging her to sell his property, but to "keep the Winchester."

There were also peace officers who might bend the law to their own wishes, such as Virgil Earp, when he appointed Wyatt and Morgan and their friend Doc Holliday as assistant city marshals, prior to the "Gunfight at the O.K. Corral." The line separating lawman from criminal was sometimes faint.

Frontier justice was administered with original style by such magistrates as Judge Roy Bean, billing himself as "Law West of the Pecos" and establishing his own fiefdom at the small rail town of Langtry, Texas. The Judge named the town after the mistress of Edward,

---

Finest peace officer badge known from West, the back inscribed PRE-SENTED/TO/Oliver C. Jackson/BY HIS FRIENDS AS A/TOKEN OF/THEIR ESTEEM AND/in recognition of his/Efficient services./SACRAMENTO.CAL/March 13th 1885." The miniature Lightning Colts in white gold, with rose-gold grips. See also dust jacket and endpaper.

Stevens 10-gauge double-barrel shotgun of Fred Dodge, Special Agent, Wells Fargo, number 927. Gun borrowed from Dodge by Wyatt Earp, and reportedly used in the killing of Curly Bill Brocius, 1882. Also believed used in shooting of outlaw Bill Doolin. Mug book used by Dodge and others; prepared for Wells Fargo. Gun featured in traveling Smithsonian Institution exhibition "America's Star: U.S. Marshals 1789–1989."

Sam Smith
Murderer & Train Robber

Tom Wind
Murderer & Train Robber

Lucius Burr
alias
Charley Elli
Murderer & Train

F. J. DODGE
SPECIAL OFFICER

Mexican mine guards, holsters carrying Model 1875 Remingtons; from scrapbook of mine operation. Mazatlán, Mexico, 1882.

Marlin lever-action rifle held by Deputy Sheriff C. H. Farnsworth, at *left*; Arizona Ranger W. K. Foster had Model 1895 Winchester. Both belts with double rows of cartridges, and holstered Colt Single Actions.

Prince of Wales (later King Edward VII), actress Lillie Langtry. Having been appointed a justice of the peace in 1882, Bean officiated from a shanty where iced beer was advertised along with "Notary Public" and "Justice of the Peace." Strapped to his side was an ivory- or pearl-handled six-shooter!

One Riot, One Ranger

"Courage is a man who keeps on coming on"—so stated one of the most courageous of all that special breed, the Texas Rangers. The man was Captain C. H.

McNelly, a post–Civil War Ranger as tough as any who ever served the force.

As an organization, the Rangers began to dole out frontier justice and deal with marauding Indians. They served Texas when it gained statehood and fought in the Mexican War. Many were on the side of the Confederacy in the Civil War, and following the war the Rangers were virtually nonexistent until 1874. A state police was established in 1870, but was a unit of oppression and murder, used by the governor for his own purposes. That force was disbanded in 1873. In the next

year the Rangers reemerged in a Frontier Battalion and a Special Force.

The Special Force was led by Civil War veteran C. H. McNelly. The Frontier Battalion was to deal with Indians in the West, while McNelly's Rangers were assigned to handle bandits and rustlers on the border with Mexico. From this revival emerged the most respected, revered, and celebrated of law enforcement organizations in the West. "One riot, one Ranger" sums up the often solitary modus of this always small but highly efficient band.

Sheriff of Anadarko, Oklahoma, and his deputies. Rack of arms and handcuffs at front even had shoulder-stocked Mauser automatic pistol! Early 1900s.

This lawman's holster carried a German Luger automatic pistol; c. 1900.

From the outlaw Sam Bass to John Wesley Hardin to Bonnie Parker and Clyde Barrow, the Rangers got their man (or woman).

A lesser-known force, but with its own history and traditions, was the Arizona Ranger. A tough cattleman, Captain Burton C. Mossman, led this select unit, which existed only from 1901 to 1909.

Private detective and police organizations also had a role in taming the frontier. Of these Pinkerton's is the best known, with a history dating back to Scotsman Allen Pinkerton, a bodyguard to President Abraham Lincoln. Under the motto "We Never Sleep," the agency made the James Gang and Butch Cassidy, the Sundance Kid, and the Wild Bunch targets for the hoosegow.

Armed for Justice

Six-gun dexterity under pressure was expected of the peace officer. Judging from photographs, the written word, and interviews, his armaments and accouterments were maintained in a ready state, some even tuned for smooth actions. Refinements might be cut-off triggerguards, tied-back triggers, hand-honed mechanisms, smoothly filed hammer knurlings, shortened barrels, and special holster or hideout rigs. When Wyatt Earp strolled down to the "O.K. Corral" showdown, his Prince Albert coat had a custom canvaslined and wax-rubbed pocket for his revolver. Wild Bill Hickok, as reported in the *Cheyenne Daily Leader* (July 1879), had "ivory handled revolvers . . . made expressly for him and . . . finished in a manner unequaled by any ever before manufactured in this or any other country. It is said that a bullet from them

never missed its mark. Remarkable stories are told of the dead shootist's skill with these guns."

Americans were fascinated with firearms, shooting matches were common throughout the country, and to a lawman (as to the gunfighter) the effectiveness of his gun was paramount. The bold men who administered the law had a wide following from the public—who were equally fascinated by the transgressors of the law (their guns too were occasionally tuned and altered like those noted above).

Whether or not guns were notched, for each man killed, is an often-asked question. Occasionally a nineteenth-century firearm is located with notched markings, but the writer has yet to see a historically associated handgun of a prominent lawman, gunfighter, or outlaw—known to have been a mankiller—boasting notches.

Occasionally notches are seen on hunting firearms, a more likely record of downed antlered or other game.* The common shooting of game in the nineteenth century, the high percentage of veterans of armed conflict with Mexicans, adversaries from the Civil War, and conflicts with Indians and fellow citizens meant there were a great many in the West who knew death intimately. So it was with famed lawman and gunfighter Bat Masterson, reminiscing in *Human Life* magazine, in a series published in 1907 (he also wrote a piece for the Savage firearms company, to help promote a new automatic pistol). Masterson had this to say about mankillers:

> I have been asked . . . to write something about the noted killers of men I am supposed to have personally known in the early days on the western frontier and who of their number I regarded as the most courageous and the most expert with the pistol. . . . I have known so many courageous men in that vast territory lying west and south-west of the Missouri River—men who would

---

* According to John M. Ryan, First Sergeant, M Company, 7th Cavalry, Captain Thomas French "had a Springfield rifle, caliber .50, breech-loader, and it was his custom, whenever he shot an Indian, to cut a notch on the stock of that gun." Ryan was present at the Little Bighorn, with Major Reno, and survived the battle.

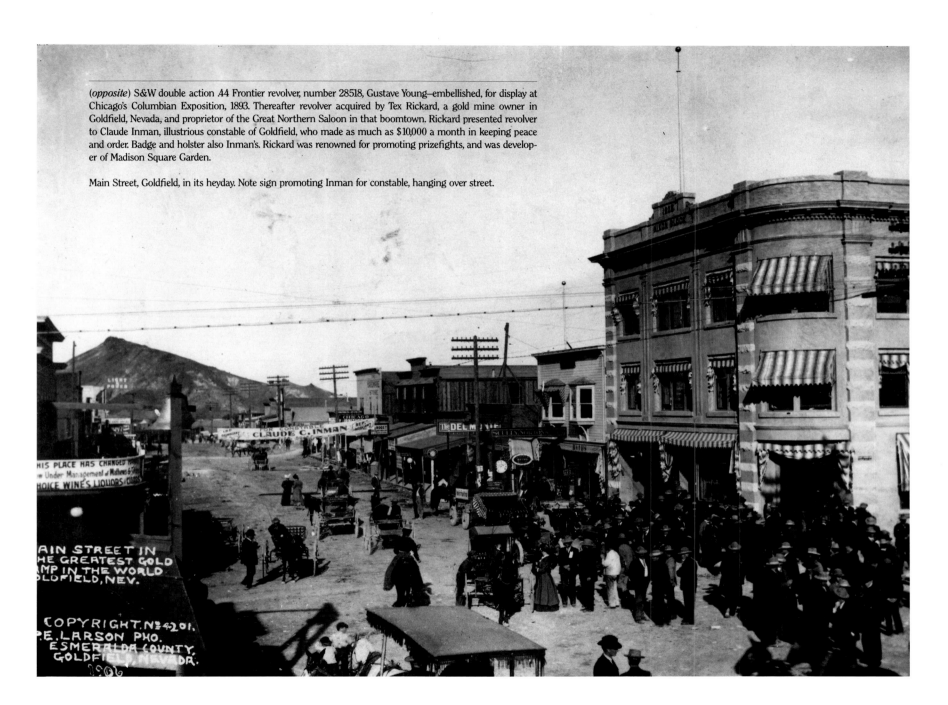

(*opposite*) S&W double action .44 Frontier revolver, number 28518, Gustave Young–embellished, for display at Chicago's Columbian Exposition, 1893. Thereafter revolver acquired by Tex Rickard, a gold mine owner in Goldfield, Nevada, and proprietor of the Great Northern Saloon in that boomtown. Rickard presented revolver to Claude Inman, illustrious constable of Goldfield, who made as much as $10,000 a month in keeping peace and order. Badge and holster also Inman's. Rickard was renowned for promoting prizefights, and was developer of Madison Square Garden.

Main Street, Goldfield, in its heyday. Note sign promoting Inman for constable, hanging over street.

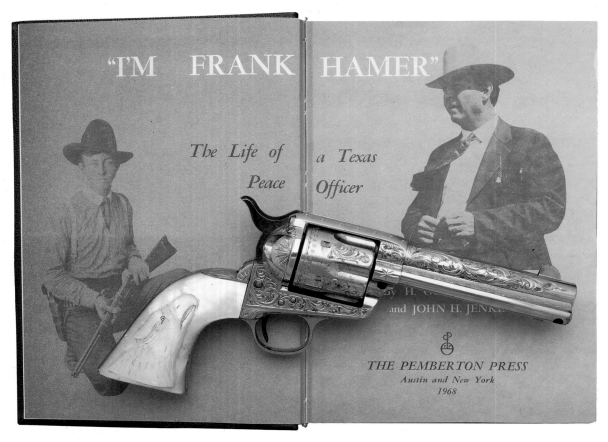

when called upon face death with utter indifference as to consequences, that it would be manifestly unjust for me even to attempt to draw a comparison.

Courage to step out and fight to the death with a pistol is but one of three qualities a man must possess in order to last very long in this hazardous business. A man may possess the greatest amount of courage possible and still be a pathetic failure as a "gun fighter," as men are often called in the West who have gained reputations as "man-killers." Courage is of little use to a man who essays to arbitrate a difference with the pistol if he is inexperienced in the use of the weapon he is going to use. Then again he may possess both courage and experience and still fail if he lacks deliberation.

Any man who does not possess courage, proficiency in the use of fire-arms, and deliberation had better make up his mind at the beginning to settle his personal differences in some other manner than by an appeal to the pistol. I have known men in the West whose courage could not be questioned and whose expertness with the pistol was simply marvelous, who fell easy victims before men who added deliberation to the other two qualities. . . .

Masterson went on to single out Wyatt Earp, Doc Holliday, Bill Tilghman, Luke Short, Rowdy Joe Lowe, and Ben Thompson as men who "would not have hesitated a moment to put up [their lives] as the stake to be played for."

Advice for the Western lawman based on experience was offered by General David J. Cook, who headed a private organization termed the Rocky Mountain Detective Association. His book *Hands Up; or, Twenty Years of Detective Life in the Mountains and on the Plains* presented five rules of survival. His opinion of the criminal element reflected a decided cynicism:

I. Never hit a prisoner over the head with your pistol, because you may afterwards want to use your weapon and find it disabled. Criminals often conceal weapons and sometimes draw one when they are supposed to have been disarmed.

II. Never attempt to make an arrest without being sure of your authority. Either have a warrant or satisfy yourself thoroughly that the man whom you seek to arrest has committed an offense.

III. When you attempt to make an arrest, be on your guard. Give your man no opportunity to draw a pistol. If the man is supposed to be a desperado, have your pistol in your hand or be ready to draw when you make yourself known. If he makes no resistance, there will be no harm done by your precaution. My motto has always been, "It is better to kill two men than to allow one to kill you."

A deluxe Colt belonging to Frank Hamer, the Ranger who tracked down Clyde Barrow and Bonnie Parker, and whose career began in 1906, at age twenty-two. He was trained by old-time Rangers like Captain John R. Hughes, and writer Walter Prescott Webb said of him: "If all criminals in Texas were asked to name the man that they would most dread to have on their trail, they would probably name Captain Frank Hamer without hesitation." Serial number 180260; gun owned and used by William H. Ford, in fatal shooting of a Dolph White, and eventually became Hamer's. Hamer documents with revolver state: "This weapon has been carried by me for a number of years while in the services as a peace officer." Another Single Action of the stalwart lawman was his favorite, "Old Lucky."

(*opposite*) Colts of modern-day lawmen. At *bottom*, Tom Threepersons' Single Action, fine-tuned and with special front sight; badge made from silver dollar. Holster design, worked out between the lawman and El Paso saddlemaker Sam Myers, named after Threepersons. The .45 Automatic was made by factory for Texas Ranger Manuel T. "Lone Wolf" Gonzaullas.

Well-known Border Patrol officer, crack shot, and contemporary gunfighter Colonel Charles Askins carried this modified .38 Colt in many skirmishes on the Mexican border. An escaped convict and a German sniper in World War II were downed with gun. Askins's weapon of choice on the border was a specially modified semiauto shotgun with nine-shot magazine. Candid autobiography carries unusual title *Unrepentent Sinner*.

Salute by Colt company to peace officers, *Tex and His Horse Patches* was painted by Frank E. Schoonover and issued by Colt's as poster, c. 1926. Some published with Spanish logo, some with Colt's logo, and some (as here) void of any company identification, except for an accompanying letter reprinted from artist.

IV. After your prisoner is arrested and disarmed, treat him as a prisoner should be treated—as kindly as his conduct will permit. You will find that if you do not protect your prisoners when they are in your possession, those whom you afterwards attempt to arrest will resist you more fiercely, and if they think they will be badly dealt with after arrest, will be inclined to sell their lives as dearly as possible.

V. Never trust much to the honor of prisoners. Give them no liberties which might endanger your own safety or afford them an opportunity to escape. Nine out of ten of them have no honor.

The lawman of the nineteenth century generally could count on help from townsfolk, when needed. Town reaction to the Dalton raid on Coffeyville, Kansas, and the James and Younger Gang assault on Northfield showed the support locals gave to their lawmen. Presentation firearms to nineteenth-century Western peace officers are also indications. What more fitting thank-you than a gun or a watch? Pat Garrett received both for ridding New Mexico of the menacing outlaw Billy the Kid.

The presence of guns in cities and towns and ranches, and on the persons of many a citizen, was a clear message to the lawless element that they could expect lead in return, should they get out of line. Some localities passed ordinances for controlling guns, such as those in Kansas cowtowns like Dodge City (1873). The *Abilene Chronicle* (June 1871) editorialized on controlling firearms:

Fire Arms. —The Chief of Police [then the renowned Wild Bill Hickok] has posted up printed notices, informing all persons that the ordinance against carrying fire arms or other weapons in Abilene, will be enforced. That's right. There's no bravery in carrying revolvers in a civilized community. Such a practice is well enough and perhaps necessary when among Indians or other barbarians, but among white people it ought to be discontinued.

The result was some checking of arms, largely by trail-driving cowboys. But smaller weapons were easy to hide, and the Texans were uncomfortable unarmed. Law officers would wear their guns openly, a warning and an indication of backing up the badge. The location of the tougher element in the trail towns was often in a "boys' town" section, meaning shootings would affect those who were in the rough part of a community. Statistics show too that numbers of homicides were less than one might expect; only forty-five men died of violent ends in the Kansas cowtowns of Abilene, Caldwell, Dodge city, Ellsworth, and Wichita from 1870–1885. The majority of these were cowboys and gamblers; their killers were most often local lawmen.

Lawlessness in the West did not stop with the civilization evident in modern towns and cities of the twentieth century. The ugly cancer of drugs and its smuggling over U.S. borders with Mexico have given a new lease on violence in the West. Most modern lawmen have traded their six-shooters for multishot automatic pistols, and horses have largely been replaced by four-wheel-drive vehicles, aided by radio contact, and the wizardry of electronic faxes and police computer networks. But the makeup of the tried and true lawmen is the same:

I will give you a description of the Texas Rangers, as they were at that time. In the first place he wants a good horse, strong saddle, double girted, a good carbine, pistol, and plenty of ammunition. He generally wears rough clothing, either buckskin or strong, durable cloth, and generally a broad-brimmed hat, on the Mexican style, thick overshirt, top boots and spurs, and a jacket or short coat, so that he can use himself with ease in the saddle.

A genuine Texas Ranger will endure cold, hunger and fatigue, almost without a murmur, and will stand by a friend and comrade in the hour of danger, and divide anything he has got, from a blanket to his last crumb of tobacco...he is not so bad after all. He generally settles down into a quiet, sober citizen.[*]

---

[*] A. J. Sowell, *Rangers and Pioneers of Texas* (San Antonio: Shepard Brothers, 1884).

COWBOYS AND RANCHERS: "SHOOTING IRONS"

Cattle and horses were introduced to the New World by the Spanish explorers. The American cowboy evolved as a mirror of the Mexican *vaqueros* of Texas, whom the pioneers first saw in the 1820s. As Texas became Americanized, the cowboys took over the cattle herds, estimated at 100,000 head by 1830.

Ranging grew as a Texas industry, and with the introduction of cattle drives, the cowboy and rancher grew to national prominence. Getting cattle to the market meant young men under the guidance of more experienced foremen, working the cattle north in the drive season, from May to September.

The drives were at their peak from 1867 to the mid-1880s, from Texas to the Kansas railheads. A herd of longhorn cattle could run 1,000 to 2,000 head, supervised by only a half-dozen to a dozen cowboys. Stampedes, river crossings, rustlers, hostile Indians, and rattlesnakes were among the obstacles the drovers had to face. One in seven of the cowboys was black, an equal proportion Mexican, and there was a contingency of British, as well as Europeans, and Americans from the East, and—the largest group—native Westerners.

It was a tough and hardy life, but offered an appeal that was both romantic and adventurous. Cowboys captured the imagination, although for decades their image back East was of uncouth roughnecks and rowdies. Soldier and ex-Westerner Richard Irving Dodge painted a picture from firsthand observation (1882, when the image was undergoing some degree of national improvement):

Frontier leather, c. 1850s to 1880s. Saddle bag and holster combination by Main & Winchester, San Francisco, established 1849. California "slim Jim" style at *left*, with matching belt, made for 1851 Navy and dating from 1850s; considered earliest style of true Western holster; note lack of cartridge loops in belt. Other three Mexican-style "loop" holsters, made from single piece of leather (*top left and center*) or with riveted loops (*right*); the pouch holding handgun fits through loops. Bridgeport gun rig at *top* patented January 1882, required special extended hammer screw on revolver. Rig at *right* was Buffalo Bill Cody's; inscription on silver disk.

Cowgirl, amply armed with Bisley Colt and a double action revolver, an unlikely combination, and possibly supplied for photograph.

207

Vaquero high-quality gear, the Colt First Model Dragoon silver-inlaid and engraved; on barrel "Por/Salda Rabia/Amozoc." Mexican silver-and-steel Bowie knife belonged to Ignacio Zaragoza, hero of Battle of Puebla, May 1862. Spurs with complicated pierced rowels, silver-inlaid, straps sewn with silver and gold thread, c. 1850s; for owner of the spread.

(*opposite*) Representing early and late *vaquero* arms, for well-to-do rancher: cased pair of Model 1860 Army Colts, ivory grips carved with Mexican eagle, to wear in holsters left and right. Model 1890 Remingtons have monogrammed holsters and monogrammed mother-of-pearl grips. Massive Mexican eagles on bridle bits.

For fidelity to duty, for promptness and vigor of action, for resources in difficulty, and unshaken courage in danger, the cowboy has no superior among men. But there is something in this peculiar life which develops not only the highest virtues, but the most ignoble of vices. It is not solitude, for the shepherds of the Plains lead lives quite as solitary, and they are generally quiet, inoffensive persons. The cow-boy, on the contrary, is usually the most reckless of all the reckless desperadoes developed on the frontier. Disregarding equally the rights and lives of others, and utterly reckless of his own life; always ready with his weapons and spoiling for a fight, he is the terror of all who come near him, his visits to the frontier towns of Kansas and Nebraska being regarded as a calamity second only to a western tornado. His idea of enjoyment is to fill himself full of bad whiskey, mount his mustang, tear through the streets, whooping, yelling, flourishing and firing his pistols until the streets are deserted and every house closed, then with a grim smile of happiness he dashes off to his comrades to excite their envy by graphic pictures of his own exploits and the terror of the timid townspeople.

Firearms were necessary on the trails for defense against Indians or the occasional cattle rustler, to kill a rattlesnake or an injured horse or steer, and for self-defense when in the cattle towns. The towns, at the end of the drive, presented temptations hard for the bedraggled cowpuncher to resist. Abilene in the spring of 1871 would count about 500 people; but by summer it would harbor some 7,000! It was a cowboy's dream:

[T]he greater number [of transients slept] under blankets spread upon the prairie. As to drink, there was probably more whiskey drank than water, and of quality that would make rabbits fight a bull dog. On the first of June, 1871, the fiery furnace of the Abilene Texas cattle trade was in full blast; it was red hot, everything sizzled. On the southwest corner of First and Cedar Streets was Jake Karatofsky's General Merchandise Store. Whiskey included in the "General" department. From this corner to the southeast corner of Mulberry and First was a solid wall of saloons, gambling houses and other [dens] of perdition. From the northeast corner of First and Cedar around to the Gulf House . . . was also a solid row of gambling dens and saloons. These dens were run 24 hours of the day and 30 and 31 days of the month and fresh relays of victims always ready to take the places of those who had lost their last penny at the wheel of fortune, or rather misfortune, and they who were lying dead drunk on the floor or sidewalk. Brass bands, string bands, piano, vocal music were installed inside and at the doors of these places to attract the passer-by and retain the sucker already in the toils, and too, the "Soiled Dove"

was there; bedizzened in her gaudy dress, cheap jewelry and high colored cosmetics, and then the Devil himself were there night and day. Talk about "Hell down below." Why, Abilene was a [seething], roaring, flaming Hell.

Thousands and tens of thousands were staked and lost and won at these gaming tables. One Texas cattle man lost $30,000 at one sitting. I have seen a hatful of gold lying loose in a pile on these tables. Some body steal it? you ask. He would have been bored full of bullets in the twinkling of an eye.[*]

In this environment cowboys and ranchers were supposed to surrender their guns, to avoid shooting confrontations. Sometimes a coin check would be traded for the hardware, to be retrieved on leaving town. Concealed weapons often were snuck into town, and sometimes were brought into play when tempers flared or drinking and carousing got out of hand.

Controlling the lawless drew editorial comment in the local press. A Wichita report (August 1873) decried the serious pounding a visiting cowboy received from local police:

If however, there is any other way in the world to persuade infractors of the city laws to desist, aside from beating them over the head with a revolver, we insist that it should be resorted to, and the knock down business only used in self preservation. It is strange with the reputation our police have far and near, for reckless daring, grit and determination to duty, even at the sacrifice of life, and that anyone should attempt to infringe the law before them, after being told to desist, unless it is done to try their mantle.

[*]Theophilus Little, "Early Days of Abilene and Dickinson County," in Adolph Roenigk, *Pioneer History of Kansas*.

(*top*) Model 1866 Winchester carbine, made for the Mexican market; gold- and nickel-plated. Number 107801. Engraving attributed to L. D. Nimschke, who had a strong Mexican and South American following.

(*bottom left*) Elegantly attired Mexican hacienda owner, 1860 Army Colt in holster.

(*bottom right*) Two Mexican friends, c. 1870s. Colt Army conversion in bikini holster; dangerously positioned (though common in Mexico at the period) for quick draw!

"Albert Edward Meredith, out West, in Montana," marked on back of this cabinet photograph. Rifle a Henry; in belt what appears to be a British bulldog revolver. Sometimes photographers supplied props, possibly the case here. Chaps of "shotgun" style, since of double-barrel shape; fringed edging copied from Indians.

Heavily armed Sawtell Ranch, Idaho, 1872, had wide complement of frontier firearms: Colt 1851 and 1860 revolvers, Remington New Model Army, Sharps and Spencer carbines, Springfield rifles, and much, much more.

(*top left*) These Arizona cowboys carried their handguns tucked into belts, possibly supplied by photographer Fly. Huge rowel spurs at *lower right* reveal Mexican influence.

(*top right*) Carbon County, Montana, ranch house. Interesting double rifle with fixed bayonet in hands of figure at *right*, his boot with Bowie knife, and hip with revolver.

(*bottom left*) From the 1880s, the "Cowboy" marked "No 6," and thus part of a series. By Cheyenne photographer, C. D. Kirkland.

(*bottom right*) L. A. Huffman's Montana prairie scene, *The Night Hawk in His Nest*. The double-loop holster held a Colt Single Action, with steerhead-carved ivory grips. According to James H. Cook's *Fifty Years on the Old Frontier*, when on cattle drives "[e]veryone went armed with a heavy revolver and a knife. But few carried rifles. One reason for this was that the added weight on one side of a horse, on those long, hard trips, was a great cause of saddle galls—something to be strictly guarded against on an eighteen-hundred-mile drive. . . . Constant practice with both knife and pistol made some of the boys very expert with these weapons."

(*opposite*) At *right*, an icon of American gunmaking, serial number 1 from production run of Colt Single Action Armys. Found by a collector in the 1930s, and acquired for sum of $4. Companion the earliest-known engraved Peacemaker, number 114; decorated by Nimschke. Both revolvers reproduced in miniature by the U.S. Historical Society, Richmond, Virginia, in special collectors' limited editions authorized by Colt company.

An advantage of cowtown lawmen was the experience of many, who were skilled shots, well armed, and cool under duress. Wyatt Earp, Wild Bill Hickok, and Bat Masterson, whose reputations were fine-tuned in rough-and-ready Kansas, were three of these men.

Carrying of firearms was common, as recalled by a cowboy with Wyoming's M-Bar Ranch (1890s):

We all carried guns. I remember that each of the six men had guns almost exactly alike. We all preferred the Colt single-action six-shooter. Some liked the Bisley model, others the Frontier model. Some were of different caliber, but all were built on a .45-caliber frame. I noticed that these men carried their guns with one empty shell in the cylinder, and five loaded cartridges. This was for safety's sake. The gun was carried with the hammer on the empty shell. . . .

Another wrote: "Guns were as natural a part of a cowhand's equipment as, say, a jackknife is of a boy's pocket kit, and only a few didn't carry them. . . ."

Cowboys as Pistol Shots

Just how competent were cowboys as pistol shots? That was the theme of an article by "A Bronco-Buster," in *The Rifle* magazine, April 1888:

To pull a .22 or .32 calibre on a person, the chances are that he would pay little attention to it. . . . If you want a man to respect you, draw a .45 on him. Some of the boys can handle a revolver with much accuracy. . . .

A cowboy's pride is to draw a revolver and turn contents loose in the shortest possible time, and yet make an effective shot. There are many tricks in handling a six-shooter. One is to have muzzle of the revolver pointed towards yourself; revolver being held upside down. Should a person get the drop on you and demand your gun, by making a pretence to give it to him, he little suspects that, by giving the pistol a sudden twirl on your forefinger, the barrel is instantly reversed and contents discharged. . . .

Most of our shooting is done at short range, both when afoot and on horseback. . . . One of the most difficult feats is to ride a "cayuse" on a gallop, making several circles around a telegraph pole, and endeavoring to make a ring of bullet-holes around same. . . .

I have often heard the question asked of people from the East, why it is that a cowboy prefers a single-action revolver to a double-action, or a self-cocking one. There are several reasons. One is, when discharging the self-cocking pistol it requires ten

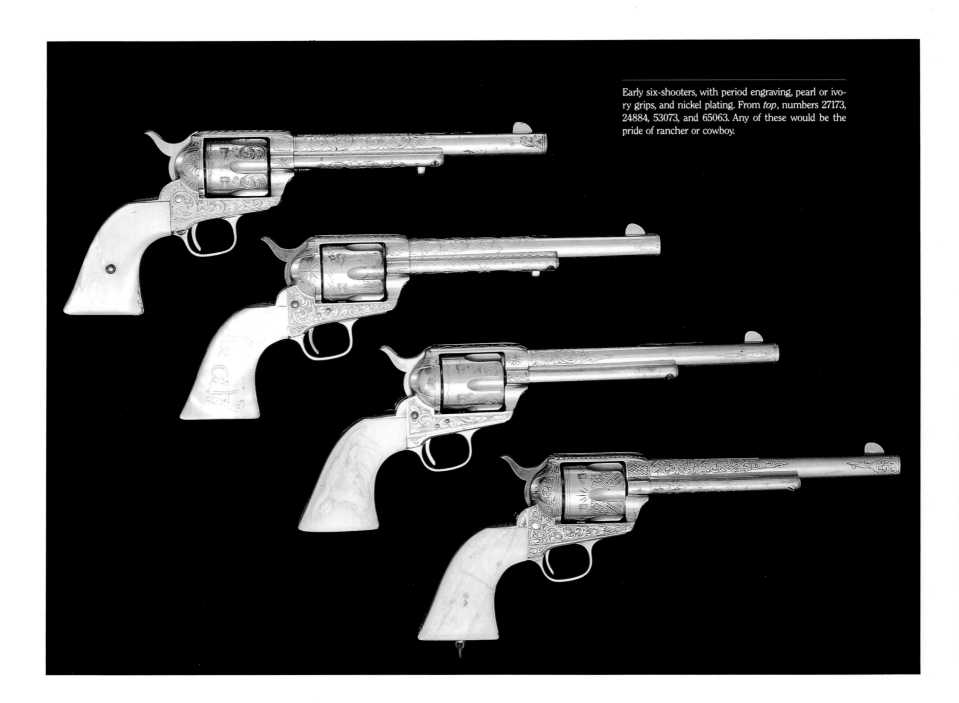

Early six-shooters, with period engraving, pearl or ivory grips, and nickel plating. From *top*, numbers 27173, 24884, 53073, and 65063. Any of these would be the pride of rancher or cowboy.

pounds or more pressure on the trigger; your aim is thus rendered uncertain. Most people who are familiar with revolvers imagine that a double-action pistol in the hands of an expert can be discharged much the quicker. It is done by fastening the trigger back to guard. The hammer is then raised by the thumb, and instantly released. By this method the trigger is not obliged to be pulled. Another way is what we call "fanning" the pistol. . . . Oh! there are lots to learn by you people in the East who think you know how to handle a six-shooter. If you doubt my word, make a trip out West, visit a Vaqueros camp, and if you have got the "sand," you will soon know all.

Until the barbed-wiring of the West began in earnest in the 1880s, the range remained open and free. Then range wars* became part of the Western saga. The two best-known were the Lincoln County War (New Mexico, 1877–78) and the Johnson County War (Wyoming, 1889–93). These disputes saw some of the bloodiest gun battles in the West.

"The Regulators"

The most extraordinary shoot-out of the Lincoln County War pitted the McSween and Chisum faction (including Billy the Kid and cohorts, the "Regulators") against that of Major L. G. Murphy. The root cause was a struggle for economic power. A five-day gunfight took place in Lincoln, starting on July 15, 1878. A posse

---

*Some "range wars" were actually mercantile wars, as was that of Lincoln County, fought over supply contracts with the army and the nearby Apache reservation.

Black cowboy, in "wooly chaps," of angora fur; gave extra warmth in colder areas of West, such as Montana, Wyoming, Idaho, and into Canada. Though prejudice and conflict existed, friction was more likely to be between white and Mexican cowboys than between white and black.

(*top right*) Two cowboys horsing around with their Colts. Holsters of Mexican loop style; cowboy on *right* preferred cross-draw.

(*bottom right*) Quiet game of cards on the ranch, c. 1895. Model 1892 Winchester carbine held by heavy drinker at *right*.

Figure at right held Sharps-Borchardt sporting rifle; his holster carried a Merwin & Hulbert, which featured a twist mechanism for automatic ejection of all cartridges at once.

Big Sandy, Montana, cowboys, early 1890s. Note gauntlets or cuffs, shotgun chaps with fringes, and shoulder holster stuffed with Model 1878 Colt double action revolver.

Elaborate credit line to frontier photographer, who captured two men armed with Remington single actions and Remington-Keene bolt-action rifles, c. 1890s.

sprayed the home of McSween with rifle fire. The Kid and a party of twelve ran from a nearby store, guns blazing, and entered the McSween house to even the odds. Other McSween supporters were in two nearby stores and an adjacent house.

Positioned against the McSween force of about sixty men were forty supporters of Major Murphy, led by Sheriff George Peppin.

For the next three days, sporadic firing took place, with one of the Regulators in the McSween house killed. A second Regulator was wounded.

On the 16th, shots nearly hit a cavalryman who was coming to advise Peppin that Colonel Nathan A. M. Dudley would not let him borrow a howitzer! The Regulators shot a Murphy man, at a tremendous distance, with a Sharps .45-120 rifle. To the rescue came three soldiers, and a doctor—and the Regulators fired on them as well.

Finally on the fifth day, Colonel Dudley openly took sides, though under orders to remain neutral, and ordered his men into position against the McSween faction. The Colonel, on horseback, led four mounted officers and eleven black cavalrymen, followed by a twelve-pound mountain howitzer and a Gatling gun, to force the McSweens into submission.

Dudley made a show of claiming to be defending women and children rather than taking sides. McSween men abandoned the two stores and adjacent house and took to the hills after Dudley trained his howitzer in their direction. Thus with his force reduced to about twenty, McSween was at a distinct disadvantage.

Peppin's men moved in closer to the McSween house and started breaking open shutters, smashing windows, and pushing over a brick barricade. When a Peppin deputy shouted to McSween that they had warrants for his arrest, McSween refused to surrender, saying he had warrants to arrest the Peppin posse. In answer to the deputy's demand to see the warrants, one of the Regulators yelled "Our warrants are in our guns, you c——k-s——g sons-of-bitches."

Chuck-wagon time had guns at the ready. New Mexico, c. 1885–90.

Sporadic gunfire continued, and a fire set near the back of the house failed to spread, finally going out. Another fire was started at the McSween stable and spread to the house.

Mrs. McSween described the scene, before she left around 5:00 P.M. to reach safety in the nearby Tunstall store, having been preceded by another woman and her children:

The boys talked to each other and McSween and I were sitting in one corner. The boys decided I should leave. They were fighting the fire in my sister's house [a wing of the same building]. McSween said he guessed that was better. . . . The Kid was lively and McSween was sad. McSween sat with his head down, and the Kid shook him and told him to get up; that they were going to make a break.

By nightfall, the Regulators had gathered together in the kitchen. Gunfire increased, and the only route of escape was out the back door, through a yard and a gate, then a vacant lot near the Tunstall store, and into woods by a river. Peppin possemen were waiting near the kitchen door. The Regulators made their way out

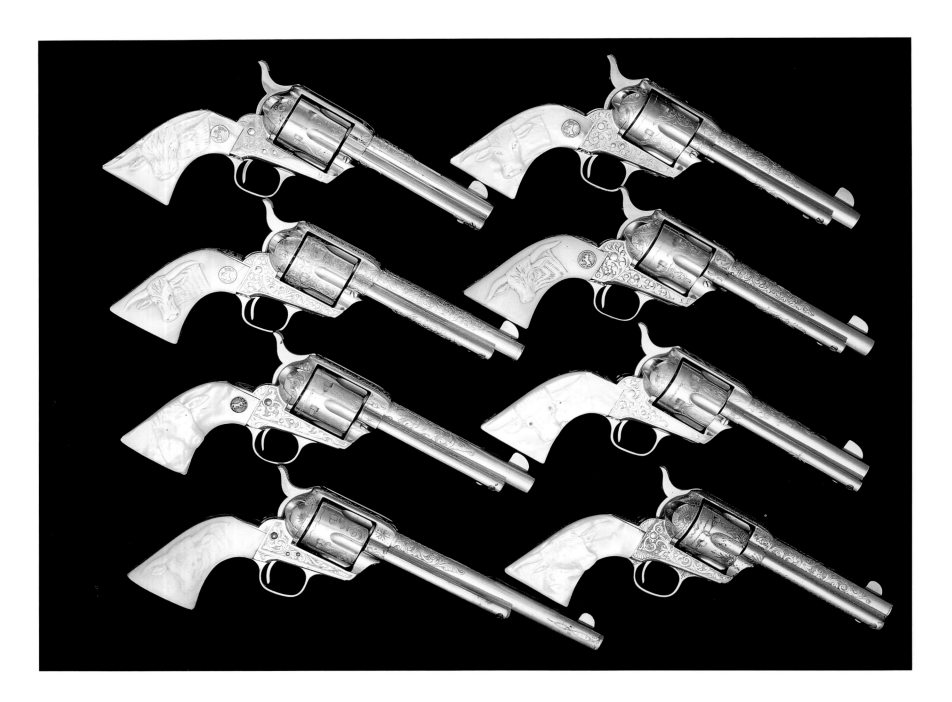

Billy the Kid, photographed in Sumner, New Mexico, c. 1879–80. An eyewitness described the young outlaw (1878): "He was supposed to be about eighteen, but looked older when you saw him closely. He was sunburned and not much to look at. . . . There were scores just like him all up and down the Pecos. Everything he had on would not have sold for five dollars—an old black slouch hat; worn-out pants and boots, spurs, shirt, and vest; a black cotton handkerchief tied loosely around his neck, the ever-ready Colt double-action .41 pistol around him and in easy reach; [and] an old style .44 rimfire brass-jawed Winchester. . . . He had a pair of gray-blue eyes that never stopped looking around." By date of this photo, the Kid was sporting a Single Action Colt and a Model 1873 Winchester. Tintype produced reversed image, and thus the Kid was wearing his Colt on right hip, showing he was right-handed.

Surpassing factory-embellished Single Actions in rarity are specials modified by frontier gunmakers or by New York dealers. Of the former, the Freund Armory of Wyoming and Colorado excelled. Pictured is the finest-known Freund custom Colt, number 83639, with faceted and engraved hammer, coin-silver front sight, game-scene-and-scroll-engraved, engraved pearl grips, inscribed on topstrap *FREUNDS ARMORY/ CHEYENNE WYO.*, and gold- and silver-plated.

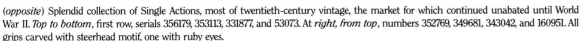

(*opposite*) Splendid collection of Single Actions, most of twentieth-century vintage, the market for which continued unabated until World War II. *Top to bottom*, first row, serials 356179, 353113, 331877, and 53073. At *right, from top*, numbers 352769, 349681, 343042, and 160951. All grips carved with steerhead motif, one with ruby eyes.

the door, and when they were into the open the flames revealed them to the posse. The gunfire became a staccato, but miraculously four of five escaped unhurt—including Billy the Kid.

The worsening fire forced McSween, still in the house with several men, to call out, "I shall surrender." Four of Peppin's men were approaching the kitchen door when suddenly McSween shouted, "I shall never surrender."

The shooting then started again. What took place was termed by a participant "the big killing"—at point-blank range, McSween and two of his henchmen were killed in a matter of seconds. Four McSween Regulators escaped, one badly wounded. One of the Peppin men died, shot through the eye.

The Kid and the rest of the Regulators had escaped, one of them claiming, "We have got out of something worse than this."

The five-day battle was the toughest shooting fray yet for Billy the Kid, and proved his coolness under fire. It was the kind of pluck and courage that would soon make him one of the most famous of Western cowboy-rustler-gunfighter-outlaws.

Nate Champion Standing Fast

The Johnson County War pitted cattle barons

Classic trail drive cowboy of 1880s might depart Texas with copy of Loving trail manual. Inside, a guide to brands and full-page ads from merchants in Kansas and Texas. R. E. Rice, Dodge City, took ad to extol virtues of his handmade saddles, gun belts, and other equipment. Belt and holster pictured typical of those by Rice, c. 1881–84. Frontier six-shooter, number 53125, too expensive for most cowboys, especially considering costs for cool drinks, square meal, and female companionship at end of the trail.

(*top right*) The Bar C roundup wagon, c. 1884. Second *from right*, standing, the heroic Nate Champion.

(*bottom right*) Still-life photograph by Roosevelt, of his Elkhorn ranch house, c. 1885. Against the large elk rack at center was TR's Model 1876 .45-75 rifle; at *bottom right* his fancy saddle; at *top right* one of his custom Colt six-shooters in hand-tooled holster.

221

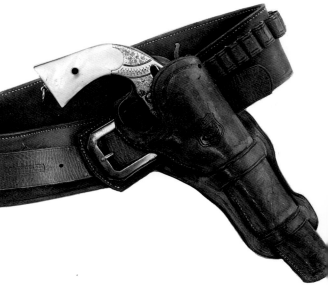

From a grateful Theodore Roosevelt to hunting guide and ranch hand William Merrifield, whose name is inscribed on backstrap, this Merwin & Hulbert was engraved and then plated in gold, and fitted in handsome J. & S. Collins & Co. holster and belt rig. Merrifield had taken TR on successful hunt for a grizzly bear. A Tiffany watch also given guide, inscribed inside lid: "If it's a black bear I can tree him; if it's a grizzly, I can bay him."

Two of Theodore Roosevelt's frequent companions in his ranching days: the Colt .44-40 termed his "best western revolver" and customized for him by L. D. Nimschke. Winchester .40-60, also by Nimschke, a favored "saddle gun for deer and antelope." Superb two-loop holster, deluxe-carved, as were TR's saddle and other equipment. Revolver number 92248; rifle number 45704.

(opposite left) From the armory of Montana rancher Granville Stuart, five-shot Webley bulldog revolver was .45 c.f. caliber and nickel-plated. Engraving likely done by Nimschke; not an English style.

(opposite right) Worthy of the most successful rancher, Sharps Model 1853 sporting rifle number 8249 was factory-engraved, had double set triggers and select walnut stocks. The letterhead from the renowned Freund Brothers, known throughout the frontier for their sights, and their craftsmanship.

against small ranchers. The most extraordinary confrontation, an all-day gun battle, saw Nate Champion, a noted gunslinger, and his friend Nick Ray trapped in a cabin by no less than fifty supporters of the powerful and ruthless Wyoming Stock Growers Association. Champion dragged the wounded Ray back into the cabin while shooting at the attackers with his Colt Single Action. Champion's account of the battle shows his cool nerve:

> Nick is shot but not dead yet. He is awful sick. I must go and wait on him. It is now about two hours since the first shot. Nick is still alive. They are still shooting and are all around the house. Boys, there is bullets coming in here like hail. Them fellows is in such shape I can't get at them. They are shooting from the stable and river and back of the house. Nick is dead. He died about 9 o'clock.

Finally the attacking ranchers torched the cabin. Champion closed his diary with:

> Well, they have just got through shelling the house like hell. I heard them splitting wood. I guess they are going to fire the house tonight. I think I will make a break when night comes, if alive. It's not night yet.
> The house is all fired. Goodbye, boys, if I never see you again.

Champion signed his name, then bolted out the back door, firing his rifle. He was struck by twenty-eight bullets. On his vest the ranchmen attached a warning: CATTLE THIEVES BEWARE.

The shoot-out was a graphic highlight of the

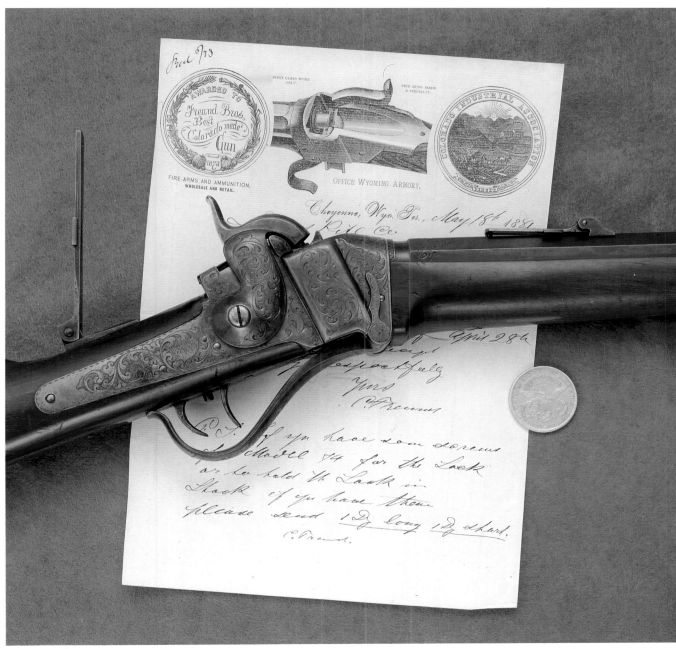

Several of Granville Stuart's frontier guns. The Winchester Model 1873 a One of One Thousand, number 7282. The 1876 profusely engraved with game scenes and scrollwork, number 10001; carrier block inscribed "Granville Stuart/1880." Sharps Sporting Rifle, number 25038, had belonged to James Stuart, and later brother Granville, and was presented by his widow to artist E. S. Paxson. The rifle was used by James on the Yellowstone Expedition of 1863. Henry rifle factory-engraved and inscribed with name "J. B. Stuart" (possibly the Confederate general, who was a first cousin of Granville and James). The Colt Model 1877 was regularly carried by Granville. Pack saddle and handcuffs also Granville Stuart's. Extensive documentation shows that Stuart was one of the keenest arms enthusiasts of any Westerner, and frequently indulged his capacity to acquire fine guns. He even sent illustrations to the Winchester factory for guiding the engravers on his Model 1876 custom rifle. On its arrival he wrote the factory: "I am satisfied with its looks. If it prooves to be as good [accurate] as it is beautiful (women seldom do) it is a world-beater."

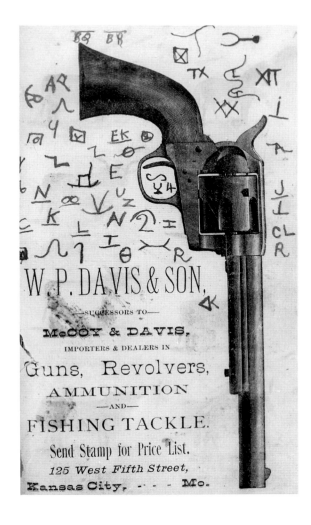

Advertisement from the 1881 edition of Loving's *Live Stock Manual*, for selling the Colt Peacemaker, and more. Brands drawn by manual owner.

(*opposite right*) Rancher James H. Cook, c. 1886–87. Colt and Winchester both deluxe, as was his deerskin outfit. Cook wrote *Fifty Years on the Frontier*, a fascinating source on the West.

Studio shot of teenage cowboy, his revolver apparently a Remington Model 1875 or 1890, with pearl or ivory grips: a luxury considering wages at the time.

This cowboy secured his raised-carved-grip Single Action in angora woolly chaps (with matching cuffs) by opening the loading gate. Only period photo known to author documenting that practice.

Michael Cimino big-budget film *Heaven's Gate*, the most expensive Western ever made.

Cowboy and Rancher Shooting Irons

No less an authority than Theodore Roosevelt wrote of the arms of the 1880s rancher, typical of many bosses, the quality of whose armory often exceeded the basics of his cowboys:

> When I first came to the plains I had a heavy Sharps rifle, 45-120, shooting an ounce and a quarter of lead and a 50 [-150] calibre, double-barrelled English express [by Webley]. Both of these, especially the latter, had a vicious recoil; the former was very clumsy; and above all they were neither of them repeaters; for a repeater or magazine gun is as much superior to a single- or double-barreled breech-loader as the latter is to a muzzle-loader. I threw them both aside. . . .

On handguns, TR summed up preferences with: "Of course, every ranchman carries a revolver, a 45 Colt or Smith & Wesson, by preference the former." In his own battery were two exquisitely engraved Single Actions, one with monogrammed and carved ivory grips, the other with mother-of-pearl grips inscribed in script *Theodore Roosevelt.*

Ranchers like Roosevelt, and Montana's Granville Stuart, were so keen on firearms that they had veritable collections. TR referred to his whole rig, saddle, bridle, spurs, guns, and more: "I now look a regular cowboy dandy, with all my equipments finished in the

(*top*) This Model 1895 Winchester, signed with buffalo head and CMR monogram, was engraved by cowboy artist Charles M. Russell for his friend Frank Linderman. Engraving done with jackknife. Dated 1913. On the other side, a buffalo bull, cow, and calf, and bull elk. When finished Russell said, "There she is. . . . Now the old gal [the rifle] will always have fresh meat in sight."

(*bottom left*) Ranch hand photographed by Blaine & Williams, Campbell, California, 1903. Chaps of batwing style, holster of Mexican double-loop pattern.

(*bottom right*) Mexican gentleman and son, c. 1880, nattily dressed, and with matching gun rigs. Father with Merwin & Hulbert, son with French or Belgian revolver.

most expensive style..." One of these specials was a
.40-60 Winchester. In describing it he summed up the
thoughts on rifles of most ranchers:

> A ranchman...with whom hunting is of secondary importance,
> and who cannot be bothered by carrying a long rifle always
> round with him on horseback, but who, nevertheless, wishes to
> have some weapon with which he can kill what game he runs
> across, usually adopts a short, light saddle-gun, a carbine, weigh-
> ing but five or six pounds, and of such convenient shape that it
> can be kept under his thigh alongside the saddle. A 40-60 Winch-
> ester is perhaps the best for such a purpose, as it carries far and
> straight, and hits hard, and is a first-rate weapon for deer and an-
> telope, and can also be used with effect against sheep, elk, and
> even bear, although for these last a heavier weapon is of course
> preferable.

Cowboy preferences in guns were the same as those
of their rancher bosses, only far less likely to be fancy,
and more often limited to a handgun (Colt Single
Action preferred), and possibly a long gun (Winchester
lever-action carbine preferred).

Barbed wire and farming nudged the cowboy and
rancher aside in the 1890s. Thereafter ranches were reduced in size (some down from millions of acres), but
the image cultivated by the entertainment industry,
and begun by Buffalo Bill's Wild West show, has remained a cherished American legacy. And it was Buffalo Bill's Wild West that would give the cowboy an
image of rustic respectability, in contrast to that of a
hell-raising roughneck.

Extremely deluxe Colts, holsters, spurs, and saddle heavily encrusted
with silver, popular with wealthy ranchers south of the border.

SODBUSTERS, SHOPKEEPERS, AND WELLS FARGO

Merchandisers of firearms and accouterments made positive contributions to westward expansion. They served not only in meeting the needs of the variety of users, but as conduits of information to makers and manufacturers for improvements in guns, accessories, and ammunition. The bigger dealers, like Tryon and Grubb of Philadelphia, Schuyler, Hartley & Graham, Spies and Kissam, and J. P. Moore's Sons of New York, B. Kittredge & Co. of Cincinnati, and Folsom of New Orleans, St. Louis, Chicago and New York, had access to the markets, and equal access to the manufacturers.

In the West itself, dealers the likes of Freund, of Colorado and Wyoming, and J. P. Lower of Denver and F. C. Zimmerman of Dodge City had stocks which could equip a small army. Freund was capable of custom gunwork and engraving, and was renowned for their own specially designed sights—devotees were keen shooters such as Generals Phil Sheridan and George Crook, millionaire Pierre Lorillard, and Theodore Roosevelt.

The commonality of gun ownership was even evident in courtrooms. An 1869 observer of a murder trial in Kansas noted: "These men were walking arsenals. Nearly all were carrying two six-shooters, and among them were rifles of many different patterns. One man could be seen with a long-barreled Hawkins rifle, while his neighbor carried an army Enfield, one a Springfield, and one man an old brassband American musket."

However, most farmers, or sodbusters as the cowboys derisively called them, were lucky to

A banking and express operation founded in New York (at the posh Astor House) in 1852, Wells, Fargo & Co. became synonymous with the Western spirit of daring and enterprise. Early express messenger 10-gauge double-barrel (*center*) made by Dean, London, inscribed on top rib *Wells Fargo & Co.* Colt Model 1862 Police with special factory snubnose 2-inch barrel similarly engraved on backstrap; serial 39251. Folding Burgess 12-gauge pump shotgun, of 1890s manufacture, was advertised for "police service, express messengers, U.S. marshals, prison and bank guards," it served distinguished W. F. & Co. special officer Fred Dodge. Treasure chest is among most sought-after of firm's memorabilia.

Wells, Fargo & Co. inscribed revolvers, for issue to agents. At *top*, S&W Schofield .45, number 1878; its marking visible on barrel. Colt .45 number 308619, roll-marked "W. F. & Co." on buttstrap. Two stalwarts of company service for many years.

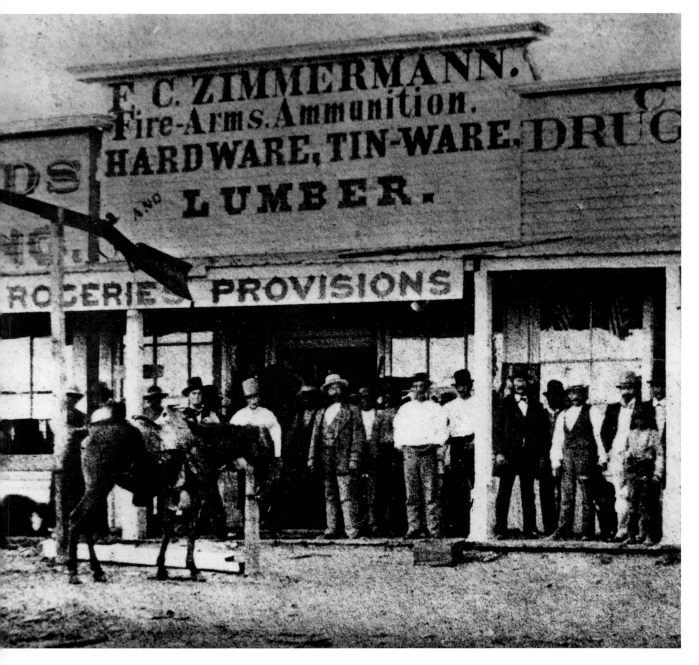

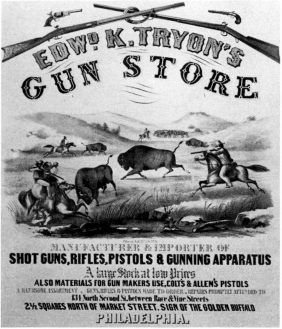

1850-era trade card for a key supplier of arms for the West. Tryon was established 1811, remained in business through five generations, celebrated 125th anniversary in 1936.

Source for guns on Front Street, Dodge City, c. 1875. Many a buffalo hunt outfitted here. Gun sign a much-desired species of Americana; most ended up at junkyard.

Deringers by A. G. Genez, New York, one of the most competent of nineteenth-century U.S. gunmakers. Pistols built for member of distinguished Napa Valley family whose vineyard is the oldest continuous winery in California, established 1877.

CALIFORNIA
BAERENBLUT
BERINGER BROS.
LOS HERMANOS VINEYARDS
ST. HELENA CAL.
CONTENTS 1/5 GALLON
250
METAL-LINED
CAPS
Made expressly for
COLT'S Pt.
Belt and Pocket
PISTOLS

Presented to the original Buffalo Bill, William Mathewson (a founder of Wichita, Kansas), in appreciation of single-handedly saving a train of 147 wagons from Indian attack. At a surprise banquet, Mathewson received the cased set. Some years later he reminisced: "You could have knocked me down with a feather when they gave me those guns with my name carved on them. I have been in tight places in my time, passed through many a danger, but nothing ever took my nerve away so completely as the presentation of those guns. I was speechless, but finally stammered some sort of appreciation and rode away over the starlit prairie that night, the proudest man on the frontier." Etching, silver plating, inscribing, ivory carving, and casing attributed to Tiffany & Co. Numbers 14143 and 14239, Model 1861 Colt Navys.

have simple arms—many times merely a musket kept from Civil War service. Arms sold by the government for emigrants were of surplus type, and sometimes used, but serviceable. Handguns of any quality were considered a luxury.

Nineteenth-century Western towns and cities had ample supplies of guns at homes and in stores, ranging from the common and inexpensive to the occasional deluxe piece of a well-to-do-banker, lawyer, doctor, or politician. Respectable urbanites would generally prefer concealable handguns, in the smaller calibers, which often gave a false sense of security, rather than the potential of self-defense. Flooding the West were literally tens of thousands of cheaply made handguns, later termed "owlheads," because of the owl motifs often molded into their hard rubber grips. European gunmakers, Belgians especially, found a ready market for the inexpensive pocket protectors, as did several American manufacturers. The Colt company complained of the cheap competitors, but fought back with its own line of hideaways and maintained a high standard of quality.

Fighting back was part of the frontier spirit. The townspeople of both Coffeyville and Northfield took on two of the toughest outlaw gangs in the West and brought them to their knees. The author remembers the memorial plaque in the treasurer's office at Carleton College to Joseph L. Heywood, the courageous cashier at Northfield's First National Bank (and employee at the college), who died from gunshots when he refused to cooperate with the James and Younger Gang. Every manner of gun in both towns was brought into play in those historic confrontations—rifles and shotguns proved the most effective.

Encouraging an interest in shooting and marksmanship in towns and cities were organized shooting clubs. The National Rifle Association was established in 1871, mainly by New Yorkers (among them New York City resident General U. S. Grant). German shooting clubs—the *Schuetzenverein*—sprang up in many communities with German-speaking residents. Spurred

"Owlhead" pistols (better known to collectors as suicide or Saturday-night specials), lesser-quality pocket protectors, some good enough only for a shot or two. From these inexpensive arms came the cliché "hotter than a two-dollar pistol." Among trade names for such arms: Terror, Red Jacket, Defender, and Swamp Angel. In .32 and .38 rimfire calibers, and by a myriad of U.S. and foreign (particularly Belgian) manufacturers. Hopkins & Allen and Forehand & Wadsworth represented here.

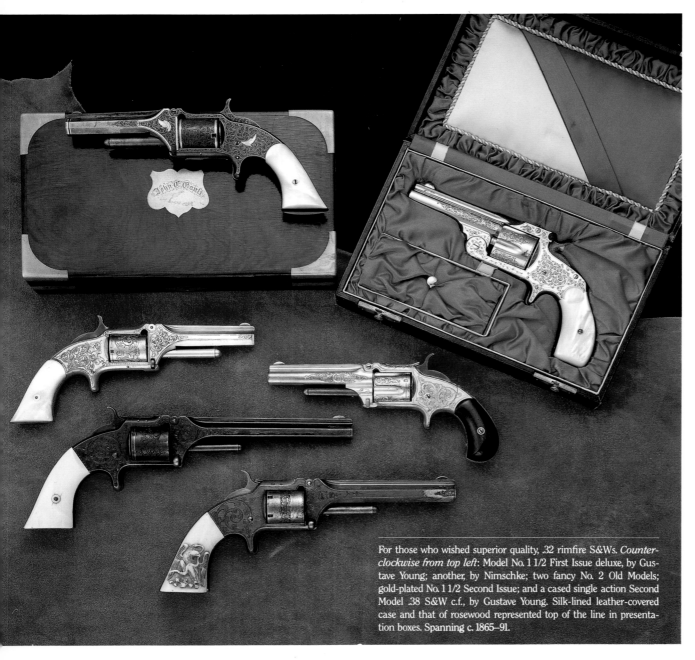

For those who wished superior quality, .32 rimfire S&Ws. *Counter-clockwise from top left*: Model No. 1 1/2 First Issue deluxe, by Gustave Young; another, by Nimschke; two fancy No. 2 Old Models; gold-plated No. 1 1/2 Second Issue; and a cased single action Second Model .38 S&W c.f., by Gustave Young. Silk-lined leather-covered case and that of rosewood represented top of the line in presentation boxes. Spanning c. 1865–91.

on by a national passion for marksmanship and firearms, target shooting was as big a sport in the nineteenth century as baseball today, even to the extent of shooting matches with large bodies of spectators. Target and trick shots like Annie Oakley, Doc Carver, and Buffalo Bill were national heroes.

An early Texas supporter of competitive rifle shooting was W. L. Cushing of Galveston, who wrote the Sharps Rifle Co. (April 1875):

> If you have any new circulars descriptive of Sharps Creedmoor Rifle I will be pleased to have you forward me same. My intention is to get up a "long range team" here. We have as fine a range as can be found in the U.S. I am now getting up a Rifle club for shooting range, to be armed with Maynard guns, have already rec'd some of the guns & orders for others. . . . Although Remington's guns seem to have occasioned considerable I must confess to being prejudiced in favor of Sharps though I have seen none of the Creedmoor guns of either make.

Cushing went on to state: "I am passionately fond of Rifle shooting, have now a Maynard, Winchester, Spencer, two Ballards, a Wesson & some 3000 rounds of Am[munition]. . . ."

The rage for shooting also saw trap competitions (at first with glass balls) evolve, from c. 1866, and touring marksmen and women. Every boy could count on a rifle, the .22-caliber types proliferating beginning in the 1880s. Even gallery shooting became increasingly popular, with indoor ranges in cities, where handgun shooting could be practiced and matches shot.

The Westerners' (and the Easterners') enthusiasm for the shooting sports continues to modern times, but because of increased urbanization, the opportunities for these sports are diminishing. And the big-city press is inclined to cover shoot-outs in the streets instead of organized competitive pistol, rifle, and shotgun shooting.

Express Agency Weaponry

From the beginning of organized transportation and the shipping of valuables, a potent defense was required. Quoting Granville Stuart just after the Civil War: "a party of passengers crowded into a coach have

Calamity Jane outfitted as a teamster, holding Sharps Model 1874 Hunter's Rifle, made in calibers .40, .44, .45, and .50. She was born Martha Jane Cannary, near Princeton, Missouri, 1852; the origin of her nickname is unknown. Enjoying alcohol and men, she led a rip-roaring life, from Kansas to Montana, and once rode a bull down the main street of Rapid City. Prior to death in 1903 she wished press and public would "leave me alone and let me go to hell my own route." Alleged marriage between Jane and Wild Bill Hickok considered apocryphal.

Leading arms dealer of Denver, renowned marksman, and promoter of target shooting John P. Lower. Such marksmanship would bring down a black bear, any day. He fired a Model 1878 Sharps-Borchardt military rifle, a type chambered for .40-70, .44-77, and .45-70 cartridges; nearly 12,000 such rifles were produced. An Officers Model also made, in .45-70, and in total of only forty-eight; sent as rifle-match prizes and presentations to military men of influence.

Charming little girl with Model 1873 Winchester. Boys and girls both learned shooting and gun safety at tender ages in the West.

With their store-bought duds and waist-high six-gun rigs, these *compadres* were likely city dudes; c. 1880s.

True dude Oscar Wilde, in a portrait painted during U.S. tour, c. 1882, in San Francisco. While in Cheyenne, Wilde was interviewed by a reporter, who described the Englishman's broad silk necktie as in a color between pink and burnt sienna, his handkerchief, hosiery, and hat lining matching. The reporter "did not investigate any further, but would bet a rusty horse pistol against a stone dwelling that his subterranean strati of apparel was of the same delicate shade."

no chance against a few 'Road Agents' armed with double barrel shot-guns."

The shotgun proved the most effective defender of passengers, mail, and valuables. Stagecoach driver J. T. Morley worked for Wells Fargo, California, in the late 1870s and early 1880s:

> We stage drivers were furnished with .45 calibre Colt revolvers and sawed off shotguns especially made in the east for the company. The shot gun barrels were charged with 7 1/2 grams of powder and loaded with 16 buck shots in four layers with four shot to the layer. . . . One of the strict rules of the company to all drivers was as follows. "Whenever you leave your stage, extract the shells from your guns and revolvers." If a driver left either his shotgun or revolver in the stage, as was frequently necessary, and returned to find either pointed at him by a bandit, the driver knew that the gun or revolver was not loaded.

Despite these formidable defenses—even some in the Black Hills outfitted with a 2-pound mountain howitzer (1877)—holdups were not uncommon. Writing of a Black Hills coach, so armed, observer Ami Frank Mulford added: "They also have twelve Winchester repeating rifles inside, with plenty of ammunition in little pockets near the windows, or rather port-holes. These stages are run [between Bismarck and] the Black Hills, and despite all their arms and caution, are very frequently held up, by white as well as red devils. . . ."

Early stage lines and expressmen depended largely on Colt revolvers and percussion shotguns, and kept up to date with evolutionary improvements in breechloaders, like the Spencer and Henry rifles. An 1867 stage depot near Fort Wallace, Kansas, was described by William Bell:

> When attacked, the men creep into [fortified] pits, and, thus protected, keep up a tremendous fire through the portholes. Two or three men, with a couple of breech-loaders each, are a match for almost any number of assailants. I cannot say how many times these little forts have been used since their construction, but during the three weeks we were in the neighborhood, the station was attacked [by Indians] twice. . . .

Some orders for guns for arming Wells Fargo were processed directly with the gun companies, through

237

Sam Langton launched private mail service, 1850, making deliveries on foot and via mule from Marysville to gold camps near Nevada City and Downieville, California. Langton's Pioneer Express grew, became family business, and had offices in several northern California towns. John Ager was a business partner, and superintendent c. 1854–61. Pistol is Ager's own Model 1851 Navy.

Adams & Co., a subsidiary of Adams Express Company, which had been established in the eastern United States, 1839. In 1849 the firm entered the California market, buying and transporting gold and shipping ledgers and goods to the East. Adams expanded in California quickly, became largest and most efficient express operation of early 1850s. For many years Adams competed with Wells Fargo. Among former's clients: the Colt company, whose engraver inscribed this Model 1849 Pocket revolver, part of an order for agents.

Colt Navys on Wells Fargo treasure chest, accompanied by California "slim Jim" period holster. At *top*, number 65897, backstrap inscribed *Geo. Chorpenning.—C. & S. L. Mail."* Fighting hostile Indians, weather, and terrain, Chorpenning ran his California and Salt Lake mail service, the "Jackass Mail," c. 1851–60. Route taken over by Russell, Majors and Waddell, after founder forced into bankruptcy. *Bottom* revolver inscribed on backstrap *P.M.S.S. Co. Sacramento,* serial number 155092. Navy carried on Pacific Mail and Steam Ship Company vessel *Sacramento.* Any such inscribed revolvers are prized mementoes of pioneer Western transportation.

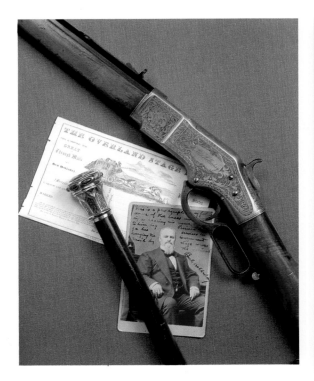

(*opposite and above*) Winchester Model 1866 rifle, presentation gold quartz cane, and silver-and-gilt punch bowl of stagecoach king Ben Holladay, founder of the Overland Mail. A trader and freighter during Mexican War, Holladay headed for California in 1850 and became associated with Russell, Majors and Waddell in 1858. Two years later he assisted in establishing the Pony Express, and in 1862 took over Russell, Majors and Waddell partnership, organizing the Overland Stage Line. With operations from California to Missouri by 1866, he sold out in that year to Wells, Fargo & Co.—partly because of losses from Indian attacks on stagecoaches, stage stops, and livestock. Subsequently Holladay invested in steamship lines and railroading. In the mid-1870s he was forced out of business by financial reverses. Living lavishly and pretentiously, Holladay built a huge mansion, Ophir, near New York City. Private stagecoach was mounted in silver; once he was robbed by a highwayman and suffered the indignity of surrendering his prized gold watch and other valuables.

Wells, Fargo & Co. stagecoaches lined up for Virginia City, Nevada, c. 1867. A July 1850 issue of *Missouri Commonwealth* described armament for stage connections between Independence and Santa Fe: "The mail is guarded by eight men, armed as follows: Each man has at his side, fastened in the stage, one of Colt's revolving rifles, in a holster below one of Colt's long revolvers, and in his belt a small Colt's revolver, besides a hunting knife; so that these eight men are ready, in case of attack, to discharge 136 shots without having to reload." Coaches continued in use into early twentieth century, were needed as connectors to railroad. Defense armament was reduced over time, as Indian depredations and lawlessness were eliminated or reduced.

Period photograph, in which stagecoach holdup was staged for camera. Handsomely inscribed gold watch rewarded stagecoach driver Shine for foiling highwaymen. Shine had noticed weakness in three outlaws, and whipped the team away. Outlaws fired on stage, but driver sped on to town. The heroic Shine was only twenty-six years of age, and gained reputation for coolness and daring. Eventually leaving stagecoaching, Shine went on to become a California state senator; was appointed U.S. Marshal for northern California and Nevada in 1898.

(*top right*) From Wells Fargo Bank History Room's collection of historic arms, Model 1860 Colt Army factory-made snub-nose, carried by company detective James B. Hume. Gun had been surrendered to Hume by stage robber and murderer Charles Dorsey, a.k.a. Charles Thorn. Once a farmer and prospector, Hume served as El Dorado County, California, sheriff and undersheriff, then joined Wells, Fargo & Co. as chief of detectives, remained in company's employ from 1873–1904. Hume was a pioneer in scientific law enforcement, later referred to as criminology. Among those he pursued and was instrumental in capturing, or killing: Black Bart the PO8, Chris Evans, and John Sontag.

agents like W. M. Ashton of New York. Markings on early guns have been observed hand-engraved: on barrels for shotguns, and on backstraps for handguns. As orders became more frequent, roll dies and stamps were employed, as was the case with orders for Colt Single Actions shipped to the attention of Ashton.

One of the biggest Wells Fargo orders was through New York dealers Schuyler, Hartley & Graham or the rival Francis Bannerman, for the Schofield .45 S&W, with barrels shortened to about 5 inches. The stamping "W.F. & Co's Ex." (with or without the 's) appears on the right side of the ejector housing on the barrel. Several hundreds of these are estimated to have been supplied, c. 1880. A number following the Wells Fargo company markings coincides with the revolver's serial number.

But individual agency employees sometimes desired their own revolvers. Colt received such a request from a Wells Fargo agent in San Francisco (1887):

> I want a .44 calibre double-action "frontier six-shooter" made with a barrel two and a half (2 1/2) inches long. Then, instead of chambering the cylinder and barrel to shoot the Winchester model '73 cartridge which the "frontier six-shooter" takes, I want both cylinder and barrel chambered to shoot the .41 calibre center-fire cartridge. . . .

The smaller-framed Colts and Smith & Wessons had a strong expressman following. These and various other guns may be found with such markings as W.F. & CO., AM. EX. CO. RY. EX. AGY., PROPERTY OF ADAMS EXPRESS CO., and so forth.

Agents in action were rewarded for heroism against Indians and highwayman, as attested to by an occasional inscribed gun, or watch. One of the first to be so

From finest private collection of W. F. & Co. treasure boxes, and shotguns. Note bullet holes in smaller box at *upper left*. Model 1866 Winchester, number 154100, with rare express company frame inscription.

Wells, Fargo & Co. Deadwood treasure wagon and armed guards, with $250,000 in gold bullion from Great Homestake Mine, c. 1890.

Shotgun of Charles E. Boles, a.k.a. Black Bart the PO8, most notorious robber of Wells, Fargo & Co. and thorn in firm's side from 1875 to 1883. In that period he committed twenty-nine holdups (according to the count of Special Officer Hume) and only once failed to obtain loot. Bart's first victim was a coach driven by John Shine. His stickup career was finally halted when Hume traced laundry mark found on handkerchief left at robbery site; Boles spent four years in San Quentin, and soon after release he vanished. Shotgun a sawed-off Loomis IXL No. 15, serial number 36822.

Treasure box used in a robbery between Fort Jones and Yreka, California, in late 1890s; note end of box hacked out. Wells Fargo shotgun, repaired at wrist. Miscellaneous loot and reward poster.

REWARD!
STAGE ROBBERY!
A REWARD OF
$500 EACH

Will be paid for the arrest and conviction of the parties concerned in the robbery of our express, on the Downieville stage, at the Oregon House, on the afternoon of June 23d, 1873, also,

One-fourth of the Amount Recovered for the Recovery of the Treasure,

CONSISTING OF

One Bar, valued at $2,200, $381 Coin and $100 in Dust.

L. F. ROWELL,
Ass't Sup't Wells, Fargo & Co.

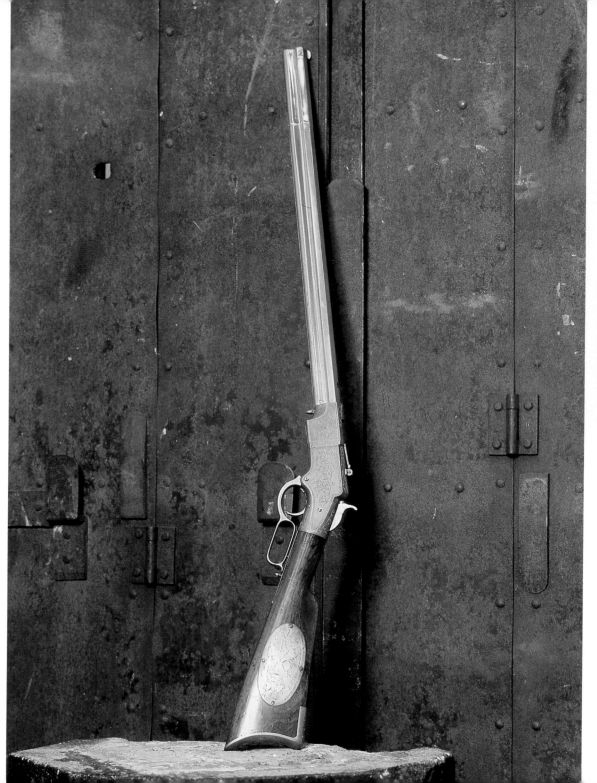

Messengers for W. F. & Co. from the 1890s, amply armed.

Deluxe Henry rifle, reward from Wells, Fargo & Co. to former Nevada City, California, town marshal Stephen Venard, for killing three road agents and recovering loot. Finest-known W.F. & Co. presentation firearm, German-silver stock plaque inscribed *Presented by* WELLS FARGO & CO. *to Stephen Venard/for his gallant conduct May 16th/1866.* Serial number 1228.

Displayed on company horse blanket, longarms for W.F.& Co. agents and messengers. *Top left*, Remington Model 1882 10-gauge shotgun, number 4607, engraved on barrel rib WELLS FARGO & CO. 256. *Bottom left*, Ithaca 12-gauge built on 10-gauge frame for heavy-duty use, number 211333. To *right*, another Ithaca, butt modified; number 240191. Some 750 Ithaca shotguns like these two were sold to W. F. & Co., from 1909 to 1917. All bore W. F. & Co. markings, followed by identification numbers. The 1886 Winchester, number 50884, marked "W. F. & Co's. Ex." on left side of barrel, in front of forearm, and on bottom of frame. Wood block used by messengers to hold shotgun shells and rifle and revolver cartridges.

honored was Stephen Venard, given an enriched Henry rifle and $3,000 for pursuing and then killing three outlaws who stuck up the Wells Fargo stagecoach near Nevada City, California. The German-silver stock plaque carries an elegant inscription and a depiction of the courageous agent shooting the bandits. It had been a Henry of Venard's that he used in the chase.

The kind of heroics that earned such awards took place in Fairbank, Arizona, 1900, when five of the Burt Alvord Gang tried to rob an express car. Little did they suspect that Wells Fargo guard and gritty sometime peace officer Jeff Milton was on hand and would spoil their plans.

The five bandits, including one "Three-Fingered Jack" Dunlap, began their holdup at dusk. A crowd had gathered and the stage for Tombstone waited for passengers. The first "Hands up!" sounded like a joke. Then came the command "Throw up your hands and come out o' there," a shot, and off flew Milton's hat. His response to that was to grab a sawed-off shotgun and shout, "If there's anything here you want, come and get it."

The outlaws fired at Milton with rifles at close range. His shirt was shredded and his left arm badly shattered, shots which spun him around and knocked

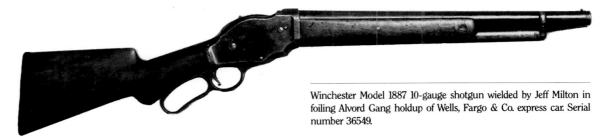

Winchester Model 1887 10-gauge shotgun wielded by Jeff Milton in foiling Alvord Gang holdup of Wells, Fargo & Co. express car. Serial number 36549.

Handguns for W. F. & Co. *Clockwise from top left*, Colt New Army, marked "W. F. & Co." on butt, number 240662. Colt Police Positive, "W. F. & Co. A. 253" on butt, number 16729. Another Colt New Army, "W. F. & Co. A. 62" on butt, number 230537. All three in .38 caliber. *Next* three in .45 caliber: Single Action, 5 1/2-inch barrel, butt marked "W. F. & Co.," number 301670. Model 1878 Frontier; on back-strap "W. F. & Co. No. 978," number 4325. S&W Schofield with barrel marking "W. F. & Co.'s Ex. 164." The firm's *Instructions* guidebook, published 1884, stated "325. In case a Messenger on a stage route leaves the coach, for meals, etc., he must retain possession of his fire-arms. 326. Messengers on all important routes are required to travel armed for defense, in case of attack. Arms and ammunition can be procured by requisition."

W. F. & Co. messengers, in mid-1890s. Iron treasure box served as seat; Marlin .22 rifles at left, and Floberts at right probably for target practice—of insufficient caliber for self-defense.

THE BRAVE EXPRESS MESSENGER
WHO DID NOT FLINCH AT HIS POST

RETURN THIS GUN To
Wells Fargo & Co. Express.

B. P. DROWN
- SCRAP BOOK -
- 1886 -

GUARD

EL ESTADO DE CHIHUAHUA
PAGARA
AL PORTADOR EN EFECTIVO
CINCO PESOS
CONFORME AL DECRETO MILITAR
DE FECHO DE FEBRERO DE 1914
CHIHUAHUA, MEXICO
BYRON P. DROWNE
EL PASO, TEX.

Wells Fargo & Co. 57

Wells Fargo & Co Express

1-15   Form 279

Wells Fargo & Co Express

From | BYRON P. DROWNE | Shipper
(City or Town)

| BYRON P. DROWNE |
Consignee

For

Street Address

City or Town   State

Value $ INSTRUCTIONS TO EMPLOYES

If the Way-bill Label cannot be pasted on the shipment, it should be pasted on
tag separate from the one bearing the only address on the shipment.

The
BALDWIN
Art Gallery
Plattsburgh,
New York

him to the floor of the car. Rushing the entrance, the gang was greeted by Milton standing up, holding the shotgun like a pistol. The blast put eleven pellets into Three-Fingered Jack, and a stray pellet hit gang member (and leader of the heist) Bravo Juan Yoas. As he fell, Jack yelled, "Look out for the son of a bitch, he's shooting to kill."

Milton, the artery in his arm cut, was able to roll shut the express car's door. He took the safe keys and flung them among several packages, and made a tourniquet for his shattered arm. Later he recalled: "I felt myself going, but I enjoyed it. I heard the most beautiful music—the most wonderful band—that I ever heard in my life. I wonder if every man does."

The door was shot through and through by the three gang members left in action, and they circled the car still shooting through its sides.

Milton had passed out, and was covered with blood. The gang forced themselves into the car, with the train's engineer, who was able to prevent further shooting by claiming that "the man's dead now." Failing to find keys on Milton, and not prepared to blow the safe, they took the wounded Dunlap with them, and rode off empty-handed.

Milton never regained normal use of his arm, which the doctors wanted to amputate. Refusing, the tough shootist checked out of the hospital instead. Dunlap was not so lucky, and would die from his wound.

Not all express agents were willing to shoot it out with road agents or Indians, but it was customary to equip them to put up a fight. The company fully expected them to shoot back when confronted with criminals. That same attitude was part of the spirit of the frontier, even with the sodbusters and shopkeepers.

The respected Jeff Milton, veteran of several gunfights, casually contemplated coiled rattlesnake in Mexican desert.

Scrapbook kept by W. F. & Co. express guard Byron P. Drowne, maker of frequent runs between Los Angeles and El Paso. Five-peso currency, stamped with his name, used as calling card. Gun, badge, shotgun shells, and tag all his. Well-used shotgun by Samuel Buckley & Co., London.

(*top right*) San Francisco Money Department of W. F. & Co. Firm's description of this photograph noted: "Here all kinds of treasure, such as jewelry, money, bullion and other valuables are handled by trusted employees in closely guarded rooms." Revolvers, shotguns, and wax seals are among objects and memorabilia.

(*bottom right*) Cabinet photograph of shackled train robber, from criminal ID card album assembled by Wells, Fargo & Co., 1898, for office use and containing over ninety similar photographs. Back of illustrated card identified criminal as "Sam Smith/Tr. Robber/Andover, Kansas July 16, 1898/Arrest Aug. 3, 1898."

Conrad Friedrich Ulrich
DIESINKER

Engraver of the highest style
Visiting Wedding & Reception cards
Bank Notes Drafts Certificates
for
Railroads & Corporations documents and
Securities representing Money or value & designer of
Monograms, Crests, Letters, Arms in Mediaeval or
Modern Splendor.

HUNTERS AND GENTLEMEN-SPORTSMEN

From the time of the Lewis and Clark Expedition and well before, a magnetic draw of the West was the seemingly limitless panorama of wildlife. Journals reveal the variety of game observed by Lewis and Clark, and those attractions were a lure as well to the trailblazers and mountain men. Further, not a few of the military were enthralled with hunting. And so were the most intriguing of all sportsmen who ever graced the West: the aristocrats.

To the blue bloods the appeal rivaled even that of the Dark Continent of Africa. Some of these foreign aficionados came in elaborate expeditions, complete with artists as chroniclers. Their adventures inspired the film *A Man Called Horse*, starring Richard Harris as an English lord.

William Drummond Stewart

In Scotsman and Battle of Waterloo veteran Stewart, reality rivaled the silver screen. On and off from 1832 to 1843, Captain William Drummond Stewart traveled the mountain man's West. His preparations for hunting and exploring the Louisiana Purchase Territory included an interview with William Clark. The escapades of Stewart and those who accompanied his expeditions served as inspiration for two autobiographical novels, *Altowan* and *Edward Warren*. Stewart attended mountain men rendezvous, shot wild animals, met numerous Indians, enjoyed the scenery, and mingled with such stalwarts of the trailblazer West as Jim Bridger, Antoine Clement, General William Ashley, William Sublette, and the missionary Marcus

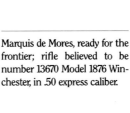

Marlin Model 1881 lever-action sporting rifle, its frame honoring the buffalo; engraved by Conrad Ulrich, and firing .40-60 cartridge. Whitney rolling-block, competitor to Remington of same action, in .32-20. Sportsmen and hunters had wide choice of single-shots and repeaters in metallic-cartridge longarms.

Marquis de Mores, ready for the frontier; rifle believed to be number 13670 Model 1876 Winchester, in .50 express caliber.

William Drummond Stewart meeting Indian chiefs, c. 1837. Quoting from *Altowan*: "The long hair floating about, as raised by the motion of the rider; and the horsetails dangling, and the dust, and the occasional shout; the flashing of the bright gun-barrels in the sun, and the fierce bearing of those who carried them—combined to form a subject alike for the painter and the moralist." Oil by Alfred Jacob Miller, 33" x 42 1/2". A trapper described Stewart: "[T]he last as come out of Independence was that ar Englishman. He'd a nor-west capote on, and a two-shoot gun rifled. Well, them English are darned fools; they can't fix a rifle any ways; but that one did shoot "some"; least *he* made it throw plum-center. . . . All the boys called him Cap'en, and he got his fixings from old Chouteau. . . . he had the best powder as ever I flashed through life, and his gun was handsome, that's a fact. Them thar locks was grand. . . ."

Lithograph from Karl Bodmer painting of well-dressed Prince Maximilian and David Dreidoppel meeting with Minataree Indians. Well-armed travelers carried double rifles; 1842. Both Miller and Bodmer pictures from the Thomas Gilcrease Institute of American History and Art, Tulsa, Oklahoma.

ZUSAMMENKUNFT DER REISENDEN MIT MONNITARRI INDIANERN   RENCONTRE DES VOYAGEURS AVEC DES INDIENS MEUNITARRI

THE TRAVELLERS MEETING WITH MINATARRE INDIANS.

From George Catlin's six-lithograph commission from Samuel Colt, published 1851, the artist taking buffalo with his rifle "Sam Colt." In *Life Amongst the Indians*, Catlin praised this gun: "'Sam! who's Sam?' Why *Sam Colt*, a six-shot little rifle [Model 1839 Paterson carbine], always lying *before* me during the day and *in my arms* during the night, by which a tiger's or alligator's eye, at a hundred yards, was sure to drop a red tear. . . ." Believed first instance of American manufacturer commissioning pictures from artist intended for product promotions, a practice repeated frequently by gun and cartridge makers later in nineteenth century.

Whitman. While in America, Stewart would inherit the titles of 7th Baronet of Murthly and 19th Baron of Grandtully, becoming a lord.

For the expedition of spring to fall 1837, Stewart hired a young Baltimore artist, Alfred Jacob Miller, to record the adventures on canvas. Among the accouterments brought along was armor to present Jim Bridger, as protection against missiles from Indians. Miller's pictures were the first artistic documentation of the Rocky Mountains. On the final expedition, from spring to fall 1843 (having returned to Scotland, accompanied by Indians, buffalo, and even a grizzly bear), Stewart had tried to persuade John James Audubon to join him. On this trip, with some sixty men (including Stewart's Scottish valet and two additional servants), the party reached the Yellowstone, hunting elk and bear, fishing, and enjoying the unmatched scenery.

An accompanying journalist, Matt Field of the *New Orleans Picayune*, wrote on their return: "We are the fattest, greasiest set of truant rogues your liveliest imagination can call up to view. We are the meanest, raggedest—perhaps you would add, the ugliest—set of buffalo butchers that ever cracked a rifle among the big hills of Wind River." Stewart was described by one of the party as "a mighty hunter and a prince among sportsmen."

Stewart had spent seven glorious summers in the Green River country of the Rockies. They were memories he savored until his death in Scotland, in 1871. Like many of his fellow travelers and hunters in the West, Stewart left an estate that was a veritable treasure trove of artifacts and souvenirs. Not the least of these was a bizarre pair of chairs, with cleverly simulated horns on the huge carved buffalo head backs, now featured in the exhibits of the Gene Autry Western Heritage Museum.

Prince Maximilian and Karl Bodmer

Still another titled foreigner was drawn to the West at about the same time as Stewart: Alexander Philip Maximilian, Prince of Wied-Neuwied, who was con-

Mid-nineteenth-century lithograph, signed Yves, of *vaqueros* and probably continental European sportsmen, in pursuit of buffalo. Double rifle has knocked down one buffalo and is about to take second.

Stirring print of Catlin downing buffalo with his Colt Dragoon. Subtitled "He writes, 'I have five shots to the right and left, four of which were fatal to the heart, and all in less than half a minute.'" Scabbard on Catlin's back held "Sam Colt." Other prints in series included *Firing His Colt's Repeating Rifle Before a Tribe of Carib Indians in South America, Relieving One of His Companions from an Unpleasant Predicament During His Travels in Brazil, Water Hunting for Deer, A Night Scene on the River Susquehanna Penn.*, and *A Mid-Day Halt on the Rio Trombutos, Brazil*.

sumed by a passion for science and knowledge. Although he had long wished to visit America, service in the Napoleonic Wars had prevented him. Prince Maximilian's research led him to depart for America in the spring of 1832, and by the spring of 1834 his expedition had begun, even meeting Captain William Drummond Stewart in St. Louis. Maximilian's most significant companion was the Swiss-German artist Karl Bodmer. The Prince's manservant, David Dreidoppel, was more like an aide-de-camp and was more the sportsman-hunter of the expedition than the scientifically oriented Maximilian. Much of their travel was by steamboat, visiting trading posts and observing the Indians. The Prince couldn't help but notice of the Crow tribe that "they have many bardashes, or hermaphrodites, among them, and exceed all the other in unnatural practices...."

The party wintered in the Dakota Territory, where the Prince nearly died, and the cold was so extreme it froze Bodmer's paints and the ink for the Prince's journals. In spring 1834 the travelers left for St. Louis. In mid-July the Prince, Bodmer, and Dreidoppel departed New York for Europe. Unfortunately the bulk of the Prince's scientific collections were lost in a tragic fire; among the losses were skins and skulls of birds and animals shot for scientific reasons. Prince Maximilian nevertheless published a landmark book on the West, *Reise in das Innere Nord-America in den Jahren 1832 bis 1834*, in two large volumes, with a companion collection of Bodmer's watercolor paintings.

Travelers, Sportsmen, and a Grand Duke

Still later came increasing numbers of travelers and sportsmen, some of whom published memoirs of their experiences. International big game hunting was a passion of the century, and the subject was commonly discussed in clubs and among the fashionable. One such sportsman was Sir St. George Gore, of Sligo, Ireland, a baronet, whose party of approximately forty had an accompaniment of 112 horses, 18 oxen, sundry milk cows, and 50 hunting dogs (Irish staghounds and greyhounds). Their goal was a three-year hunt in Texas

Gold-inlaid and engraved for a French aristocrat, Model 1851 Navy number 1873 was specially prepared by Colt Hartford and London factories, "in the white," for embellishments by Parisian gunmaker and dealer Guenault. The extraordinary set is a reflection of continental and British fascination with Sam Colt's revolvers and with the American West.

(*opposite*) Buffalo Bill Cody (*left*) with three unidentified companions. The young hunter held the .50-caliber Springfield trapdoor "Lucretia Borgia" across his lap. Gun presently displayed at Buffalo Bill Historical Center, but lacking buttstock, which with trigger assembly, broke off and was lost. Remington revolver at Cody's waist believed to be that illustrated on page 293.

Magnificent presentation Model 1876 Winchester half-magazine rifle, from General William E. Strong to Phil Sheridan, in .50-95 caliber, engraved by John Ulrich and so signed. A horseback buffalo hunt scene on other side may have commemorated Sheridan's role in Grand Duke Alexis hunt. A close friend of Sheridan, Strong had ordered exquisite Model 1873 Winchester for himself, also gold-plated and engraved by John Ulrich. Likely Sheridan's admiration of the 1873 led to the presentation Model 1876.

Grand Duke Alexis (*right*) with Lieutenant Colonel George A. Custer, on the occasion of their grand buffalo hunts in Nebraska and Colorado. Alexis's revolver likely the $400 presentation Russian Model he received from the S&W factory, December 1871. As reported in the *Springfield Daily Republican*: "Wholly informal, but thoroughly successful, was the reception of the Grand Duke which took place in this city, yesterday afternoon.... The procession...moved down Main Street amid salutations of white handkerchiefs, and hearty cheers from the many eager spectators, and proceeded...to Smith & Wesson's pistol factory. The party were received without parade by Messrs. Smith and Wesson, and were shown into their private office, where an elegant pistol, inlaid with gold [by Gustave Young], having pearl butt upon which were the coat of arms of America and Russia, and inclosed into a rosewood case, bearing the inscription 'From S & W to A.A.' was presented to the Duke by Mr. Wesson, and the appropriate thanks returned."

S&W Old Russian .44, one of 3,000 refused by Russian government, but quickly sold to New York dealer. Number 4514 had barrel reduced from 8-inch length, is Nimschke-engraved, nickel-plated, and fitted with carved ivory grips. On occasion of Grand Duke's visit to S&W, his principal aide, Admiral Poissett, was given a nickeled No. 3 revolver, and others in the party lesser revolvers.

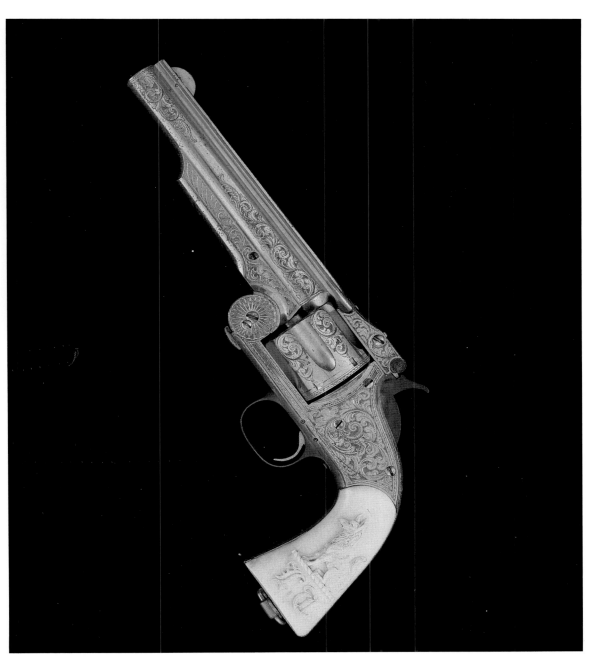

Best-quality London shotgun bears gold plaque inlay on bottom of stock inscribed FROM/EARL DUNRAVEN/TO/TEXAS JACK/1874. Inscription suggests Dunraven humored Texas Jack, who appears to have considered "Earl" his lordship's first name!

George A. Custer's Remington Creedmoor .44 rolling-block sporting rifle, with personal effects. A deluxe .50-caliber Remington inspired Custer to write factory (October 1873), stating accuracy and performance on a three-month expedition to the Yellowstone that summer: "During this period...I carried the rifle...on every occasion, and the following list exhibits but a portion of the game killed by me: Antelope, 41; buffalo 4; elk, 4; blacktail deer, 4; American [whitetail] deer, 3; white wolf, 2; geese, prairie chickens, and other feathered game in large numbers....I rarely obtained a shot at an antelope under 150 yards, while the range extended from that distance up to 630 yards." The .50 Remington was profusely engraved, and is believed to have been taken by Indians at the Little Bighorn.

"Earl Dunraven/from Texas Jack" inscribed on backstrap of S&W American (*top*). Plain revolver, same model, simply engraved on frame. TEXAS JACK/COTTON WOOD SPRING/1872. Both .44s, pistols contrast the blue-blood Earl with his friend and hunting guide frontiersman Jack Omohundro.

(*opposite*) Custer with his first grizzly bear, shot with Remington rolling-block rifle, on Black Hills expedition, 1874. *From left,* scout Bloody Knife, Private Noonan, and Captain William Ludlow. Springfield trapdoor carbine (*left*) in .50 caliber, of period. Parker 12-gauge shotgun, c. 1880, type first in West in late 1860s, chambered for reloadable brass breech-loading centerfire cartridges. Parker was destined to become foremost U.S. maker of side-by-side double shotguns, and many officers in the West owned them, including General Nelson A. Miles.

Arkansas toothpicks, Sheffield-made for the American market. *Left,* c. 1840 by W. & S. Butcher, with 9-inch etched blade. *Right,* spearpoint blade marked JOSEPH HOLMES NO 5/I SMITH FIELD SHEFFIELD/ARKANSAS TOOTH PICK; iron crossguard. *From top*: marked by W. N. S. Butcher; coffin-shaped handle; blade etched with decorations and ARKANSAS TOOTH PICK. Next marked MANUFACTURED FOR F. C. GOERGEN, NEW ORLEANS and with large etched blade panel; grips of ebony. Ivory-gripped knife by R. Bunting & Sons, and also marked W. GREAVES & SONS. Sheath with toothpick marking. Stag-handled knife by Marshes & Shepherd; unusually wide blade; gold-embossed sheath bears toothpick legend. *Bottom* knife crisply marked on blade and by crossguard. Mountings of most knives were done in German silver, and most date in 1850s and 1860s.

Tin sign c. 1880. A major supplier of gunpowder, Hazard's powder mills were in Hazardville, Connecticut. Operations of owner Colonel Augustus C. occupied 400 acres near the Connecticut river. Hazard built twenty-seven-room French Colonial mansion in Enfield and hobnobbed with the likes of Daniel Webster and Sam Colt (for whom he made cartridge packets). At one time firm rivalled Du Pont, with which Hazard was known to rig prices and production, dominating powder business in the United States. Rifle Colt Model 1855 Sidehammer in .44 caliber, with desirable scope sight; pistol a Remington Model 1871 Army .50 c.f. rolling-block; either gun could down a buffalo.

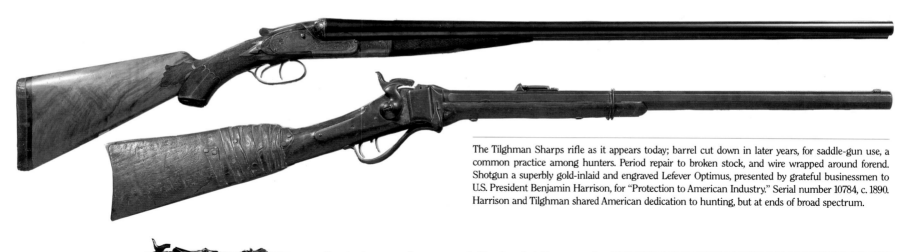

The Tilghman Sharps rifle as it appears today; barrel cut down in later years, for saddle-gun use, a common practice among hunters. Period repair to broken stock, and wire wrapped around forend. Shotgun a superbly gold-inlaid and engraved Lefever Optimus, presented by grateful businessmen to U.S. President Benjamin Harrison, for "Protection to American Industry." Serial number 10784, c. 1890. Harrison and Tilghman shared American dedication to hunting, but at ends of broad spectrum.

Springfield Officers Model .45-70 used by Billy Dixon, a scout under General Nelson A. Miles and a guide for surveying parties in Texas Panhandle; he won Medal of Honor for heroism at Battle of Buffalo Wallow, pitting six soldiers and scouts against large number of Indians. Dixon was a hero also (as were all participants) at Second Battle of Adobe Walls, one of the most Hollywood of Indian-and-white confrontations. The deadly week-long fight pitched hide hunters and post operators against a force of about 700 Comanches, Kiowas, and Cheyennes, joined by a few Arapahos and Apaches. A young Comanche medicine man, Isatai (Little Wolf), was the chief instigator, telling a war council that a special warpaint he mixed would ward off bullets. A leader in the predawn attack, planned and organized over a period of several days, was the halfbreed Quanah Parker, whose white mother had been captured by Comanches as a little girl.

Billy Dixon, then twenty-three and already an experienced buffalo hunter, spotted the first attacking wave, early in the morning of June 27, 1874. He fired his new .50-caliber Sharps buffalo rifle and ran to the post's saloon, yelling warnings to the others. Two hunters were asleep in their wagons and were killed and scalped, as was their Newfoundland dog.

Everyone else took cover in the saloon and in two stores. These buildings had not been built as forts, so shooting by the defenders was through windows and doors and cracks in the walls. Among the hunters present was a youthful W. B. "Bat" Masterson.

Twenty-six men and one woman held out against the waves of war-painted attackers. The animated warriors, screaming and firing guns and shooting bows and arrows, laid siege to the post. In the first waves they rode right up to the buildings. Soon the withering fire from the deadly accurate buffalo rifles (most of them Sharps) took their toll. Several Indians were killed or wounded; among the dead was a son of Chief Stone Calf. A bugler who blew calls for the attackers was killed. Quanah Parker was hit by a spent bullet and his horse shot out from under him. Isatai, watching the melee from a distance, had his horse (covered with the magic war paint) shot too. The most amazing of all marksmanship—still talked about among rifle shooters—was Billy Dixon's killing of a warrior from 1,538 yards, using a Sharps buffalo rifle in .50 2 1/2-inch caliber. Dixon himself admitted that his had been a "scratch shot."

Only two more whites were killed (one by accident), and by the sixth day more hunters had reinforced the post, its defenders swelling to about a hundred.

The Indians had managed to drive off the post's horses; they took supplies from some wagons and did force the post's abandonment. The whites returned to Kansas, while the Indians split into smaller bands and raided parts of Texas, New Mexico, Kansas, and Colorado. These attacks killed about eighty whites that summer.

Years later it was learned that certain men at Adobe Walls knew in advance the attack was coming, but did not warn the hide hunters, for fear they would abandon the post. Only one of those who knew the attack was coming stayed at the post—and he managed to warn the hunters by firing a pistol to awaken the men (pretending a ridgepole was breaking in the saloon) on the morning he expected the attack—and then he kept them awake with free drinks.

The disgraced Isatai's English name, Lone Wolf, was derisively changed by some Indians to Coyote Droppings. His reputation as a medicine man was over.

and the territory occupied by today's Montana, Colorado, and Wyoming.

Yet another aristocratic adventure was the celebrated tour of the Grand Duke Alexis, a son of Czar Alexander II. The Grand Duke, first Romanov to visit America, was on a goodwill junket. However, as a devoted huntsman, he was enchanted by the opportunity to pursue the beasts of the West.

Young Alexis, all 6 feet 2 inches of him, was handsome and energetic, and only twenty-one years of age. A splendid parade in New York greeted him on arrival. He dined with President U. S. Grant and the keen hunter General Phil Sheridan at the White House, and visited the Smith & Wesson factory in Springfield, Massachusetts, inspecting revolvers in production for the Russian army and receiving a superbly gold-inlaid and engraved Russian Model for his own collection.

While at the White House, Alexis was enthralled of descriptions by Sheridan and Grant of the Great West. Having recently organized a hunt for *New York Herald* owner James Gordon Bennett and other millionaires, Sheridan filled Alexis in on their experiences. Before leaving the White House, Alexis was advised by Sheridan that he could hunt the West, with the U. S. Army at his beck and call.

Site of the first hunt would be Nebraska, near Fort McPherson and North Platte. To guarantee success, Sheridan arranged as guide a young hunter then mak-

---

(*opposite, bottom right*) Buffalo hunters Jim Elder (*left*) and Bill Tilghman, c. 1874. Factory records show Tilghman's Sharps Model 1874 sporting rifle shipped to F. C. Zimmerman, Dodge City, June 1874: 40-70 Sharps c.f., 32-inch octagonal barrel, double set triggers, open sights, oiled stocks, $42. Tilghman hunted buffalo c. 1870–75, during which time his total kill was just under 12,000. Crack hunters enjoyed solid income and social prestige. Among the best-known: New Yorkers Josiah and John Mooar, Bat and Edward Masterson, Wyatt Earp, "Prairie Dog Dave" Morrow, and O. A. "Brick" Bond. Bond was regarded by Tilghman as "most remarkable" of all, killed 200,000 buffalo in four years. Another hunter, Tom Nixon, was close under Bond's record and according to Tilghman "killed 120 buffalo in 40 minutes at one stand, which kept the barrel of his Sharps so hot it burned out in the process."

267

The highly touted Sharps. *From left*, Model 1850 or Second Model rifle and the Model 1849 or First Model rifle, both types standard in .36 and .44 calibers; Model 1853 shotgun; Model 1853 sporting rifle, in .36, .44, and .52 calibers; and the metallic-cartridge Model 1874 target rifle. The 1874 was built in a wide variety of types, and of calibers, barrel lengths and weights, finishes, sights, buttplates, and stocks.

ing a national name for himself: William F. "Buffalo Bill" Cody.

Camp Alexis was established, with Chief Spotted Tail of the Sioux agreeing to put on a show with 1,000 Indians! A special train for the expedition, stocked with exotic game food and spiritous beverages, bore the Grand Duke's party and General Sheridan. They were soon joined by the flamboyant Lieutenant Colonel George Armstrong Custer, as the hunt's grand marshal and official escort to Alexis. On arrival of the special

Cheyenne shop of Freund's Wyoming Armory, c. 1880.

A Hold Up on the Prairie, an oil painting by Robert O. Lindneux, a friend of fellow artist Charles M. Russell and of Buffalo Bill Cody.

(*opposite*) Gentlemen-sportsmen, after successful buffalo hunt. Guide at *center* armed with Spencer carbine. Double rifle at *right*; balance of sportsmen appear to have preferred Remington rolling-blocks. C. 1870s.

train to North Platte, January 12, 1872, the entourage (greeted the next morning by the whole town) was some 500 strong: military officers, two companies each of infantrymen (in wagons) and cavalrymen, the regimental band of the 2nd Cavalry, a variety of other support personnel, and no less than three wagons full of wine, champagne, and liquor.

That evening, at a festive dinner, the Duke was given pointers on hunting buffalo by an exuberant Cody. Out on the plains the next morning, buffalo by the thousands were visible to the hunting party. Alexis rode Buffalo Bill's horse, Buckskin Joe, and proceeded to attempt killing his prey on the run. However, Joe was trained to dart after another buffalo on hearing one shot (all it took for Cody to make a kill), and Alexis emptied two revolvers without downing a single beast. Cody then rode up to Alexis and gave him "Lucretia Borgia," Cody's buffalo-killing Springfield trapdoor rifle:

[I] told him to urge his horse close to the buffaloes, and I would give him word when to shoot. At the same time I gave old Buckskin Joe a blow with my whip, and with a few jumps the horse carried the grand duke to within about ten feet of a big buffalo bull. "Now is your time," said I. He fired, and down went the buffalo.

The generally self-composed Alexis then became animated with the thrill of his triumph. An eyewitness captured the moment:

The Grand Duke leaped from the saddle in a transport of astonishment, turned the horse loose, threw the gun down, cut off the tail as a souvenir, and then, sitting down on the carcass, waved the dripping trophy, and let out a series of howls and gurgles like the death-song of all the foghorns and calliopes ever born. The Russians galloped up and he poured out excitement in a strange northern tongue, so steadily and so volubly that Cody reeled in his saddle. His countrymen embraced and hugged him. The gory trophy went from hand to hand till all were plastered with blood and dirt.

Next was celebratory champagne, and an elaborate luncheon on the prairie. During lunch an Indian killed a buffalo with a bow and arrow, demonstrating to the Duke the effectiveness of these weapons (Alexis had

269

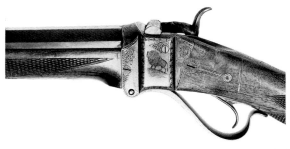

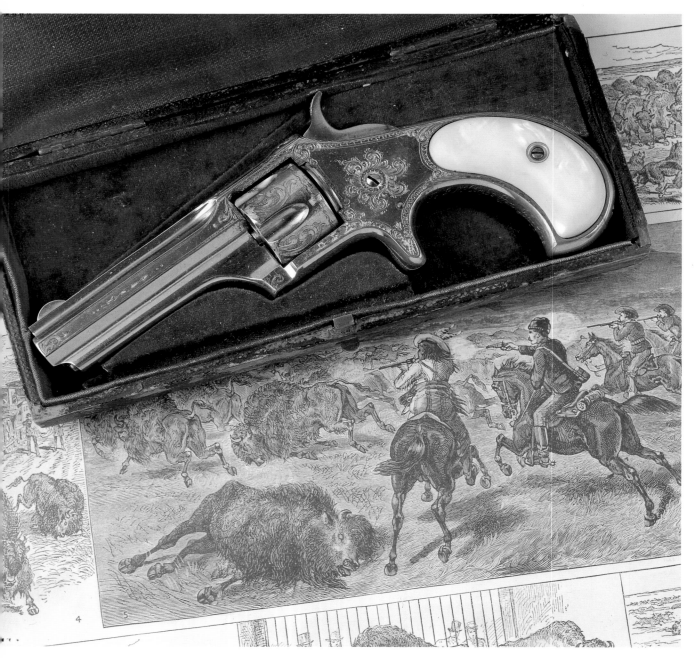

A custom Sharps rifle, by Freund; the buffalo engraved in primitive style. A catalogue of F. W. Freund and his Wyoming Armory, from the mid-1880s, noted on the cover: "The F. W. Freund's Patent Rifle/Acknowledged to the Best in the World./Military Men of Highest Rank, Long Range Shootists, Miners, Stockmen, Tourists/And Frontiersmen of the Far West, all say the same." Among those whose testimonials were quoted: Generals Phil Sheridan, George Crook, and W. E. Strong, Pierre Lorillard, and E. Remington (Ilion, New York).

Buffalo hunters skinning hide, 1874. Carbine by Sharps.

Remington pocket revolver, cased in Sharps rifle sight box; inscribed on inside curve of grip frame *to J McCombs from John Poe/Ft. Griffin Texas 1874*. Joe S. McCombs and John William Poe were buffalo hunters who set out on a hunt, December 25, 1874, from Fort Griffin, Texas. By the following May1, the hunters (working with a third professional, John C. Jacobs) had taken 1,300 hides.

"Antelope" Ernst Bauman, market hunter, Denver lawman, Indian scout, champion rifle shot, and amateur artist. Bauman's Sharps Model 1874 sporting rifle, number 155798, fitted with sights marked by J. P. Lower, Denver. Amber lenses in shooting glasses, the right frosted except for very center; left covered over with pasted-on paper. Antelope-skin rifle case may relate to Bauman's nickname. These Bauman items, the buckskin suit, and more are in Gene Autry Western Heritage Museum collection.

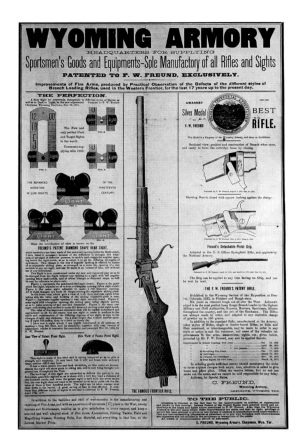

One side of Freund brochure, promoting sights and guns. Other side quoted letters of recommendation, more on sights, advantages of Wyoming Armory arms, and new improved rifle, *"made entirely by hand."* c. 1882.

Sharps rifle converted c. 1870s by gunsmith in Montana Territory, from Civil War cavalry carbine. Heavy 24-inch octagon barrel, marked A.B. CHARPIE/HELENA/M.T., .50 c.f. caliber, 11 1/2-pound weight. Bowie knife with J. P. Lower & Son, Denver, markings. Brass buckle of period promoted Lower's Sportsmen Depot; belt holds thirty-eight cartridges in metal containers. Rival C. Gove & Sons buckle, with belt holding twenty-eight cartridges. U.S. Army issue map printed on cloth; compiled 1869.

TR and his favorite Model 1876 Winchester; Bowie knife by Tiffany & Co. tucked into cartridge belt, c. 1885.

termed them "absurd toys") and presented the arrow —which had gone through the buffalo—to Alexis.

With a revolver at thirty yards, Alexis killed his second buffalo that afternoon, upon which more champagne flowed. Buffalo Bill coyly remarked: "I was in hopes that he would kill five or six more before we reached camp, especially if a basket of champagne was to be opened every time he dropped one." Alexis would kill another six buffalo, and the total from two days' shooting came to fifty-six.

A grateful and elated Alexis showered Cody with a number of presents, including gold cuff links. The hunt was something of a trial run for Buffalo Bill's first Wild West show. The event also received enormous press coverage and became another thrilling episode in the rapidly evolving legend of Buffalo Bill.

Still another buffalo hunt was organized for Alexis when he was feted in Denver. Led by Alexis and Custer, the party of some hundred cavalrymen and civilians charged into a herd of buffalo, firing at will. This time 200 were killed, 62 of them by Alexis! The Grand Duke was so thrilled that he hugged and kissed Lieutenant Colonel Custer. Becoming fast friends, Custer (and his wife Elizabeth) accompanied Alexis on much of the rest of the tour.

Devoting the rest of his life to aristocratic pleasantries, rich food and fine drinks, and the company of his mistresses, Alexis spent most of his later years in St. Petersburg and Paris; he died at age fifty-eight. The great hunt in America, with Buffalo Bill and officers Custer and Sheridan, was likely the adventurous highlight of his entire life.

The Earl of Dunraven

Though not as celebrated in America as the Grand Duke Alexis, every bit as enthusiastic over the West and its hunts was Windham Thomas Wyndham-Quin, Fourth Earl of Dunraven. An adventurous soul, Dunraven had vivid dreams:

> I was young—not twenty-eight years of age [1869]; and my boyish brain-cells were stored to bursting with tales of Red Indians

and grizzly b'ars; caballeros and haciendas, prairies and buffaloes, Texans and Mexicans, cowboys and voyageurs, and had not yet discharged or jettisoned their cargo. I was in search of such sport and adventure as, under the circumstances, were to be found.

Arriving in America in 1869, Wyndham-Quin cavorted and socialized in the East on a honeymoon with his wife, to the point of collapsing from sunstroke. He sailed back to England and would not return to America until 1872. By then he was Lord Dunraven, having inherited his title on the death of his father.

Heading quickly West, he had a meeting with General Phil Sheridan to discuss plans for an ambitious hunt. With his companion, private physician George Henry Kinsley, Dunraven rode by train to North Platte, Nebraska, to meet with the guides suggested by Sheridan: Buffalo Bill Cody and Texas Jack Omohundro.

Dunraven's description of the two showed instant admiration, and referred to Texas Jack's armaments: "Round his waist was a belt supporting a revolver, two butcher knives, and, in his hand he carried his trusty rifle, the 'Widow'—now in my possession. . . ."

The month-long hunt was a resounding success, with a fine elk trophy taken for the Earl's estate. On returning to North Platte, the party was described by Dunraven himself as "about the dirtiest, most blood-stained, hungriest, happiest, most contented, and most disreputable crowd to be found anywhere in the great territories of the West."

In the fall of 1872, Dunraven and Kingsley returned for still another hunt. Cody and Omohundro took them after buffalo, but that trip did not prove successful. After a bighorn sheep hunt and other adventures, the two British gentlemen reached Denver at Christmastime. Later, hunting elk and sight-seeing, the Earl decided to acquire his own hunting preserve in the United States. A real estate agent was given the task of putting a purchase together, while his lordship and Kinsley returned to Ireland.

The party was back in the West again in 1874, now with an estate in Estes Park, Colorado, of some 4,000 acres. For various reasons, including lack of the freedom and privacy the Earl had anticipated, Estes Park

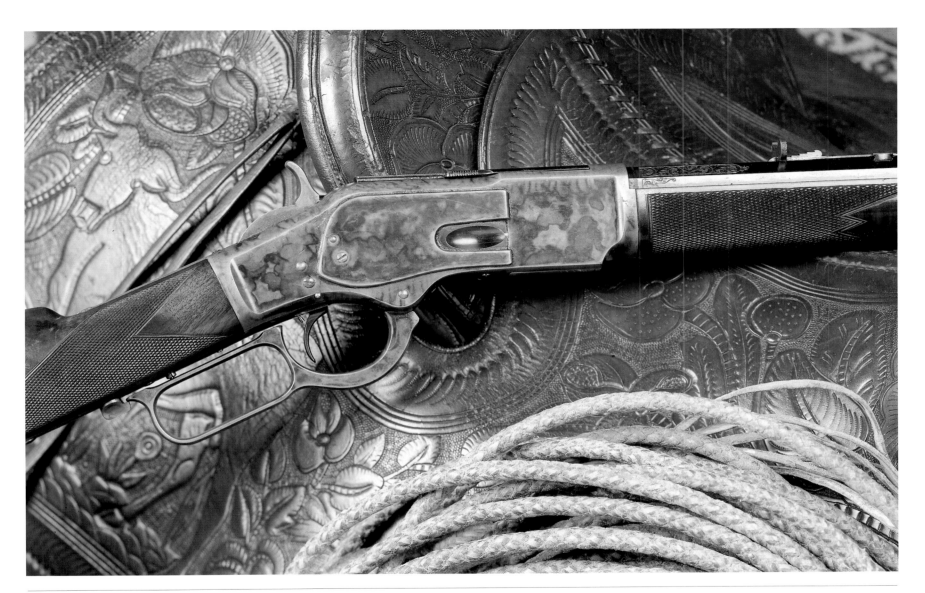

Finest-known Winchester Model 1873 "One of One Thousand" rifle, number 40633. Shipped from factory, November 25, 1879, as folows: rifle, octagon barrel of 26-inch length, case-hardened, checkered stock, set trigger, 1 of 1000. The factory's 1875 catalogue referred to the process of selection: "All of those barrels that are found to make targets of extra merit will be made up into guns with set-triggers and extra finish, and marked as a designating name 'one of thousand,' and sold at $100." These rifles came to be the best-known custom guns in the history of Winchester.

(*opposite*) Theodore Roosevlet's deluxe Model 1876 (*left*), A5-75, number 38647, one of his finest rifles. With this he "killed every kind of game…from a grizzly bear to a big-horn." Companion rifle a presentation to guide and friend Bill Merrifield; bears brand of TR's Maltese Cross Ranch.

Determined hunter, Bowie knife, and Model 1873 Winchester on the mark.

Hunters, bears, bear traps, and guns, in Carbon County, Montana, at ranch of Paul Bretesche; late 1880s. Pump rifle the large-frame Colt Lightning, in express caliber. Rifle at *left* appears to be a light-caliber English single-shot—unsafe for pursuit of bear.

Tiffany & Co. skinning sets for sportsmen, as displayed by the firm in the Paris Exposition of 1900. Both sets liberally marked with Tiffany & Co. stamps, on knives, saws, sharpening rod, and leather cases. Stag grips with silver escutcheons. Firm has long history of association with fine guns and accessories, begun before the Civil War, and continuing through to World WarI, reintroduced again c. 1983.

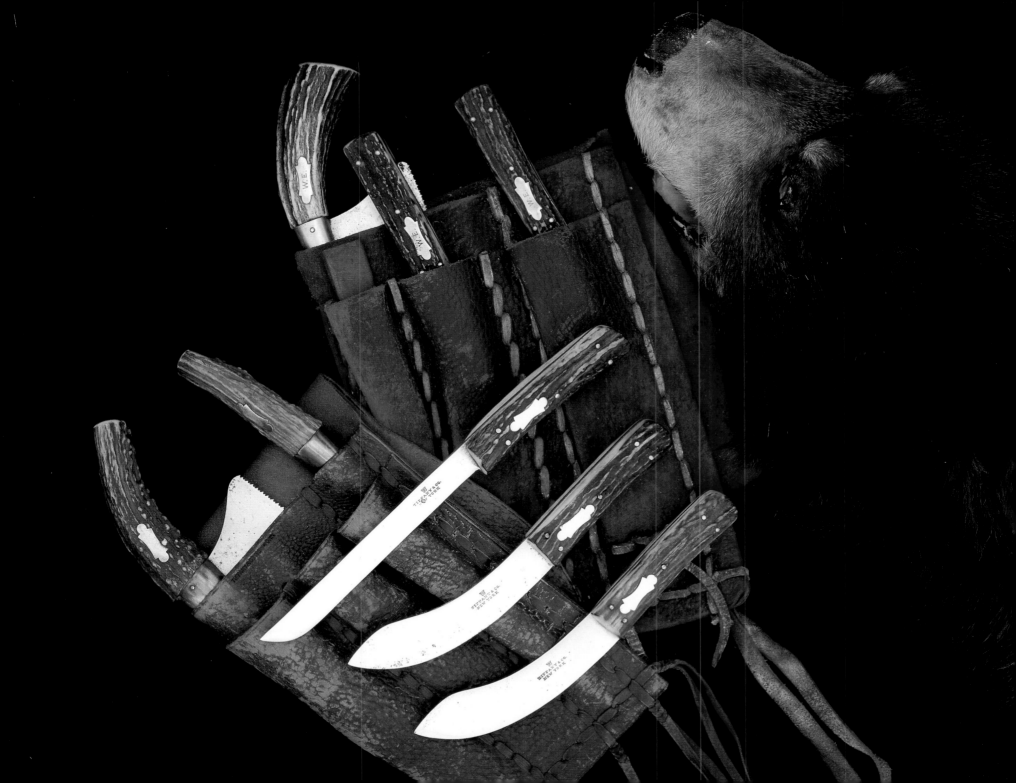

After hanging the meat; hunting party in Colorado, c. 1885. Deer, elk, mountain sheep, mountain lion, and bear all taken. Hunters armed with Winchester and Sharps rifles.

became a real estate investment rather than a hunting preserve.

Among those the Earl met during his adventures in America was the artist Albert Bierstadt, who was along on the Estes Park expedition of 1874 and painted pictures for the Earl's homes in America and Ireland. Squatters on Estes Park and real estate problems were quashing the Earl's hopes for the park's development. When he left the area, discouraged, his landholdings were 6,600 acres, leased by him in 1883, and finally sold out nearly a quarter of a century later.

Dunraven's memories of the West remained cherished until his death in 1926, aged eighty-five. Among reminders of his adventures were guns given him by Texas Jack, inscribed to Earl, as if that were Dunraven's first name!

The Buffalo Hunters

The last of the rendezvous of the mountain men was held in 1838, at Popo Agie Creek, not far from the Wind River Mountains, Wyoming. The beaver market had collapsed, and the majority of mountain men had to turn to other livelihoods. Some of them became buffalo hunters.

The near extermination of the buffalo presents the most shocking example of wildlife excess in American history, and served as the impetus to organize a public and government campaign to save wildlife and its habitat.

The efforts of only a few hundred professional market hunters, from the years 1865 to 1882, were needed to kill off millions of buffalo. At one time over 100 million roamed North America, from Canada to Mexico and nearly from coast to coast. Most of the beasts were on the Great Plains, living in roughly circular migrating patterns to renewing grasslands, pursued by wolves and grizzly bears and intermingled with pronghorn antelope.

As early as 1832, the diary of artist Karl Bodmer recorded 43,000 buffalo hides being shipped from Fort Union, Dakota Territory, to St. Louis, mostly from Indian dealings with traders.

The herds were then still massive, far more than the Indians could ever have killed off themselves. Among those who hunted buffalo the Indian way, coursing from horseback, was John James Audubon. In the summer of 1843, along the Missouri River, the aging artist survived a charge by a buffalo bull.

As late as 1871 a herd observed by Major R. I. Dodge in Colorado was estimated at some 4 million strong, spread over an area of about 50 by 200 miles. In October 1871, during blizzard weather along the Smokey Hill River, Colorado, a group of soldiers saw part of that herd; an officer described it:

> For six days we continued our way through this enormous herd, during the last three days of which it was in constant motion across our path. I am safe in calling this a single herd, and it is impossible to approximate the numbers that composed it. At times they pressed before us in such numbers as to delay the progress of our column, and often a belligerent bull would lower and shake his craggy head at us when we passed him a few feet distant.

As the railroad penetrated the West, transportation accessed the hunters readily to markets. Buffaloes were also shot by hunters like young W. F. Cody, to feed construction crews, and later for dining passengers.

Cody was hired as a professional hunter, contracted for by the Kansas Pacific Railway. Beginning in 1867, "Buffalo Bill," over an eighteen-month period, killed 4,280 buffalo. His record for one day was sixty-nine, in a mounted contest against another hunter, whose count was forty-six.

But most buffalo were killed for their hides, by hunters firing at distances with high-powered rifles. The buffalo would continue to graze until the hunters had killed the number they wished. The wagons and skinners would then move in to take the commercial parts. As the hide and meat markets subsided, with tongues a delicacy, vast numbers were killed for tongues only. In 1865 an estimated 1 million buffalo were slaughtered. In each of the years 1871 and 1872, approximately 5 million were killed. By 1881, most of the millions had been killed off, except for north of the Platte River, with about 1,500,000 beasts left.

The "Double W" cartridge board, c. 1897, exhibited choice of Winchester's cartridges; an A. B. Frost print at *center*, above H honoring memory of Civil War–era mechanic and inventor, B. Tyler Henry. Wide spectrum of advertising art commissioned by Winchester, Remington, Marlin, Colt, and other gun and cartridge firms, often with Western themes and often employing artists known for Western subjects, among them Frederic Remington, W. R. Leigh, N. C. Wyeth, and Philip R. Goodwin.

Some states attempted to limit the killing, but the military was in opposition—to them the end of the buffalo meant the end of the Indian. And to the railroad, buffalo hunting was good for business.

As a source of income, buffalo hunters had shot out the herds by 1882. The last surviving group in significant numbers from the Great Plains became that at Yellowstone National Park. Another savior of the species, ironically, was Buffalo Bill himself, who had a collection performing in his Wild West show.

Expert James B. Trefethen has termed the destruction of the immense migrating buffalo herds as "the most brutal and wasteful chapter in the history of America's wildlife." Further, what happened with the buffalo shocked thoughtful people into doing something to prevent anything like that from happening again. Thus, the tragic chapter gave impetus to a growing conservation movement.

Although market hunting in the West had largely ended with destruction of the great buffalo herds, set-

By L. Villegia, San Francisco, superb shotgun testifies to demand for fine guns; c. 1860. San Francisco dealer Charles Curry offered the following distinguished makers (mainly English), August 1860: "Wm Greener, Westley Richards, J. Manton, Moore & Harris, Robert Chaplain, Chas. Jones, John Wiggans, Bentley & Son, Robert Adams, Middleton, J. Parker, Mortimer, Thos. Stevens; also, J. M. Evans and W. W. Keyes of Philadelphia, besides other makers too numerous to mention.

(*opposite*) John Krider's trade card is one of the most beautiful from nineteenth-century American gunmaking. At *left*, a Colt Model 1883 hammerless shotgun, and the presentation Lefever Optimus of President Benjamin Harrison: examples of quality worthy of comparison with most contemporary European makers.

tlers and sportsmen brought in via railroads continued, on a smaller scale, the killing of wildlife. Limits on animals were nonexistent; shooting bags were left to the individual to determine.

After the Buffaloes

Still another of the foreign blue bloods who were keen on the West and enjoyed the hunt was the Marquis de Mores. At twenty-four, in 1883, he hoped to set up a cattle empire in the Dakota Badlands. An aristocrat with an American wife, the Marquis had a heroic view of life, was a French army officer, and felt he could make a fortune in the beef business. Assisting him in these endeavors was his father-in-law, Baron Louis von Hoffmann. The Baron's daughter, Medora, loved to shoot; she had a fine-quality arsenal and her own hunting palace, a wagon complete with bathroom and other conveniences. The Marquis even said that her shooting with a rifle beat his.

The ranch plan proved to be a bust, and an expensive one at that. Besides building his own town, appropriately named Medora, the Marquis built a packing plant to allow shipping of meat to markets in ice-packed railroad cars.

The Marquis had quite an aristocratic demeanor, and according to the *Detroit Free Press*, "Around his waist [was] a leather belt filled with gun cartridges; it also held two long-barrelled Colt's revolvers of heavy calibre and a bowie knife which would bear inspection even in Arkansas. His gun was double-barrelled, made in Paris, a breechloader of plain but accurate finish, having a rubber shoulder piece at the butt to take up the shock of the recoil. The arrangement of the locks permitted instant firing." As evident from photographs, the Marquis was fond of the Model 1876 Winchester rifle, like his neighbor, one Theodore Roosevelt.

De Mores was not particularly popular in the Badlands, in part because his ranching operation threatened to interfere with guided hunts for visiting dudes. After he had invested over $1 million in the Medora business, the enterprise collapsed, and the Marquis, his wife and children, and his valet abandoned the town.

Bad luck plagued the Marquis until he was killed by tribesmen in northern Africa in 1896. In the heroic style he so admired, de Mores fought the attackers with his Badlands Colt revolvers, killing three before succumbing to knife and sword wounds.

American Huntsmen

Besides the British and continental blue bloods, America's own aristocrats, the upper crust of society, were captivated by the West and devoted to the hunt. Foremost among these devotees was Theodore Roosevelt, who credited his experiences in the West with much of his success in a quite remarkable life.

Clearly TR's hunts and his awareness of the pressures on Western wildlife led to the unequaled leadership role he took in conservation. While completing *Ranch Life and the Hunting Trail*, second of his books on hunting, he was instrumental in establishing a national organization dedicated to the outdoors and to wildlife conservation: the Boone and Crockett Club (1887).

Prominent among the club's charter members were artist Albert Bierstadt, naturalist George Bird Grinnell, and TR's brother Elliott (father of Eleanor Roosevelt). TR wrote the club's constitution and was its first president. Members had to have taken in fair chase "at least one individual of one of the various kinds of American large game." The species listed covered all those then in the West (including Canada): "bears, buffalo (bison), mountain-sheep, caribou, cougar, musk-ox, white goat, elk (wapiti), wolf (not coyote), prong-horn antelope, moose, and deer." Membership was limited to one hundred, but the club's influence on wildlife conservation, hunting, and forest preservation in America was unequaled. The New York Zoological Society, Glacier National Park, and innumerable federal game preserves are among the achievements of the Boone and Crockett Club.

Still another organization of achievement and pioneering leadership in wildlife conservation in America was The Camp Fire Club of America (1897), of which TR was an active member. Both organizations remain

Visiting sportswomen from Worcester, Massachusetts, Mrs. Houghton and Mrs. Marble, by Northern Pacific observation car, game bag, and retrievers, 1876.

(*opposite*) A day shooting wild turkeys, the Cherokee Strip, Oklahoma, 1890s. Species, once going the way of buffalo, has been returned in numbers to forty-nine states and boasts largest populations since before 1800. A triumph of sound game management and conservation practices, spearheaded by hunters and sportsmen.

vigorously devoted to conservation to this day.

The author's book *Theodore Roosevelt Outdoorsman* chronicles the unique legacy of Theodore Roosevelt in conservation, and much of what he accomplished was inspired by his many years of hunting in the West. The very first of these hunts after big game demonstrates TR's pluck and sportsmanship. His guide, Joe Ferris, took TR off into the Badlands, looking for buffalo (1883). TR carried a .45-120-caliber Sharps rifle. After a week of tracking and searching, through rain and mud, with their horses temporarily running away in fright from what appeared to be coyotes, TR finally got a buffalo with "a dandy shot. . . . Roosevelt was like a boy just out of school and so was I. I never saw any one so enthused in all my life and by golly, I was enthused for more reasons than one. I was plumb tired out and he was so eager to shoot his first buffalo that it somehow got into my blood and I wanted to see him kill his first one as badly as he wanted to. . . ." Roosevelt was so ecstatic that he improvised an Indian war dance around the fallen hulk and then gave a flabbergasted Ferris $100 in cash!

TR's preference for the Winchester Model 1876, and for Winchesters in general, was described in *Hunting Trips of a Ranchman*, his first outdoors book (1885):

The Winchester [Model 1876 .45-75], stocked and sighted to suit myself, is by all odds the best weapon I ever had, and I now use it almost exclusively, having killed every kind of game with it, from a grizzly bear to a big-horn. It is as handy to carry, whether on foot or on horseback, and comes up to the shoulder as readily as a shot-gun; it is absolutely sure, and there is no recoil to jar and disturb the aim, while it carries accurately quite as far as a man can aim with any degree of certainty; and the bullet, weighing three quarters of an ounce, is plenty large enough for any thing on this continent. . . . the Winchester is the best gun for any game to be found in the United States, for it is deadly, accurate, and handy as any, stands very rough usage, and is unapproachable for the rapidity of its fire and the facility with which it is loaded.

TR's firearms battery for his Western hunts quickly concentrated on the lever-action Winchester. The ever-growing Roosevelt arms collection ran through the entire range of the lever-action Winchesters: the 1873, 1876, 1886, 1892, 1894 and 1895, in calibers from as small as .32-20 to as large as .45-90. His expertise was based on wide practical experience, from years of hunting in North America, mainly the West. He owned over fifty firearms, primarily rifles, and could discuss guns, ammunition, and hunting, as well as wildlife and conservation, with any contemporary expert. TR had even mastered hand-loading, which he is known to have done while President. His legacy to generations of sportsmen and hunter-conservationists has no equal.

The writings of Roosevelt and other Americans, as well as those of continental and British sportsmen, have left a thorough literature on the hunters and gentlemen-sportsmen of the West.

Crusading for Wildlife

In contrast to the ofttimes regal sportsmen and most of the settlers, ranchers, cowboys, military peace officers, shopkeepers, and others were the market hunters, that breed not inclined to think in terms of conservation and intent on exploiting wildlife for profit.

At the time TR became deeply engaged in hunting the West, the great buffalo herds had been decimated and other game species were threatened. The stage was set for the beginnings of the world's most effective conservation programs, the roots of which date back to America's sportsmen.

The responsible sportsmen and hunters became saviors of the wildlife, in a movement which remains active in modern times and which has returned several species to populations exceeding their numbers at the close of the nineteenth century. Whitetail and mule deer, wild turkey, elk, pronghorn antelope, black bear, wild sheep, and buffalo all owe their rejuvenation to generations of sportsmen more than to any other segment of our population.

Inspired by such leaders as Theodore Roosevelt, wildlife management in America rapidly developed in the late nineteenth century and made great strides in the early twentieth. By the First World War, almost all states had offices established to administer conservation projects for wildlife protection. Publicly and privately the movement remains powerful and effective, in contrast to sham private conservation and wildlife protective groups which are effective mainly as self-serving fund-raisers.

Hunting licenses helped in financing the state offices and their staffs. And in 1937 the Pittman-Robertson Act was passed, by which a 10 percent excise tax on firearms and ammunition sales was earmarked to fund wildlife projects on state and federal levels.

Hunting in the West today is a multimillion-dollar business, considering license fees, costs of guns and ammunition, luggage and equipment, travel costs, lodging, guide fees, and more.

And for some species, groups like the Foundation for North American Wild Sheep have auctions in which a hunt for a specific game animal brings over $75,000, all of which is earmarked for conservation projects.

Some of the most spectacular sporting guns ever made were intended to raise funds for conservation projects. Adorned with wildlife scenes and scroll engraving and usually richly gold-inlaid, these and less deluxe guns have raised millions of dollars for conservation. Much of the funding has been raised for spending in the West, but these projects have worldwide application. Fund-raising has been undertaken in the main by the Boone and Crockett Club, The Camp Fire Club of America, the Foundation for North American Wild Sheep, the Rocky Mountain Elk Foundation, Ducks Unlimited, the National Wild Turkey Federation, the National Shooting Sports Foundation, Safari Club International, and the National Rifle Association of America.

Today's West remains a sportsman's paradise, thanks to the traditions of conservation and sportsmanship established by pioneers like Theodore Roosevelt and the spirit of conservation brought to America by the aristocrats and adventurers like William Drummond Stewart and the Earl of Dunraven.

Marlin Model 1889 Centennial rifle, gold-inlaid and engraved, with deluxe walnut stocks, as fund-raiser for National Shooting Sports Foundation, Riverside, Connecticut. Offered at NSSF's 1989 Shooting and Hunting Outdoor Trade Show, proceeds from which were earmarked for organization's educational activities in schools. NSSF has raised hundreds of thousands of dollars from similar special guns and from cartridge boards donated by firearms and ammunition manufacturers. Cased rifle donated by Marlin Firearms Co.; engraving and inlaying by A. A.White of American Master Engravers, Inc., stock by Fred Wenig of Reinhart Fajen, Inc. Realized $21,400 at auction.

WILD WEST SHOWMEN, AND WOMEN

P. T. Barnum's one-day "Grand Buffalo Hunt" in Hoboken, New Jersey, is recognized by many as the earliest Wild West show. The buffaloes had been brought down from Boston, after dedication ceremonies of the Bunker Hill monument. Sundry circus groups put on shows with hints of Wild West programs, and then there was James Capen "Grizzly" Adams's California Menagerie—presented to New Yorkers with the cooperation of P. T. Barnum.

Stage performances by Buffalo Bill, sometimes with Wild Bill Hickok, date as early as 1869. Hickok got into some mischief, not being able to resist the temptation of firing blanks from his Colt Navys at the legs of actors playing Indian roles. Cody's melodramatic performances presented a spectacle of shooting and marksmanship, horses, and fireworks. Besides Wild Bill Hickok and (briefly) Ned Buntline, stars were Texas Jack Omohundro, his girlfriend and later wife Mlle. Morlacchi, and a troupe of Indians, both real and made-up.

In the off-season Cody would often guide hunting parties and sometimes serve as Army scout. He killed the Indian Chief Yellow Hand in 1876, and that led to more fame, and the melodrama *The Red Right Hand; or, Buffalo Bill's First Scalp for Custer*. Still another stage performer with Cody was Captain Jack Crawford, known as the Poet Scout.

The first successful Wild West show was that created by Buffalo Bill. The buffalo hunt for the Grand Duke Alexis, organized at the request of General Phil Sheridan, and with George A. Custer, was a hint of an institution to come. Cody's hunting forays with publisher James Gordon Bennett and friends and the Earl of Dunraven were also preludes to the main event.

Buffalo Bill remained dominant personality and star in Wild West genre for over forty years. Mementoes of the epoch: silver-mounted and Indian-trade-bead-decorated holster rig by George E. Robbins, Miles City, Montana; S&W of Texas Jack; Cody's 12-gauge Westley Richards shotgun; Indian peace medal of President James A. Garfield term; Cody gauntlets and Wild West show program; and presentation tomahawk of Cody chum "White Beaver," actually Dr. David Franklin Powell.

Unidentified character, whose costume and pose suggest show business association. Back of photograph marked "Old Death on the Trail."

As a scout, Cody in buckskins, his rifle an English best-quality sporting arm of the type the Earl of Dunraven would have brought on his American hunts.

William F. Cody, c. 1871; already known as "Buffalo Bill" for at least four years. A jingle coined while making his reputation:

    Buffalo Bill, Buffalo Bill,
    Never missed and never will,
    Always aims and shoots to kill,
    And the company pays his buffalo bill.

Tintype believed made at Fort McPherson.

Ned Buntline Sharps rifle and leather carrying case; invoiced to E. Z. C. Judson, Stamford, New York, May 4, 1877. Sharps president E. G. Wescott agreed to "our best trade discount which we never give except on rifles by the case and to the trade; assuming that you will become so greatly impressed with its merits, that you will be unable to resist the temptation to tell the *dear public* in some of your 'yarns' as to what you think of Sharps' OLD RELIABLE." Model 1874 sporting, in .45 2 7/8-inch caliber, 30-inch barrel, double set triggers, number 160009. Inset photo shows Buntline with Cody, Mme. Giuseppina Morlacchi, and Texas Jack, during engagement of *The Scouts of the Prairie*, written for Cody by Buntline and performed in winter 1872–73 season.

Looking the role of a cavalier with his plumed hat, Cody occupied center stage, with Elisha Green and Wild Bill Hickok at *left*, and Texas Jack Omohundro and Eugene Overton at *right*. The occasion was theatrical tour of *The Scouts of the Plains* in the fall and winter 1873–74 season.

But what propelled Cody into Wild West shows in a serious way was the Fourth of July celebration he organized for North Platte, Nebraska, in 1882. A thousand cowboys competed for prizes in shooting, riding, roping, and bronco busting, and Cody put on a demonstration (with blanks) of pursuing and killing buffalo from horseback. The outdoor event was such a success that authority Don Russell hails it as "the beginning of both the Wild West Show and the rodeo."

Cody then put together a troupe and performed in the 1882–83 season. While on tour he met with showman Doc Carver, in New Haven, Connecticut. Carver, known as the "Champion Rifle Shot of the World," had already done a tour of Europe (1879–82) and would take on all comers in a shooting match. Carver was also known as the "Evil Spirit of the Plains." Briefly, Cody and Carver toured as partners.

Another Cody rival and sometime partner was Captain A. H. Bogardus, a former market hunter who would pioneer the sport of trap shooting. Other showmen associated with Cody in the early years were the Indian fighter Major Frank North, Pawnee Bill Lillie, and cowboys Johnny Baker ("The Cowboy Kid"), and Buck Taylor ("King of the Cowboys").

On tour in 1883, the show was billed as "The Wild West, Hon. W. F. Cody and Dr. W. F. Carver's Rocky Mountain and Prairie Exhibition," with the spectacular opening at Omaha's Fair Grounds, in May. Before the public's very eyes was the Deadwood stagecoach under attack, buffalo coursing, the Pony Express, races, bronc riding, roping, steer riding, and the "Grand Hunt on the Plains." Featured wild animals were buffalo, bighorn sheep, deer, and elk, as well as longhorn steers and wild horses. That first season saw the show play as far east as Newport, Rhode Island, and Boston.

In Hartford, the *Courant* was so taken by the Wild West that Cody was hailed as "an extraordinary figure" who "sits on a horse as if he were born to the saddle. His feats of shooting are perfectly wonderful. . . . " It was "the best open-air show ever seen," and Cody "out-Barnumed Barnum."

Doc Carver and Winchester 1873 rifle. Subheading to caption reads: "As he appeared before H. R. H. the Prince of Wales at Sandringham, April 15th 1879, on which occasion he broke one hundred glass balls consequtively with rifle."

From a grateful Cody to dime-novel writer Colonel Prentiss Ingraham, butt of Remington over-and-under deringer neatly inscribed, number 5181. Another deringer known, inscribed on backstrap *Wm Fielder./from/Buffalo Bill*. Engraved, silver-plated, pearl-gripped, and in a silk-lined leather case.

Bogardus & Sons, still more Champion Shots of the World. The Captain's practice of shooting glass balls launched from traps (instead of live birds released from boxes) led to sport of trapshooting. But not in time to save passenger pigeon from extinction, because of heavy demand for delicacy of squab.

Buffalo Bill's Colt Burgess lever-action .44-40 rifle, inscribed on other side "Hon. Wm. F. Cody July 26 1883/with Compliments of Colts Co." Presented to Cody while on tour, in Hartford. The Colt company was always anxious to accommodate Buffalo Bill and his contemporaries. Among Colt handguns made for Cody were specials in single action, double action, and semiautomatic mechanisms. Saddle of c. 1890–95, by Collins and Morrison, Omaha, inscribed with Cody's name and decorated with round conchos of 1881 silver dollars.

Card at *right center* is Cody's own documentation of Remington New Model Army revolver (number 73293), presented to Charles Trego, intimate friend and business associate over some thirty years. A wealth of material documents the revolver as Cody's personal working handgun from scout, Indian fighter, and buffalo hunter days. Trego was foreman of Cody's Scout's Rest Ranch and for years looked after his show horses; also traveled as general manager of the Wild West show. Trego was the model for Frederic Remington's only monumental bronze, *The Cowboy*, in Philadelphia's Fairmount Park (1908), and is believed to have served as model for other of the artist's works as well. Revolver, memorabilia, and documents from collection of Charles Trego family.

Cody's various partners, for a number of reasons, soon left. But he persevered to become the archetypal Wild West show performer and entrepreneur, and the international superstar of contemporary show business. He was, after all, a real-life hero: Pony Express rider, hunter, Army scout, Union Civil War soldier, professional hunting guide, and veteran of some sixteen Indian fights. His instincts as a showman were superb.

Although Ned Buntline (Edward Z. C. Judson) wrote a handful of dime novels with Buffalo Bill as hero, and they performed together briefly on the stage, Buntline played a minor role in the career of Buffalo Bill. Far more deserving of credit for promoting Cody was Prentiss Ingraham, a prolific author credited with over 1,000 dime novels. For Cody, Ingraham wrote *The Knight of the Plains; or, Buffalo Bill's Best Trail*, a play that premiered in New Haven, with Buffalo Bill as star. As a ghost writer for Cody, Ingraham penned approximately eighty-five dime novels, but it was apparently Cody himself who wrote the first autobiography, *The Life of Hon. William F. Cody* (c. 1879).

Cody played eleven seasons of melodramatic stage appearances before his Wild West outdoors career took off with the Omaha Fair Grounds July 4, 1883, event. These stage performances included shootings and marksmanship, horses, and fireworks.

1888 poster revealed Cody biography, left nothing of positive image out. One of grandest of numerous Buffalo Bill posters. Note Model 1873 Winchester rifle; Cody preferred Winchesters, and stated in a 1902 program: "As you know, I always use Winchester rifles and ammunition. I have used both exclusively for over twenty years for hunting and in my entertainments."

Gold-plated handguns flashed in sun as Annie Oakley opened their leather case at center arena; were gifts from husband, Frank Butler. Single-shot at *left* a Stevens-Gould No. 37, other single-shot a First Model S&W; revolver a S&W Model No. 3. Ensemble put together by Butler as presentation, in the 1890s. L. C. Smith shotgun (by Hunter Arms Co.) a 12-gauge "Trap" grade; portraits of Miss Oakley on lockplates, and her signature gold-inlaid on triggerguard; embellishment attributed to Tiffany & Co. Glass targets were popularized by Miss Oakley and other trick and competition shots.

An Oakley show specialty, firing over shoulder by aiming in mirror. Among other feats was shooting cigarettes out of mouths of dignitaries, among them Kaiser Wilhelm of Germany. After World War I began, Annie announced she wished she had opportunity to do trick again, and this time she would miss the cigarette, but not the Kaiser!

Stevens rifle, number 25640, inscribed on other side *NUTLEY/N.J.* One of the most elegant of her firearms collection. Referring to herself as a "crack shot in petticoats," the world-famed performer did much for the cause of women, not the least of which was beating men at their own game. For her, the woman's place was not at home.

Annie Oakley show belt, and husband's table cover. Cards struck by her .22 r.f. bullets; show tickets came to be commonly known as "Annie Oakleys" from holes punched in them by ticket-takers. A rival of Annie was Miss Lillian F. Smith, "The California Girl," another prodigy. At fifteen she fired demonstration before editor of *The Rifle* magazine, who declared she was "a wonder, and it will be difficult, if not impossible, to find her equal in many styles of shooting with the rifle." Recruited by Buffalo Bill, and accompanied the troupe to England in 1887. Though a gifted shot, she never attained the star status of Miss Oakley.

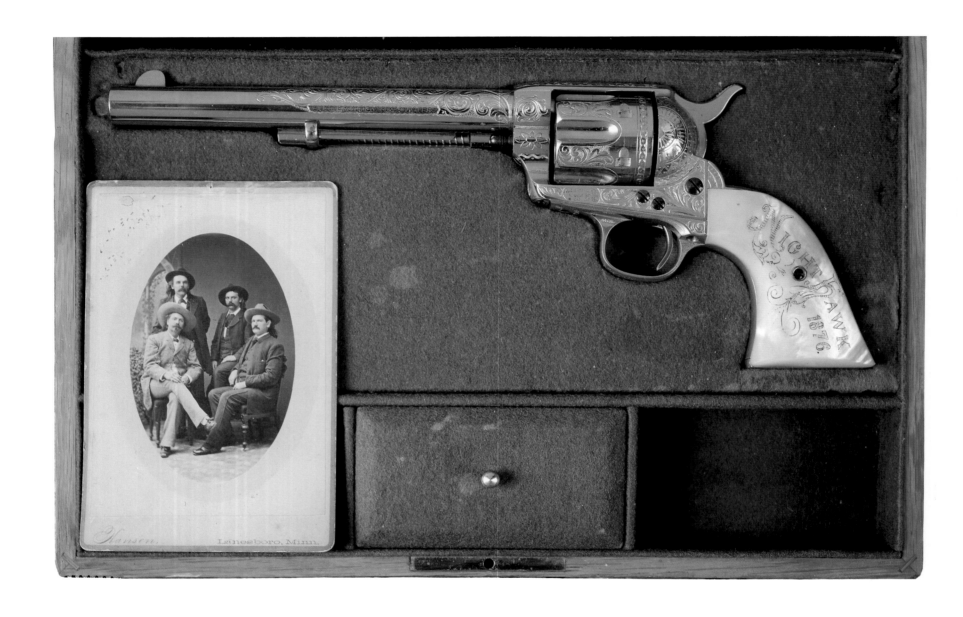

The "Night Hawk" Colt 44-40, number 127109. A gift from Buffalo Bill to Dr. George Powell, "Night Hawk," standing at *left* in c. 1885 photograph. Standing *right*, brother Dr. William Powell, known as "Blue Eyed Bill" or "Broncho Bill." Seated *right*, another brother, Dr. David Franklin Powell, "White Beaver." Seldom-observed engraved pearl grips. Powells let public believe their Indian names and associations gave merit to patent medicines they hawked.

Presentation Model 1874 Sharps sporting rifle inscribed on butt *Texas Night Hawk/to his brother/White Beaver/1877*. On top of buttplate, further inscribed *Col. Prentiss Ingraham/From D F Powell. M.D./1881*. Gifts of firearms within circle of Buffalo Bill and his friends were a part of their friendship; firearms were objects of great moment and meaning in their lives as frontiersmen or enthusiasts of the frontier.

Buck Taylor, original "King of the Cow-Boys." Taylor, all 6 feet 5 inches of him, became a national hero; could pick up handkerchief from ground while riding full-speed on horseback, rode bucking broncos, and threw steers. Subject of first dime novel with a cowboy as hero, written by Prentiss Ingraham (1887).

Photographed on Staten Island, 1886, among these Wild West show cowboys was the seventeen-year-old Johnny Baker, reclining at *left*. Known as the "Cowboy Kid," Baker was virtually Cody's adopted son, and became an expert shot, often performing with Annie Oakley—but never outshooting her. Baker stayed with Cody to the end and organized a "Buffalo Bill Wild West Show Co., Inc." for a year after Cody's death.

When the outdoor Wild West show gathered steam, Cody's troupe at various times featured Chief Sitting Bull, stagecoach driver John Y. Nelson, and, beginning in 1885, Little Miss Sure Shot, Annie Oakley, with her husband, Frank Butler.

Annie, a child prodigy shot, had been a market hunter at age fifteen (1875), and had beaten the traveling marksman Frank Butler, who then became her partner, manager, and husband, in their own performing act. A leading press agent gave this admiring description:

> [Annie] was a consummate actress, with a personality that made itself felt as soon as she entered the arena. Even before her name was on the lips of every man, woman, and child in America, the sight of this frail girl among the rough plainsmen seldom failed to inspire enthusiastic plaudits. Her entrance was always a very pretty one. She never walked. She tripped in, bowing, waving, and

wafting kisses. Her first few shots brought forth a few screams of fright from the women, but they were soon lost in round after round of applause. It was she who set the audience at ease and prepared it for the continuous crack of firearms which followed.

It was Chief Sitting Bull, in 1885, who gave Annie the nickname "Little Sure Shot." She was also known as "the Peerless Wing and Rifle Shot." Another performer who joined the troupe was trick rider Antonio Esquivel, a brilliant horseman billed as the champion *vaquero*.

Competitors of Cody were legion. One of the most bitter rivals was Doc Carver, of Carver's Wild West. Libel suits abounded, and Carver even put out a "list of failures" to squash competition. At the top of the list, Carver put Buffalo Bill. On the bottom was another marksman, Captain E. E. Stubbs, whose billing was "Champion Wing-Shot of the West."

The popularity of Cody's Wild West was such that in one July week, 1885, the total attendance was 193,960! Some appearances lasted months, since moving the show around was a logistic nightmare. Shooting would always remain an important part of the program, and bristling with firearms, somehow Cody and company traveled about America without headaches from the police. England, however, would be another matter.

In 1887 the Wild West had its biggest break, with an engagement to perform in London as part of the American Exhibition of the fiftieth Anniversary of Queen Victoria's reign. Over 200 crew and cast set off by steamer from New York. But when they disembarked in London, Her Majesty's Customs confiscated the specially loaded ammunition (except the low-powered cartridges firing bullets), requiring the troupe to use blanks supplied by the Woolwich Arsenal. The

Cody stood at *center* in front row of London show troupe photograph. At *top center*, next to American flag, stagecoach driver John Y. Nelson, wearing Colt 44s. Blowup revealed special holsters with inscribed metal plates.

(*opposite*) Silver-mounted Colt grip butt inscribed *De sus amigos/Los Charros/Mexico 1881* and *para el mejor Charro/Don/Vincente Oropeza*. Number 35521. Brilliant roper, Oropeza was also sometime chief of *vaqueros* of the Wild West; taught Will Rogers roping tricks.

London Agency of Colt's Patent Fire Arms Manufacturing Co., Inc., accommodated the Wild West for upkeep of the firearms.

Among the royalty who enjoyed the show were Edward, Prince of Wales, and, at her first attendance of a command performance since the death of her husband, Prince Albert, Queen Victoria. Cody hailed the tour as "an expedition to prove to the center of old world civilization that the vast region of the United States was finally and effectively settled by the English-speaking race."

In another command performance, Buffalo Bill drove the Deadwood coach with four European kings and the Prince of Wales as passengers. The Prince said to Cody, newly commissioned a colonel (by the governor of Nebraska), "Colonel, you never held four kings like these before." To which Cody replied, "I've held four kings, but four kings and the Prince of Wales makes a royal flush, such as no man ever held before."

Cody and his show were the hit of London, and he was, to quote the *Times*, the "hero of the London season." An American observer wrote that "the greatest, most unapproachable, thoroughly howling success that America ever sent to London was Buffalo Bill. . . ." The show ran from early May to the end of October, and then did engagements elsewhere in England, returning to the United States in May. The popular Annie Oakley left the show at the end of the London engagement, in response to an invitation from Crown Prince Wilhelm (later the Kaiser) in Berlin.

In 1888, Buffalo Bill's Wild West reopened in the United States, while that same year saw the premier of the Pawnee Bill Historical Wild West Exhibition and Indian Encampment. A former showman with Buffalo Bill, Pawnee Bill had bouts of good and bad luck with his troupe, and for a while he teamed up with Annie Oakley and Frank Butler.

In 1889, Cody and his troupe went on a four-year tour, beginning by returning to Europe. Among the distinguished fans were the Shah of Persia and Queen Isabella of Spain. This tour brought the Wild West to

Custom gold-inlaid and cased for Johnny Baker, Colt Model 1889 .38 New Army and Navy revolver was shipped in 1895, along with a richly embellished Colt .44 Bisley Target revolver, gold-inlaid "Col. W. F. Cody/ Buffalo Bill." Performers like Cody and Baker normally used shot charges in shows, since lead bullets had much longer trajectory. Standard 44-40 charge was approximately 20 grains black powder and 1/2 ounce No. 7 1/2 chilled shot. Most shots taken at 20 yards, often from galloping horse; at that range the pattern was only about 2 to 3 inches—still calling for considerable marksmanship. Colt ledgers show Baker was shipped a smoothbore .44 New Service revolver, with 7 1/2-inch barrel.

(*opposite, bottom left*) G. W. "Pawnee Bill" Lillie's Colt 44-40 smoothbore, custom-built on his order by Colt Factory and shipped April 1891; number 140472. Factory ledgers indicate revolver made with "slightly choked" barrel, and that several pairs of similar smoothbore Colt's were made for Lillie. In 1902 Colt's gave Lillie a pair of Single-Actions with pearl grips, a gift repeated in 1906.

Showman and Cody colleague Nate Salsbury owned this engraved and gold-inlaid Colt New Army and Navy double action revolver, number 14669. Made as a cased set, like the Johnny Baker Colt, gun was never fired. Salsbury played a key role in Cody Wild West show career, and their association was considered an ideal partnership. Stepped down as active manager at end of 1894 season, about time revolver was made.

Alice McGowen, a performer in Buffalo Bill's Wild West. Her rifle a Marlin .22 lever-action, her revolvers Colts.

Mrs. G. W. Lillie, the former May Manning, a Philadelphia girl taught to shoot and made into a Wild West performer by Pawnee Bill.

Center rifle a Marlin Model 1881 inscribed on frame "Capt. E. E. Stubbs/Champion Rifle Shot of the/World," in .38-55 caliber, silver-plated and blued; number P934. Winchester, Whitney-Kennedy, and other Marlin rifles known similarly inscribed. Marlin (*top*) and Winchester rifles used by sharpshooter T. H. Ford, whose real name was Thomas M. Pringle. The Marlin a .22 r.f. Model 1892, engraved, and inscribed from factory on barrel; number 123275. The Winchester a Model 1892 specially made in smoothbore, silver-plated and in .32-20 caliber.

(*opposite left*) Ford's letterhead quoted Captain Bogardus, Pawnee Bill Lillie, and others, endorsing claims of marksmanship and showmanship. Bogardus held Ford to be "sober and reliable."

(*opposite right*) T. H. Ford aiming his pump Winchester .22 with a mirror.

Lyon, Marseilles, Barcelona, Naples, Rome (with a blessing from Pope Leo XIII), Verona, Florence, Bologna, Milan, and Venice. Later the show performed in Innsbruck, Munich, Vienna, Berlin, Dresden, Leipzig, and other German cities, with the final performance in Stuttgart. Competitors of Cody also appeared in Europe, among them Doc Carver and his Wild American show, which even toured Australia.

Cody took a break from the European tour, during which he was recruited by General Nelson A. Miles to attempt peacefully extricating Chief Sitting Bull from the situation that would result in the chief's death two weeks before the Battle of Wounded Knee.

The European tour continued in 1891, with the addition of international horsemanship, making the troupe the "Congress of Rough Riders of the World." Touring Germany, then Holland, then returning to England and Wales, the show stayed on to 1892, and returned to London. Finally, the finest outdoor Wild West show in history returned to the United States, in October, and prepared for the 1893 season as the biggest entertainment draw at the Columbian Exposition in Chicago. Actually, the show was located adjacent to the Exposition, but was not an official part of it. Cody and company cleared somewhere between $700,000 and $1 million in the season, an enormous profit.

Buffalo Bill's Wild West had its heyday from 1887 to 1896, and the numbers of imitators during and after were numerous. Pawnee Bill and his shows merged

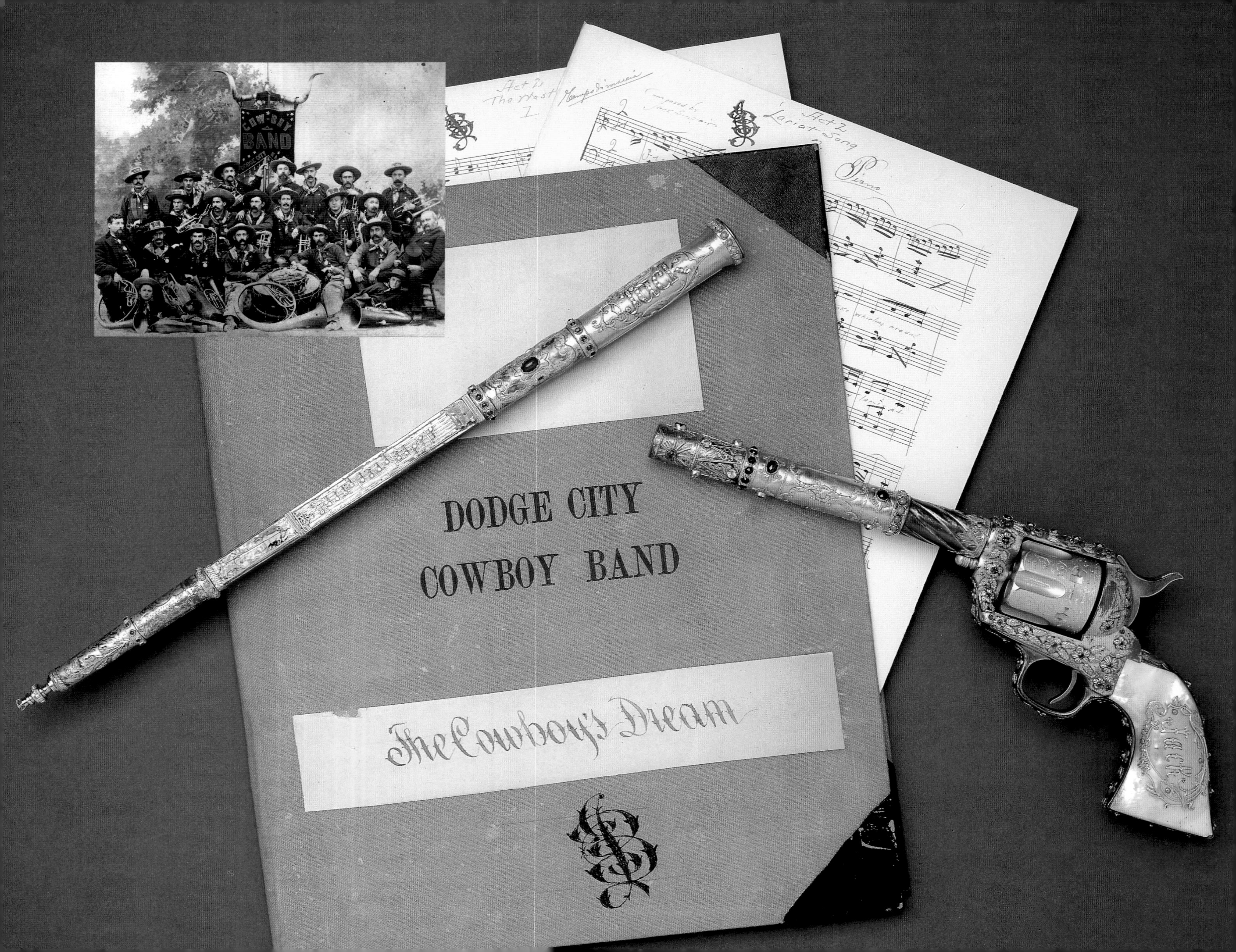
COW-BOY
BAND
Act 2
Lariat Song
Piano
DODGE CITY
COWBOY BAND
The Cowboy's Dream

Showman Arizona Joe holding Winchester Model 1873 presented by factory; frame inscribed *Arizona Joe from W.R.A. Co.* Rifle had been acquired by Englishman Lord Huntington, after watching Joe perform. Remained in England for many years. One of Col. Ingraham's dime novels entitled *Arizona Joe, The Boy Pard of Texas Jack*; subtitled "*History of the strange life of Captain Joe Bruce, a Young Scout, Indian Fighter, Miner, and Ranger, and the Protege of J. B. Omohundro, the famous Texas Jack.*" Little is presently known about Joe, apparently an intriguing character of his day.

Baton and Colt of Dodge City Cowboy Band's leader, Jack Sinclair. Band formed in 1881, later moved to Pueblo, Colorado, and still later headquartered in Los Angeles. Performed at wide variety of stock shows, and at inauguration of President Benjamin Harrison. Revolver presented to Sinclair by friends, 1892, and often used to lead band, occasionally fired to punctuate a tune and "to shoot the first man who plays a false note." On the baton, a musical bar from "Auld Lang Syne." (*Inset*) Dodge City Cowboy Band, 1886. These heavily armed musicians are well prepared to deal with music critics.

Frank Chamberlin and wife, Myrtle, billed themselves as first trick roping act to appear in Wild West shows. At *left*, Frank checks chambers of his S&W Schofield revolver; sidekick held Model 1892 Winchester.

Unidentified shootist, aiming cocked Colt; elaborate Indian pipe bag hung from belt; Winchester at feet.

with Cody for several years; Buck Taylor formed his own short-lived show; Colonel Frederic T. Cummins put together his Indian Congress (featuring Geronimo, Chief Joseph, and Red Cloud); and there was even the Cole Younger and Frank James Wild West (1903). Innumerable Wild West shows performed around the country by the early twentieth century. Some of these outfits were part of circus and carnival acts. An occasional train wreck or other disaster would wreak havoc on a show; a head-on collision with a freight train in 1901 killed a hundred of Cody's horses and injured Annie Oakley so badly she was unable to perform for a year.

1902 saw the beginning of the last European tour of Buffalo Bill's Wild West. Cody was saddled with debt because of a string of bad investments: the town of Cody, Wyoming; a project in Mexico; an Arizona gold mine; patent medicine with Dr. David F. Powell (White Beaver); and a Nebraska ranching operation. Fortunately, in 1895 the Wild West had worked an arrangement with James A. Bailey, of Barnum & Bailey fame, to help with travel logistics and general business. Bailey had the circus and Buffalo Bill's Wild West share the use of tour equipment while in America and Europe.

Finally in 1909 Buffalo Bill's Wild West merged with Pawnee Bill's Great Far East, known to performers as the "Two Bills Show." An upcoming rival, however, was the Miller Brothers 101 Ranch, featuring the black cowboy Bill Pickett, creator of bulldogging. The Miller Brothers 101 Ranch also headlined such stars as Tom Mix, Lucille Mulhall (the first cowgirl), and Will Rogers. Even Geronimo put in an appearance at a 1905 event, on the Millers' Oklahoma ranch.

The 101 Ranch became a national sensation and in the 1912 season put on no fewer than 421 performances, in twenty-two states and three provinces in Canada. During their English tour, 1914, the outbreak of World War I ended the 101 Ranch's string of successes. The Millers were served an order impressing their "horses and vehicles . . . for public service." The war brought an end to the Wild West outdoor shows on the grand scale of the previous thirty years.

For Cody his last performances were as part of the 1914 and 1915 seasons of the Sells-Floto Circus and Buffalo Bill's Wild West, and then in the "Buffalo Bill (Himself) and 101 Ranch Wild West, Combined with the Military Pageant Preparedness." The latter was a production of the Miller and Arlington Wild West Show Co. The tour ended in November 1916, and Buffalo Bill died in Denver on January 10, 1917. Even in death his show business career continued: reportedly his body was sold for $10,000, so that it would be buried at Lookout Mountain, near Denver, and serve as a tourist attraction.

Historian Don Russell's book *The Wild West, or A History of the Wild West Shows* lists 116 such shows within the period 1883 to 1957. Such entertainments have been largely succeeded by rodeos, which rarely include firearms. But marksmanship and gunfire were a feature of a majority of the pre-1914 Wild West performances.

The role of the gun in the West was a theme which played in outdoor arenas throughout America and Europe, in Canada, and even in Australia. An arsenal of guns and blank (and often live) ammunition accompanied the troupes. It was marksmanship which gave stardom to the premier female performer of all these shows, Annie Oakley. And it was marksmanship which was a primary focus of the image of the preeminent male superstar, Buffalo Bill.

These shows also established the cowboy as an American hero, helped reveal to the world the mystique of the noble mounted Indian warrior, and launched the West as legend.

Buffalo Bill announced switch to automatics, although he had already been presented a Colt Model 1902 Military automatic gold-inlaid with his name. Savage .32 bore number 33177, and COL. W. F. CODY inscribed on backstrap. Given to the aging showman in 1911.

Believed to be trick-shooting team, Eagle Eye and wife, Neola, handsomely attired and well armed. Among later-era exhibition shooters, best-known were Ad Topperwein and wife, Plinky. Employed by Winchester factory, Topperweins were billed as "World's Greatest Shooting Team." For over sixty years he held world record of shooting 72,491 2 1/2-inch wooden blocks thrown as aerial targets; record set in 1907, over ten-day period.

Gear used by George Gardiner, a cowboy in Buffalo Bill's Wild West in the 1890s, rodeo performer into early 1920s, and law officer in Sheridan, Wyoming. Spurs so-called gal-leg design, silver-mounted. Trophy bronc belt proved prowess as rodeo cowboy. His Colt is number 224513, a .38-40 Single Action, on hip in photograph.

WORLDS CHAMPION
BEST ALL ROUND COWBOY
GLENDIVE ROUNDUP 1919
Won by
Geo. T. Gardner.

Gene Autry earned his popularity via live performances, recordings, radio shows, films, and television. Usually he carried two 45s: one in his holster, the other a D45 model Martin guitar. This picture features the first Martin of that design ever made. His silver-mounted gun belt carried one Colt 45, sometimes the gold version with floral motifs by Kuhl, San Francisco, and custom trigger and wide hammer spur, other times the engraved and plated version, with gold GA monogram on backstrap and gold signature on bottom of barrel.

ARMING THE FICTIONAL WEST

F ittingly, the first American film with both creative drama and realism was a Western, the widely heralded Thomas Edison company production *The Great Train Robbery* (1903). Though Edison had filmed *Cripple Creek Barroom* five years before, it was only a short glimpse of life in the West. Buffalo Bill Cody had also been captured on film, as had other performers—Annie Oakley among them.

The Great Train Robbery, filmed in New Jersey, relied on a prop that would remain as essential to the Western genre as the horse and the cowboy: guns. One of the most dramatic scenes in the movie had one of the outlaws aim his revolver directly into the camera, and thus at the audience. Soon after those early days of film, the industry moved to the West Coast.

More than 4,200 feature-length Western films have been made, with as many as 227 in 1925 (silent) and 143 in 1940 (sound). The count of Western television series exceeds 150, with thousands of episodes. One series, *Gunsmoke*, holds the record for consecutive seasons: twenty. Locations for film and TV productions were largely in temperate California, but also in Nevada, New Mexico, Arizona, and Texas.

To the devotee of guns and accessories, a distinct evolutionary pattern is evident: early productions were much more likely to be authentic in firearms and their use, and in such accessories as holsters, rifle scabbards, cartridge belts, spurs, saddles, and clothing. Some of the actors and extras were real cowboys, with shooting and riding experience. In some cases advisers were called in to lend their expertise. For example, Wyatt Earp did so for William S. Hart, and a fascinating correspondence developed between the two, who became fast friends. Lawman Bill Tilghman directed the production of a Western film, based on a subject in which he had considerable expertise: *The Passing of the Oklahoma Outlaws*. He too was a friend of William S. Hart, as were Bat Masterson and Pat O'Malley (an outlaw once part of the Al Jennings gang). Another true-life character of the West, who lived in California, was Emmett

Tom Horn, perfectly cast with Steve McQueen as the doomed hero. One of screenwriters, Tom McQuane, is a devoted sportsman and enthusiast of firearms. Note rifle, a Model 1876 Winchester—seldom seen on the big screen.

Dalton. William S. Hart was so enamored of the West and its heroes and legends that he put together a collection of art and guns. Among the latter he prized what he thought was an authentic Billy the Kid Colt six-shooter.

Tom Mix had a firsthand knowledge of the arms and accouterments of the West, but his flamboyant approach led to romanticized gear. Guns made for him were highly embellished, replete with brands, his signature, Wild West scenes, deluxe grips, and profuse scrollwork. His appreciation of fine guns became known, and the Remington Arms Co. built a special rifle given

(*top left*) Bandit blazed away at screen to amazement of audience of pioneer picture *The Great Train Robbery*.

(*top right*) Still from Bill Tilghman's road-show film *Passing of the Oklahoma Outlaws* (c. 1915). Hailed by an evangelist as "the greatest silent sermon ever preached on 'The Wages of Sin is Death.'" The *Los Angeles Evening Herald* noted (February 1920): "William (Bill) Tilghman . . . is here to present a motion picture which he filmed himself, telling the story of the old West as it really was. He states that many of the scenes are enacted by the same persons that played the parts under more trying circumstances in the old days. . . . [His] rooms at the King Edward Hotel resemble a small armory. He is the possessor of some 15 guns, all of them having belonged to famous bandits, some of them being notched, denoting the number of men killed by the former owner before he fell afoul of the law. . . ." No print of film has survived.

(*bottom left*) Douglas Fairbanks squared off against this pair of pistol-packing desperadoes in *Wild and Woolly*, a 1917 Western comedy filmed in Arizona, and in Burbank and Hollywood.

(*bottom right*) William S. Hart held Colt he thought Billy the Kid's, during break in filming of King Vidor's *Billy the Kid* (1930). Hart was technical adviser; at *left*, star Johnny Mack Brown. Gun enthusiast Hart wrote to Colt factory, December 1924, enclosing photographs of fancy Single Actions (numbers 342963 and 346014) made for son, then two years and four months old: "When the little fellow has grown to manhood and his [Dad] has crossed the Big Divide, he will be a Two Gun Bill—just as his Dad was. When I was a boy on the Frontier I saw many guns that had been (inlaid) by some of those who liked fancy shootin' irons, but I never saw anything as handsome as the guns now owned by my son."

(*top*) From *The Terror*, starring Tom Mix in a "thrilling match of wits, horsemanship and daring of the American Cowboy versus the Russian Cossack."

(*bottom*) In *The Plainsman* (1936), Gary Cooper portrayed Wild Bill Hickok, and thus the butts-forward presentation of his Colt revolvers. Film was directed by arms collector Cecil B. De Mille and centered on post–Civil War West. Among other characters were Calamity Jane and Buffalo Bill Cody. Heavies of film were arms dealers selling guns to Indians, and the Indians themselves.

(*right*) Tom Mix's tooled leather boots and familiar white Stetson were sure signatures, as was the pearl-handled Colt. Finely engraved Remington Model 8 semiautomatic rifle was a present to him from performers in Miller Brothers 101 Ranch show. Silver-plated mascot sculpted by French artist Pallet and cast in London; it adorned the radiator cap of one of Mix's fine cars.

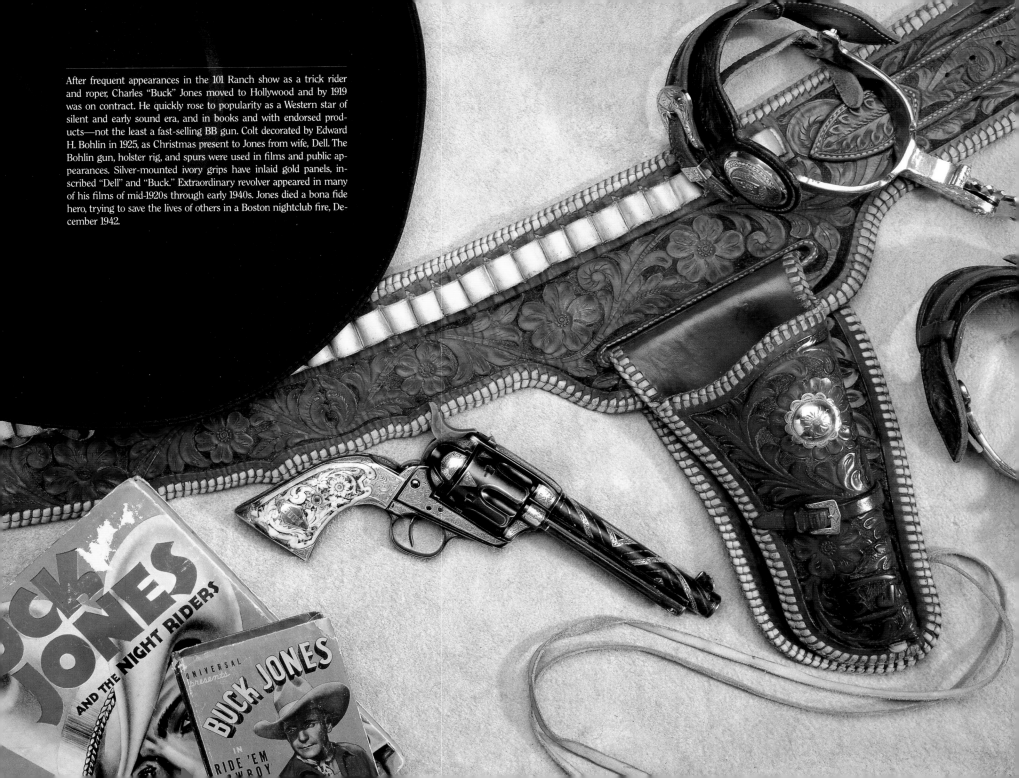

After frequent appearances in the 101 Ranch show as a trick rider and roper, Charles "Buck" Jones moved to Hollywood and by 1919 was on contract. He quickly rose to popularity as a Western star of silent and early sound era, and in books and with endorsed products—not the least a fast-selling BB gun. Colt decorated by Edward H. Bohlin in 1925, as Christmas present to Jones from wife, Dell. The Bohlin gun, holster rig, and spurs were used in films and public appearances. Silver-mounted ivory grips have inlaid gold panels, inscribed "Dell" and "Buck." Extraordinary revolver appeared in many of his films of mid-1920s through early 1940s. Jones died a bona fide hero, trying to save the lives of others in a Boston nightclub fire, December 1942.

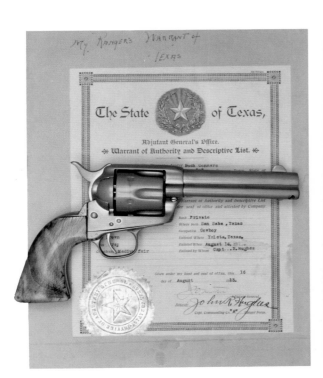

Colt .45 of Buck Connors, who, like Jones, was a real-life hero and genuine Westerner. Connors lived cowboy life even a Hollywood writer could not have created: in U.S. Army and Navy during Spanish-American War, cited for bravery, and nominated for Medal of Honor; a performer in Buffalo Bill's Wild West and in Pawnee Bill's show; Texas Ranger, and commissioned to enter Mexico and film revolution; fought in some of its battles. Entered Hollywood film community in 1920s, and appeared as character actor, often as sidekick of Buck Jones or Bob Steele. Favorite Colt a gift from widow of Texas Ranger who had been killed in a gunfight. Connors still carried revolver when he dropped dead on street as a Yuma County, Arizona, sheriff, 1947. Serial numbers 50979 (on gripstraps, from a black-powder Colt) and 186272.

Nicknamed the "Duke," John Wayne became an American icon, a towering symbol of masculinity, American-style. Role as Ringo Kid in John Ford's *Stagecoach* (1939) established stardom. Number-one male box-office draw in United States, 1950–65. Appeared in nearly ninety Western films. Still shot from *Red River* shows Wayne wearing bib-front shirt; hat his original; neckerchief another trademark. Holster and belt rig by Bianchi, made as limited-issue commemorative. Revolver the 5 1/2-inch .38-40, used in 1930s B Westerns.

to him by friends—just as had been done for colorful figures like General Custer decades before.

Although the studios either developed armories for firearms and related props or could call on rental companies, the stars began to vie with one another for elaborate shooting irons. William S. Hart had a richly inlaid and engraved pair of Single-Action Colts, with 7 1/2-inch barrels, and grips scrolled and bearing WSH initials in gold. Among Tom Mix's Colts was a .45 auto-

In Columbia's *Last of the Pony Riders* (1952), Gene wore a silver-mounted gun rig and wielded an engraved Colt from his growing gun collection. Gene's "Ten Cowboy Commandments" were a "Code of the West" for his film and TV fans, ranged from fair play and integrity to abstinence and patriotism. The first "Singing Cowboy," Gene had an advantage as an actor: he always played himself. Film career spanned the years 1934 to 1959.

Crusty U.S. Marshal Rooster Cogburn, one of Wayne's most popular roles, carried this large-loop Model 1892 Winchester carbine. Gun became a trademark; type first used by Wayne in *Stagecoach*. Paramount Pictures publicity still from *True Grit* (1969), for which he was given Oscar. Eyepatch worn in film. Carbine number 501892. Two other large-loop carbines in National Cowboy Hall of Fame Collection, also used in Wayne pictures. The 5-in-1 blanks of type commonly used in Westerns, fit .44 and .45 calibers.

From *Rooster Cogburn*, sequel to *True Grit*, costarring Katharine Hepburn, an ardent admirer of the Duke, who in *Me* rated him: "Of the style of man who blazed the trails across our country." Stars surrounded with explosives in this Universal Pictures still.

Presentation Colt 45s, from President Fred A. Roff of Colt's to Gene Autry and Gail Davis, at height of their popularity in early days of television. Davis appeared in more Autry films than any other leading lady and starred in Autry Flying-A Productions TV series *Annie Oakley*.

Some stars from the B Westerns, so called because they were made for the bottom half of a twin bill—the top half being A productions. The type took off in the 1930s, and *clockwise* from Gene Autry–Metropolitan Museum of Art/Christie's 1985 auction Colt .45 are Clayton Moore (later the Lone Ranger) in *Tomahawk Territory*, Guy Madison in *The Charge at Feather River*, Hopalong Cassidy with heavy Robert Mitchum in *Leather Burner*, Roy Rogers brandishing pair of Colt six-shooters, Audie Murphy in *The Guns of Fort Petticoat*, Jimmy Wakeley in *West of Alamo*, at *center* Joel McCrea in *Cattle Drive*, Rex Allen and his horse Koko, *above* "The Gene Autry Story" cassette tape, and Johnny Mack Brown with Bohlin holster rig and saddle. Gene Autry Western Heritage Museum is a Mecca for anyone who loves the genre, whether the West of fact or of fiction.

B Western star Ken Maynard's Bohlin-gripped pair of Colts, and double Bohlin holster rig. The set appeared in his circus show, and late in his film career. A gifted rider, Maynard had been in Wild West shows and was one of most skilled horseman of Westerns. His action-packed feats on horseback and terra firma had broad appeal. In circus, he rode a Bohlin saddle that matched the gun rig.

(opposite) Movie revolvers and holsters lay above prop Gatling gun, in original movie crate. Gatling made up of brass, iron, and other metals (painted to simulate brass); fully wired and fitted to work on acetylene. Appeared in dozens of films, including *100 Rifles* and *The War Wagon*. Double rig with pair of Colts used by Don "Red" Barry in several B Westerns of late 1930s into 1940s, including those in his role as Red Ryder. Center rig used by Russ Hayden as supporting player in several Hopalong Cassidy films and in short-lived TV series with Jackie Coogan: *Cowboy G Men*. Well-used Colt and holster at *right* saw service in early silent era by leading actor Art Accord.

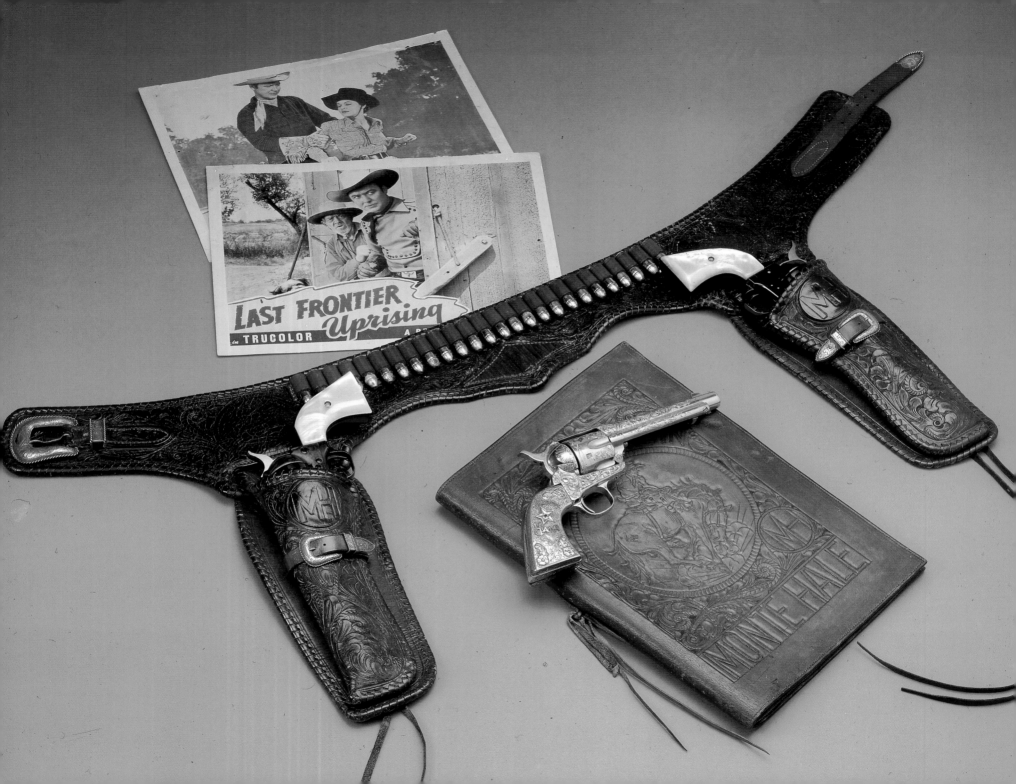

Pair of Audie Murphy's Model 1894 Winchesters, the stocks overlaid with silver and gold. Made to mount on automobile; note monograms on stocks. Winner of the Medal of Honor and most decorated American soldier of World War II, Murphy was leading star of Bs after the war. Career spanned 1948–69; killed in plane crash, 1971.

Texan Monte Hale debuted in Westerns in 1944 and starred in a B series produced by Republic pictures; was groomed as possible Roy Rogers replacement. After demise of Bs, he toured as singing cowboy, made rodeo appearances, and appeared on television. Made over twenty-five Westerns, and was also featured in *Giant*. Double gun belt and script cover made by Bob Brown, used by Hale in several films in 1940s and early 1950s. Monte and wife Joanne played key role with Gene and Jackie Autry in creating Gene Autry Western Heritage Museum.

matic with TM brand in gold on the ivory grips; he also had a handsome design for a superb Single-Action, by renowned engraver R. J. Kornbrath. The drawing shows profuse engraving and gold and platinum inlaying. Dated 1932, the revolver was to bear portraits of Mix and his horse Tony, the TM brand, Western scenes, and elaborate border motifs.

Some stars, like Gene Autry, acquired factory-decorated Single-Action Colts, and company ledgers record shipments to the film studios of Lasky, Columbia, Fox, and Republic. But *the* artist in saddles and gear was Ed Bohlin. Buck Jones and Ken Maynard are but two of the stars who had Bohlin-enriched guns. Even more had Bohlin holster and belt rigs, some dripping with silver and gold. The saddles and bridles were particularly deluxe, almost to the point of provoking groans from the stars' horses.

Colt Single-Actions have predominated throughout the history of the Western, as they actually did in the post-1873 real West. The Colt remains the film and TV arm of choice. For longarms, the number-one choice remains the Winchester.

Simple comparison of movie stills with nineteenth-century photographs reveals the freedoms the film industry has taken with accuracy during most of the history of filmmaking. These liberties are not only in the authenticity of the guns, but in the period of use. Hollywood created its own West, and tended to outfit the supposed nineteenth-century hero with a Bohlin special six-shooter in a silver-and-gold-mounted rig. An original ensemble would have been a plain or scroll-engraved Single-Action with a relatively plain holster and belt.

Hollywood's own style also meant elaborate costumes for the stars, especially in Grade B films. The garish clothes were in keeping with their silver-and-gold-mounted holster and belt rigs and richly decorated Colts.

The lack of authenticity carried over to the guns themselves, which were plain, but on which excesses like stag grips were used. Holsters became the bus-

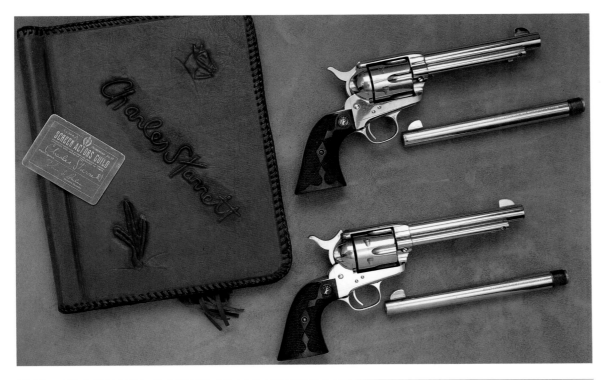

Script book, Screen Actors Guild card, and unusual Colts of Charles Starret, best remembered for portrayal of Durango Kid in several B Westerns of 1930s and 1940s. He was one of ten founding members of the Guild; the solid-gold card commemorated his contributions to that organization. The 5 1/2-inch barrels rifled and meant for .44 special cartridges; interchangeable barrels are .44-40 smoothbores.

(*opposite*) Wild Bill Elliott Colt .45, number 350594, cattle brand engraved by Cole Agee. Ivory grips silver-mounted. Plated in chrome, a durable finish longer-lasting than nickel; seen from time to time on film guns. Elliott's Western screen career began with *The Arizona Wildcat* (1927), and his last film was *The Forty-Niners* (1954). Known for wearing his Colts with butts forward.

cadero* type, with tie-downs for the leg, and—an innovation of the quick-draw era beginning in the 1950s—steel linings to allow cocking the hammer and revolving the cylinder of the six-shooter even before it had cleared leather.

The Colt company capitalized on the post–World

War II explosion of interest in the West, and its dramatization on TV, by returning the Single-Action Army to production (1955). Company President Fred A. Roff personally knew many of the stars, and gave them revolvers—reaping considerable publicity. Quick draw became a popular sport, with clubs springing up, and a national championship, held in Las Vegas.

Holster makers also got into the act. One of them, John Bianchi, was so caught up in the Western theme that in 1977 he established his own museum: the

Frontier Museum Historical Center. In 1985, the museum was sold to Gene Autry, and became the nucleus (with Gene's own collection) of the Gene Autry Western Heritage Museum.

Arvo Ojala's patented steel-lined holster was a favorite of a number of 1950s–1970s performers. For over forty years, Ojala has been Hollywood's fast-draw coach, and has become a legend in the process.

Entire generations of Western history buffs and gun collectors got hooked on the West by watching the movies. Many of these fans were also captivated by the Saturday-matinee B Westerns, and by the serials that sometimes accompanied the features.

Cap pistols and matching holster sets were a high-volume business. If the fan was old enough and lived where law permitted, the real gun could be acquired. Not a few fans watched TV with holster and belt strapped to waist, trying to outdraw good guy or bad. In the opening sequence of *Gunsmoke*, the devotee could try his hand against the quickest of them all, fast-draw coach Arvo Ojala going up against hero Marshal Matt Dillon.

In the mid-1950s, Colts and Winchesters remained reasonable enough in price so that old guns were still used by performers. The time would come when skyrocketing collectors' prices would make studio gun collections worth substantially more than their rental potential, at which point all the studios sold their collections. Now the remaining source of prop guns is Stembridge Gun Rental and its crosstown counterpart, Ellis Mercantile, both of Los Angeles.

The introduction of replica guns in the 1950s and 1960s gave film studios a new source of hardware. Firms like Uberti & Co. and Armi San Marco, of Brescia, Italy, manufacture copies of Colt and other makes and have supplied quantities of guns for the film and TV industry. Uberti became the gunmaker to "spaghetti Western" director Sergio Leone, turning out thousands for that client alone. Leone became so fascinated with *il padrone* Aldo Uberti that he shot a documentary special on him for Italian television. Val Forgett's Navy Arms Company became the major U.S. importer

---

*Holster attached to cartridge belt by looping through special slot, system first used in the early twentieth century.

Alligator holster set by Bohlin, for Jack Holt, Western star in his own right, and father of B star Tim Holt. Tooled outfit, also by Bohlin, was Leo Carrillo's, worn in role as Pancho in the Cisco Kid series, costarring Duncan Renaldo. Belt and holster rigs of this pattern remained the standard for movie and TV gunfighters until early 1950s, when designs by Arvo Ojala and others transformed the public's expectations in such matters.

Familiar black Bailey hat, silk scarf, Bohlin waist belt and buckle, Hamley double-gun rig, and Colts used by William Boyd in his portrayal of Hopalong Cassidy. Revolvers factory-engraved, and shipped in 1928; first appeared on film in 1935; were carried by Boyd into 1950s. Originally blued, guns were silver-plated during film career.

Alan Ladd and Brandon De Wilde in *Shane*, a ranchers vs. sodbusters saga ranked high on lists of favorite Westerns.

of these replicas and itself became a manufacturer. When the Western was replaced on TV by police shows and situation comedies, the big-screen Westerns and TV shows subsided, but the genre did not die.

The 1990 TV production of Larry McMurtry's epic novel *Lonesome Dove* was one of the most popular TV programs of the year. In the same year the three-hour feature film *Dances with Wolves* became a smash hit, and went on to dominate the Oscars. *Wolves* has gone on to record-setting videocassette rentals and sales. Authenticity was evident in the firearms of both productions; the Walker Colt was used in *Lonesome Dove* and an Uberti-made Henry rifle in *Dances with Wolves*.

Another hit Western was *Young Guns*, followed by *Young Guns II*, starring hot young actors like Emilio Estevez, Kiefer Sutherland, Lou Diamond Phillips, and Charlie Sheen. Their guns were by Uberti (Single Actions and Model 1873 Winchester look-alikes), though Billy the Kid (played by Estevez) sometimes used an original Colt Model 1877 Lightning double action—a type with an action too complex to make it a profitable product for a replica firm.

The list of performers, screenwriters, directors, and producers who became gun collectors is impressive: besides William S. Hart, Tom Mix, Gene Autry, and Roy Rogers, the author is aware of Cecil B. De Mille, John Wayne (and sons Michael and Patrick), George Montgomery, Charlton Heston, Scott Glenn, and John Milius, as well as virtuoso performer Sammy Davis, Jr., comedian-actor Buddy Hackett, and singer-songwriter-actor Mel Torme. Mel owns nearly a hundred Single Action Colts, among them a rarity acquired from props while he was appearing on the Lucille Ball TV show! John Milius has been putting together a Single-Action collection, partly for use in a feature film in production on McNelly's Rangers. Milius has long been considering a film on mountain man Jedediah Smith, and another on Theodore Roosevelt as a young rancher-hunter in the Dakota Badlands.

Students of quick-draw coach Arvo Ojala often

have become keen devotees of shooting and gun handling. Sammy Davis, Jr., sometimes did six-shooter tricks in his Las Vegas act. Jerry Lewis became another enthusiast (and keen shooter). Kirk Douglas could twirl Colts with the best of them, as can Kevin Costner, Steve Martin, and Scott Glenn.

Manufacturers like Colt and Winchester long ago recognized the debt they owe to TV and film Westerns

Hollywood gun coach Arvo Ojala, with his dream assignment: teaching Marilyn Monroe about the six-shooter. Film was Otto Preminger's *River of No Return*, with Robert Mitchum and Rory Calhoun.

Panorama of Westerns, most in the A category, from the 1940s, 1950s, and 1960s. For details see Appendix.

Some major stars of the TV Western, *top row, from left*: Clayton Moore as the *Lone Ranger*, John Russell in *Lawman*, Nick Adams in *The Rebel*, Chuck Connors in *The Rifleman*, Wade Preston as Christopher Colt in *Colt .45*, Richard Boone as Palladin in *Have Gun, Will Travel*, Gene Barry as *Bat Masterson*, Will Hutchins in *Sugarfoot*, Hugh O'Brian in *The Life and Legend of Wyatt Earp*, and Gail Davis in *Annie Oakley*.

in promoting their brands and firearms. Sometimes programs even used the marque name, such as *Colt 45* and *Winchester '73*. For the latter film, released in 1950, a nationwide promotion was launched by Universal Studios and Winchester—a search for antique One of One Thousand Model 1873 rifles. Each reported owner of an original rifle was awarded a Model 94 Winchester carbine.

Though there are fewer TV and film Western productions today than in their heyday, a reflection of their eternal popularity is the Western section of video stores and catalogues. Books on the Western continue to be published, some learned treatises by scholars. The best reference so far is by the British Film Institute, *The BFI Companion to the Western* (1988).* The quality of the Western today is more likely to be of a higher standard, and more realistic. Authenticity in props, and even speech, has improved, and realism in action, even sounds, is more in demand than at any time in the history of film or of television.

In effect, the Western has gone full circle, and its guns and accouterments, indeed the whole genre, are closer now to reality than ever before yet still largely retain the imaginary Hollywood vision of a West that never was. Nevertheless, the result is a screen West that not infrequently presents to the viewer the closest he will ever come to realizing that fantasy of stepping back in time to a lost world.

---

*The book claims the total number of Westerns at over seven thousand!

The Lone Ranger. Top gun rig by Bohlin; used by radio star Brace Beemer in public appearances, and by Clayton Moore, 1940s and early 1950s. *Middle* holster set used by Moore, c. 1950–56. *Bottom* outfit used by Moore from 1956 on. The *center* Colt a Frontier model bought by Moore in 1949, for public appearances. The other Colts were all used in movies and TV by Clayton Moore in the 1950s and 1960s. Spurs by Bohlin, c. 1950s.

Steve McQueen as Josh Randall, bounty hunter in *Wanted Dead or Alive*. The 44-40 hybrid pistol a cut-down Model 1892 Winchester carbine, referred to as the "Mare's Leg." Large lever identifies gun as one of three versions used in series at different times.

(*opposite*) *Bonanza*, one of the longest-playing of TV Westerns, 1959–63. From *left*, Colts and holster sets of Pa Cartwright and his sons Hoss and Little Joe, roles played by Lorne Greene, Don Blocker, and Michael Landon. Some sequences were directed by Robert Altman, who would go on to make *Buffalo Bill and the Indians*, starring Paul Newman.

James Arness wore badge, hat, and holster rig and wielded Colt .45 as Marshal Matt Dillon in *Gunsmoke*. The longest-running dramatic episode program in television history (excluding soap operas), program was carried on CBS from 1955 to 1975. Quick-draw holster and belt designed by Arvo Ojala; appeared on program for first several years, when another Ojala outfit took over.

A lineup of late-1950s TV Western stars, all on contract with Warner Brothers. *From left*, Will Hutchins, Peter Brown, Ty Hardin, Jack Kelly, James Garner, Wade Preston, and John Russell. All were students of Arvo Ojala, and all used Ojala holsters. Note Peter Brown's trousers, under holster: consequence of cooking off a few blank rounds before revolver cleared leather!

(*top left*) Robert Redford starring in *Jeremiah Johnson*, script by mountain man buff John Milius, with Edward Anhalt. 1972 production admired for its visual magnificence and captivating adventure.

(top right) Richard Boone's Peacemaker, and the famous business card of the character he played, in *Have Gun, Will Travel*. Ran 1957–63.

(*opposite left*) At *right*, the Model 1892 Winchester regularly used by Chuck Connors as Lucas McCain in *The Rifleman* TV series; number 985658. Presentation Model 1894, number 2405000, gift from a grateful Winchester factory, c. 1959. The Connors show ran 1958–63 and began from a 1958 program on *Dick Powell's Zane Grey Theater*, in an episode entitled "The Sharpshooter." Script for the sequence was by Sam Peckinpah, later to make series of very tough, but realistic, Western films.

(*opposite right*) Chuck Connor's matched pair of Alvin White-engraved and gold-inlaid Colt .45s, presented to the actor to replace the pair he gave to Leonid Brezhnev, at San Clemente, 1974. Numbers CC-1 and CC-2; long grips to accomodate the actor's large hands. The Colt Peacemakers given to Brezhnev were used by the Russian for boar hunting!

Trick shooter, quick-draw expert, and showman Joe Bowman, with Robert Duvall, on the set of *Lonesome Dove*. Successes like the demand for Bowman's shooting exhibitions and the broad popularity of Larry McMurtry's novel and its television dramatization are evidence of the eternal appeal of the West.

The cinema Western in the 1970s and '80s. Three of the author's favorite Westerns displayed with two videos, produced by Sony and BBC-TV, on Sam Colt and his guns. Henry and Model 1873 Winchester replicas by Uberti & Co. For further details see Appendix.

Presentation Winchester Model 1892 carbine from Pawnee Bill to Jimmie Rogers, a smoothbore used in trick shooting. Gun accompanied by traveling case, marked with hand-lettered "Pawnee Bill's Pioneer Days Co." Only known presentation firearm to famed country-and-western singer, and equally rare gift from Pawnee Bill. Number 378806; .44-40. The Model 1873 is a standard carbine, with desirable nickel-plated finish.

339

For a Few Dollars More, from the spaghetti Westerns of Sergio Lione, dating from mid-1960s to mid-1970s. Films gave boost to replica arms business of Aldo Uberti, Gardone, Val Trompia, Italy. For further details, see Appendix.

Young Guns and *Young Guns II* are two contemporary Westerns using Italian-made replica arms. "Arkansas Dave" Rudabaugh, played by Christian Slater, from Billy the Kid's gang in both films, holds Single Action Army of Uberti & Co. manufacture. For *Young Guns II*, Uberti supplied thirty Colt and Winchester replicas. Number 83636, shown here, is the gun Slater used in film. Other recent Westerns in which Uberti guns have been used are *City Slickers*, *Silverado*, *White Fang*, and *Dances with Wolves*.

Devoted collector of firearms and lover of the West Cecil B. De Mille. The renowned director admiring his pair of Colt Single Actions, received from the Colt company, 1956. A letter to Colt's from the director's executive assistant noted: "[Mr. De Mille] was as delighted as his own grandson might have been with a new cap pistol. . . . It might interest you to know that among his rather large collection of firearms are two nickel plated single action Colts which are reliably reputed to have belonged to Wild Bill Hickok about whom he made a picture in the mid-1930s called *The Plainsman*, and in which these two weapons were used." Several pieces from the De Mille gun collection were sold by Christie's, New York, October 1988.

Uberti-made Henry rifle (chambered for .44-40), fired by Kevin Costner in *Dances with Wolves*. Buffalo-hunting sequences in film captured spirit of that risky undertaking.

Ridin' hard in typical Wild West fashion is Phil Spangenberger and his wife, Linda. Often assisted by Linda, Spangenberger performs several times a year as a mounted sharpshooter and fancy gun handler. Working with his Colt Peacemakers, he has traveled all over the world recreating the shooting and riding skills of the old-time Westerner.

Colt Texas Paterson revolver from the Johnny Cash collection, donated by him to Christie's benefit auction for the Arms and Armor Department, Metropolitan Museum of Art, New York, October 1985. Serial number 614 on barrel, wedge, and cylinder; 607 on various other parts. Cash also donated signed Martin guitar, books, Colt belt buckle, and set of U.S. cavalry saddlebags. Cash is one of several country-and-western singers keen on guns; among others, Randy Travis, Willy Nelson, Glenn Campbell, and Hank Williams, Jr.

Arvo Ojala, Hollywood's legendary gun coach, whose forty-year career has been saluted by a "Gunsmoke" issue, of which twenty-five Single Action Colts were produced (at *right*, with red-cloth-lined walnut case), and by the one-of-one "Arvo Ojala Commemorative," at *left*. Special Ojala-designed fast-draw holster and belt fitted with sterling-silver buckle; made by his own leather-making factory. Celebrity students beginning *clockwise from left* of photo of Arvo with longtime friend Roy Rogers: Michael J. Fox, Gary Cooper, Sammy Davis, Jr., Paul Newman, Cliff Robertson, Frank Sinatra, Scott Glenn, Steve Martin, and Kevin Costner. Red-covered booklet published by Listerine, with quick-draw instructions, and firearms safety tips from Arvo. Revolvers numbers SA91494 (one of one) and SA92541.

ON THE TRAIL OF THE PEACEMAKERS

Collectors who enter the arena of the American West will rarely have a boring moment on earth. In no other area of collecting is there such a continual reinforcement and rebirth of enthusiasm—from fellow collectors, from museums, from traveling to the sites (like the Custer Battlefield, a guaranteed lifetime fix), even from Western films and television programs. Most important, however, are the objects themselves—if only they could talk.

The collectors' items with the most to say, and often with the loudest "voices," are the peacemakers, the arms of the American West. Each category in this realm of collecting could occupy a devotee's lifetime of leisure. And each presents its own challenges, and pitfalls. In all of them the collector is part curator and researcher, part detective, part archivist, part conservator, part dealer, part bird dog, and part dreamer.

A Note on Authenticity

In researching *The Peacemakers*, the author has carefully selected each object for illustration. Every firearms collector, dealer, museum specialist, and researcher has to be equally careful.

A specialty of the author's profession is the authentication of collectors' firearms, particularly American antiques. In order to keep ahead of makers and purveyors of fake material, the author has purposely avoided publishing every detail to watch for in collecting arms. The buyer has to proceed with caution to avoid being taken in by fraudulent pieces. A cardinal rule

Greg Martin in San Francisco lair, the Winchester 1873 a presentation to Captain Jack Crawford. Inscribed on sideplates from factory, and with poem: *Hold me, guide me, guard/me, then tell me true, if/you love me as I love you. Your Dearie.* Finding such treasures has been a specialty of Martin since being bitten by collecting bug as a boy.

See page 372

OVERLAND STAGE LINE
ATCHISON
OMAHA
NEBRASKA
CITY
BEN HOLLADAY
EXPRESS
Wells Fargo & Co

Corner of a private museum, where the old West reigns, despite presence of African wart hog and safari skins.

Cover photograph from Butterfield & Butterfield auction catalogue of Parker Lyon–William Harrah Pony Express Museum collection of Western Americana, sold in July 1986. Mel Tormé's foreword provided background on the collection: "William Parker Lyon, of van and storage fame, enjoyed stamp collecting as a hobby until he purchased a genuine old western stagecoach [the Ben Holladay Overland as pictured] back in 1915. Instantly bitten by the rabid bug known as American Western History, he set about expanding his newfound interest into a 400 ton, three building archive of historic gems, rivaled only by the treasure trove of San Simeon's landlord, another William, whose last name was Hearst. . . . [In 1955] another William—this time Bill Harrah, himself a world-class collector—decided the acquisition of the Pony Express Museum was irresistible. . . . [It was exhibited] within the environs of Harrah's [Reno] Casino, and from the moment I beheld that extraordinary display, I never looked back." Collection acquired by Greg Martin (whose wife, Petra, models period gown in photo), who stated: "Nothing in my life as a collector has been of greater excitement or fascination to me than the purchase of the Lyon-Harrah Pony Express Museum."

Thomas Eakins portrait of renowned ethnologist Frank Hamilton Cushing, surrounded by Zuni Indian memorabilia and dressed in costume of Zuni priest. Shows nineteenth-century fascination with Indian artifacts and culture. Oil on canvas 90 x 60 inches; c. 1895. A masterpiece displayed at the Thomas Gilcrease Institute of American History and Art.

New England rifles, of the 1820s and 1830s; types which were tried in the West. *From left*, by G. B. Fogg, Manchester, New Hampshire; A. Barrows, Castleton, Vermont; and H. Pratt, Roxbury, Massachusetts. The Fogg and Barrows rifles are silver-wire-inlaid.

Hawken rifle, with 4- to 5-pound hand-forged traps of type used by mountain men in search of beaver. Belt knife of period, as is top hat of beaver felt.

Replicas of Hawken rifle and pistol, made by Michael C. Hayes for collector Thomas A. Conroy. Rifle barrel by Bill Large; .58-caliber; lock, trigger, and furniture from the Hawken Shop, St. Louis, established by Art Ressel. Pistol barrel by Sharon Barrel Works, .62 smoothbore.

always is to buy only from sources one trusts. If possible, equally desirable is a guarantee of full refund should any item later prove not as advertised or described.

Above all, a collector should be cautious if he is buying alleged high-value guns at a bargain. There is no reason for a collector to be cheated if he buys judiciously and uses good common sense. An investor depends on expert advice when buying stocks; an arms collector should depend on correspondingly expert advice when buying weaponry. Not to do so could mean severe financial loss and great personal disappointment in an otherwise grand hobby.

Indian Arms

Ironically, New York City and Washington, D.C., house the most remarkable collections of American Indian material. Because of the fascination with Indian culture, collectors like oilman George Heye, the staff of the Smithsonian Institution, and the prescient and curious (Thomas Jefferson among them) sought objects

George A. Custer and Libbie, in library, Fort Abraham Lincoln, November 1873. Presentation Smith & Wesson, and other guns from collection, in rack at *right*.

Gold-inscribed Model 1895 Winchester, presented to Miles by his friend and fellow collector John R. Hegeman, Jr. Similar carbine made up for Hegeman; guns bore numbers 22417 and 20990, respectively.

350

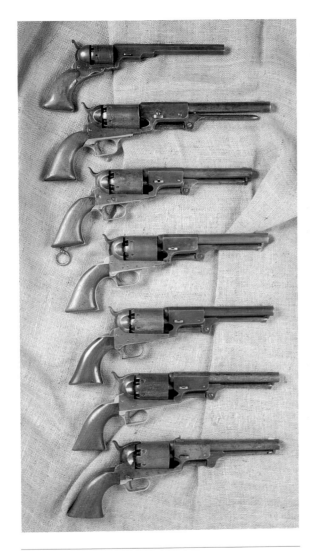

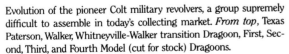

Evolution of the pioneer Colt military revolvers, a group supremely difficult to assemble in today's collecting market. *From top*, Texas Paterson, Walker, Whitneyville-Walker transition Dragoon, First, Second, Third, and Fourth Model (cut for stock) Dragoons.

Colt Second Model Dragoons, cased pair of an officer. Miraculously survived military use in superb condition. Winner of coveted silver medal from NRA Annual Meetings.

Tenth Anniversary of the Custer Battle, June 25, 1886. Skirmish line, firing in reenactment, on actual battlefield site. A film was made by William Selig, on site in 1909, but no print survives. An ambitious and reasonably authentic 1912 Thomas Ince production, *Custer's Last Fight*, has survived, and is available on videotape. Both films were billed as including Indians who were participants in the original battle.

Lee-Metford rifle and hippo-gripped Remington .44-40 revolver of Major Frederick Russell Burnham, D.S.O. Books authored by Burnham, and Matabele artifacts captured by him. On this heroic figure of the West, and of Africa, Theodore Roosevelt wrote: "I know Burnham. He is a scout and a hunter of courage and ability, a man totally without fear, a sure shot, and a fighter. He is the ideal scout, and when enlisted in the military services of any country he is bound to be of the greatest benefit." Burnham survived Indian attack as a boy in Minnesota, was mounted messenger in California at thirteen, cowboy in Texas, Arizona pioneer, gold prospector, professional meat hunter, stagecoach guard; sailed to Africa (1893) and served under Cecil Rhodes in first Matabele War, survived numerous blood-curdling experiences in Africa; fellow of Royal Geographical Society, gold miner in Klondike, appointed "Chief of Scouts" in British Army in Africa, given Distinguished Service Order for heroism during Boer War, served in Mexico in last days of Porfirio Díaz, was oil prospector, etc. Burnham's career represents extraordinary link between frontier America and frontier Africa, of which there are numerous parallels.

at the time the Indians were still using them. The Heye Foundation alone has over 450 tomahawks (more than half from the West). In the nineteenth century, weapons not only came east, but went to Great Britain and continental Europe. At this writing, auction houses and antique dealers are still repatriating specimens from across the Atlantic.

The national fascination with the Indian, a rebirth of Indian pride, and the active promotion of collecting by galleries like Sherwood's Spirit of America (Beverly Hills, California) and the Alexander Gallery (New York City) and auction houses like Christie's, Sotheby's, and Butterfield & Butterfield have whipped the enthusiasm of collectors into a frenzy of activity. The annual Ethnographic and Indian Market shows in Santa Fe, New Mexico, are musts for the collector, and most better-quality antique arms shows offer Indian weaponry.

The 1911 discovery of Ishi, last of the California Yahi tribe, rekindled the interest in hunting with the bow and arrow. Although the bows and arrows used today contrast significantly with the comparatively primitive equipment of the Indians, the basic techniques of stalking to a close range and of outwitting the prey remain unchanged over centuries.

Authenticity and provenance are paramount in collecting Indian weaponry. Beware of tacks added to poor-conditioned guns (usually Winchester 1866 and 1873 Models) to pass them off as Indian originals. A knowledge and understanding of iron and brass tacks will help in ferreting out authentic weapons so decorated.

Trailblazers and Mountain Men

Thomas Jefferson's private museum at Monticello

California knives, most by Will & Finck and Michael Price, San Francisco. I. H. Schintz knife (with badge) presented to San Francisco chief of police M. J. Burke, 1861. Walrus-ivory hilt decorated with silver studs, solid-gold escutcheons, and gold trim; other side of scabbard inscribed *M. J. Burke. Chief of Police*; overall length 11 3/4 inches. Some of most captivating of Western artifacts have San Francisco associations.

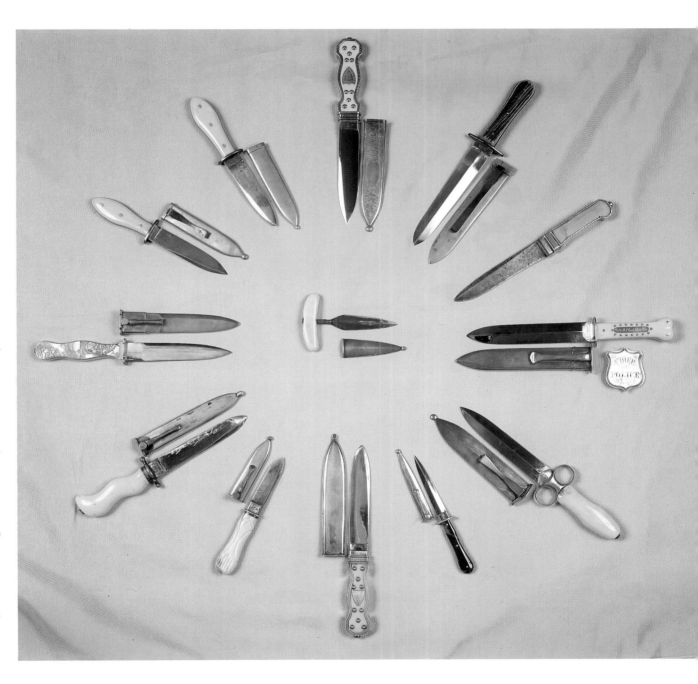

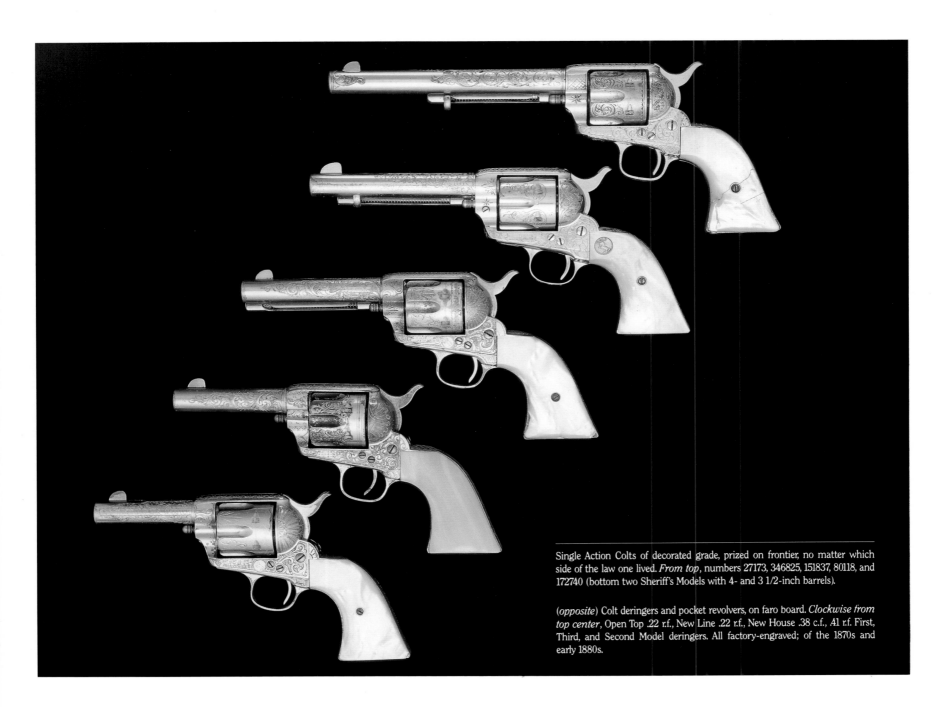

Single Action Colts of decorated grade, prized on frontier, no matter which side of the law one lived. *From top*, numbers 27173, 346825, 151837, 80118, and 172740 (bottom two Sheriff's Models with 4- and 3 1/2-inch barrels).

(*opposite*) Colt deringers and pocket revolvers, on faro board. *Clockwise from top center*, Open Top .22 r.f., New Line .22 r.f., New House .38 c.f., .41 r.f. First, Third, and Second Model deringers. All factory-engraved; of the 1870s and early 1880s.

featured elements from the culture in the West, brought to him from the Lewis and Clark Expedition and from other sources. His interests in firearms and field sports are well known. As he wrote to George Washington, "one loves to possess arms. . . ." Surely he was familiar with and admired the firearms and other weaponry used by Lewis and Clark. Unfortunately, in the clearing of his estate soon after he died, Jefferson's collection of arms was broken up.

The re-creation of the Frederic Remington Studio, at the Buffalo Bill Historical Center, shows Remington's dedicated collecting of mountain man and Indian memorabilia, and of the pioneer West in general, in part as props for his art. The Museum of The American Fur Trade, Chadron, Nebraska, more than any other institution reveals the world of the mountain man.

Only a handful of Hawken rifles with original owner documentation are known to the author; the rarity of such specimens, the scarcity of Hawken guns in general, and the high mortality rate in any weaponry

Bat Masterson Colt .45, number 112737, subject of one of his letters sent to Colt factory, ordering Single Actions. This one shipped July 30, 1885, to Opera House Saloon, Dodge City, address.

Single Actions of frontier interest; note entry on docket for "Theft of a Colt." *From top*, numbers 21698, 90166, and 16647.

from that era make such arms among the hardest to obtain. Some guns terminated as crowbars, some with cut-down barrels, broken stocks and other parts, and varied alterations, making discovery of a "mint-condition" Hawken nearly impossible.

Adding to the appeal of these arms and this era are groups like the Buckskinners and the National Muzzle Loading Rifle Association. Shooting events and organized rendezvous allow competition in target matches and encourage (or require) participants to be dressed in period costumes. At rendezvous, TVs and radios, portable phones, and other modern amenities are no-

Cowboy and cowgirl, perhaps visiting East from the West. Woolly chaps match angora-covered saddlebags.

Hunting World's silk scarf, celebrating the Colt Single Action; designed from author's book *Colt: An American Legend*. Bob Lee also commissioned his designers to create companion scarf, based on author's *Winchester: An American Legend*.

Double rows of cartridges adorn Texas Ranger Walter Rowe's belt and holster rig; ammunition not interchangeable between Model 1895 Winchester and Colt Single Action.

Masterpieces by Bill Cleaver, Vashon Island, Washington, king of reproduction holster and leather-gear makers. Meanea-style (Cheyenne) holster with sterling-silver conchos and hand-stamped border, accompanied by matching cartridge-money belt, commissioned by author.

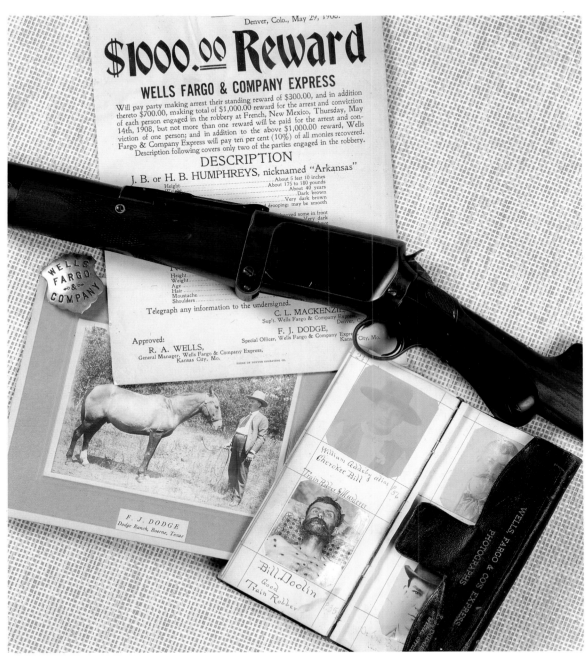

From 1872 through 1915, Lower's Sportsmen's Depot dispensed goods to an eager clientele. One of few dealers to use die stamp markings on some of guns going through their hands. Vertically hung trade sign a mammoth double rifle, accurately depicted in wood and metal.

Special Officer Fred J. Dodge's Burgess 12-gauge folding shotgun (number 3033), his personal mug book, and related memorabilia. Bill Doolin and Cherokee Bill pursued by Dodge; both paid with lives for lawless ways.

ticeably absent. Dress and arms are authentic, and the public is permitted at set hours to visit and get a feel for the old days.

As with Indian arms, collectors of mountain man pieces need to exercise particular caution to avoid acquiring cleverly altered originals or patinated replicas.

The Army

Soldiers like generals Custer and Miles number among the early collectors of weaponry from the frontier. Of course, soldiers from time immemorial have accumulated collections, some with "liberated" goods. The Army itself was active in collecting, and several posts are still standing around the West, not a few with on-site museums. Arms were also sent to other posts outside the West. The Rock Island Arsenal has an important collection, not only of Army weapons, but of captured guns from Indians, particularly postdating the Little Bighorn. The West Point Museum is another repository of the rare and the standard in Western military arms.

The victory of U.S. forces in the short-lived Gulf War of 1991 rekindled an interest and pride in the military, whose sophisticated modern weaponry and tactics overwhelmed the Iraqis. The names of several makers

The eminent collector of Western Americana Parker Lyon (*left*), being presented with Colt revolver by Emmett Dalton. A September 1932 newspaper article covered the donation: "[Dalton] presented Mr. Lyon with the .45 Colt pistol used by Bill Doolin, famous outlaw, and agreed to help Mr. Lyon entertain delegates to the American Legion convention tomorrow. Legionnaires will see many famous relics of the Old West on the outside of the museum, a nominal charge being fixed for entrance to the building itself." Whereabouts of the Doolin Colt presently unknown; gun engraved, nickel-plated, and ivory-gripped.

Young man's first buck deer; c. 1880s. Marlin and Whitney rifles of like period. The .40-60 cartridge casing was fired by author in Theodore Roosevelt's Model 1876 Winchester saddle gun, of which TR wrote that: "it carries far and straight, and hits hard, and is a first-rate weapon for deer and antelope, and can also be used with effect against sheep, elk, and even bear, although for these last a heavier weapon is of course preferable."

Captain Jack presented Model 1895 Winchester carbine to his doctor; S&W double action Fourth Model revolver inscribed by Jack to publisher of his poetry —verse which might charitably be characterized as flamboyant and archaic.

LARIATTES

LITTLE ONES PRAYING AT HOME.—A Song

A BOOK OF POEMS AND RECITATIONS BY

Captain Jack Crawford,

"THE POET SCOUT."

and the weapons themselves hark back to the Army in the West: Colt (M-16 rifles), Winchester (ordnance shells and small-arms ammunition), the Apache and Scout helicopters, and the Sidewinder, Chaparral, Maverick, and Tomahawk missiles.

Collectors of military arms often term the field "U.S. martials." Since there are regimented groupings of types and models, with standard markings, one can take a focused approach. After the Civil War, the use of serial numbers became standard on these guns, an aid in dating them. A useful reference is *Flayderman's Guide to Antique American Firearms and Their Values*, with a clear-cut presentation of all types, providing quantities, standard markings, and pricings.

In Search of Glitter

The lot of a great many miners was to die destitute. Few hit "pay dirt" as did Silver King John Mackay. He sent 14,719 ounces of silver from the Comstock Lode to Tiffany & Co., to have made the most elaborate silver set in the firm's history. Although Mackay's son

From the arms collection of Annie Oakley, Marlin Model 1889 presented by inventor. Among other Marlins owned by Annie were the Model 1891 .22 r.f. (with which she fired an amazing target of twenty-five shots in twenty-seven seconds, at a 36-foot distance; the group measured less than 1 inch in diameter), and Model 1893 and 1897 rifles. The 1893 was gold-and-platinum-inlaid and engraved, and was a .38-55 takedown.

Buffalo Bill's 16-gauge British shotgun, marked on top rib *WESTLEY RICHARDS, 170, NEW BOND ST, LONDON. MADE FOR THE HON. W. F. CODY [BUFFALO BILL] NEBRASKA*. Number 6625. The coat also Cody's, of buffalo hide.

Clarence became one of the great American collectors of arms and armor, whereabouts of his father's guns have eluded the author. Documented prospector-miner guns are quite rare. Ed Scheiffelin's Sharps rifle is an exception to that; his deluxe S&W pistols in their elegant holsters remain undiscovered—for now!

Metal detectors at ghost-town sites will trace buried arms, and relic miner-type guns found at antique arms shows are sometimes not in much better condition. Since so many U.S. prospectors followed the lure of Australian nineteenth-century gold rushes, an abundance of American arms of the period are still down under. One of the best books on Bowie knives is by Australian Ken Burton, and most of the knives pictured were found by the author in his native land, many brought in by miners as well as shipped in by importers for the burgeoning market.

The strike-it-rich glamour of mining arms transcends the tired and patinated condition of most specimens. Such accouterments as gold and silver scales, gold nuggets, mining gear, and gold quartz jewelry all add to the glitter.

Gunfighters, Gamblers, and Outlaws

Of all Western themes of arms collecting the guns of the gunfighters and outlaws hold the greatest public fascination, and are generally the most costly and appealing to the collector. But these stand also as the most fraught with risk: bogus weapons and documents and fake inscriptions are not unusual. In the author's extensive authenticating work, he has seen all too many attempts at fraud. However, when the piece is genuine, as are those throughout the present book, it often speaks for itself, and requires little or no documentation.

But corroboration is often critical. Court records, for example, document the Colt .44 Single Actions carried by Frank McLaury (number 46338) and Billy Clanton (number 52196) at the O.K. Corral shoot-out. And Colt's serial ledgers have served to identify three Bat Masterson Single Actions, out of the eight he ordered.

On the other hand, the author has seen a 7 1/2-

inch-barrel Single Action Colt with lots of accompanying papers—but none of the documents prove the gun to have belonged to Wyatt Earp, whose name is inscribed on the backstrap in script.

The National Organization for Outlaw and Lawman History (NOLA) has an annual convention, publishes a journal, and concentrates on the dynamics of outlaws and gunfighters. Original research is encouraged, and NOLA's journal helps to dispel not a few of the legends of the West, while proving others to be actually true. A splinter group has also formed, known as the Western Outlaw–Lawman History Association.

Peace Officers

Collecting in this field covers any number of organizations, municipalities, and locations. Most of the renowned law enforcement groups still exist: U.S. Marshals, Texas Rangers, the sheriffs of many locales and counties, and police forces of towns and cities. Some of these forces have their own historians, as does the U.S. Marshals Service, and their own museums, as do the Texas Rangers (Fort Fisher, at Waco). The Texas Ranger Museum bristles with guns and knives, has a strong collection of related memorabilia, a library and research center, and living quarters for members of Company F. A 1991 addition was the library of James E. Michener, a good friend of founder and first museum curator the late Gaines de Graffenried.

In recognition of peace officers and of their gunfighter adversaries or sometime associates, Colt and Winchester and groups like the U.S. Historical Society and Franklin Mint have issued a number of commem-

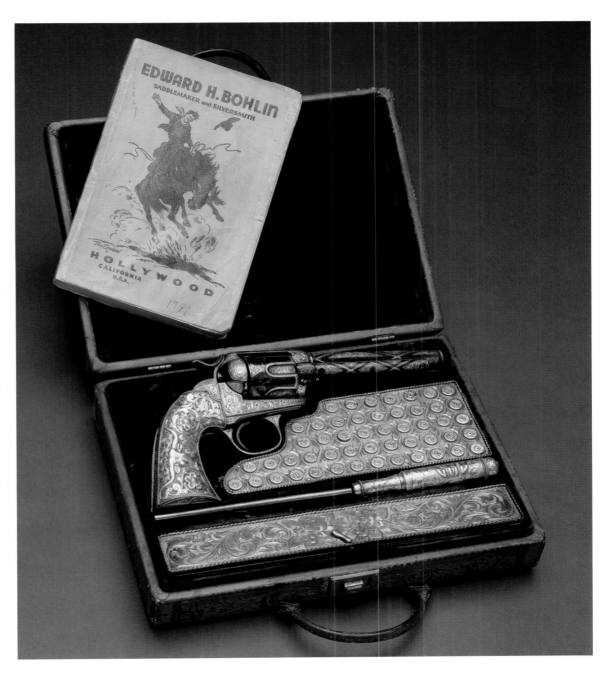

Bohlin of Hollywood catalogue; Colt Bisley was Bohlin's own revolver. Most of his clients were from film and rodeo world; some firearms of particularly lavish garnitures were for the Rose Parade and similar events. Bohlin proclaimed that "it's the High Class Merchandise that Really Counts."

(opposite) Super .38 Colt Automatic of Tom Mix, ivory grips with gold-inlaid brand, echoed on boot tops. Multigallon hat a Mix trademark.

orative guns. Authorization for these issues have sometimes been by the U.S. Marshals Foundation, the Texas Rangers or Texas Rangers Museum, and institutions like the Gene Autry Western Heritage Museum. Special issues have also been made for law enforcement agencies. The author's books *Colt: An American Legend* and *Winchester: An American Legend* have listed a number of these. With some issues only law enforcement personnel qualify for purchase.

Accouterment collectors have a field day with badges. Many a collector keen on peace officer guns is equally smitten with the fascinating array of stars and shields. Elvis Presley was one such devotee.

Cowboys and Ranchers

Of all the species of characters from the West, the cowboy remains king, worldwide. Home on the range, tough, but with a heart of gold, kindly to women and children, nevertheless ready to whoop and holler after finishing chores or trail ride—and always with his trusty six-shooter and Winchester. Ranchers too have their image, represented more by the deluxe engraved Colts and equally fancy Winchesters. Levi's, Stetsons, the Marlboro Man, even two Presidents are part and parcel of the cowboy/rancher identification: Theodore

Best-known of the radio-era Lone Rangers, Brace Beemer owned this double rig, and used it in personal appearances. Son Bob remembered that the "LR on [Dad's] boots stood for honesty, fair play, and the basic goodness of man." Mask a prop, and not the carefully regulated style approved for Lone Ranger use.

Honoring the Wild West, Colt Dragoon embellished by Tiffany & Co., as birthday present from Jackie Autry to Gene, on his eighty-first birthday (1988). Congratulatory letter accompanying gift, from Tiffany chairman William R. Chaney, noted: "Tiffany has enjoyed a long and close involvement in the design and manufacture of decorative firearms. . . . The design was inspired by the work of two renowned western artists, Frederic Remington and George Catlin. All detail is expressed in profuse gold and silver inlay and engraving. The grip, executed in vermeil, was based upon the skin of a rattlesnake." Another Dragoon model made by Tiffany's for author, embellished with gold inlays based on Indian pictograph paintings of the Battle of the Little Bighorn.

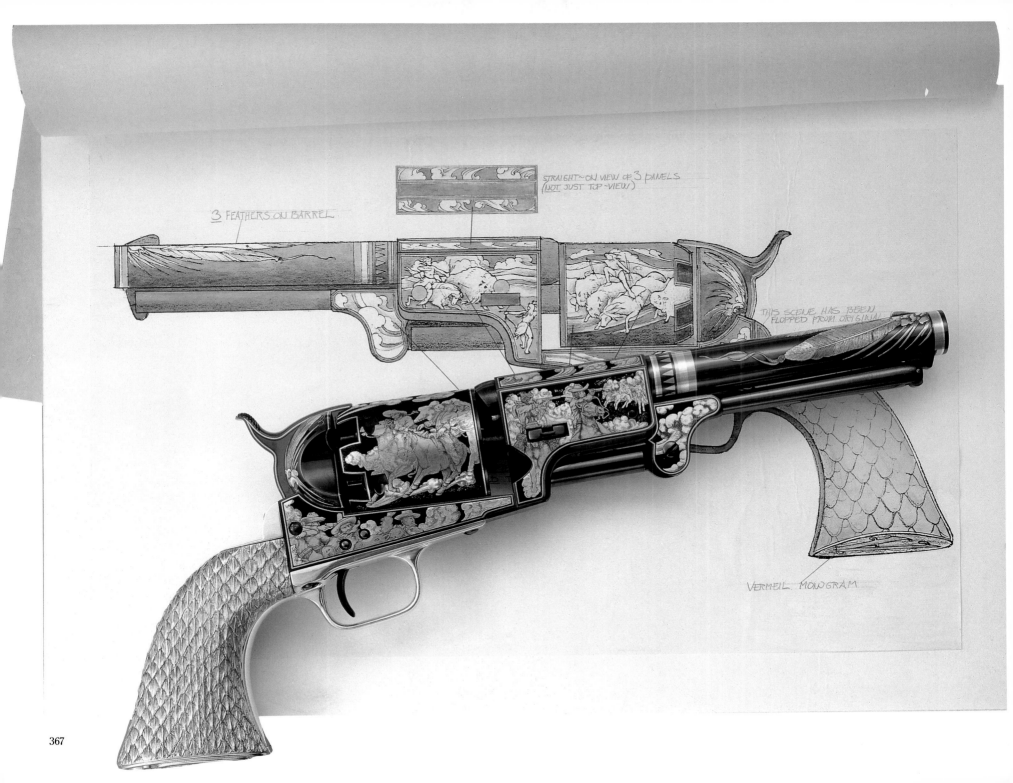

STRAIGHT~ON VIEW OF 3 PANELS
(NOT JUST TOP~VIEW)

3 FEATHERS ON BARREL

THIS SCENE HAS BEEN
FLOPPED FROM ORIGINAL

VERMEIL MONOGRAM

Contemporary Dragoon saluting Colt's contributions to American history, particularly the West. Jointly embellished by Alvin A. White and associate Andrew Bourbon, for Thomas A. Conroy. Colt factory and office on barrel lug; Texas Ranger and Indian cylinder scene accentuated in gold. Some of most exquisite decorations in history of firearms are done by modern-day craftsmen.

Superbly decorated Colt Single Actions, by A. A. White and Andrew Bourbon, with Wild West and Civil War motifs, in 18- and 24-karat gold. Revolvers and spare cylinders were fitted in an equally deluxe velvet-lined rosewood case.

Roosevelt (the real thing) and Ronald Reagan (both real and cinema star to boot).

Many of the great ranches still exist, though diminished in size. Some, like the King Ranch, have a store purveying saddles, holsters, and other paraphernalia and a line of Western clothes and luggage. Another Texas spread, the YO Ranch, celebrated its centennial (1980) with richly decorated Colt Single-Actions and with a handsome illustrated catalogue offering a line of collectors' items. New York City boasts the Billy Martin store, on fashionable Madison Avenue, with an array of duds and accessories, all celebrating our fascination with the West. Even Ralph Lauren has adopted the Western style, and he has his own ranch in Colorado.

Museum shops in the National Cowboy Hall of Fame, Gene Autry Western Heritage Museum, Buffalo Bill Historical Center, and other cowboy-oriented institutions have a ready market with eager visitors. Cowboy hats and boots are common in New York, and have a universal market, carrying the Western spirit internationally. Gun shows in the West feature Western arms and accessories, primarily antique. At arms shows in the rest of the country, many also carry guns and memorabilia with cowboy-rancher associations.

Some ranches and organizations, like the YO and the Cowboy Artists of America, have trail rides, on which participants can bring their firearms. And the Texas Gun Collectors Association has a contingent which meets informally from time to time, at the YO Ranch, with card games and shoot-outs (using black-powder blanks) inspired by the West of old.

One of the most elegant luggage and fashion chains in the world, Bob Lee's Hunting World, carries exquisite cowboy belts and scarves, the latter featuring

Showy guns and gear favored by dudes discovering the West and expanding dude ranch market in the 1920s and 1930s. Colt engraved by Wilbur Glahn and bears silver-inlaid inscription of name on backstrap; ruby-inlaid eyes on steerhead pearl grips. Larry Larom's Valley Ranch, near Cody, Wyoming, had tie-in with Brooks Brothers clothing family, recruited guests using office in New York store for many years.

Bohlin saddles, Colt Single-Actions, and Winchesters.

Books like *Old West Antiques and Collectables* and *Cowboy and Gunfighter Collectables* feature guns and holsters, accompanied by memorabilia and accessories—the collecting of which makes any gun room sparkle with color and romance.

High-quality-replica makers, king of whom is "Wild Bill" Cleaver, can manufacture *signed* copies of originals which are equal in quality to any holsters, chaps, or cowboy accessories ever made. Old West Outfitters, Scottsdale, Arizona, has a color catalogue of outdoor wear and gear, and bills itself as "direct merchants of authentic frontier dry goods."

Wells, Fargo *Et. Al.*

Keeping the spirit of Wells, Fargo & Co. alive is one of America's largest banks: Wells Fargo. Descended from the original Wells, Fargo & Co., the San Francisco –based firm maintains a richly appointed museum at its Montgomery Street facility, and still another museum on Grand Avenue in Los Angeles. Further, the bank has a fleet of stagecoaches, ready for parades and for highly effective commercials on TV.

Like cowboy, mountain man, and prospector guns, those of expressmen are generally rather tired and used. But those W.F. & CO., ADAMS EXPRESS, and other markings are magic. They are also tempting to the trickery of fakers. Colt has records on express guns which left the factory marked. The Ithaca Gun Company has similar records, and the Wells Fargo History Room, San Francisco, can also be helpful.

Shopkeeper weapons will often be crisp in condition, since they were seldom used, but those of sodbusters are commonly quite patinated.

A feeling for old-time frontier gunshops can be gleaned from the re-creation in the Cody Firearms Museum, as well as from a shop at the National Cowboy Hall of Fame. The film *Heaven's Gate* presented an authentic general-store scene, with customers picking out their shooting irons and ammunition.

Period advertising signs, store cabinets, and related memorabilia fit in smartly in the gun room of any col-

lector seeking a Western flavor. Parker Lyon's Frontier Museum displayed the all-time unequaled collection— impossible to duplicate today. His claim of over a million objects was no idle boast.

Hunters and Gentlemen-Sportsmen

Many public museums recognize the hunters-sportsmen of the West with exhibits, but only one major museum deals with the theme exclusively: the Museum of the Fur Trade. Other institutions which feature displays on the subject are the Gene Autry Western Heritage Museum; the Buffalo Bill Historical Center (log cabin with the National Collection of Heads and Horns, in the Cody Firearms Museum); the National Firearms Museum of the National Rifle Association, Washington, D.C.; the J. M. Davis Gun Museum, Claremore, Oklahoma; and the Remington Gun Museum, Ilion, New York.

The memory of the conservation-oriented sportsman-hunter is honored by organizations like the Boone and Crockett Club (which oversees Theodore Roosevelt's Gun Room at Sagamore Hill and the Heads and Horns at the Cody Firearms Museum), The Camp Fire Club of America, and the many other conservation organizations alluded to in Chapter IX. All honor the sportsman-hunter tradition and carry on with the message of their patron, Theodore Roosevelt.

The arms of the hunters-sportsmen are still available at gun shows, though the more deluxe specimens of the likes of Theodore Roosevelt's are either already in museums or destined to be placed there in time.

Today's responsible sportsman hunts game descended from species hunted, stalked, and tracked by those hardy and dedicated nineteenth-century gentlemen, common folk, and aristocrats.

Wild West Showmen and Women

No institutions have a better grasp on the Wild West show world than the Buffalo Bill Historical Center and the Gene Autry Western Heritage Museum. The former has an immense collection in the Buffalo Bill Museum, and even has museum patrons who are descen-

Marlin saluted the milestone of 2 million Model 39 rifles by having that gun gold-inlaid and engraved by Alvin White. Horse-and-rider logo from painting done for factory by Frederic Remington.

The art of anvil firing, as practiced by Dynamite Deke Sonnichsen, head of International Society of Anvil Firers, Menlo Park, California. Institution has European origins; in United States dates from colonial times. Came to West with gold rush; continuous events held in California since 1850s; usually tied in to celebrating anniversary of California's admission to Union, September 9. Deke claims: "To see the loading, gasketing and lighting, using fuse or forge-heated iron rod, to witness the explosion, and floating top anvil amid the billowing cloud of dense, white smoke, while the concussion of the low level shock wave hits your chest with a friendly thump as you try to listen for the humming ring of the 'flyer,' is indeed inspirational, if not singularly stupendous!"

Security for collectibles recommended, against fire as much as theft. Fort Knox of Orem, Utah, favorite brand of author.

dants of Buffalo Bill. Gene Autry himself began in show business (long before he bought the California Angels baseball team, radio and TV stations, real estate, etc.); he knew 101 Ranch star Tom Mix, Will Rogers, and many more.

The Woolaroc Museum, Bartlesville, Oklahoma, has significant 101 Ranch and Will Rogers displays, and historical societies around the United States—especially in the East and Midwest, where the shows performed —sometimes display memorabilia and literature, or at least have material in their collections.

Discoveries by collectors can also be made in Europe and England, in locales where engagements were played. The author found John Y. Nelson's deluxe pair of Colt Single Action revolvers in England, complete with fancy holsters bearing plaques inscribed:

John Y. Nelson
Buffalo
Bill's
Wild West

The outfit had belonged to a descendant who remained in England after the Wild West had left the country.

Several Wild West show performers spent their final years in the East or Midwest; to this day their treasure troves of memorabilia and arms are waiting for the collector to find them.

The late Robert Coe, Standard Oil heir and ambassador, told the most wonderful stories of his boyhood, when he and his brother would be allowed to take a day off from school, to watch Buffalo Bill's Wild West set up for its New York performances. The next day the two brothers would sell Buffalo Bill autographs to their schoolmates for $1 apiece!

Since Buffalo Bill himself was an inveterate collector, visitors to the Buffalo Bill Museum are quite overwhelmed by the wealth of the collections. Royal gifts abound, as do show gear, costumes, guns, saddles and bridles, letters and programs—enough to transfix any admirer of the inimitable Cody.

Smoothbore rifles or revolvers are a collector's treasure. The smoothbore Colt Single-Actions ordered by Pawnee Bill have eluded collectors for years; only one from the original dozen or more is known to the author. The use of smoothbore firearms was a vignette in the film *Buffalo Bill and the Indians*, in which Sitting Bull fires Cody's revolver at a covered wagon, leaving a pattern of shot in the canvas, to the amusement of the Indians and the annoyance of Cody—delightfully protrayed by Paul Newman.

The Fictional West

The West that remains the most alive is that of film and television: its breadth and scope is universal, and with videos the audience is ever greater. For the privileged with a theater screen at home, video equipment by Eiki and other makers will project VHS cassettes on screen as if they were 35mm movies!

The collecting of guns by screen stars is a rather exclusive passion. Foremost in that realm is the Gene Autry Museum, many of whose specimens are featured in Chapter XI. Of course, guns lent by firms like Stembridge have played roles in any number of Westerns—and generally are in poor condition as a result. Documented film or TV guns need strong letters from participants, or clear film stills for identification, or a video record—even a star or bit player holding a gun, recorded on video reminiscing.

Film memorabilia like lobby cards, posters, stills, programs, T-shirts, caps, and autographs are ideal accompaniments to the guns.

Toys for kids, like Roy Rogers and Gene Autry cap guns, holster and belt rigs, Sky King and Lone Ranger compasses, cereal box prizes, *ad infinitum*, are all part of the fictional West's TV and film lore.

Film festivals for Westerns are held in theaters around the country with stars like Monte Hale feted and present to sign autographs. Collector newspapers are published (e.g., *Big Reel*, *Classic Images*, and *Westerns and Serials*) for the buying, selling, and trading of films and videos, programs, lobby cards, and more. And the Gene Autry Museum regularly has film presentations, in the Wells Fargo Theater. Periodically the museum also presents seminars, frequently with guest stars from the films present.

The Golden Boot Awards, annual "Oscars" for Western film and TV performers and production hands, are a fan's delight. The first one attended by the author was at the Sportman's Lodge, Los Angeles. James Stewart was the honoree, and the stars present were from as early as Yakima Canutt to as recent as Patrick Wayne. As guests of Jackie and Gene Autry, the author shared a table with Monte and Joanne Hale, Mr. and Mrs. Ricardo Montalban, Ernest Borgnine (who bought a Colt auction gun that evening), and Jan Michael Vincent and friends. The evening closed with Gene Autry leading the house in singing "Back in the Saddle Again."

With such dedication and enthusiasm to the real West and fictional West, the passion for the West and the Western will never die. The genre is as American as motherhood, apple pie, and the Colt and the Winchester. Despite the wishful thinking of some self-appointed arbiters of taste (some with a political agenda to boot),* the West and the Western have a permanency in our culture which is eternal.

And the hardware of the West—those Peacemakers—will remain forever as symbols of the free life of the open range, and as the ultimate in collectibles of frontier America.

---

*See J. Hoberman, "How the West Was Lost," *The Village Voice*, August 27, 1991, pp. 49–53.

(*top left*) Exterior view, Gene Autry Western Heritage Museum, Los Angeles; interior views to *right*.

(*top center*) Detail from the Colt Gallery.

(*top right*) Overview of the Colt Gallery, primarily exhibiting the former Colt Industries Museum and George A. Strichman collections.

(*bottom left*) Portion of the Spirit of Conquest Gallery.

(*bottom right*) From the Spirit of Community Gallery, relating to law and order.

APPENDIX

Chapter I, Indians: Arms and the First Americans

Shorter bows were best for use from horseback, with their maneuverability and safety, since a rider could be impaled from a fall. In their ultimate evolution the Indian bow measured 40 inches or less. Lengths were variable based on the individual archer's size, on the importance of concealability, or on whether the bow was for use on foot or horseback. One rule of thumb was to make the bow equal in length to the distance from the shooter's right shoulder across the chest and outstretched left arm to the fingertips of the left hand. Another was to make it equal to the distance from the shooter's waist to the ground, and still others were based on other anatomical points of reference.

The skilled archer could shoot an arrow through a buffalo, and even through two. Admiring the Indian's facility with the bow and arrow, some whites became proficient enough to kill buffalo from horseback.

The arrow could be shot with a velocity of 150 feet per second and had a striking force of about 25 pounds, at short distances (15 yards or less preferred). Within its range, a bow and arrow was as good at killing a big animal, or a human, as a bullet.

In construction the two types of bows were the self bow—one piece of wood—and the compound—layers of wood, and sometimes bone and/or horn, held together by glue and wrappings. Both types were customarily reinforced with sinew.

It was artist Alfred Jacob Miller's contention that the smartest of the Yankees could not attempt to make a bow of compound type. And one would bring two quality horses in a trade.

Osage orange was a wood preferred for making bows. Also popular were ash, white elm, ironwood, cedar, dogwood, willow, mulberry, and hazelwood. Obtainable from white traders were hickory, oak, and yew. Various tribes had individual preferences.

Heat from campfires was useful in shaping and bending the bow, a process that was at times quite lengthy. It might take a month to build a bow, and the warrior would need several in his collection, in case of loss or breakage in war and hunting. Some bows were made with a tip at one end, allowing an added function as a spear.

Bow decoration might be paint, pieces of horse mane, and possibly a scalp. Bowstrings were made from deer or buffalo sinew, twisted together, three-ply being preferred. Sometimes rawhide strips or twisted vegetable fiber were used. Bear gut would also do, as would squirrel hides. When not in use, the string could be loosened from one end, relaxing the bow and the sinew.

Plains Indian arrows were of ash, birch, cane, chokecherry, currant, dogwood, Juneberry, willow, and wild cherry. Gooseberry was a Sioux favorite, and serviceberry wood shoots were favored by Blackfoot Indians.

Among methods for determining arrow lengths were measuring from one's elbow to finger tip, with small finger length added: measuring the distance from the archer's breastbone to where his middle fingers touched with both arms extended in front and angled together in a triangle; and holding a stick with its butt at the bottom of the left hand and then grasping hand over hand a total of six times.

Most Plains Indian arrow lengths measured about 25 1/2 inches and were about 5/16 to 1/2 inch in diameter. Arrows for war were heavier than those for hunting; an average arrow weighed about an ounce.

The shape and size of the nock for the bowstring revealed matters about the archer such as how he held the bow and arrow and what material was used for the bowstrings (V-shape meant a fiber string; U-shape meant rawhide or sinew). Arrowheads were glued and tied in place with sinew, in a notch on the arrow tip.

Grooving was common on Plains Indian arrows, usually wavy or somewhat zigzag. Various theories of the purpose of grooving have been offered: to keep the arrows flying straight to target, to represent lightning (magic for speed and power), to make the wound bleed more freely. It appears the grooving primarily had a religious purpose, to bring good luck to the archer.

Cresting, or marking with identifying colors, gave an individuality to each archer's arrows. The variety of colored markings was endless. Colors such as a dull red with about four inches of yellow at the tip were used on Sioux war arrows.

The feathering or fletching on arrows relied largely on eagle and wild turkey feathers, but hawk, owl, and parrot feathers were also used. The fletching was done at an angle to give arrows a spin, such as the rifling in a gun barrel imparts to a bullet. The majority of hunting and war arrows had three feather fletchings, equally attached at the butt end, and usually measuring about one fourth the shaft's length. Wet sinew was used in securing both arrow feathers and arrowheads. When the sinew dried, the grip was tight and secure.

Arrowheads already on the Plains, in the eighteenth and

nineteenth centuries, were customarily of iron or steel, obtained from white traders. Flint or stone points were also used, but these were found by Indians of this period, not made by them. Some bone and sinew points were used for hunting, and there were also wooden points for small animals and birds.

Iron points from traders were common, but metal from banded wooden barrels, from frying pans and other cooking utensils, and even from stove parts was serviceable. The Indians were ingenious in their adaptations. Files obtained from traders made fine arrowheads.

Shapes of the heads indicate their use. Tapering blades, fairly long, were for hunting. Heads for war were sharp-edged, with shoulders angled to form barbs. Unlike hunting blades, which were securely fastened to shafts, the war head was loosely attached, to allow it to come off and remain in the wound. A hunting head could be pulled out of the wound, but a war head had to be pushed through to the other side or removed surgically. Aggravating the situation was the splitting of the war arrow's shaft on hitting the victim.

Arrowheads usually measured 2 to 3 1/2 inches long, with double-edge sharpening. Occasionally smaller points are found, as short as 1 inch long. Some tribes used poisons on war arrow heads. Rust was not unusual on iron, and that or other substances could lead to infection. Tribal variations do occur in arrows, and some tips were for games and target shooting. Buffalo-sinew points are known to have been used for buffalo hunting.

Quivers and Cases

Quivers for arrows and cases for bows were made by Plains Indians. What began in centuries past as simple, undecorated buckskin or rawhide containers for bow and arrows evolved to complex and quite handsomely embellished designs. Sometimes otter and other exotic skins were employed, with tail in place, and with porcupine quills and bead embellishments. Fringed edges were also popular.

A case was important for ease in carrying, but also to keep bows and arrows dry. Quivers became status symbols in time, and indicative of the warrior's fighting skills. The ultimate skin was that of the mountain lion. The best of these quivers were by the Comanche and Kiowa tribes, the fur rich and thick, the edgings and other decoration colorful with cloth, beads, and sinew. Fringes and porcupine quills added to their beauty.

A stick framework inside the quiver kept the arrows from warping. The kit fit on the Indian's back, and was comfortably light.

About twenty arrows would be carried in the quiver. When on horseback, the archer would position the quiver at the side for drawing out the arrows. But when on foot he would carry it on his back, at an angle to allow quick access. When on the attack, the archer could hold about five arrows in his bow hand, and a couple clenched in his teeth, at the ready.

Warriors had the advantage in firepower over single-shot firearms, but they had to use their stalking skills, and call on sheer courage, to get close. To this day, archers who hunt prefer to get within about 15 yards of their target.

Note: For a profusely illustrated, indispensably valuable source on the Indians of the West, the writer recommends Thomas E. Mails's classic work *The Mystic Warriors of the Plains.*

Chapter XI, Arming the Fictional West

(*Illus.*, page 329) The Western in the 1940s, 1950s, and 1960s: 1940 film *The Outlaw* credited with introducing sex to the Western, while *The Ox-Bow Incident* (1942) spotlighted social themes and was harbinger of so-called adult Westerns. *Top to bottom, from left to right:* Gregory Peck in *The Gunfighter*; Barbara Stanwyck in 1952 rerelease of the 1935 film *Annie Oakley*; Gary Cooper and Burt Lancaster in *Vera Cruz*. Charlton Heston in *Major Dundee*; Robert Taylor in *The Last Hunt*; Fess Parker in Walt Disney's *Davy Crockett*; another scene from *The Last Hunt* with hero aiming his Sharps rifle. Gregory Peck, Burl Ives, and Chuck Connors in *The Big Country*; Charlton Heston as Buffalo Bill in *Pony Express*; Sterling Hayden in *The Iron Sheriff*; Gary Cooper and Grace Kelly in the classic Academy Award Winner *High Noon*; George Peppard and Richard Widmark in *How the West Was Won*. Sam Peckinpah's rawly realistic *The Wild Bunch*, featuring Ben Johnson, Warren Oates, William Holden, and Ernst Borgnine; *Maverick Queen*, starring Barry Sullivan and Barbara Stanwyck; James Stewart in *Winchester '73, above* photograph of doyen of contemporary Western artists Harry Jackson, completing his 26-foot-tall monumental sculpture of John Wayne (at Great Western Bank headquarters, Wilshire Boulevard, Beverly Hills); Colt .45 a prototype of the John Wayne commemora-

tive, serial number SA53865. Steve McQueen, Yul Brynner, and friends in *The Magnificent Seven*; Lee Marvin, Claudia Cardinale, and Burt Lancaster in *The Professionals*; Paul Newman and Robert Redford in *Butch Cassidy and the Sundance Kid*; and Ven Heflin in the remake of *Stagecoach*.

(*Illus.*, page 338) The Western in the 1970s and 1980s: *From top left,* Glenn Ford in *Man from the Alamo*; Kirk Douglas showing his six-gun magic (holster by Ojala); Harry Belafonte and Sidney Poitier in *Buck and the Preacher*; Fernando Lamas in *100 Rifles* (also starred Raquel Welch and Burt Reynolds); Clint Eastwood in *Joe Kidd* (with broomhandle Mauser pistol). *From bottom left,* Jim Brown in *The Legend of Nigger Charley*; Robert Culp and Raquel Welch in *Hannie Caulder*; Susan Clark and Burt Lancaster in *Valdez is Coming*; and Eastwood again in *Pale Rider* (using Remington New Model Army).

(*Illus.*, page *340*) Re. Aldo Uberti: Daughter Maria, now president of Uberti U.S.A. Inc., recalls: "Sergio Leone came to our house when I was maybe six or seven years old. . . . He came to order some 'special' guns for a movie he was working on: *A Fistful of Dollars*, I believe it was. He bought a large amount of 'modified' guns (he and my father spent hours figuring out how they had to be modified for his very particular needs); my mother still remembers that his first order was for about $80,000 worth of guns, which at the time was quite a respectable sum. After that first film, Leone kept getting guns especially made for him. Another big order was put together for *The Good, the Bad, and the Ugly,* where there were some Civil War scenes with hundreds of our guns. Naturally using our guns opened the doors to the whole of the Italian-made Western movies and since then we have been providing thousands of guns to Cinecittà."

BIBLIOGRAPHY

Research materials included original newspapers and periodicals; city, state, and regional directories; unpublished memoirs and correspondence; photographic sources; miscellaneous museum, historical society, and library archival materials; government reports; dealer and jobber advertising and factory serial number shipping ledgers; order books; and twentieth-century reference periodicals and journals. Research also involved personal examinations of tens of thousands of weapons, and correspondence and interviews with numerous collectors, dealers, curators, historians, and students, and with descendants of original owners and users of arms.

Abbott, E.C. ("Teddy Blue"), and Helena Huntington Smith. *We Pointed Them North: Recollections of a Cowpuncher.* New York: Farrar and Rinehart, 1939.

Adams, Ramon F. *The Cowman Says It Salty.* Tucson: University of Arizona Press, 1971.

_____. *The Old-Time Cowhand.* New York: Macmillan, 1961.

_____. *Six-Guns and Saddle Leather: A Bibliography of Books and Pamphlets on Western Outlaws and Gunmen.* Norman: University of Oklahoma Press, 1969.

Ahlborn, Richard E., ed. *Man Made Mobile: Early Saddles of Western North America.* Washington, D.C.: Smithsonian Institution, 1980.

Alter, J. Cecil. *Jim Bridger.* Norman: University of Oklahoma Press, 1973.

Altmayer, Jay P. *American Presentation Swords.* Mobile, Ala.: Rankin Press, 1958.

Arganbright, Bob. *The Fastest Guns Alive.* St. Louis: published by the author, 1978.

Asbury, Herbert. *Sucker's Progress: An Informal History of Gambling in America from the Colonies to Canfield.* New York: Dodd, Mead, 1938.

Athearn, Robert G. *William Tecumseh Sherman and the Settlement of the West.* Norman: University of Oklahoma Press, 1956.

Baird, John D. *Fifteen Years in the Hawken Lode.* Chaska, Minn.: Buckskin Press, 1971.

_____. *Hawken Rifles: The Mountain Man's Choice.* Big Timber, Mont.: Buckskin Press, 1974.

Baker, T. Lindsay, and Billy R. Harrison. *Adobe Walls: The History and Archeology of the 1874 Trading Post.* College Station: Texas A & M University Press, 1986.

Ball, Larry D. *The United States Marshals of New Mexico and Arizona Territories, 1846–1912.* Albuquerque: University of New Mexico Press, 1986.

Barnhart, Jacqueline Baker. *The Fair But Frail: Prostitution in San Francisco, 1849–1900.* Reno: University of Nevada Press, 1986.

Beatie, Russel H. *Saddles.* Norman: University of Oklahoma Press, 1981.

Beebe, Lucius, and Charles Clegg. *U.S. West: The Saga of Wells Fargo.* New York: Dutton, 1949.

Benton, Captain J. G. *A Course Of Instruction in Ordnance and Gunnery Composed and Compiled for Use of Cadets of the U. S. Military Academy.* New York: Van Nostrand, 1861.

Berry, Don. *A Majority of Scoundrels: An Informal History of the Rocky Mountain Fur Company.* New York: Harper & Brothers, 1961.

Boessenecker, John. *Badge and Buckshot: Lawlessness in Old California.* Norman and London: University of Oklahoma Press, 1988.

Bourke, John G. *On the Border with Crook.* New York: Scribner's, 1891.

Branch, E. Douglas. *The Hunting of the Buffalo.* New York: D. Appleton and Co., 1929.

Breakenridge, William M. *Helldorado: Bringing the Law to the Mesquite.* Boston: Houghton Mifflin, 1928.

Brophy, Lt. Col. William S. *Krag Rifles.* North Hollywood, Calif.: Beinfeld Publishing, 1980.

_____. *Marlin Firearms.* Harrisburg, Penn.: Stackpole, 1989.

_____. *The Springfield 1903 Rifles.* Harrisburg, Penn., Stackpole, 1985.

Brown, Mark H. *The Plainsmen of the Yellowstone: A History of the Yellowstone Basin.* New York: Putnam's, 1961.

Brown, Robert L. *Saloons of the American West.* Silverton, Colo.: Sundance Books, 1978.

Brown, Stuart E., Jr. *The Guns of Harpers Ferry.* Berryville, Va.: Virginia Book Company, 1968.

Bryan, Howard. *Wildest of the Wild West.* Santa Fe, N.M.: Clear Light Publishers, 1988.

Buscombe, Edward, ed. *The BFI Companion to the Western.* New York: Atheneum, 1988.

Calhoun, Frederick S. *The Lawmen: U.S. Marshals and Their Deputies, 1789–1989.* Washington and London: Smithsonian Institution, 1990.

Carpenter, Charles H., Jr., with Mary Grace Carpenter. *Tiffany Silver.* New York: Dodd, Mead, 1978.

Carter, Capt. R.G. *On the Border with Mackenzie; or, Winning West Texas from the Comanches.* New York: Antiquarian Press, 1961.

Carter, Harvey Lewis. *"Dear Old Kit" The Historical Christopher Carson: With a New Edition of the Carson Memoirs.* Norman: University of Oklahoma Press, 1968.

Chapman, Arthur. *The Pony Express: The Record of a Romantic Adventure in Business.* New York and London: Putnam's, 1932.

Cleland, Robert Glass. *This Reckless Breed of Men: The*

Trappers and Fur Traders of the Southwest. New York: Knopf, 1950.

Cook, James H. *Fifty Years on the Old Frontier.* New Haven: 1923.

Cope, Kenneth L. *Stevens Pistols and Pocket Rifles.* Ottawa, Ontario: Museum Restoration Service, 1971.

Current, Karen. *Photography and the Old West.* New York: Abradale/Harry N. Abrams, 1986.

Custer, Elizabeth B. *"Boots and Saddles" or, Life in Dakota with General Custer.* Norman: University of Oklahoma Press, 1962.

Custer, General George Armstrong. *My Life on the Plains or, Personal Experiences with Indians.* Norman and London: University of Oklahoma Press, 1962.

Dary, David. *Cowboy Culture: A Saga of Five Centuries.* New York: Knopf, 1981.

_____. *Entrepreneurs of the Old West.* New York: Knopf, 1986.

Dedera, Don. *A Little War of Our Own: The Pleasant Valley Feud Revisited.* Flagstaff, Ariz., Northland Press, 1988.

Demeritt, Dwight B., Jr. *Maine-Made Guns and Their Makers.* Hallowell, Me.: Maine State Museum, 1973.

Dillon, Richard. *Wells, Fargo Detective: A Biography of James B. Hume.* Reno: University of Nevada, 1986.

Dippie, Brian W., ed. *Nomad: George A. Custer in "Turf, Field and Farm."* Austin and London: University of Texas Press, 1980.

Dodge, Colonel Richard Irving. *Our Wild Indians: Thirty-three Years' Personal Experience Among the Red Men of the Great West.* Hartford: A. D. Worthington and Company, 1882.

du Mont; John S. *Custer Battle Guns.* Canaan, N.H.: Phoenix Publishing, 1988.

Dunlap, Jack. *American British and Continental Pepperbox Firearms.* Los Altos, Calif.: published by the author, 1964.

Dykstra, Robert R. *The Cattle Towns.* Lincoln and London: University of Nebraska Press, 1968.

Edwards, William B. *Civil War Guns.* Harrisburg, Penn.: Stackpole, 1962.

Egan, Ferol. *Fremont: Explorer for a Restless Nation.* Garden City, New York: Doubleday, 1977.

Estergreen, M. Morgan. *Kit Carson: A Portrait in Courage.* Norman: University of Oklahoma Press, 1962.

Fenin, George N., and William K. Everson. *The Western from Silents to the Seventies.* New York: Grossman Publishers, 1973.

Flayderman, Norm. *Flayderman's Guide to Antique American Firearms . . . and Their Values.* 5th ed. Northbrook, Ill.: DBI Books, 1990.

Foxley, William C. *Frontier Spirit Catalogue of the Collection of The Museum of Western Art.* Denver, Colo.: Museum of Western Art, 1983.

Frazer, Robert W. *Forts of the West.* Norman: University of Oklahoma Press, 1965.

Friedman, Michael, *Cowboy Culture: The Last Frontier of American Antiques.* West Chester Penn.: Schiffer Publishing, Ltd., 1992

Frost, Lawrence A. *The Custer Album: A Pictorial Biography of General George A. Custer.* Seattle: Superior Publishing, 1964.

Frost, Richard I., Leo A. Platteter, and Don Hedgpeth. *The West of Buffalo Bill.* New York: Abrams, 1970.

Fuller, Claud E. *The Breech-Loader in the Service 1816–1917: A History of All Standard and Experimental U.S. Breech-Loading Magazine Shoulder Arms.* Topeka, Kans.: Arms Reference Club of America, 1933. Reprinted 1965, New Milford, Conn.: N. Flayderman, 1965.

_____. *Springfield Shoulder Arms 1795–1865.* New York: Francis Bannerman Sons, 1930.

_____. *The Whitney Firearms.* Huntington, W. Va.: Standard Publications, 1946.

Fulton, Maurice Garland, ed. *Pat F. Garrett's Authentic Life of Billy the Kid.* New York: Macmillan, 1927.

Garavaglia, Louis A., and Charles G. Worman. *Firearms of the American West 1803–1865.* Albuquerque: University of New Mexico Press, 1984.

_____. *Firearms of the American West 1866–1894.* Albuquerque: University of New Mexico Press, 1985.

Gard, Wayne. *Frontier Justice.* Norman: University of Oklahoma Press, 1949.

_____. *The Great Buffalo Hunt.* New York: Knopf, 1959.

_____. *Rawhide Texas.* Norman: University of Oklahoma Press, 1965.

Goetzmann, William H. *The Mountain Man.* Cody, Wyo.: Buffalo Bill Historical Center, 1978.

Goodnight, Charles, Emanuel Dubbs, John A. Hart, and others. *Pioneer Days in the Southwest, 1850–1879.* Guthrie, Okla.: State Capital Company, 1909.

Goodson, Joe, ed. *Old West Antiques and Collectables.* West Austin, Tex.: Great American Publishing, 1979.

Graham, Colonel W. A. *The Custer Myth: A Source Book of Custeriana.* New York: Bonanza Books, 1953.

Grant, Ellsworth Strong. *Yankee Dreamers and Doers.* Chester, Conn.: Pequot Press, 1973.

Grant, James J. *Boys' Single-Shot Rifles.* New York: Morrow, 1967.

_____. *More Single-Shot Rifles.* New York: Morrow, 1959.

_____. *Single-Shot Rifles.* New York: Morrow, 1947.

_____. *Still More Single-Shot Rifles.* Union City, Tenn.: Pioneer Press, 1979.

Gray, John S. *Centennial Campaign: The Sioux War of 1876.* Fort Collins, Col.: Old Army Press, 1976.

Greer, James Kimmins. *Colonel Jack Hays: Texas Frontier Leader and California Builder.* New York: E. P. Dutton, 1952.

Greever, William S. *The Bonanza West: The Story of the Western Mining Rushes, 1848–1900.* Norman: University of Oklahoma Press, 1963.

Grinnell, George Bird. *The Fighting Cheyennes.* New York: Scribner's, 1915.

Guild, Thelma S., and Harvey L. Carter. *Kit Carson: A Pattern for Heroes.* Lincoln: University of Nebraska Press, 1984.

Hafen, LeRoy R. *Broken Hand, The Life of Thomas Fitzpatrick: Mountain Man, Guide and Indian Agent.* Denver: Old West Publishing Company, 1973.

_____, ed. *The Mountain Man and the Fur Trade of the Far West.* Ten volumes. Glendale, California: Arthur H. Clark Company, 1965–72.

Haley, J. Evetts. *Jeff Milton: A Good Man with a Gun.* Norman: University of Oklahoma Press, 1948.

Hammond, George P., and Edward H. Howes, ed. *Overland to California on the Southwestern Trail 1849: Diary of Robert Eccleston.* Berkeley and Los Angeles: University of California Press, 1950.

Hanson, Charles E., Sr. *The Plains Rifle.* Harrisburg, Penn.: Stackpole, 1960.

Harmon, S. W. *Hell on the Border: He Hanged Eighty Men.* Fort Smith, Arkansas: Phoenix Publishing Company, 1898.

Heide, Robert, and John Gilman. *Box-Office Buckaroos.* New York: Abbeville Press, 1982.

Hicks, Major James E. *Notes on United States Ordnance, Vol. 1, Small Arms 1776–1940*; Vol. 2, *Ordnance Correspondence Relative to Muskets, Rifles, Pistols and Swords*. Mt. Vernon, N. Y.: published by the author, 1940. Vol. 1 reprinted as *U.S. Military Firearms 1776–1956*, LaCanada, Calif.: James E. Hicks & Sons, 1962.

Hobsbawm, Eric. *Bandits*. New York: Pantheon, 1981.

Hodge, Frederick Webb, ed. *Handbook of American Indians North of Mexico*. Smithsonian Institution Bureau of American Ethnology, Bulletin 30. Published in two parts. Washington, D.C.: U.S. Government Printing Office, 1912.

Horn, Tom. *Life of Tom Horn, Written by Himself.* Denver: Louthian Book Company, 1904.

Howard, Major General O. O. *My Life and Experiences Among Our Hostile Indians*. Hartford: A. D. Worthington & Company, 1907.

Hungerford, Edward. *Wells Fargo: Advancing the American Frontier.* New York: Random House, 1949.

Hunt, Aurora. *Major General James Henry Carleton, 1814–1873: Western Frontier Dragoon*. Glendale, Calif.: Arthur H. Clark Co., 1958.

Hunter, J. Marvin (comp.). *The Trail Drivers of Texas*. Two volumes. New York: Argosy-Antiquarian, Ltd., 1963.

Huntington, R. T. *Hall's Breechloaders*. York, Penn.: George Shumway, 1972.

Hutslar, Donald A. *Gunsmiths of Ohio—18th and 19th Centuries. Vol. 1, Biographical Data*. York, Penn.: George Shumway, 1973.

Hutton, Paul Andrew. *Phil Sheridan and His Army*. Lincoln: University of Nebraska Press, 1985.

Inman, Colonel Henry. *Buffalo Jones's Forty Years of Adventure*. Topeka: Crane & Company, 1899.

Jahns, Pat. *The Frontier World of Doc Holliday: Faro Dealer from Dallas to Deadwood*. New York: Hastings House, 1957.

Jamieson, G. S. *Bullard Arms*. Erin, Ontario: Boston Mills Press, 1988.

Jenkins, John H., and H. Gordon Frost. *"I'm Frank Hamer."* Austin and New York: Pemberton Press, 1968.

Jinks, Roy G. *125 Years with Smith & Wesson*. North Hollywood, Calif.: Beinfeld Publishing, 1977.

Katz, D. Mark. *Custer in Photographs*. New York: Bonanza Books, 1985.

Katz, William Loren. *The Black West*. Seattle: Open Hand Publishing, 1987.

Keleher, William A. *Violence in Lincoln County 1869–1881*. Albuquerque: University of New Mexico Press, 1982.

Lavender, David. *Bent's Fort*. Garden City, N. Y.: Doubleday, 1954.

_____. *The Way to the Western Sea: Lewis and Clark Across the Continent*. New York: Harper & Row, 1988.

Levine, Bernard R. *Knifemakers of Old San Francisco*. San Francisco: Badger Books, 1978.

Lewis, Berkeley R. *Small Arms and Ammunition in the United States Service*. Smithsonian Miscellaneous Collections, Vol. 129. Washington, D.C.: Smithsonian Institution, 1956.

Kindig, Joe, Jr. *Thoughts on the Kentucky Rifle in Its Golden Age*. Wilmington, Del.: George N. Hyatt, 1960. Republished, various editions. York, Penn.: George Shumway.

Kopec, John A., Ron Graham, and C. Kenneth Moore. *A Study of the Colt Single Action Army Revolver*. Dallas, Tex.: Taylor Publishing, 1976.

Logan, Herschel C. *Underhammer Guns*. Harrisburg, Penn.: Stackpole, 1960.

Loomis, Noel M. *Wells Fargo: An Illustrated History*. New York: Bramhall House, 1968.

McGrath, Roger D. *Gunfighters, Highwaymen & Vigilantes: Violence on the Frontier*. Berkeley, Los Angeles, and London: University of California Press, 1984.

McHugh, Tom. *The Time of the Buffalo*. New York: Knopf, 1972.

McIntire, Jim. *Early Days in Texas: A Trip to Hell and Heaven*. Kansas City, Missouri: McIntire Publishing Company, 1902.

McKennon, C. H. *Iron Men: The Saga of the Deputy United States Marshals Who Rode the Indian Territory*. Garden City, New York: Doubleday, 1967.

Mackin, Bill. *Cowboy and Gunfighter Collectibles*. Missoula, Mont.: Mountain Press, 1989.

Mails, Thomas E. *The Mystic Warriors of the Plains*. Garden City, N.Y.: Doubleday, 1972.

Marcot, Roy M. *Spencer Repeating Firearms*. Irvine, Calif.: Northwood Heritage Press, 1983.

Marquis, Thomas B. *Keep the Last Bullet for Yourself: The True Story of Custer's Last Stand*. New York: Two Continents Publishing, 1976.

Maxwell, Samuel L., Sr. *Lever-Action Magazine Rifles Derived from the Patents of Andrew Burgess*. Bellevue, Wash.: published by the author, 1976.

Mayer, Frank H., and Charles B. Roth. *The Buffalo Harvest.* Denver: Sage Books, 1958.

Mead, James R. *Hunting and Trading on the Great Plains, 1859–1875*. Norman: University of Oklahoma Press, 1986.

Meadows, E. S. *U.S. Military Holsters and Pistols and Pistol Cartridge Boxes*. Dallas, Tex.: Taylor Publishing, 1987.

Metz, Leon C. *Pat Garrett: The Story of a Western Lawman*. Norman: University of Oklahoma Press, 1974.

_____. *The Shooters*. El Paso: Mangan Books, 1976.

Miles, Nelson A. *Personal Recollections and Observations of General Nelson A. Miles*. Chicago: Werner Co., 1896.

_____. *Serving the Republic*. New York: Harper & Brothers, 1911.

Miller, Nyle H., and Joseph W. Snell. *Why the West Was Wild: A Contemporary Look at the Antics of Some Highly Publicized Kansas Cowtown Personalities*. Topeka: Kansas State Historical Society, 1963.

Moody, Ralph. *Stagecoach West*. Burlingame, Calif.: Promontory Press, 1967.

Morgan, Dale L. *Jedediah Smith and the Opening of the West*. Indianapolis: Bobbs-Merrill, 1953.

Mouillesseaux, Harold R. *Ethan Allen, Gunmaker: His Partners, Patents and Firearms*. Ottawa, Canada: Museum Restoration Service, 1973.

Mowbray, Andrew, ed. *Guns at the Little Bighorn: The Weapons of Custer's Last Stand*. Lincoln, R. I.: Andrew Mowbray, 1988.

Mullin, Kevin J. *Let Justice Be Done: Crime and Politics in Early San Francisco*. Reno: University of Nevada Press, 1989.

Mullin, Robert N. *Maurice Garland Fulton's History of the Lincoln County War*. Tucson: University of Arizona Press, 1980.

Nevins, Allan. *Fremont: Pathmarker of the West*. New York: D. Appleton-Century Company, 1939.

Newman, Kim. *Wild West Movies*. London: Bloomsbury, 1990.

Norton, Brigadier General Charles B. *American Inventions and Improvements in Breech-Loading Small Arms, Heavy Ordnance, Machine Guns, Magazine Arms, Fixed*

Ammunition, Pistols, Projectiles, Explosives, etc. Boston, Mass.: Osgood, 1882.

Oliva, Leo E. *Soldiers on the Santa Fe Trail.* Norman: University of Oklahoma Press, 1967.

O'Neal, Bill. *Encyclopedia of Western Gunfighters.* Norman: University of Oklahoma Press, 1979.

_____. *Henry Brown: The Outlaw-Marshal.* College Station, Tex.: Creative Publishing, 1980.

Parkman, Francis. *The California and Oregon Trail.* New York, 1849.

Parsons, John E. *The First Winchester: The Story of the 1866 Repeating Rifle.* New York: Winchester Press, 1969.

_____. *Henry Deringer's Pocket Pistol.* New York: Morrow, 1952.

_____. *The Peacemaker and Its Rivals.* New York: Morrow, 1950.

_____. *Smith & Wesson Revolvers: The Pioneer Single-Action Models.* N.Y.: Morrow, 1957.

Pelzer, Louis. *The Cattlemen's Frontier.* Glendale, Calif.: Arthur H. Clark Company, 1936.

Penzig, Edgar. *Bullets, Blades and Bravery Stories and Weapons of Australia's Wild Colonial Days.* Katoomba, N.S.W., Australia: Tranter Enterprises, 1990.

Perkins, Jim. *American Boys' Rifles 1890–1945.* Pittsburgh, Penn.: RTP Publishers, 1976.

Peterson, Harold L. *American Indian Tomahawks.* Vol. 19 of *Contributions from the Museum of the American Indian,* Heye Foundation. New York: Museum of the American Indian, Heye Foundation, 1965.

_____. *American Knives: The First History and Collectors' Guide.* New York: Scribner's, 1958.

_____. *The American Sword 1775–1945.* New Hope, Penn.: Robert Halter, River House, 1954.

Phillips-Wolley, Clive. *Big Game Shooting, The Badminton Library of Sports and Pastimes,* Vol. 1. London: Longmans, Green, 1894.

Prassel, Frank Richard. *The Western Peace Officer.* Norman: University of Oklahoma Press, 1972.

Prucha, Francis Paul. *Indian Peace Medals in American History.* Lincoln: University of Nebraska Press, 1971.

_____. *The Sword of the Republic: The United States Army on the Frontier, 1783–1846.* New York: Macmillan, 1969.

Quaife, Milo Milton, ed. *Kit Carson's Autobiography.* Chicago: Lakeside Press, 1935.

Quinn, John Philip. *Gambling and Gambling Devices.* Canton, Ohio: J. P. Quinn, 1912.

Rattenbury, Richard C. *Packing Iron: A Survey of Military and Civilian Gunleather on the Western Frontier.* Millwood, N.Y.: ZON International Publishing, in press.

_____. and Thomas E. Hall. *Sights West: Selections from the Winchester Museum Collection.* Cody, Wyo.: Buffalo Bill Historical Center, and Lincoln, Neb.: University of Nebraska Press, 1981.

Reedstrom, Ernest Lisle. *Bugles, Banners and War Bonnets.* Caldwell, Id.: Caxton Printers, 1977.

Reilly, Robert M. *United States Martial Flintlocks.* Lincoln, R. I.: Andrew Mowbray, 1986.

_____. *United States Military Small Arms 1816–1865.* Baton Rouge, La.: Eagle Press, 1970.

Richardson, Rupert Norval. *The Comanche Barrier to South Plains Settlement.* Glendale, Calif.: Arthur H. Clark Company, 1933.

Roberts, Gary L. *Death Comes for the Chief Justice: The Slough-Rynerson Quarrel and Political Violence in New Mexico.* Niwot: University Press of Colorado, 1990.

Roosevelt, Theodore. *Hunting Trips of a Ranchman.* New York and London: Putnam's, 1885.

_____. *Ranch Life and the Hunting Trail.* New York: Century, 1888.

_____. *Theodore Roosevelt: An Autobiography.* New York: Macmillan, 1913.

Rosa, Joseph G. *The Gunfighter: Man or Myth.* Norman: University of Oklahoma Press, 1969.

_____. *Guns of the American West.* New York: Crown, Inc., 1985.

_____. *They Called Him Wild Bill.* Norman: University of Oklahoma Press, 1982.

_____. *The West of Wild Bill Hickok.* Norman: University of Oklahoma Press, 1982.

_____. *Buffalo Bill and His Wild West.* Lawrence: University of Kansas Press, 1989.

_____, and Robin May. *Cowboy: The Man and the Myth.* London: New English Library, 1980.

_____. *Gunsmoke: A Study of Violence in the Old West.* London: New English Library, 1977.

Rosebush, Waldo E. *Frontier Steel: The Men and Their Weapons.* Appleton, Wis.: C. C. Nelson, 1958.

Ross, Marvin C., ed. *George Catlin Episodes from "Life Among the Indians" and "Last Rambles."* Norman: University of Oklahoma Press, 1959.

Rossi, Paul, and David C. Hunt. *The Art of the Old West from the Collection of the Gilcrease Institute.* New York: Knopf, 1971.

Russell, Carl P. *Firearms, Traps, and Tools of the Mountain Men.* New York: Knopf, 1967.

Russell, Charles M. *Good Medicine: Memories of the Real West.* Garden City, N.Y.: Garden City Publishing, 1930.

Russell, Don. *The Lives and Legends of Buffalo Bill.* Norman: University of Oklahoma Press, 1960.

Rye, Edgar. *The Quirt and The Spur: Vanishing Shadows of the Texas Frontier.* Chicago: W.B. Conkey, 1909.

Sabin, Edwin L. *Kit Carson Days.* Two volumes. New York: The Press of the Pioneers, Inc., 1935.

Sandoz, Mari. *The Buffalo Hunters: The Story of the Hide Men.* New York: Hastings House, 1954.

_____. *Hostiles and Friendlies.* Lincoln and London: University of Nebraska Press, 1959.

Savage, William W., Jr. *Cowboy Life: Reconstructing An American Myth.* Norman: University of Oklahoma Press, 1975.

Scott, Douglas D., Richard A. Fox, Jr., Melissa A. Connor, and Dick Harmon. *Archaeological Perspectives on the Battle of the Little Big Horn.* Norman and London: University of Oklahoma Press, 1989.

Sell, DeWitt E. *Collector's Guide to American Cartridge Handguns.* Harrisburg, Penn.: Stackpole, 1963.

Sellers, Frank. *American Gunsmiths.* Highland Park, N.J.: Gun Room, 1983.

_____. *Sharps Firearms.* North Hollywood, Calif.: Beinfeld Publishing, 1978.

Senkewicz, Robert M., S. J. Senkewicz. *Vigilantes in Gold Rush San Francisco.* Stanford: Stanford University Press, 1985.

Sharpe, Philip B. *The Rifle in America.* New York: Funk & Wagnalls, 1947.

Shelton, Lawrence P. *California Gunsmiths 1846–1900.* Fair Oaks, Calif.: Far Far West Publishers, 1977.

Shillingberg, William B. *Wyatt Earp and the "Buntline Special" Myth.* Tucson: Blaine Publishing Company, 1976.

Shirley, Glenn. *Guardian of the Law.* Austin, Tex.: Eakin Press, 1988.

_____. *Law West of Fort Smith: A History of Frontier Justice in the Indian Territory, 1834–1896.* Lincoln: University of Nebraska Press, 1968.

Sinclair, Andrew. *John Ford.* New York: Dial Press, 1979.

Smith, Helena Huntington. *The War on Powder River.* New York: McGraw-Hill, 1966.

Smith, Samuel E., and Frank M. Sellers. *American Percussion Revolvers.* Ottawa, Ontario: Museum Restoration Service, 1971.

Smith, Waddell F. *The Story of the Pony Express.* San Rafael, Calif.: Pony Express History and Art Gallery, 1964.

Sprague, Marshall. *A Gallery of Dudes.* Lincoln and London: University of Nebraska Press, 1967.

Steckmesser, Kent Ladd. *The Western Hero in History and Legend.* Norman: University of Oklahoma Press, 1965.

Steward, Edgar I. *Custer's Luck.* Norman: University of Oklahoma Press, 1955.

Streeter, Floyd Benjamin. *Ben Thompson: Man with a Gun.* New York: Frederik Fell, 1957.

_____. *Prairie Trails and Cow Towns.* Boston: Chapman and Grimes, 1936.

Taylor, Lonn, and Ingrid Maar. *The American Cowboy.* New York: Harper & Row, 1983.

Thorp, Raymond W. *"Wild West" Doc Carver: Spirit Gun of the West.* London: W. Foulsham, 1957.

Thrapp, Dan L. *The Conquest of Apacheria.* Norman: University of Oklahoma Press, 1967.

Trefethen, James B. *An American Crusade for Wildlife.* New York: Winchester Press, 1975.

Tuska, Jon. *The Filming of the West.* Garden City, N.Y.: Doubleday, 1976.

Utley, Robert M. *Billy the Kid.* Lincoln and London: University of Nebraska Press, 1989.

_____. *Cavalier in Buckskin: George Armstrong Custer and the Western Military Frontier.* Norman and London: University of Oklahoma Press, 1988.

_____. *Frontier Regulars: The United States Army and the Indian, 1866–1891.* New York: Macmillan, 1973.

_____. *Frontiersmen in Blue: The United States Army and the Indian, 1848–1865.* New York: Macmillan, 1967.

_____. *High Noon in Lincoln: Violence on the Western Frontier.* Albuquerque: University of New Mexico Press, 1987.

_____. *The Indian Frontier of the American West 1846–1890.* Albuquerque: University of New Mexico Press, 1984.

_____, and Wilcomb E. Washburn. *The American Heritage History of the Indian Wars.* New York: American Heritage, 1977.

Viola, Herman J. *After Columbus: The Smithsonian Chronicle of the North American Indians.* Washington, D.C.: Smithsonian Institution, 1990.

_____. *Exploring the West.* Washington, D.C.: Smithsonian Books, 1987.

Virgines, George. *Western Legends and Lore.* Wauwatosa, Wis.: Leather Stocking Books/Pine Mountain Press, 1984.

Wahl, Paul, and Don Toppel. *The Gatling Gun.* New York: Arco, 1978.

Wallace, Ernest. *Ranald S. Mackenzie on the Texas Frontier.* Lubbock: West Texas Museum Association, 1964.

Walton, W. M. *Life and Adventures of Ben Thompson, the Famous Texan.* Austin: W. M. Walton, 1884.

Webb, W. E. *Buffalo Land.* Cincinnati: E. Hannaford & Company, 1872.

Webb, Walter Prescott. *The Texas Rangers.* Austin: University of Texas Press, 1965.

_____. *The Great Plains.* Boston: Gin and Company, 1933.

Weber, David J. *The Taos Trappers: The Fur Trade in the Far Southwest, 1540–1846.* Norman: University of Oklahoma Press, 1971.

Webster, Donald B., Jr. *Suicide Specials.* Harrisburg, Penn.: Stackpole, 1958.

Westermeier, Clifford P., ed. *Trailing the Cowboy: His Life and Lore as Told by Frontier Journalists.* Caldwell, Idaho: The Caxton Printers, Ltd., 1955

Westerners, Members of the Potomac Corral. *Great Western Indian Fights.* Lincoln: University of Nebraska Press, 1960.

White, G. Edward. *The Eastern Establishment and the Western Experience.* New Haven and London: Yale University Press, 1968.

Wilder, Mitchell A., et al. *The Wild West.* Fort Worth, Tex.: Amon Carter Museum of Western Art, 1970.

Williamson, Harold F. *Winchester—The Gun That Won the West.* New York: A. S. Barnes; London: Thomas Yoseloff, 1952.

Wilson, R. L., and R. Q. Sutherland, *The Book of Colt Firearms.* Kansas City: Published by R. Q. Sutherland, 1971.

Wilson, R. L. *Colt: An American Legend.* New York: Abbeville Press, 1985.

_____. *Colt Engraving.* North Hollywood, Calif.: Beinfeld Publications, 1982.

_____. *Theodore Roosevelt Outdoorsman.* New York: Winchester Press, 1971.

_____. *Winchester: An American Legend.* New York: Random House, 1991.

_____. *Winchester Engraving.* Palm Springs, California: Beinfeld Publications, 1990.

_____. *Winchester: The Golden Age of American Gunmaking and the Winchester 1 of 1000.* Cody, Wyo.: Winchester Arms Museum, Buffalo Bill Historical Center, 1983.

_____, and L. D. Eberhart. *The Deringer in America,* 2 vols. Lincoln, R. I.: Andrew Mowbray, 1985, 1992.

Wilson, R. L., and P. R. Phillips. *Paterson Colt Pistol Variations.* Dallas: Jackson Arms, 1979.

Winant, Lewis. *Pepperbox Firearms.* New York: Greenberg, 1952.

Woods, Lawrence M. *British Gentlemen in the Wild West.* New York: Free Press/Macmillan, 1989.

Wright, Robert M. *Dodge City, the Cowboy Capital and the Great Southwest.* Wichita: Wichita Eagle Press, 1913.

Young, Harry (Sam). *Hard Knocks: A Life Story of the Vanishing West.* Chicago: Laird and Lee, 1915.

Youngblood, Charles L. *A Mighty Hunter: The Adventures of Charles L. Youngblood.* Chicago: Rand, McNally, 1890.

Yost, Nellie Snyder. *Buffalo Bill: His Family, Friends, Fame, Failures, and Fortunes.* Chicago: Swallow Press, 1979.

ACKNOWLEDGMENTS, PHOTOGRAPHIC NOTE, AND OWNER CREDITS

To Gene and Jackie Autry, Chairman and President, the Gene Autry Western Heritage Museum, to Monte Hale, of the Board of Directors, and to Mrs. Joanne D. Hale, Executive Director of the Museum, to James Nottage, Chief Curator, to Mary Ellen Hennessey Nottage, Collections Manager, to Dr. John Langellier, Director of Research and Publication; to Jim Wilke, Assistant Curator, to Susan Deland, Director of Merchandise Operations, and to Museum volunteer Sonia Russell. Special appreciation to James Nottage and John Langellier, for assistance and encouragement above and beyond the call of duty.

To Greg and Petra Martin, premier collectors and devotees of Americana, specializing in *The West*.

To Al and Carol Cali, collectors nonpareil of Wells Fargo, arms, and gaming equipment.

To Peter De Rose, James B. Smith, Richard Ulbrich, and John K. Watson, Jr., for lending prized pieces from their collections for the Peter Beard shoot at Hadlyme.

To James and Theresa Earle for highlights from their outlaw and gunfighter collection.

To Norm Flayderman for Buffalo Bill, Bowie knife, tomahawk, and related memorabilia, from his Americana archives.

To Lee A. Silva for the wealth of photographic images in the Greg Silva Memorial, Old West Archives.

To Matthew R. Isenburg for daguerreotypes from his extensive collection.

To Peter Buxtun, George Jackson, Tom Martin, and Herb Peck, Jr., for photographic images from their expansive collections.

To Dr. Edward C. Ezell, Curator, and Harry Hunter, Museum Specialist, Department of Military History, National Museum of American History, Smithsonian Institution.

To Thomas A. Thornber, Vice President, Castle View Productions, and to Jean R. Alexander, author's assistant and secretary, for valued editorial and production support.

To Rhonda Redd, for editorial insights and for considerable patience during the creation of this tome. And to her mother, Christine Fajors, for her insights and counsel on word processing.

To Alexander Acevedo, the Alexander Gallery.

To Michael and Carol Kokin, Sherwood's Spirit of America gallery.

To Martin J. Lane, American Antique Firearms, New York City.

To Charles E. Hanson, Jr., Curator, Museum of the Fur Trade.

To Phil Spangenberger, Blackpowder Editor, *Guns & Ammo* magazine.

To Frederick S. Calhoun, Historian, U.S. Marshals Service, and to Ana-Marie Sullivan.

To Richard Rattenbury, Curator of History, National Cowboy Hall of Fame and Western Heritage Center.

To Dr. Paul Fees, Curator, Buffalo Bill Museum, and to Elizabeth Holmes, Assistant Registrar, Buffalo Bill Historical Center.

To Robert J. Chandler, Historical Officer, Wells Fargo Bank.

To the late Gaines de Graffenried, first Curator, Texas Ranger Museum and Hall of Fame.

To Don Snoddy, Director, Union Pacific Railroad Museum.

To Arthur J. Ressel, Jeff Faintich, Gregg Grimes, and anonymous friend K.R.

To Kitty Deernose, Museum Curator, Custer Battlefield National Monument, and to Lieutenant Colonel James Pyatt, Secretary, Little Big Horn Associates.

And to Howard L. Blackmore, Blair Clark, Thomas A. Conroy, Chris de Guigne IV, Richard Ellis, Louis A. Garavaglia, John Gilchriese, Enrique Guerra, Roy G. Jinks, R. L. Moore, Jr., M.D., Virgil Mylin, Brig and Louise Pemberton, Peter and Sandra Riva, William B. Shillingberg, S. P. Stevens, Glen Swanson, Donald B. Tharpe, Maria Laura Uberti, Arno and Peter Werner, William R. Williamson, Heidi, Christopher, and Stephen Wilson, John and Judy Woods, Charles G. Worman, and Donald M. Yena.

To Donald I. Greene, President, P&B Office Machines of Connecticut (Pawcatuck), and to his immensely patient and helpful son, David, for introducing the author to the miraculous world of word-processing equipment, in time to complete the manuscript for this book.

And to Robert Loomis and colleagues at Random House, and to Martin Moskof and Associates, designers, who produced a complex volume in record time.

PHOTOGRAPHIC NOTE

Peter Beard's work has appeared in *Vogue*, *Life*, *Playboy*, and a number of other publications, and his books to date are *The End of the Game*, *Eyelids of Morning*, and *Longing for Darkness*. Books in progress are *Beyond Gauguin* and *Last Word from Paradise*.

His photographic technique for this project was creative design and layout for some sixty 4×5 transparencies, of over 250 objects, at interior and exterior locations, with occasional interruptions by whitetail deer and inquisitive children, and a steady video background diet of Robert Altman's *Buffalo Bill and the Indians*. Allan Brown assisted with his equipment as described below.

Allan Brown's work has appeared in the editorial pages of *Outdoor Life*, *Audubon*, *Colonial Homes*, *The Saturday Evening Post*, *Yankee*, *The American Rifleman*, *Man at Arms*, *Quest*, and numerous other periodicals and books. For firearms photography, Brown uses a 4×5 Combo View Camera almost exclusively. He prefers Kodak Ektachrome film (either daylight for outdoors or tungsten for studio work) for consistent quality. Of as much importance as the film is finding a quality lab to process it. Much of the work for *The Peacemakers* was by R. J. Phil, of East Hampton, Connecticut.

For lighting, Brown uses Lowell tungsten lights, 3200 Kelvin, in the studio. The combination of these lights along with various diffusion materials and reflectors produces the lighting he finds complimentary to firearms. Tungsten lights have the added benefit over strobes of allowing one to see the exact lighting that the film will record.

Susan Einstein's studio is in Los Angeles. She has specialized in the photography of art objects for museums, galleries, collectors, and artists for about twenty years. Formerly on the staff of the J. Paul Getty Museum and the Fowler Museum of Cultural History at UCLA, she has a master's degree in art history from the University of California, Berkeley. Her work has appeared in several art books, catalogues, and periodicals.

Miss Einstein uses a 4×5 Toyo View Camera, daylight Ektachrome film, and strobe lighting.

Douglas Sandberg is a graduate of California College of Arts and Crafts, in Oakland. Much of his skill in photographing works of art was learned at the auction gallery Butterfield & Butterfield, San Francisco, where he was Director of Photography for seven years. In 1987 he created his own Comprehensive Photography company in South Park, San Francisco. His clients range from Christie's to WordStar, Pebble Beach Co., to Electronic Arts, and more. An artist as well with a brush, his paintings of antique and modern cameras have been on show at galleries. Equipment used for this book was primarily a Toyo 4×5 View Camera and Balcar Electronic Flash system. Strong and direct lighting were used to bring out subtleties of engraving, with soft low-light filling in shadow detail. His choice of film: Ektachrome 100 Plus.

Most of the photographs in *The Peacemakers* were shot by Peter Beard, Allan Brown, Susan Einstein, and Douglas Sandberg. Balance of color photography by Thomas A. Conroy, Larry Faeth, John Fox, Roger Fuhr of ROLANDesign, Paul Goodwin of Richard Ellis Publications, Sid Latham, Stephen Lee, Eric Long, Staff Photographer, National Museum of American History, Smithsonian Institution, Louise Pemberton, Bruce Pendleton, Gary C. Putnam, Rick Oltmans, Barry Slobin, Steve Smith, S. P. Stevens and Turk Takano of *Gun* magazine of Tokyo.

OWNER CREDITS

American Museum of Natural History, New York, 66; Arizona Historical Society, 20 (photo *at left*), 34, 102 (*right*), 105, 142 (*bottom*), 181, 185, 198 (*right*), 249 (*top*), 251 (*left*); author's collection (primarily memorabilia), 2, 42, 44 (*left*, game bag, pistol), 64 (*bottom right*), 81, 82, 95 (sword), 117 (advertising), 118, 122 (*left*), 130, 134, 205, 223 (letter, coin), 230 (*right*), 252 (Ulrich card and ivory), 267, 268 (*right*), 270 (*top*), 281, 289, 311, 312 (*left* and *bottom*), 313 (*bottom left*), 317 (*right*), 319, 329, 330, 337 (*left*), 338, 339 (*left*), 340 (*right*), 341, 347 (*left*), 358 (*left*), 360, 373 (*right*); Gene Autry, 367; Gene Autry Western Heritage Museum, 70, 87, 98, 107, 123, 146, 160, 161 (*top right*), 171 (*right*), 172 (*left*), 173 (*right*), 175 (*right*), 177, 203, 204, 220, 222 (*left*), 244 (*left*), 256, 257 (*bottom*), 271, 289 (rifle, case), 291 (*right*), 292 (*right*), 295, 299 (*top left*), 303 (*right*), 306, 309, 310, 312, 313 (*right*), 314, 317 (*left*), 318, 319, 320, 321, 322, 325, 326, 327, 329, 330, 331, 332, 333, 334, 337 (*right*), 338, 339 (*right*), 348 (*left*), 362, 365, 366, 370, 375; Bancroft Library, University of California, 122 (*center*); Robert B. Berryman, 182-183, 307 (*left*); Joe Bishop, 165; Boone | & | Crockett | Club, \ Buffalo |' Bill | Museum, I 274; | Buffalo | Bill Historical Center, front of dust jacket, 258, 291 (*left*), 294, 297 (*left*), 299 (*bottom left, right*); Butterfield & Butterfield, 346; Peter J. Buxton, 142 (*top*), 170 (*top right*), 252 (b & w photo), 361 (b & w photo); Al and Carol Cali, 127 (*right*), 136, 140 (*right*), 145 (*bottom*), 149, 150, 151, 152, 155 (*right*), 169, 229, 242 (*left*), 244 (*right*), 245, 247, 248, 249 (*bottom*), 250, 251 (*top right*), 354, 359 (*right*); Amon Carter Museum, 212 (*bottom right*); Dwight Chapin, 118 (deringer), 134 (*right*), 163 (*bottom right*); Christie's, 342 (*left*); "Wild Bill" Cleaver, 358 (*left*); Colt Collection of Firearms, Connecticut State Library, 158; Colorado Historical Society, 49 (*center*); Connecticut Historical Society, 300; Thomas A. Conroy, 349, 368; Custer Battlefield National Monument, 48 (*bottom*), 93, 102 (*left*), 261 (*left*), 350 (*left*), 352 (*right*); Daughters of the Republic of Texas (knife), 60; Michael Del Castello, 275 (rifle); Denver Public Library, Western History Department, 33, 63 (*bottom right*), 109, 170 (*top center*), 225 (*left*), 235 (*right*), 269, 278, 290, 359 (*left*); Peter de Rose, 76, 95, 112 (*top*), 141, 154 (*right*), 211 (*right*, pistol), 288 (S & W); Chris de Guigne IV, 61, 353; Jim and Theresa Earle, 159 (*bottom, right, and left*), 162 (*bottom left*), 173 (*bottom left*), 174 (*top*), 176, 356 (*right*); Richard Ellis, 77, 84 (*right*), 86, 114; Jeff Faintich, 51, 52, 53; Norm Flayderman, 6 (*bottom right*), 10, 54 (*left*), 62-63, 96 (*right*), 137, 139, 166, 202, 251 (*bottom right*), 264, 272, 273 (*left*), 277, 293, 324, 350 (*right*); Ft. Laramie Historical Association, 104, 112 (*bottom*); John E. Fox, 73, 224 (*left*); William C. Foxley, 259; Paul Friedrich, 168 (*right*), 231, 238; Thomas Gilcrease Institute of American History and Art, 6 (*left top* and *bottom*), 37, 40 (*bottom left*), 145 (*top*), 254, 255, 257 (*top*), 268 (*left*), 347 (*right*); W. H. D. Goddard, 200, 201, 261 (*right*); Gregg Grimes, 51, 52, 53; Enrique Guerra, 117, 208, 210 (*bottom left* and *right*), 226 (*bottom right*); Hagley Museum and Library, 40 (*top left*); Hugh E. Hayes, 153 (*left*); Ralph Heinz, 23; Hunting World, Inc., 357 (*right*); Matthew R. Isenburg (daguerreotypes and/or daguerreotype copper plate), 11, 16

(and New Orleans *Picayune*), 30, 36, 43 (*right*), 83, 118 (daguerreotypes, Currier and Ives print, diary), 126, 130, 201, 126, 130, 201, 262, 288 (*left*), 361; George Jackson, 200 (badge); Harry Jackson, Wyoming Foundry Studios, Cody, 373 (*right*); Kansas State Historical Society, 21 (*bottom right*), 67 (*right*), 87 (b & w photo), 88 (*left*), 147, 157 (*bottom left*), 168 (*left*), 189 (*top left* and *right*), 191 (*top left*), 230 (*left*), 282; Michael D. Kokin (Sherwood's Spirit of America), 3, 7, 8, 100 (*left*); Martin J. Lane, *frontis.*, front of dust jacket, 4, 5, 17, (war bonnet), 44 (*left*, memorabilia), 49 (rifle, *top*), 82 (bow, arrows), 89, 106 (*left*), 108, 173 (*top left*), 225 (*right*), 287, 356 (*left*); Robert M. Lee, 357 (*right*); Dr. Harmon C. Leonard, 15 (*bottom*), 19 (*right*); Library of Congress, 92 (*left*) 103 (*right*); Lincoln County Heritage Trust, 219 (*right*); Los Angeles County Museum of Natural History, 178 (revolver); Jack Lott, 352 (*left*); Dr. Paul McCombs, 351 (*right*); A. I. McCroskie, 260; John McWilliams, 60 (daguerreotype, ambrotype), 67 (*left* and *bottom left*), 84 (Walker and Californians, daguerreotypes *left* and *right*); Dr. Richard C. Marohn, 174 (*bottom*), 175 (*left*), 195 (*top left*); Marlin Firearms Company, 284-285, 345, 363 (*left*), 372; Greg Martin, front endpaper, badge from back endpaper and back of jacket, 12, 14, 55 (*top right, top*), 92 (*right*), 94, 100 (*left*), 106 (*left*), 110, 121, 124, 128, 129 (*right*), 135, 138, 162 (*top left* and *right*), 164, 167, 173 (*top left*), 184, 185, 186 (*left*), 187, 190, 194, 195 (*right*), 196, 197, 206, 207, 210, 215, 216, 217, 219, 228, 237, 239, 240, 241, (*left*), 243; 263 (*right*), 270 (*left*), 275 (saddle), 280, 286, 296, 297 (*right*), 298, 303 (*bottom left*), 304, 305, 308 (*right*), 323, 336 (*left*), 344, 363 (*right*), 364; Tom Martin, 54 (*top left*), 64 (*bottom left*), 152, 155, 211 (*left*), 212 (*left*), 225 (*center*), 226 (*bottom left*), 276 (*right*); Milwaukee Public Museum, 55 (*top right, top*); Minnesota Historical Society, 65; Monroe County Historical Society, 263 (*center*); Montana Historical Society, 27 (*left*), 48 (rifle), 113 (*top*), 212 (*top right*) 223 (*left*), 276 (*left*), 283; Montezuma Masonic Lodge No. 1, Santa Fe, 46, 47; Dr. R. L. Moore, Jr., 17 (*left*); Museum of the Fur Trade, 55 (*top right, bottom*); Museum of the American Indian, Heye Foundation, 21 (*left*); National Archives (photos), 11, 30, 31, 32, 36, 68, 71, 103 (*left*), 106 (*right*), 211 (*right*), 262 (b & w photo); National Cowboy Hall of Fame and Heritage Center, 1 vi, 159 (*top right*), 192 (*right*), 226 (*top left*), 266 (Sharps); National Museum of American History, Smithsonian Institution, 18, 22, 26 (*bottom*), 45, 56, 78, 85, 88 (*right*), 90, 91, 96 (*top*), 111; Nebraska State Historical Society, 288 (*right*); Arvo Ojala, 328 (*right*), 335, 338, 343; The Old Print Shop, Inc., 6 (*top right*), 9, 43 (*left*), 44 (*right*), 55 (*bottom right*); Colonel William Orbello, 50; Oregon Historical Society, 55 (*left* and *top right, center*); Panhandle Plains Historical Museum, 191 (*bottom left*), 266 (*bottom left*); Patton Museum of Cavalry and Armor, Fort Knox, Kentucky, 113 (*bottom*); Herb Peck, Jr., 20 (photo, *right*), 35, 120 (*top*), 127 (*left*), 129 (*left*), 155 (*left*) 236 (*left*), 288 (b & w photo, *left*); N. Brigham Pemberton, 189 (*bottom*), 214, 218, 355; Petersen Publishing Company, 315, 316, 340 (*left*), 352; David R. Phillips, 96; Carl Press, 336 (*right*); William H. Reisner, Jr., 49 (*bottom left*); Glode and Jody Requa, 132-133, 134, 163; Arthur J. Ressel, 51, 52, 53; Theodore Roosevelt National Historic Site, 274 (*right* rifle); Theodore Roosevelt Collection, Harvard University Library, 221 (*bottom*), 273 (*right*); Joseph G. Rosa, 119, 159 (*top left*), 161 (*bottom left*), 172 (*right*); Royal Canadian Mounted Police, 21 (*top right*); Dr. William Schultz, 84 (*left*); J. Logan Sewell, 131; Lee Silva and the Greg Silva Memorial Old West Archives, 35, 95 (*left*), 117, 140 (b & w, *left* photo), 142, 143, 170 (*top left*), 178 (badge), 179, 193 (b & w photo), 195 (*bottom left*), 198 (*left*), 199 (*right*), 235 (*left*), 236 (*right*), 292 (*right*), 303 (*bottom center*), 307 (*right, top and bottom*), 308 (*left*), 315 (*left*), 357 (*left*); James B. Smith, 64 (*bottom right*), 67 (*top left*), 76, 83, 267; Deke Sonnichsen, 373 (*left*); Southwest Museum,

120 (*bottom*), Phil Spangenberger, 233, 315 (*right*), 316, 340 (*left*), 342 (*right*); State Historical Society of North Dakota, 19 (*left*), 26 (*top*), 144, 253; State Historical Society of Wisconsin, 64 (*top left*); Buck Stevens, 115, 148, 156, 213, 227, 232, 301, 313 (*top left*), 351 (*left*); Arthur and Joe Swann, 38; Glen Swanson, 25; Fred Sweeney, 192 (*left*); Margo Sweet, 44 (*left*, traps); the late Wiliam O. Sweet, 13, 24, 64 (*top right*); Tennessee State Museum, 38 (Arthur and Joe Swann Collection); Texas Ranger Hall of Fame and Museum, Waco, Texas, 359 (*right*); Tiffany & Co., Corporate Division, 367; Time-Life and West Point Museum, 79; Richard J. Ulbrich (Indian peace medals, weaponry), 2, 11, 16, 17, (*right*, *top* and *bottom*), 20, 30, 36, 39 (*right*), 40 (*right*), 41, 42, 43 (*right*), 44 (muskets, knife), 118 (knife, gun, accessories), 125, 126, 130, 140 (*left*), 141 (knife), 163 (knives, Lewis & Tomes pistols), 252, 262, 265, 281 (*left*), 288 (rifle, knife), 348 (*right*), 361; University of Oklahoma Library, Western History Collections, 161 (*top left*), 180, 188, 199 (*left*), 266 (*right*), 270 (*top right*), 312 (*top right*); University of Wyoming Western Heritage Center, 327; John K. Watson, Jr., 17 (*right, upper* gun), 30 (gun), 76, 81, 82, 83, 95 (*right*), 265, 267; Michael Wayne, 315 (*right*), 316; Wells Fargo Bank History Room, 241 (*right*), 242 (*right*), 246; Paul R. Wells, 279; West Point Museum, 100 (*left*); A. A. White (period photograph), 5; Christopher T. Wilson (memorabilia), 20, 30, 36; C. B. Wilson, 157 (*top*); David S. Woloch, 63 (*top*), 117 (pistol), 302; Wyoming State Archives and History Department, 170 (*bottom left*), 221 (*top*); Yale University, Beinecke Library, 263 (*top*), 303 (*top*); Yale University, Peabody Museum of Natural History, 69; Donald M. Yena, 15 (*top*), 29, 39 (*left*), 59, 153 (*right*), 154 (*left*), 186 (*bottom right*), 191 (*right*); private collections, 51, 74, 75, 186 (*top right*), 222 (*right*), 223 (*right*), 266 (*top*), 281 (*right*), 369.

INDEX

References to illustrations are in *italics*

Back endpaper: Icons of the West, from the Gene Autry Western Heritage Museum (badge from the Greg Martin Americana Collection). Winchester Model 1876 short rifle custom-built for rancher–sportsman Theodore Roosevelt, his "saddle gun for deer and antelope," number 45704; *below at right* Dodge City Cowboy Band leader Jack Sinclair's elaborate Colt Single Action Army revolver, garishly embellished, and guaranteed to keep the musicians in line; the Remington double deringer presentation inscribed from Buffalo Bill Cody to dime-novel writer Colonel Prentiss Ingraham, number 5181; gold-plated Smith & Wesson Model No. 3 part of a three-pistol cased set presented to Annie Oakley by her husband and manager, Frank Butler, number 27941; silver-plated and Tiffany-etched S & W (*above* badge) one of cased pair presented to George Armstrong Custer by hunting friends from Michigan, 1869; extraordinary gold badge presented to Sacramento Police Chief Oliver Cowdery Jackson, 1885; Colt Single Action at *left* a Christmas present from Dell Jones to her trick rider and film star husband, Buck (1925), embellishments by saddlemaker Edward H. Bohlin; Bohlin also made Buck's spurs. For contrasting images of most of the above, see back of dust jacket.